CRIME

A SERIOUS AMERICAN PROBLEM

ISSN 1532-2696

CRIME

A SERIOUS AMERICAN PROBLEM

Thomas Wiloch

INFORMATION PLUS® REFERENCE SERIES
Formerly published by Information Plus, Wylie, Texas

Detroit • New York • San Francisco • San Diego • New Haven, Conn. • Waterville, Maine • London • Munich

Crime: A Serious American Problem

Thomas Wiloch
Paula Kepos, Series Editor

Project Editor
John McCoy

Editorial
Danielle Behr, Ellice Engdahl, Michael L. LaBlanc, Elizabeth Manar, Daniel Marowski, Charles B. Montney, Heather Price, Timothy J. Sisler

Permissions
William Sampson, Sue Rudolph, Edna Hedblad, Jacqueline Key, Lori Hines, Denise Buckley, Sheila Spencer

Composition and Electronic Prepress
Evi Seoud

Manufacturing
Keith Helmling

For more information, contact
Thomson Gale
27500 Drake Rd.
Farmington Hills, MI 48331-3535
Or you can visit our Internet site at
http://www.gale.com

LIBRARY OF CONGRESS CATALOGING-IN-PUBLICATION DATA

ISBN 0-7876-5103-6 (set)
ISBN 0-7876-9069-4
ISSN 1532-2696

This title is also available as an e-book.
ISBN 0-7876-9269-7 (set)
Contact your Thomson Gale sales representative for ordering information.

Printed in the United States of America
10 9 8 7 6 5 4 3 2 1

TABLE OF CONTENTS

PREFACE

Crime: A Serious American Problem is part of the Information Plus Reference Series. The purpose of each volume of the series is to present the latest facts on a topic of pressing concern in modern American life. These topics include today's most controversial and most studied social issues: abortion, capital punishment, care for the elderly, crime, health care, the environment, immigration, minorities, social welfare, women, youth, and many more. Although written especially for the high school and undergraduate student, this series is an excellent resource for anyone in need of factual information on current affairs.

By presenting the facts, it is Thomson Gale's intention to provide its readers with everything they need to reach an informed opinion on current issues. To that end, there is a particular emphasis in this series on the presentation of scientific studies, surveys, and statistics. These data are generally presented in the form of tables, charts, and other graphics placed within the text of each book. Every graphic is directly referred to and carefully explained in the text. The source of each graphic is presented within the graphic itself. The data used in these graphics are drawn from the most reputable and reliable sources, in particular from the various branches of the U.S. government and from major independent polling organizations. Every effort has been made to secure the most recent information available. The reader should bear in mind that many major studies take years to conduct, and that additional years often pass before the data from these studies are made available to the public. Therefore, in many cases the most recent information available in 2004 dated from 2001 or 2002. Older statistics are sometimes presented as well, if they are of particular interest and no more recent information exists.

Although statistics are a major focus of the Information Plus Reference Series, they are by no means its only content. Each book also presents the widely held positions and important ideas that shape how the book's subject is discussed in the United States. These positions are explained in detail and, where possible, in the words of their proponents. Some of the other material to be found in these books includes: historical background; descriptions of major events related to the subject; relevant laws and court cases; and examples of how these issues play out in American life. Some books also feature primary documents, or have pro and con debate sections giving the words and opinions of prominent Americans on both sides of a controversial topic. All material is presented in an even-handed and unbiased manner; the reader will never be encouraged to accept one view of an issue over another.

HOW TO USE THIS BOOK

The United States of America has among the highest crime and incarceration rates in the industrialized world. It comes as no surprise then that many Americans are very interested in crime, its causes, and how to prevent it. A tremendous number of studies are conducted every year on criminals, victims, law enforcement, the criminal justice system, and prisons and jails. This book gathers together and explains information from the largest, most recent, and most reputable of these studies, in order to provide a complete picture of crime in the United States.

Crime: A Serious American Problem consists of nine chapters and three appendices. Each of the chapters is devoted to a particular aspect of crime in the United States. For a summary of the information covered in each chapter, please see the synopses provided in the Table of Contents at the front of the book. Chapters generally begin with an overview of the basic facts and background information on the chapter's topic, then proceed to examine sub-topics of particular interest. For example, Chapter 6: Sentencing and Corrections begins with an overview of the types of sentences American criminals generally receive. It then closely examines the controversies surrounding the death penalty. Discussed next are growing incarceration rates and the demographic characteristics of prisoners. Probation, parole, and recidivism are covered, and the chapter ends with a discussion of the effectiveness of incarceration as a deterrent to crime. Readers can find their way through a chapter by looking for the section and sub-section headings, which are clearly set off from the text. Or, they can refer to the book's extensive index if they already know what they are looking for.

Statistical Information

The tables and figures featured throughout *Crime: A Serious American Problem* will be of particular use to the reader in learning about this issue. These tables and figures represent an extensive collection of the most recent and important statistics on crime, as well as related issues—for example, graphics in the book cover workplace homicides, hate crime offenses, arrest rates for juvenile criminals, international incarceration rates, and average length of imprisonment for possession of illegal drugs. Thomson Gale believes that making this information available to the reader is the most important way in which we fulfill the goal of this book: to help readers understand the issues and controversies surrounding crime in the United States and reach their own conclusions about them.

Each table or figure has a unique identifier appearing above it, for ease of identification and reference. Titles for the tables and figures explain their purpose. At the end of each table or figure, the original source of the data is provided.

In order to help readers understand these often complicated statistics, all tables and figures are explained in the text. References in the text direct the reader to the relevant statistics. Furthermore, the contents of all tables and figures are fully indexed. Please see the opening section of the index at the back of this volume for a description of how to find tables and figures within it.

Appendices

In addition to the main body text and images, *Crime: A Serious American Problem* has three appendices. The first is the Important Names and Addresses directory. Here the reader will find contact information for a number of government and private organizations that can provide further information on aspects of crime. The second appendix is the Resources section, which can also assist the reader in conducting his or her own research. In this section, the author and editors of *Crime: A Serious American Problem* describe some of the sources that were most useful during the compilation of this book. The final appendix is the index. It has been greatly expanded from previous editions, and should make it even easier to find specific topics in this book.

ADVISORY BOARD CONTRIBUTIONS

The staff of Information Plus would like to extend their heartfelt appreciation to the Information Plus Advisory Board. This dedicated group of media professionals provides feedback on the series on an ongoing basis. Their comments allow the editorial staff who work on the project to continually make the series better and more user-friendly. Our top priorities are to produce the highest-quality and most useful books possible, and the Advisory Board's contributions to this process are invaluable.

The members of the Information Plus Advisory Board are:

- Kathleen R. Bonn, Librarian, Newbury Park High School, Newbury Park, California
- Madelyn Garner, Librarian, San Jacinto College—North Campus, Houston, Texas
- Anne Oxenrider, Media Specialist, Dundee High School, Dundee, Michigan
- Charles R. Rodgers, Director of Libraries, Pasco-Hernando Community College, Dade City, Florida
- James N. Zitzelsberger, Library Media Department Chairman, Oshkosh West High School, Oshkosh, Wisconsin

COMMENTS AND SUGGESTIONS

The editors of the Information Plus Reference Series welcome your feedback on *Crime: A Serious American Problem*. Please direct all correspondence to:

Editors
Information Plus Reference Series
27500 Drake Rd.
Farmington Hills, MI, 48331-3535

CHAPTER 1

CRIME—AN OVERVIEW

CRIME

The U.S. Department of Justice defines crime as all behaviors and acts for which society provides formally approved punishments. Written law, both federal and state, defines which behavior is criminal and which is not. Some behaviors—murder, robbery, and burglary—have always been considered criminal. Other actions, such as domestic violence or driving under the influence of drugs or alcohol, were only recently added to the list of criminal offenses. Other changes in our society have also influenced crime. For example, the widespread use of computers provides new opportunities for white-collar crime, as well as adding a new word—"cybercrime"—to our vocabulary.

Two main government sources collect crime statistics. The Federal Bureau of Investigation (FBI) annually compiles the Uniform Crime Reports (UCR). The UCR collects data from about 17,000 city, county, and state law enforcement agencies, whose jurisdictions contain approximately 95 percent of the total U.S. population. The *National Crime Victimization Survey* (NCVS), prepared by the Bureau of Justice Statistics (BJS), bases its findings on an annual survey of 100,000 people.

Criminal behavior can range from actions as simple as taking chewing gum from a store without paying to those as tragic and violent as murder. Most people have broken the law, wittingly or unwittingly, at some time in their lives. Therefore, the true extent of criminality is impossible to measure. Researchers can keep records only of what is reported by victims or known to the police.

FACTORS IN THE RATE OF CRIME

The FBI lists many factors that can influence the rate of crime in a particular area, including:

- Population density and degree of urbanization (big city growth).
- Variations in the makeup of the population, particularly where youth is most concentrated.
- Stability of the population—residents' tendencies to move around (mobility), commuting patterns, and length of time residing in the area (transient factors).
- Types and condition of transportation and highway systems available.
- Economic conditions, including average income, poverty, and job availability.
- Cultural conditions, such as educational, recreational, and religious characteristics.
- Family conditions with respect to divorce and family togetherness.
- Climate and weather.
- Effectiveness of law enforcement agencies.
- Policies of other parts of the criminal justice system (prosecutorial, judicial, correctional, and probational).
- Attitudes of residents toward crime.
- Crime-reporting practices of the citizens.

CRIME ON THE DECLINE

In the 1990s much of the public believed the crime rate was increasing. The randomness of crime (drive-by shootings, driveway robberies), along with sensational news reporting, fed this belief. The BJS reported, in *Perceptions of Neighborhood Crime, 1995* (Carol J. DeFrances and Steven K. Smith, Washington, D.C., 1998), that about 7.3 percent of U.S. households reported crime as a major problem in their neighborhoods. Not surprisingly, households in central cities were twice as likely (14.5 percent) to feel that crime was a serious problem. In 1995 19.6 percent of black central-city households identi-

TABLE 1.1

Percent change in Crime Index by population group and region for the period January to June 2003 and by two-year trends from 1999 to 2002

By population group

Population group	Number of agencies	Population	Violent crime	Murder	Forcible rape	Robbery	Aggravated assault	Property crime	Burglary	Larceny-theft	Motor vehicle theft	Arson
Total	**9,908**	**209,448,333**	**−3.1**	**+1.1**	**−4.0**	**−0.5**	**−4.4**	**−0.8**	**−1.0**	**−1.1**	**+0.9**	**−10.0**
Cities:												
Over 1,000,000	10	24,682,265	−4.4	+5.7	+2.3	+0.5	−8.3	−0.9	+1.2	−1.1	−2.1	−10.5
500,000 to 999,999	20	13,651,785	−4.1	−3.9	−10.5	+0.8	−6.4	−1.0	−2.2	−1.4	+2.2	−0.8
250,000 to 499,999	37	12,889,909	−4.3	+1.5	+0.7	−4.4	−4.9	−2.1	−3.4	−1.2	−3.8	−8.1
100,000 to 249,999	157	23,617,458	−2.6	+8.3	−3.4	−1.8	−3.3	−0.3	−0.8	−0.9	+3.4	−12.6
50,000 to 99,999	282	19,431,570	+0.6	−0.3	−3.2	+0.9	+0.9	−1.2	−0.5	−1.8	+1.7	−9.1
25,000 to 49,999	568	19,782,085	−1.1	+2.3	−1.9	−1.2	−1.0	−0.2	0	−0.7	+3.2	−13.3
10,000 to 24,999	1,253	19,918,282	−1.6	+2.1	−7.3	+0.6	−1.6	−0.5	−0.4	−0.6	+0.3	−6.9
Under 10,000	4,749	15,660,302	−3.5	+6.0	−8.1	+6.8	−5.2	+0.7	−0.1	+1.0	+0.3	−15.7
Counties:												
Suburban[1]	929	38,642,490	−1.1	−3.4	−4.0	−0.8	−0.8	−0.5	−1.1	−1.8	+7.5	−12.6
Rural[2]	1,903	21,172,187	−5.7	−17.6	−8.7	+3.1	−5.8	−2.5	−2.4	−2.6	−2.8	−5.7

[1]Includes crimes reported to sheriff's departments, county police departments, and state police within Metropolitan Statistical Areas.
[2]Includes crimes reported to sheriff's departments, county police departments, and state police outside Metropolitan Statistical Areas.

By geographic region

Region	Violent crime	Murder	Forcible rape	Robbery	Aggravated assault	Property crime	Burglary	Larceny-theft	Motor vehicle theft	Arson
Total	**−3.1**	**+1.1**	**−4.0**	**−0.5**	**−4.4**	**−0.8**	**−1.0**	**−1.1**	**+0.9**	**−10.0**
Northeast	−2.4	+4.3	−3.5	+0.9	−4.6	−5.6	−7.4	−5.3	−4.2	−11.8
Midwest	−6.2	−1.9	−5.4	−4.7	−7.2	−2.7	−4.4	−2.3	−2.0	−8.6
South	−3.2	+1.8	−5.4	+0.2	−4.6	−0.2	+0.2	0	−2.1	−11.1
West	−1.1	+0.3	−1.1	+0.7	−2.0	+2.3	+3.2	+0.7	+7.2	−9.0

For consecutive years

Years	Violent crime	Murder	Forcible rape	Robbery	Aggravated assault	Property crime	Burglary	Larceny-theft	Motor vehicle theft	Arson
2000/1999	−0.3	−1.8	+0.7	−2.6	+0.7	−0.3	−2.4	+0.1	+1.2	−2.7
2001/2000	−1.3	+0.3	−1.7	+0.8	−2.4	−0.2	−1.2	−0.4	+2.6	+2.9
2002/2001	−1.7	+2.3	+1.8	−0.4	−2.8	+1.7	+4.2	+0.5	+4.2	−2.6
2003/2002	−3.1	+1.1	−4.0	−0.5	−4.4	−0.8	−1.0	−1.1	+0.9	−10.0

SOURCE: "Table 1: Crime Index Trends by Population Group and Area," "Table 2: Crime Index Trends by Geographic Region," and "Table 3: Crime Index Trends, Two-Year Trends," in *Crime in the United States, Uniform Crime Reports January–June 2003,* Federal Bureau of Investigation, Washington, DC, December 15, 2003

fied crime as a neighborhood problem, compared to 13 percent of white central-city households.

According to FBI, state, and city reports, however, the crime rate has been dropping steadily since 1991. During that period the number of crimes in the United States declined from 14.9 million crimes in 1991 to 13.7 million in 2002, a decrease of 8 percent.

That general trend continued through the first six months of 2003, although more modestly than in previous years, according to preliminary UCR data released by the FBI. The violent crime index total was down by 3.1 percent in 2003 from the same time period in 2002, while the property crime index decreased by 0.8 percent. (See Table 1.1.) While these trends were encouraging, no society has ever been totally free of crime. James Alan Fox, dean of the College of Criminal Justice at Boston's Northeastern University, notes, "We're moving in the right direction, but we have a long way to go still before we can claim victory over our crime problem."

Why the Decline?

Experts have attempted to identify key factors contributing to the marked trend. The statistics suggest that as the baby boomers (the generation born between 1946 and 1965) outgrew their prime crime years, the crime rate began to decline. Some observers also attribute this decline to other factors, including:

- More money spent on law enforcement.
- Stiffer sentences handed down by the courts.
- The growing number of neighborhood watch programs.
- The declining number of neighborhood bars.

Others argue the decline in crime was due to the increases in incarcerations (people being jailed). From 1980 through 1995 the population in federal and state prisons more than tripled from 329,821 to 1,104,074. At midyear 2002 the number of prisoners, including city and county jail inmates, reached just over 2 million. Between 1990 and 2002 the annual incarceration rate—the number of persons in custody per 100,000 residents—rose from 458 to 702, an increase from a rate of 690 in 2001.

Urban police officers attribute the decline in crime to an increase in the number of police officers and the creation of gang and violent-crime task forces. They also praise citizens who joined crime watch organizations. In a 1995 Chicago study, researchers found that urban neighborhoods with a strong sense of community and shared values had markedly lower rates of violence (Robert J. Sampson et al., "Neighborhoods and Violent Crime: A Multilevel Study of Collective Efficacy," *Science,* vol. 277, August 15, 1997). Of special importance, the study noted, was the "willingness of residents to intervene in the lives of children," especially in the areas of truancy, graffiti, and teenage gang participation, such as hanging out on neighborhood street corners. Others posit that the booming economy of the 1990s, with its low unemployment figures and rising wages, had some effect on crime. Other theories maintain that it is a combination of these or other factors.

Causes of the Earlier Crime Increase

If crime actually declined through the 1990s, what factors lay behind the apparent increase in crime that started in the 1960s and continued through the 1980s? Experts differ as to whether the increase in reported crime for that period was real. Some believe the increase only reflected better record-keeping and participation of more local law enforcement agencies in the FBI reporting system. Others attribute the long-term increase in the crime rate to the growing up of the baby boom generation. As this population bulge entered its juvenile years, it was only natural, they argue, that the crime rate would increase. In general, males between the ages of 15 and 24 commit the most crimes. Males born during the postwar baby boom—that is, from 1945 through 1964—would be between the ages of 15 and 24 from 1960 through 1988.

Neither the FBI nor the BJS has provided official interpretations as to why the crime rate increased in the late 1980s. Unofficial observations generally attributed the increase to the influence of drug use and drug trafficking, especially involving "crack" cocaine. A large proportion of convicted offenders were on drugs while committing the crimes for which they were sentenced.

Many crimes, including murder, are committed during drug transactions. Various theories have been proposed to explain why youth gangs exist; however, many gangs exist to conduct business: drug trafficking. While some gangs restrict their activities primarily to drug dealing, other gangs deal drugs as a means of earning money to engage in other activities. The development of crack (a less expensive, more marketable form of cocaine) in the 1980s provided gangs throughout the United States with a money-making commodity. Gang wars over territory or "turf" led to many deaths of gang members and innocent bystanders. Some gangs, often with strong ethnic ties such as the Chinese "tongs" or the Jamaican "posses," became dedicated to the drug trade and participated in brutal crimes.

INCREASES PREDICTED

Some criminologists predict that all crime rates will increase through the early years of the twenty-first century, as the children of the baby boomers (the "boomerang" or "boomlet" generation) become teenagers and young adults. Experts such as Dr. James Alan Fox think that a resurgence in juvenile crime, in particular, may be imminent based on the projected growth of the juvenile population. According to estimates by the U.S. Census Bureau, the population of juveniles 15 to 17 years of age—the group responsible for two-thirds of all juvenile arrests—will increase by 19 percent by 2007. Recent statistics indicate a diminishing rate of decline in juvenile crime. Juvenile crime declined by 50 percent from 1994 to 1999, and declined 5 percent from 1999 to 2000. For the first two months of 2002, gang homicides in Los Angeles tripled from the same period in 2001, as reported in *The New York Times.*

DECREASES NOTED IN 2003

The general trend of a declining crime rate in recent years continued in 2003, according to preliminary UCR data released by the FBI in 2003. (See Table 1.1.) For the nation as a whole, in the first 6 months of 2003 data indicated a 3.1 percent decrease in violent crime and a decrease of 0.8 percent in property crime since 2002.

According to the preliminary data for 2003 for violent crimes, robbery decreased by 0.5 percent, murder rose by 1.1 percent, forcible rape decreased by 4.0 percent, and aggravated assault decreased by 4.4 percent. Among property crimes, the FBI's 2003 preliminary data showed an increase of 0.9 percent in motor vehicle theft, a 1.0 percent decrease in burglary, a 10.0 percent decrease in arson, and a decrease of 1.1 percent in larceny-theft since 2002.

By region, preliminary violent crime totals for 2003 decreased by 6.2 percent in the nation's Midwest, by 3.2 percent in the South, by 2.4 percent in the Northeast, and by 1.1 percent in the West. Violent crime offenses decreased in the nation's cities, as well, with the largest decrease of 4.4 percent recorded in cities with populations of over one million. The only increase, 0.6 percent, was recorded in cities with populations from 50,000 to 99,999. (See Table 1.1.)

THE UNIFORM CRIME REPORTS

The FBI compiles various sets of crime statistics. In one category the FBI tracks the number of crimes by type as reported by local police. The more serious crime types are included in the Crime Index. A second category tracks cleared offenses. Cleared offenses are crimes for which at least one person is arrested, charged, and turned over to the court for prosecution. This does not necessarily mean the person arrested is guilty or will be convicted of the crime.

The Crime Index tabulates the violent crimes of murder, forcible rape, robbery, and aggravated assault, and the property crimes of burglary, larceny-theft, motor vehicle theft, and arson. Arrest statistics include information on many different crimes, such as drug violations, fraud, runaways, and vagrancy. Various trends and patterns can be interpreted from these statistical categories.

Highest Rates in the Cities

While crime is certainly not limited to the cities, it is far more likely to occur in urban areas than in rural areas. According to the Crime Index, crime rate in metropolitan statistical areas during 2002 was 4,409.1 per 100,000 inhabitants. (As defined by the U.S. Census Bureau, a "metropolitan statistical area," or MSA, is an urbanized area including a central city of 50,000 residents or more, or a Census Bureau-defined urbanized area of at least 50,000 inhabitants and a total metropolitan population of 75,000 in New England and at least 100,000 elsewhere.) In cities outside the metropolitan areas (a city or urbanized area not meeting the qualifications for an MSA) the rate was 4,524.0 per 100,000, over 2.25 times higher than in rural areas (1,908 per 100,000 inhabitants). (See Table 1.2.) The crime with the greatest disparity between MSAs and rural rates, robbery, occurred about 11 times more often in metropolitan areas than in rural areas. The incidence of motor vehicle theft was about 3.5 times higher in MSAs than in rural areas.

Crime Index total rates in smaller cities, while just slightly higher than those in metropolitan areas, displayed different characteristics. In 2002 the overall rate of violent crime was higher in metropolitan areas (545.6 per 100,000 residents) than in smaller cities (403.1). In all categories of violent crime except forcible rape, the rate was higher in metropolitan areas. The rate of property crime was higher in cities outside metropolitan areas than within metropolitan areas (4,121.0 and 3,863.5 per 100,000, respectively). Among property crimes, larceny-theft occurred at a significantly higher rate in smaller cities (3,107.9 per 100,000 residents) than in metropolitan areas (2,596.4).

URBAN RATES. According to the Crime Index, the nation's largest cities (over one million in population) reported a 4.4 percent decrease in violent crimes from January to June 2003. (See Table 1.1.) By comparison, during that same period, the rate of violent crime was down by 2.6 percent in cities with populations between 100,000 and 249,999.

In the first six months of 2003, murders were up by 5.7 percent in cities with over one million in population, compared to the same period in 2002. The largest increase in murders during this time was 8.3 percent in cities with populations between 100,000 and 249,999, closely followed by a 6.0 percent increase in murders in cities with under 10,000 in population. In contrast, murders declined by 3.9 percent in cities with populations of between 500,000 and 999,999. The percentage of forcible rapes during the first six months of 2003 were highest in cities with over one million in population (2.3 percent), while forcible rapes were down by as much as 10.5 percent in cities of 500,000 to 999,999.

Property crimes such as larceny-theft and motor vehicle theft also declined in large cities of one million or more residents, while rising in cities with under 10,000 population. The only increase in burglaries (1.2 percent) occurred in cities with populations over one million. Motor vehicle thefts were up by 3.4 percent in cities with populations between 100,000 and 249,000, followed by an increase of 3.2 percent in cities with populations between 25,000 and 49,999.

Regional Differences

Distinct crime patterns are also commonly evident between different regions of the nation. In 2002 the South, the most populous region, had the highest crime rates for both violent crimes (571.0 per 100,000 residents) and property crimes (4,151.0 per 100,000). The Northeast, the least populous region, had the lowest property crime rate (2,472.6 per 100,000) and the lowest violent crime rate (416.5 per 100,000). (See Figure 1.1.)

ARRESTS

In 2002 law enforcement agencies nationwide made 13.7 million arrests for all criminal infractions excluding traffic violations. This figure includes all offenses reported by local law enforcement agencies to the FBI, including crimes not counted in the FBI's tabulations on specific crimes. There were 620,510 arrests for Crime Index violent crimes and 1.6 million arrests for Crime Index property crimes in 2002, for a total of 2.2 million arrests. Of the arrests for Crime Index offenses, larceny-theft arrests accounted for the greatest number (1.16 million), followed by aggravated assault (472,290), burglary (288,291) and motor vehicle theft (148,943). Non-Crime Index arrests for drug abuse violations (1.53 million), driving under the

TABLE 1.2

Index of Crime, 2002

Area	Population[1]	Crime Index	Modified Crime Index[2]	Violent crime[3]	Property crime[3]	Murder and non-negligent man-slaughter	Forcible rape	Robbery	Aggravated assault	Burglary	Larceny-theft	Motor vehicle theft	Arson[2]
United States total	**288,368,698**	**11,877,218**		**1,426,325**	**10,450,893**	**16,204**	**95,136**	**420,637**	**894,348**	**2,151,875**	**7,052,922**	**1,246,096**	
Rate per 100,000 inhabitants		4,118.8		494.6	3,624.1	5.6	33.0	145.9	310.1	746.2	2,445.8	432.1	
Metropolitan Statistical Area	**231,376,218**												
Area actually reporting[4]	94.3%	9,482,136		1,163,636	8,318,500	13,100	72,708	369,834	707,994	1,658,078	5,570,764	1,089,658	
Estimated total	100.0%	10,201,622		1,262,359	8,939,263	14,235	78,236	401,140	768,748	1,778,174	6,007,505	1,153,584	
Rate per 100,000 inhabitants		4,409.1		545.6	3,863.5	6.2	33.8	173.4	332.3	768.5	2,596.4	498.6	
Cities outside metropolitan areas	**22,475,044**												
Area actually reporting[4]	85.5%	881,650		79,845	801,805	617	7,464	11,981	59,783	157,232	603,408	41,165	
Estimated total	100.0%	1,016,773		90,586	926,187	717	8,679	13,746	67,444	181,014	698,507	46,666	
Rate per 100,000 inhabitants		4,524.0		403.1	4,121.0	3.2	38.6	61.2	300.1	805.4	3,107.9	207.6	
Rural counties	**34,517,436**												
Area actually reporting[4]	84.7%	582,496		65,962	516,534	1,046	6,937	5,045	52,934	169,192	306,754	40,588	
Estimated total	100.0%	658,823		73,380	585,443	1,252	8,221	5,751	58,156	192,687	346,910	45,846	
Rate per 100,000 inhabitants		1,908.7		212.6	1,696.1	3.6	23.8	16.7	168.5	558.2	1,005.0	132.8	

[1]Populations are Bureau of the Census provisional estimates as of July 1, 2002.
[2]Although arson data are included in the trend and clearance tables, sufficient data are not available to estimate totals for this offense.
[3]Violent crimes are offenses of murder, forcible rape, robbery, and aggravated assault. Property crimes are offenses of burglary, larceny-theft, and motor vehicle theft.
[4]The percentage reported under "Area actually reporting" is based upon the population covered by agencies providing 3 months or more of crime reports to the FBI.

SOURCE: "Table 2: Index of Crime, United States, 2002," in *Crime in the United States 2002,* Federal Bureau of Investigation, Washington, DC, 2003

FIGURE 1.1

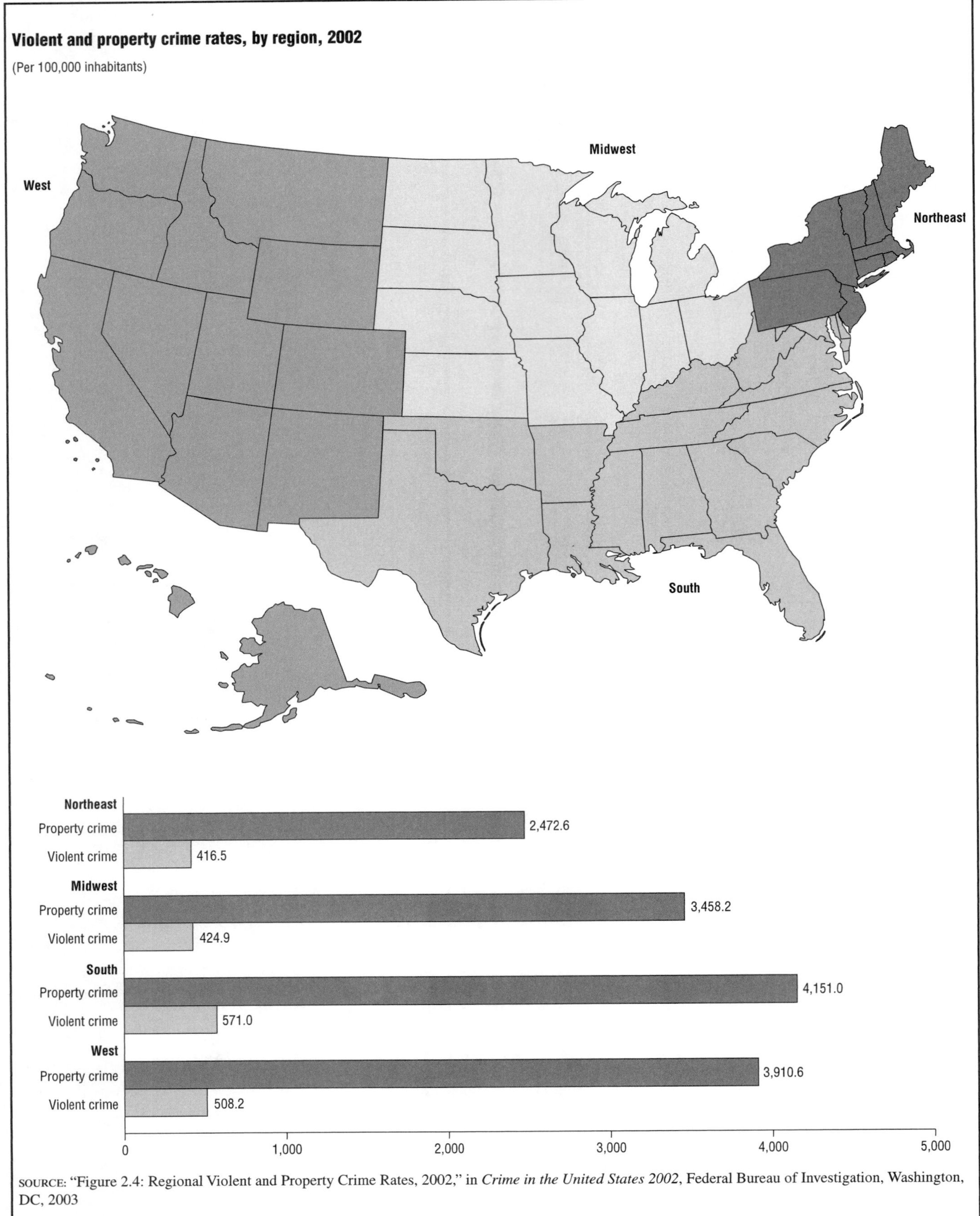

SOURCE: "Figure 2.4: Regional Violent and Property Crime Rates, 2002," in *Crime in the United States 2002*, Federal Bureau of Investigation, Washington, DC, 2003

TABLE 1.3

Estimated arrests, 2002

Offense	Arrests	Offense	Arrests
Total[1]	**13,741,438**	Embezzlement	18,552
		Stolen property; buying, receiving, possessing	126,422
Murder and nonnegligent manslaughter	14,158	Vandalism	276,697
Forcible rape	28,288	Weapons; carrying, possessing, etc.	164,446
Robbery	105,774	Prostitution and commercialized vice	79,733
Aggravated assault	472,290	Sex offenses (except forcible rape and prostitution)	95,066
Burglary	288,291	Drug abuse violations	1,538,813
Larceny-theft	1,160,085	Gambling	10,506
Motor vehicle theft	148,943	Offenses against the family and children	140,286
Arson	16,635	Driving under the influence	1,461,746
		Liquor laws	653,819
Violent crime[2]	620,510	Drunkenness	572,735
Property crime[3]	1,613,954	Disorderly conduct	669,938
Crime Index[4]	2,234,464	Vagrancy	27,295
		All other offenses	3,662,159
Other assaults	1,288,682	Suspicion	8,899
Forgery and counterfeiting	115,735	Curfew and loitering law violations	141,252
Fraud	337,404	Runaways	125,688

[1]Does not include suspicion.
[2]Violent crimes are offenses of murder, forcible rape, robbery, and aggravated assault.
[3]Property crimes are offenses of burglary, larceny-theft, motor vehicle theft, and arson.
[4]Includes arson.

SOURCE: "Table 29: Estimated Arrests, United States, 2002," in *Crime in the United States 2002,* Federal Bureau of Investigation, Washington, DC, 2003

influence (1.46 million), and public drunkenness (572,735) accounted for over one-fourth (25.7 percent) of all arrests in 2002. (See Table 1.3.)

Age

In 2002 arrestees under the age of 25 accounted for 46.4 percent of persons arrested for all criminal offenses nationwide, and 54.2 percent of persons arrested for Crime Index offenses. (See Table 1.4.) Arrestees under 21 accounted for 31.3 percent of all arrests and 41.1 percent of arrests for Crime Index offenses. Persons under 18 comprised 16.5 percent of all arrests and 25.7 percent of arrests for Crime Index offenses in 2002, while persons under 15 accounted for 5.2 percent of all arrests.

In 2002 persons under 25 accounted for 43.7 percent of violent crime arrests and 58.2 percent of property crime arrests. People in this young age group represented a large percentage of those arrested for many crimes:

- Arson (67.8 percent)
- Burglary (62.6 percent)
- Liquor law violations (78.9 percent)
- Motor vehicle theft (63.8 percent)
- Robbery (61.4 percent)
- Vandalism (68 percent)

Arrests of persons under 18 years of age (considered juveniles by most states) fell 10.9 percent from 1993 to 2002. This compares to virtually no change in arrestees over 18 years of age during the same 10-year period. (See Table 1.5.) Embezzlement violations accounted for the largest increase (73.1 percent) in arrests of persons under 18 between 1993 and 2002, followed by an increase of 59.1 percent increase for drug abuse offenses, and 48 percent for offenses against the family and children. Because curfew/loitering and running away are considered status offenses (crimes for juveniles but not for adults), they are not measured for persons over 18 years of age. Despite these increases, Crime Index arrests for juveniles declined. Arrests for violent crimes like murder and rape dropped significantly in this age group (64.3 and 26.5 percent respectively), as did some types of property crime, like motor vehicle theft (50.4 percent).

Gender

In 2002 men were arrested 3.3 times more often than women. Overall, males accounted for about 6.5 million arrests in 2002, compared to 1.9 million arrests of females. However, from 1993 to 2002, the number of males arrested for all offenses declined by 5.9 percent, while female arrests for all offenses increased by 14.1 percent. While arrests for males under 18 declined by 16.4 percent, arrests for females under 18 increased by 6.4 percent between 1993 and 2002. (See Table 1.6.)

From 1993 to 2002 drug abuse violations accounted for the largest percentage increase in non-status offense arrests for all males (34.5 percent), while for females embezzlement showed the largest increase (80.5 percent). For males and females under the age of 18, arrests for drug abuse violations between 1993 and 2002 increased by 51.2 percent and 120.0 percent, respectively. Offenses against family and children (domestic violence and child abuse) increased by 53.0 percent for all females and 8.1 percent for all males between 1993 and 2002. In 2002

TABLE 1.4

Arrests of persons under 15,18, 21, and 25 years of age, 2002

Offense charged	Total allages	Number of persons arrested				Percent of total all ages			
		Under 15	Under 18	Under 21	Under 25	Under 15	Under 18	Under 21	Under 25
Total	**9,819,501**	**510,226**	**1,624,192**	**3,077,565**	**4,556,104**	**5.2**	**16.5**	**31.3**	**46.4**
Murder and nonnegligent manslaughter	10,107	101	973	2,915	5,161	1.0	9.6	28.8	51.1
Forcible rape	20,162	1,243	3,361	6,324	9,302	6.2	16.7	31.4	46.1
Robbery	77,342	4,323	17,893	34,409	47,460	5.6	23.1	44.5	61.4
Aggravated assault	339,437	15,846	44,281	82,137	133,400	4.7	13.0	24.2	39.3
Burglary	206,136	22,389	61,843	100,886	129,124	10.9	30.0	48.9	62.6
Larceny-theft	845,009	95,090	248,861	378,668	475,903	11.3	29.5	44.8	56.3
Motor vehicle theft	107,187	8,227	32,544	52,623	68,394	7.7	30.4	49.1	63.8
Arson	11,833	3,728	5,851	7,108	8,022	31.5	49.4	60.1	67.8
Violent crime[1]	447,048	21,513	66,508	125,785	195,323	4.8	14.9	28.1	43.7
Property crime[2]	1,170,165	129,434	349,099	539,285	681,443	11.1	29.8	46.1	58.2
Crime Index[3]	1,617,213	150,947	415,607	665,070	876,766	9.3	25.7	41.1	54.2
Other assaults	921,676	71,697	168,996	261,254	390,153	7.8	18.3	28.3	42.3
Forgery and counterfeiting	83,111	457	3,652	15,737	30,841	0.5	4.4	18.9	37.1
Fraud	233,087	1,178	6,434	29,905	66,714	0.5	2.8	12.8	28.6
Embezzlement	13,416	90	1,005	3,581	5,887	0.7	7.5	26.7	43.9
Stolen property; buying, receiving, possessing	91,280	5,044	18,819	36,064	50,878	5.5	20.6	39.5	55.7
Vandalism	198,550	32,888	75,955	108,498	134,926	16.6	38.3	54.6	68.0
Weapons; carrying, possessing, etc.	118,312	8,647	25,288	46,491	67,458	7.3	21.4	39.3	57.0
Prostitution and commercialized vice	58,758	165	1,095	6,259	13,818	0.3	1.9	10.7	23.5
Sex offenses (except forcible rape and prostitution)	67,833	7,226	13,877	21,313	29,049	10.7	20.5	31.4	42.8
Drug abuse violations	1,103,017	21,836	133,754	342,204	540,142	2.0	12.1	31.0	49.0
Gambling	7,525	171	1,114	2,496	3,845	2.3	14.8	33.2	51.1
Offenses against the family and children	97,716	2,442	6,572	13,227	25,566	2.5	6.7	13.5	26.2
Driving under the influence	1,020,377	370	15,214	110,849	294,898	*	1.5	10.9	28.9
Liquor laws	463,849	10,132	106,014	331,409	366,125	2.2	22.9	71.4	78.9
Drunkenness	413,808	1,679	13,529	53,504	116,051	0.4	3.3	12.9	28.0
Disorderly conduct	482,827	56,314	139,048	203,997	277,201	11.7	28.8	42.3	57.4
Vagrancy	19,678	402	1,519	3,325	5,294	2.0	7.7	16.9	26.9
All other offenses (except traffic)	2,606,294	76,025	282,025	626,786	1,063,824	2.9	10.8	24.0	40.8
Suspicion	7,670	294	1,171	2,092	3,164	3.8	15.3	27.3	41.3
Curfew and loitering law violations	103,155	29,070	103,155	103,155	103,155	28.2	100.0	100.0	100.0
Runaways	90,349	33,152	90,349	90,349	90,349	36.7	100.0	100.0	100.0

[1] Violent crimes are offenses of murder, forcible rape, robbery, and aggravated assault.
[2] Property crimes are offenses of burglary, larceny-theft, motor vehicle theft, and arson.
[3] Includes arson.
* Less than one-tenth of 1 percent.

SOURCE: "Table 41: Arrests of Persons under 15, 18, 21, and 25 Years of Age, 2002," in *Crime in the United States 2002,* Federal Bureau of Investigation, Washington, DC, 2003

men were arrested most often for drug abuse violations (798,695) and driving under the influence (727,089). Women were arrested most often for larceny-theft (270,467), although the number of women arrested for larceny-theft declined by 14.0 percent from 1993 to 2002.

Race and Ethnicity

Although whites are arrested more often in total numbers, blacks are over-represented in almost all areas of arrests in relation to their proportion of the general population. Hispanics are counted by the government as an ethnic group, not a race, and therefore do not always appear as a separate category in statistics. Hispanics, like blacks, are also arrested more often in relation to their proportion of the population than are non-Hispanics.

According to the U.S. Census Bureau, in 2001 whites comprised 77 percent of the population, while blacks and Hispanics accounted for 12.9 and 12.5 percent respectively. In 2002, of some 9.8 million arrests nationwide, about 70.7 percent of those arrested were white and 26.9 percent were black. (See Table 1.7.) American Indians accounted for 1.3 percent and Asians/Pacific Islanders accounted for another 1.1 percent of arrests. About 50 percent of those arrested for murder were black, while 47.7 percent were whites; 63.4 percent of those arrested for forcible rape were white, while 34.0 percent were black. Similarly, 63.4 percent of those arrested for aggravated assault were white, while 34.2 percent were black. Of those arrested for burglary in 2002, 70.4 percent were white and 27.5 percent black. For larceny-theft, 67.9 percent of arrestees were white, while 29.3 percent were black.

Whites were much more likely to be arrested for driving under the influence, other liquor law violations, and running away. American Indians comprised 2.3 percent of all arrests for drunkenness, while Asian or Pacific Islanders accounted for less than 1 percent of such arrests. Driving under the influence accounted for the highest per-

TABLE 1.5

Ten-year arrest trends, 1993–2002

	Number of persons arrested								
	Total all ages			Under 18 years of age			18 years of age and over		
Offense charged	1993	2002	Percent change	1993	2002	Percent change	1993	2002	Percent change
Total[1]	**8,581,290**	**8,413,983**	**−1.9**	**1,564,326**	**1,393,752**	**−10.9**	**7,016,964**	**7,020,231**	*
Murder and nonnegligent manslaughter	15,125	8,933	−40.9	2,485	886	−64.3	12,640	8,047	−36.3
Forcible rape	23,509	17,394	−26.0	3,928	2,887	−26.5	19,581	14,507	−25.9
Robbery	96,877	69,405	−28.4	26,505	16,338	−38.4	70,372	53,067	−24.6
Aggravated assault	320,814	299,286	−6.7	49,427	38,082	−23.0	271,387	261,204	−3.8
Burglary	253,751	178,477	−29.7	89,511	54,393	−39.2	164,240	124,084	−24.4
Larceny-theft	959,452	729,825	−23.9	307,926	216,434	−29.7	651,526	513,391	−21.2
Motor vehicle theft	128,552	94,608	−26.4	57,740	28,664	−50.4	70,812	65,944	−6.9
Arson	12,646	10,055	−20.5	6,451	4,957	−23.2	6,195	5,098	−17.7
Violent crime[2]	456,325	395,018	−13.4	82,345	58,193	−29.3	373,980	336,825	−9.9
Property crime[3]	1,354,401	1,012,965	−25.2	461,628	304,448	−34.0	892,773	708,517	−20.6
Crime Index[4]	1,810,726	1,407,983	−22.2	543,973	362,641	−33.3	1,266,753	1,045,342	−17.5
Other assaults	733,037	782,294	+6.7	126,489	143,933	+13.8	606,548	638,361	+5.2
Forgery and counterfeiting	66,364	71,842	+8.3	5,341	3,070	−42.5	61,023	68,772	+12.7
Fraud	218,695	195,925	−10.4	6,449	5,258	−18.5	212,246	190,667	−10.2
Embezzlement	7,910	11,815	+49.4	510	883	+73.1	7,400	10,932	+47.7
Stolen property; buying, receiving, possessing	101,613	76,137	−25.1	28,808	15,766	−45.3	72,805	60,371	−17.1
Vandalism	209,095	169,842	−18.8	97,968	65,360	−33.3	111,127	104,482	−6.0
Weapons; carrying, possessing, etc.	175,998	104,418	−40.7	42,530	22,615	−46.8	133,468	81,803	−38.7
Prostitution and commercialized vice	61,811	51,275	−17.0	755	958	+26.9	61,056	50,317	−17.6
Sex offenses (except forcible rape and prostitution)	69,072	59,193	−14.3	13,387	12,198	−8.9	55,685	46,995	−15.6
Drug abuse violations	710,922	974,082	+37.0	73,413	116,781	+59.1	637,509	857,301	+34.5
Gambling	10,348	6,500	−37.2	1,715	1,053	−38.6	8,633	5,447	−36.9
Offenses against the family and children	67,930	79,059	+16.4	3,520	5,208	+48.0	64,410	73,851	+14.7
Driving under the influence	984,141	879,210	−10.7	8,878	12,921	+45.5	975,263	866,289	−11.2
Liquor laws	316,919	385,611	+21.7	75,836	88,574	+16.8	241,083	297,037	+23.2
Drunkenness	509,543	362,979	−28.8	11,705	11,452	−2.2	497,838	351,527	−29.4
Disorderly conduct	483,676	398,728	−17.6	103,747	112,844	+8.8	379,929	285,884	−24.8
Vagrancy	13,581	15,702	+15.6	2,254	1,346	−40.3	11,327	14,356	+26.7
All other offenses (except traffic)	1,834,511	2,209,668	+20.4	221,650	239,171	+7.9	1,612,861	1,970,497	+22.2
Suspicion	6,231	2,252	−63.9	1,239	708	−42.9	4,992	1,544	−69.1
Curfew and loitering law violations	68,042	91,984	+35.2	68,042	91,984	+35.2	–	–	–
Runaways	127,356	79,736	−37.4	127,356	79,736	−37.4	–	–	–

[1]Does not include suspicion.
[2]Violent crimes are offenses of murder, forcible rape, robbery, and aggravated assault.
[3]Property crimes are offenses of burglary, larceny-theft, motor vehicle theft, and arson.
[4]Includes arson.
*Less than one-tenth of 1 percent.

SOURCE: "Table 32: Ten-Year Arrest Trends: Totals, 1993–2002," in *Crime in the United States 2002,* Federal Bureau of Investigation, Washington, DC, 2003

centage of arrests among whites (87.8 percent), while gambling accounted for the highest proportion of arrests among African-Americans (68.3 percent). Among American Indians, liquor law violations accounted for the highest proportion of arrests (2.5 percent of all arrests for this offense). Gambling was the crime for which the most Asians/Pacific Islanders (4.2 percent) were arrested.

Offenses Cleared by Arrest

The more violent the crime, the more likely it is that a suspect will be arrested. According to the FBI, for the crimes reported to law enforcement agencies nationwide in 2002, 64.0 percent of all murders, 56.5 percent of all aggravated assaults, 44.5 percent of forcible rapes, and 25.7 percent of robberies were cleared by arrest. Property crimes, such as larceny-theft (18.0 percent), motor vehicle theft (13.8 percent), and burglary (13.0 percent), were least likely to be cleared by arrest in 2002. The fact that a crime is cleared by arrest does not mean that the individual arrested is guilty of the crime or will be convicted of the offense in criminal or juvenile court.

THE "TAKE" FROM EACH CRIME

In 2002 the value of the goods taken in the average crime varied. Generally, the value of goods taken is very low compared to the risk and consequences of the crime. The majority of those arrested in 2002 netted less than $200. In 37.8 percent of cases the value of the goods taken was under $50 and in 22.6 percent of cases it was between $50 and $200. It was over $200 in 39.6 percent of property crimes. Motor vehicle thefts, which are calculated separately, had the highest average loss of all property crimes in 2002—$6,701—up by 2.2 percent from 2001. The average bank robbery in 2002 netted $4,763, down by 6.5

TABLE 1.6

Ten year arrest trends, by sex, 1993–2002

Offense charged	Male						Female					
	Total			Under 18			Total			Under 18		
	1993	2002	Percent change	1993	2002	Percent change	1993	2002	Percent change	1993	2002	Percent change
Total[1]	**6,891,398**	**6,486,470**	**+5.9**	**1,186,822**	**992,153**	**−16.4**	**1,689,892**	**1,927,513**	**+14.1**	**377,504**	**401,599**	**+6.4**
Murder and nonnegligent manslaughter	13,656	7,986	−41.5	2,326	795	−65.8	1,469	947	−35.5	159	91	−42.8
Forcible rape	23,201	17,141	−26.1	3,856	2,782	−27.9	308	253	−17.9	72	105	+45.8
Robbery	88,326	62,330	−29.4	24,263	14,908	−38.6	8,551	7,075	−17.3	2,242	1,430	−36.2
Aggravated assault	272,381	238,780	−12.3	41,055	29,127	−29.1	48,433	60,506	+24.9	8,372	8,955	+7.0
Burglary	227,422	154,642	−32.0	80,681	48,136	−40.3	26,329	23,835	−9.5	8,830	6,257	−29.1
Larceny-theft	645,065	459,358	−28.8	212,145	130,798	−38.3	314,387	270,467	−14.0	95,781	85,636	−10.6
Motor vehicle theft	112,582	78,955	−29.9	49,534	23,777	−52.0	15,970	15,653	−2.0	8,206	4,887	−40.4
Arson	10,847	8,507	−21.6	5,685	4,393	−22.7	1,799	1,548	−14.0	766	564	−26.4
Violent crime[2]	397,564	326,237	−17.9	71,500	47,612	−33.4	58,761	68,781	+17.1	10,845	10,581	−2.4
Property crime[3]	995,916	701,462	−29.6	348,045	207,104	−40.5	358,485	311,503	−13.1	113,583	97,344	−14.3
Crime Index[4]	1,393,480	1,027,699	−26.2	419,545	254,716	−39.3	417,246	380,284	−8.9	124,428	107,925	−13.3
Other assaults	600,914	596,196	−0.8	93,725	97,759	+4.3	132,123	186,098	+40.9	32,764	46,174	+40.9
Forgery and counterfeiting	42,342	43,190	+2.0	3,482	1,949	−44.0	24,022	28,652	+19.3	1,859	1,121	−39.7
Fraud	120,506	105,140	−12.8	4,270	3,472	−18.7	98,189	90,785	−7.5	2,179	1,786	−18.0
Embezzlement	4,631	5,898	+27.4	296	506	+70.9	3,279	5,917	+80.5	214	377	+76.2
Stolen property; buying, receiving, possessing	88,634	63,261	−28.6	25,671	13,551	−47.2	12,979	12,876	−0.8	3,137	2,215	−29.4
Vandalism	183,817	141,782	−22.9	88,566	56,527	−36.2	25,278	28,060	+11.0	9,402	8,833	−6.1
Weapons; carrying, possessing, etc.	162,611	96,141	−40.9	39,160	20,123	−48.6	13,387	8,277	−38.2	3,370	2,492	−26.1
Prostitution and commercialized vice	22,728	18,078	−20.5	320	331	+3.4	39,083	33,197	−15.1	435	627	+44.1
Sex offenses (except forcible rape and prostitution)	63,068	54,249	−14.0	12,148	11,084	−8.8	6,004	4,944	−17.7	1,239	1,114	−10.1
Drug abuse violations	594,006	798,695	+34.5	65,051	98,383	+51.2	116,916	175,387	+50.0	8,362	18,398	+120.0
Gambling	9,314	5,954	−36.1	1,670	1,022	−38.8	1,034	546	−47.2	45	31	−31.1
Offenses against the family and children	55,344	59,802	+8.1	2,242	3,229	+44.0	12,586	19,257	+53.0	1,278	1,979	+54.9
Driving under the influence	846,497	727,089	−14.1	7,584	10,416	+37.3	137,644	152,121	+10.5	1,294	2,505	+93.6
Liquor laws	252,565	289,770	+14.7	54,032	58,648	+8.5	64,354	95,841	+48.9	21,804	29,926	+37.3
Drunkenness	452,805	313,451	−30.8	9,842	9,047	−8.1	56,738	49,528	−12.7	1,863	2,405	+29.1
Disorderly conduct	384,867	301,613	−21.6	80,673	79,064	−2.0	98,809	97,115	−1.7	23,074	33,780	+46.4
Vagrancy	11,470	12,696	+10.7	1,893	1,023	−46.0	2,111	3,006	+42.4	361	323	−10.5
All other offenses (except traffic)	1,498,770	1,730,296	+15.4	173,623	175,833	+1.3	335,741	479,372	+42.8	48,027	63,338	+31.9
Suspicion	5,200	1,748	−66.4	1,024	512	−50.0	1,031	504	−51.1	215	196	−8.8
Curfew and loitering law violations	49,007	63,454	+29.5	49,007	63,454	+29.5	19,035	28,530	+49.9	19,035	28,530	+49.9
Runaways	54,022	32,016	−40.7	54,022	32,016	−40.7	73,334	47,720	−34.9	73,334	47,720	−34.9

[1]Does not include suspicion.
[2]Violent crimes are offenses of murder, forcible rape, robbery, and aggravated assault.
[3]Property crimes are offenses of burglary, larceny-theft, motor vehicle theft, and arson.
[4]Includes arson.

SOURCE: "Table 33: Ten-Year Arrest Trends by Sex, 1993–2002," in *Crime in the United States 2002,* Federal Bureau of Investigation, Washington, DC, 2003

percent from 2001. Robberies of convenience stores resulted in an average of $665 taken in 2002. The average burglary in 2002 resulted in a loss of $1,549, while pocket-picking and purse-snatching accounted for losses averaging $328 and $332, respectively. (See Table 1.8.)

When a criminal steals money, as in the case of a bank robber or purse-snatcher, he or she can usually spend the stolen cash. However, in the case of burglary or motor vehicle theft the criminal almost never collects the total value of the stolen property. While the value of the stolen goods in a typical burglary might be $1,549, the thief has no way to sell it for its real value. He or she usually takes it to a fence (a person who buys and sells stolen goods). The fence may pay as little as 10 percent of the value of the item or items, depending on how easily he or she feels it will be to find a buyer for the stolen property. Thus, a $400 VCR could be worth as little as $40 to the thief.

Recovery Rate for Stolen Property

In 2002 only 36.1 percent of the value of stolen property was recovered. The recovered value of motor vehicles in 2002 was highest, at 63.1 percent, followed by livestock (19.0 percent), clothing and furs (12.5 percent), consumable goods (10.6 percent), and firearms (8.9 percent). Recovery rates for jewelry, precious metals, and office equipment averaged around 5.5 percent in 2002, while theft victims recovered televisions, stereos, and other electronics only 4.2 percent of the time. (See Table 1.9.)

THE FEDERAL GOVERNMENT'S ROLE

Federal spending accounts for only about 10 percent of all law enforcement resources. State and local governments have always played the central role in controlling crime. The federal government is required to enforce only laws within its jurisdiction, such as forgery and espionage,

TABLE 1.7

Arrests by race, 2002

Offense charged	Total arrests: Total	White	Black	American Indian or Alaskan Native	Asian or Pacific Islander	Percent distribution[1]: Total	White	Black	American Indian or Alaskan Native	Asian or Pacific Islander
Total	**9,797,385**	**6,923,390**	**2,633,632**	**130,636**	**109,727**	**100.0**	**70.7**	**26.9**	**1.3**	**1.1**
Murder and nonnegligent manslaughter	10,099	4,814	5,047	115	123	100.0	47.7	50.0	1.1	1.2
Forcible rape	20,127	12,766	6,852	240	269	100.0	63.4	34.0	1.2	1.3
Robbery	77,280	34,109	41,837	471	863	100.0	44.1	54.1	0.6	1.1
Aggravated assault	338,850	214,992	115,789	4,069	4,000	100.0	63.4	34.2	1.2	1.2
Burglary	205,873	144,958	56,647	1,992	2,276	100.0	70.4	27.5	1.0	1.1
Larceny-theft	843,066	572,515	246,946	10,345	13,260	100.0	67.9	29.3	1.2	1.6
Motor vehicle theft	107,031	64,625	39,114	1,156	2,136	100.0	60.4	36.5	1.1	2.0
Arson	11,808	9,067	2,537	100	104	100.0	76.8	21.5	0.8	0.9
Violent crime[2]	446,356	266,681	169,525	4,895	5,255	100.0	59.7	38.0	1.1	1.2
Property crime[3]	1,167,778	791,165	345,244	13,593	17,776	100.0	67.7	29.6	1.2	1.5
Crime Index[4]	1,614,134	1,057,846	514,769	18,488	23,031	100.0	65.5	31.9	1.1	1.4
Other assaults	919,691	610,946	286,787	12,201	9,757	100.0	66.4	31.2	1.3	1.1
Forgery and counterfeiting	82,882	57,125	24,148	458	1,151	100.0	68.9	29.1	0.6	1.4
Fraud	232,336	157,763	71,538	1,431	1,604	100.0	67.9	30.8	0.6	0.7
Embezzlement	13,379	9,153	3,959	64	203	100.0	68.4	29.6	0.5	1.5
Stolen property; buying, receiving, possessing	91,150	53,535	35,986	611	1,018	100.0	58.7	39.5	0.7	1.1
Vandalism	198,139	150,437	42,757	2,804	2,141	100.0	75.9	21.6	1.4	1.1
Weapons; carrying, possessing, etc.	118,148	73,140	42,810	879	1,319	100.0	61.9	36.2	0.7	1.1
Prostitution and commercialized vice	58,659	33,650	23,455	364	1,190	100.0	57.4	40.0	0.6	2.0
Sex offenses (except forcible rape and prostitution)	67,761	50,378	15,745	680	958	100.0	74.3	23.2	1.0	1.4
Drug abuse violations	1,101,547	728,797	357,725	6,848	8,177	100.0	66.2	32.5	0.6	0.7
Gambling	7,525	2,033	5,136	38	318	100.0	27.0	68.3	0.5	4.2
Offenses against the family and children	97,393	66,440	28,180	1,266	1,507	100.0	68.2	28.9	1.3	1.5
Driving under the influence	1,017,504	893,395	99,548	15,460	9,101	100.0	87.8	9.8	1.5	0.9
Liquor laws	462,215	405,275	41,204	11,397	4,339	100.0	87.7	8.9	2.5	0.9
Drunkenness	412,735	345,448	55,598	9,563	2,126	100.0	83.7	13.5	2.3	0.5
Disorderly conduct	481,932	321,117	149,393	7,883	3,539	100.0	66.6	31.0	1.6	0.7
Vagrancy	19,669	12,223	6,888	419	139	100.0	62.1	35.0	2.1	0.7
All other offenses (except traffic)	2,599,658	1,751,450	778,558	37,377	32,273	100.0	67.4	29.9	1.4	1.2
Suspicion	7,647	4,130	3,128	108	281	100.0	54.0	40.9	1.4	3.7
Curfew and loitering law violations	103,054	70,738	29,717	1,083	1,516	100.0	68.6	28.8	1.1	1.5
Runaways	90,227	68,371	16,603	1,214	4,039	100.0	75.8	18.4	1.3	4.5

and to operate prisons for those convicted of federal crimes. Yet the federal government at times has responded to increased public concern over violent crime (like after the terrorist attacks on the Pentagon and the World Trade Center in New York on September 11, 2001) by expanding its law enforcement role. Federal agencies can encourage cooperation among state and local governments and act with foreign governments to curb threats such as the spread of terrorism, drug-related crime, and organized crime. The federal government is better able than the states to collect national crime statistics and give out information. It also develops and promotes new technologies, such as crime databases, fingerprint facilities, and DNA-testing laboratories, to serve both national and local needs.

2002 Federal Budget

The Federal Budget for fiscal year 2002 allocated a proposed $4.2 billion to assist state and local governments in fighting crime. Although this level of spending was $1 billion less than in fiscal year 2001, federal assistance to state and local governments for criminal justice expenditures increased by 500 percent from 1992 to 2001.

Of the $36 billion in the Federal budget proposed for administration of justice in fiscal year 2002, nearly half was allocated for law enforcement. (See Table 1.10.) Some of the law enforcement and crime prevention priorities reflected in the FY 2002 budget included funding to prevent terrorism and support for programs to tighten border and transportation security.

The administration's 2002 budget also proposed new funding for prison construction, modernization, and the activation of newly constructed federal prisons. See Table 1.11 for a detailed look at the allocation of Office of Justice program funds from 1990 to 2001, which shows that budget requests for 2001 were about 5.5 times those for 1990.

Violent Crime Control and Law Enforcement Act of 1994

The Violent Crime Control and Law Enforcement Act of 1994 (PL 103-322) included several "get tough on crime" provisions:

- A ban on some semiautomatic assault-style rifles.
- A "three strikes and you're out" provision. This provision requires a mandatory life sentence without parole

TABLE 1.7
Arrests by race, 2002 [CONTINUED]

	Arrests under 18					Percent distribution[1]				
Offense charged	Total	White	Black	American Indian or Alaskan Native	Asian or Pacific Islander	Total	White	Black	American Indian or Alaskan Native	Asian or Pacific Islander
Total	**1,620,594**	**1,158,776**	**415,854**	**20,383**	**25,581**	**100.0**	**71.5**	**25.7**	**1.3**	**1.6**
Murder and nonnegligent manslaughter	972	446	487	23	16	100.0	45.9	50.1	2.4	1.6
Forcible rape	3,355	2,079	1,207	37	32	100.0	62.0	36.0	1.1	1.0
Robbery	17,878	6,895	10,537	91	355	100.0	38.6	58.9	0.5	2.0
Aggravated assault	44,185	26,877	16,217	535	556	100.0	60.8	36.7	1.2	1.3
Burglary	61,754	44,680	15,558	689	827	100.0	72.4	25.2	1.1	1.3
Larceny-theft	248,202	173,910	65,667	3,443	5,182	100.0	70.1	26.5	1.4	2.1
Motor vehicle theft	32,487	18,949	12,428	445	665	100.0	58.3	38.3	1.4	2.0
Arson	5,837	4,711	1,026	48	52	100.0	80.7	17.6	0.8	0.9
Violent crime[2]	66,390	36,297	28,448	686	959	100.0	54.7	42.8	1.0	1.4
Property crime[3]	348,280	242,250	94,679	4,625	6,726	100.0	69.6	27.2	1.3	1.9
Crime Index[4]	414,670	278,547	123,127	5,311	7,685	100.0	67.2	29.7	1.3	1.9
Other assaults	168,641	106,119	58,518	1,942	2,062	100.0	62.9	34.7	1.2	1.2
Forgery and counterfeiting	3,644	2,845	711	33	55	100.0	78.1	19.5	0.9	1.5
Fraud	6,418	4,242	2,051	47	78	100.0	66.1	32.0	0.7	1.2
Embezzlement	1,004	696	287	1	20	100.0	69.3	28.6	0.1	2.0
Stolen property; buying, receiving, possessing	18,769	10,612	7,761	134	262	100.0	56.5	41.4	0.7	1.4
Vandalism	75,781	61,373	12,594	919	895	100.0	81.0	16.6	1.2	1.2
Weapons; carrying, possessing, etc.	25,239	16,945	7,751	207	336	100.0	67.1	30.7	0.8	1.3
Prostitution and commercialized vice	1,094	479	597	6	12	100.0	43.8	54.6	0.5	1.1
Sex offenses (except forcible rape and prostitution)	13,857	9,986	3,603	107	161	100.0	72.1	26.0	0.8	1.2
Drug abuse violations	133,494	97,766	33,208	1,152	1,368	100.0	73.2	24.9	0.9	1.0
Gambling	1,114	127	955	0	32	100.0	11.4	85.7	*	2.9
Offenses against the family and children	6,554	4,837	1,541	56	120	100.0	73.8	23.5	0.9	1.8
Driving under the influence	15,155	14,138	628	267	122	100.0	93.3	4.1	1.8	0.8
Liquor laws	105,652	97,372	4,629	2,656	995	100.0	92.2	4.4	2.5	0.9
Drunkenness	13,508	12,155	995	258	100	100.0	90.0	7.4	1.9	0.7
Disorderly conduct	138,847	88,761	47,261	1,708	1,117	100.0	63.9	34.0	1.2	0.8
Vagrancy	1,518	1,147	346	14	11	100.0	75.6	22.8	0.9	0.7
All other offenses (except traffic)	281,184	210,704	62,641	3,261	4,578	100.0	74.9	22.3	1.2	1.6
Suspicion	1,170	816	330	7	17	100.0	69.7	28.2	0.6	1.5
Curfew and loitering law violations	103,054	70,738	29,717	1,083	1,516	100.0	68.6	28.8	1.1	1.5
Runaways	90,227	68,371	16,603	1,214	4,039	100.0	75.8	18.4	1.3	4.5

when an offender has been convicted of at least three serious or violent felony crimes and/or serious or violent drug-related crimes.

- Resources for more police, and grants to help involve community organizations in crime prevention programs.

The act also expanded the federal death penalty to apply to more than 50 offenses and provided funding for prison construction projects. A new trust fund—the Violent Crime Reduction Trust Fund—supported these new programs.

VIOLENCE AGAINST WOMEN. The U.S. Department of Justice's Office on Violence Against Women has distributed more than $1 billion worth of grants since its creation in 1995 to state, local, and tribal governments and community-based agencies to assist in efforts to prevent violence against women. In October of 2003 the President's Family Justice Center Initiative was established to help victims of domestic violence by combining often uncoordinated and disjointed local services into Family Justice Centers where medical, legal, counseling, and other assistance can be offered in a central location.

STATE CORRECTIONS BUDGETS

According to the National Association of State Budget Officers, total state spending for corrections in fiscal year 2002 was $38.5 billion, an increase of some 2.6 percent from 2001. Corrections accounted for about 7 percent of all state general-fund spending in 2002. Despite a declining crime rate, the rise in state prison populations accounted for much of the increase, with the construction of new correctional facilities accounting for much of the increase, in addition to juvenile justice programs and such alternatives to incarceration as probation and parole.

States in the Far West had the largest increase in spending for corrections in 2002, at 7.9 percent, followed by the Rocky Mountain states (6.1 percent). States in the Mid-Atlantic spent less in 2002 than they had in 2001, with a decrease of almost 1 percent.

TABLE 1.7

Arrests by race, 2002 [CONTINUED]

Offense charged	Arrests 18 and over					Percent distribution[1]				
	Total	White	Black	American Indian or Alaskan Native	Asian or Pacific Islander	Total	White	Black	American Indian or Alaskan Native	Asian or Pacific Islander
Total	**8,176,791**	**5,764,614**	**2,217,778**	**110,253**	**84,146**	**100.0**	**70.5**	**27.1**	**1.3**	**1.0**
Murder and nonnegligent manslaughter	9,127	4,368	4,560	92	107	100.0	47.9	50.0	1.0	1.2
Forcible rape	16,772	10,687	5,645	203	237	100.0	63.7	33.7	1.2	1.4
Robbery	59,402	27,214	31,300	380	508	100.0	45.8	52.7	0.6	0.9
Aggravated assault	294,665	188,115	99,572	3,534	3,444	100.0	63.8	33.8	1.2	1.2
Burglary	144,119	100,278	41,089	1,303	1,449	100.0	69.6	28.5	0.9	1.0
Larceny-theft	594,864	398,605	181,279	6,902	8,078	100.0	67.0	30.5	1.2	1.4
Motor vehicle theft	74,544	45,676	26,686	711	1,471	100.0	61.3	35.8	1.0	2.0
Arson	5,971	4,356	1,511	52	52	100.0	73.0	25.3	0.9	0.9
Violent crime[2]	379,966	230,384	141,077	4,209	4,296	100.0	60.6	37.1	1.1	1.1
Property crime[3]	819,498	548,915	250,565	8,968	11,050	100.0	67.0	30.6	1.1	1.3
Crime Index[4]	1,199,464	779,299	391,642	13,177	15,346	100.0	65.0	32.7	1.1	1.3
Other assaults	751,050	504,827	228,269	10,259	7,695	100.0	67.2	30.4	1.4	1.0
Forgery and counterfeiting	79,238	54,280	23,437	425	1,096	100.0	68.5	29.6	0.5	1.4
Fraud	225,918	153,521	69,487	1,384	1,526	100.0	68.0	30.8	0.6	0.7
Embezzlement	12,375	8,457	3,672	63	183	100.0	68.3	29.7	0.5	1.5
Stolen property; buying, receiving, possessing	72,381	42,923	28,225	477	756	100.0	59.3	39.0	0.7	1.0
Vandalism	122,358	89,064	30,163	1,885	1,246	100.0	72.8	24.7	1.5	1.0
Weapons; carrying, possessing, etc.	92,909	56,195	35,059	672	983	100.0	60.5	37.7	0.7	1.1
Prostitution and commercialized vice	57,565	33,171	22,858	358	1,178	100.0	57.6	39.7	0.6	2.0
Sex offenses (except forcible rape and prostitution)	53,904	40,392	12,142	573	797	100.0	74.9	22.5	1.1	1.5
Drug abuse violations	968,053	631,031	324,517	5,696	6,809	100.0	65.2	33.5	0.6	0.7
Gambling	6,411	1,906	4,181	38	286	100.0	29.7	65.2	0.6	4.5
Offenses against the family and children	90,839	61,603	26,639	1,210	1,387	100.0	67.8	29.3	1.3	1.5
Driving under the influence	1,002,349	879,257	98,920	15,193	8,979	100.0	87.7	9.9	1.5	0.9
Liquor laws	356,563	307,903	36,575	8,741	3,344	100.0	86.4	10.3	2.5	0.9
Drunkenness	399,227	333,293	54,603	9,305	2,026	100.0	83.5	13.7	2.3	0.5
Disorderly conduct	343,085	232,356	102,132	6,175	2,422	100.0	67.7	29.8	1.8	0.7
Vagrancy	18,151	11,076	6,542	405	128	100.0	61.0	36.0	2.2	0.7
All other offenses (except traffic)	2,318,474	1,540,746	715,917	34,116	27,695	100.0	66.5	30.9	1.5	1.2
Suspicion	6,477	3,314	2,798	101	264	100.0	51.2	43.2	1.6	4.1
Curfew and loitering law violations	–	–	–	–	–	–	–	–	–	–
Runaways	–	–	–	–	–	–	–	–	–	–

[1]Because of rounding, the percentages may not add to 100.0.
[2]Violent crimes are offenses of murder, forcible rape, robbery, and aggravated assault.
[3]Property crimes are offenses of burglary, larceny-theft, motor vehicle theft, and arson.
[4]Includes arson.
*Less than one-tenth of 1 percent.

SOURCE: "Table 43: Arrests by Race, 2002," in *Crime in the United States 2002,* Federal Bureau of Investigation, Washington, DC, 2003

TABLE 1.8

Number and percent change of offenses, by type, 2001–02

[12,524 agencies; 2002 estimated population 236,622,152]

Classification	Number of offenses 2002	Percent change over 2001	Percent distribution[1]	Average value
Murder	**12,904**	+2.2	–	
Forcible rape	**77,639**	+4.2	–	
Robbery:				
Total	**324,938**	**–1.1**	**100.0**	**$1,281**
Street/highway	139,037	–2.9	42.8	1,045
Commercial house	47,344	–1.3	14.6	1,676
Gas or service station	8,690	–7.6	2.7	679
Convenience store	20,990	–4.8	6.5	665
Residence	43,800	+4.4	13.5	1,340
Bank	7,485	–6.5	2.3	4,763
Miscellaneous	57,592	+2.7	17.7	1,340
Burglary:				
Total	**1,793,362**	**+2.0**	**100.0**	**1,549**
Residence (dwelling):	1,180,063	+3.0	65.8	1,482
Night	348,538	+2.4	19.4	1,177
Day	561,688	+4.3	31.3	1,567
Unknown	269,837	+1.3	15.0	1,698
Nonresidence (store, office, etc.):	613,299	–0.1	34.2	1,678
Night	260,525	*	14.5	1,449
Day	190,651	+0.1	10.6	1,525
Unknown	162,123	–0.4	9.0	2,227
Larceny-theft (except motor vehicle theft):				
Total	**5,808,133**	*	**100.0**	**699**
By type:				
Pocket-picking	26,707	–5.0	0.5	328
Purse-snatching	32,011	+3.0	0.6	332
Shoplifting	811,709	+2.2	14.0	187
From motor vehicles (except accessories)	1,536,453	+2.9	26.5	692
Motor vehicle accessories	622,384	+4.7	10.7	432
Bicycles	227,970	–3.5	3.9	257
From buildings	727,395	–5.4	12.5	1,013
From coin-operated machines	43,103	+1.8	0.7	250
All others	1,780,401	–2.2	30.7	984
By value:				
Over $200	2,301,455	+0.7	39.6	1,682
$50 to $200	1,310,879	–1.5	22.6	114
Under $50	2,195,799	+0.1	37.8	18
Motor vehicle theft	**1,039,490**	+2.2	–	6,701

[1]Because of rounding, the percentages may not add to 100.0.
*Less than one-tenth of 1 percent.

SOURCE: "Table 23: Offense Analysis, Number and Percent Change, 2001–2002," in *Crime in the United States 2002,* Federal Bureau of Investigation, Washington, DC, 2003

TABLE 1.9

Property stolen and recovered, by type and value, 2002

[12,007 agencies; 2002 estimated population 228,033,072]

Type of property	Value of property: Stolen	Value of property: Recovered	Percent recovered
Total	**$13,731,306,278**	**$4,958,923,288**	**36.1**
Currency, notes, etc.	977,139,529	40,078,922	4.1
Jewelry and precious metals	998,967,252	54,599,943	5.5
Clothing and furs	240,855,326	30,152,611	12.5
Locally stolen motor vehicles	6,569,478,599	4,146,165,060	63.1
Office equipment	466,027,464	25,132,680	5.4
Televisions, radios, stereos, etc.	932,644,149	39,517,884	4.2
Firearms	92,717,808	8,258,690	8.9
Household goods	205,369,049	9,693,633	4.7
Consumable goods	121,826,909	12,945,137	10.6
Livestock	17,122,092	3,253,959	19.0
Miscellaneous	3,109,158,101	589,124,769	18.9

SOURCE: "Table 24: Property Stolen and Recovered, by Type and Value, 2002," in *Crime in the United States 2002,* Federal Bureau of Investigation, Washington, DC, 2003

TABLE 1.10

Federal criminal justice budget authorities, 2002 (actual) and 2003–2008 (estimated)[1]

(In millions of dollars)

Type of program	2002 actual	Estimated					
		2003	2004	2005	2006	2007	2008
Total	**$36,177**	**$37,151**	**$40,602**	**$37,682**	**$38,644**	**$39,636**	**$40,695**
Discretionary, total	34,676	33,610	34,596	35,501	36,472	37,488	38,570
Federal law enforcement activities, total	16,607	15,632	16,138	16,589	17,077	17,591	18,124
Criminal investigations[2]	5,712	5,217	5,385	5,541	5,702	5,872	6,047
Bureau of Alcohol, Tobacco, Firearms, and Explosives	781	762	788	812	838	863	892
Border and transportation security directorate activities[3]	7,131	6,883	7,099	7,281	7,490	7,708	7,937
Equal Employment Opportunity Commission	311	310	322	333	345	356	369
Tax law, criminal investigations[4]	429	436	457	475	493	514	534
U.S. Secret Service	1,022	945	979	1,010	1,043	1,077	1,112
Other law enforcement activities	1,221	1,079	1,108	1,137	1,166	1,201	1,233
Federal litigative and judicial activities, total	8,304	8,278	8,529	8,767	9,017	9,278	9,570
Civil and criminal prosecution and representation	3,540	3,478	3,584	3,683	3,786	3,892	4,019
Representation of indigents in civil cases	329	329	334	339	344	350	357
Federal judicial and other litigative activities	4,435	4,471	4,611	4,745	4,887	5,036	5,194
Correctional activities[5]	4,618	4,468	4,618	4,753	4,896	5,043	5,198
Criminal justice assistance, total	5,147	5,232	5,311	5,392	5,482	5,576	5,678
Crime victims' fund	68	0	0	0	0	0	0
High-intensity drug trafficking areas program	187	226	229	233	237	241	245
Law enforcement assistance, community policing, and other justice programs	4,259	4,243	4,308	4,373	4,446	4,522	4,605
Terrorism prevention initiative[3]	633	763	774	786	799	813	828
Mandatory, total	1,501	3,541	6,006	2,181	2,172	2,148	2,125
Federal law enforcement activities, total	−267	−860	852	650	606	558	510
Border and transportation security directorate activities	2,419	2,606	2,692	2,570	2,587	2,604	2,622
Immigration fees	−1,852	−2,583	−2,261	−2,321	−2,384	−2,449	−2,514
Customs fees	−1,229	−1,314	−5	−5	−6	−6	−7
Treasury forfeiture fund	178	221	221	221	221	221	221
Other mandatory law enforcement programs	217	210	205	185	188	188	188
Federal litigative and judicial activities, total	975	1,050	1,041	984	1,018	1,041	1,065
Treasury forfeiture fund	345	422	377	380	387	395	402
Federal judicial officers' salaries and expenses and other mandatory programs	630	628	664	604	631	646	663
Correctional activities	−3	−3	−3	−3	−3	−3	−3
Criminal justice assistance, total	796	3,354	4,116	550	551	552	553
Crime victims' fund	606	605	1,706	500	500	500	500
September 11 victims' compensation	60	2,700	2,361	0	0	0	0
Public safety officers' benefits	198	49	49	50	51	52	53
Mandatory programs	−68	0	0	0	0	0	0

Note: These data are from the budget submitted by the President to Congress in 2003.
[1]Detail may not add to total because of rounding.
[2]Includes Drug Enforcement Administration, Federal Bureau of Investigation, Department of Homeland Security, Financial Crimes Enforcement Network, and interagency crime and drug enforcement programs.
[3]Department of Homeland Security.
[4]Internal Revenue Service.
[5]Federal prison system and detention trustee program.

SOURCE: "Table 1.10: Federal Criminal Justice Budget Authorities, 2002 (Actual) and 2003–2008 (estimated)," in *Sourcebook of Criminal Justice Statistics 2002,* U.S. Department of Justice, Bureau of Justice Statistics, Washington, DC, 2003.

TABLE 1.11

Allocation of Office of Justice programs' funds by type of justice activity, fiscal years 1990–2001[1]

In thousands of dollars

Type of budget activity	1990[2]	1991[2]	1992	1993	1994	1995	1996	1997	1998[3]	1999[3]	2000[3]	2001[4]
Total	**$762,358**	**$845,021**	**$865,689**	**$997,023**	**$848,960**	**$1,267,660**	**$2,702,011**	**$3,251,347**	**$3,733,066**	**$3,743,045**	**$3,919,611**	**$4,175,721**
Executive direction and control	24,240	25,169	26,641[5]	27,219	29,600	31,702	28,696	30,579	35,039	38,103	44,103	47,728
Research, evaluation, and demonstration programs	22,766	23,929	23,739	22,995	22,500	27,000	30,000	30,000	41,148	46,148	43,448	69,846
Justice statistical programs	20,879	22,095	22,095	21,373	20,943	21,379	21,379	21,379	21,529	25,029	25,505	28,991
State and local assistance programs												
Alcohol and crime in Indian country	NA	NA	NA	NA	NA	NA	NA	NA	NA	NA	NA	4,989
Anti-drug abuse formula (Byrne grants)	395,101	423,000	423,000	423,000	358,000	450,000	475,000	500,000	505,000	505,000	500,000	498,900
Anti-drug abuse discretionary	49,636	66,994	73,500	223,000[6]	116,500	62,000	60,000	60,000	46,500	47,000	52,000	78,377
Counterterrorism	NA	NA	NA	NA	NA	NA	NA	17,000	19,000	0	152,000	220,494
Criminal records upgrade	NA	NA	NA	NA	0	100,000	25,000	50,000	45,000	45,000	0	0
DNA identification State grants	NA	NA	NA	NA	NA	NA	1,000	3,000	12,500	15,000	0	0
Drug courts	NA	NA	NA	NA	NA	11,900	0	30,000	30,000	40,000	40,000	49,890
Family support	NA	NA	NA	NA	NA	NA	1,000	1,000	1,000	1,500	1,500	1,497
Indian tribal courts program	NA	NA	NA	NA	NA	NA	NA	NA	NA	5,000	5,000	7,982
Law enforcement block grants	NA	NA	NA	NA	NA	NA	503,000	523,000	523,000	523,000	497,885[7]	521,849
Motor vehicle theft prevention	NA	NA	NA	NA	NA	NA	500	750	750	1,300	1,300	1,297
Public Safety Officers' Benefits Program	24,818	26,075	27,144	28,524	30,821	29,717	30,608	32,276	33,003	31,809	32,541	35,619
Regional Information Sharing System[8]	13,402	14,000	14,500	14,491	14,491	14,500	14,500	14,500	20,000	20,000	20,000	24,945
State and local correctional facilities grants	NA	NA	NA	NA	0	24,500	617,500	670,000	720,500	720,500	653,533[7]	684,990
State criminal alien assistance program	NA	NA	NA	NA	NA	130,000	300,000	330,000	420,000	420,000	420,000	399,120
State prison drug treatment	NA	NA	NA	NA	NA	NA	27,000	30,000	63,000	63,000	63,000	62,861
Telemarketing fraud prevention	NA	NA	NA	NA	NA	NA	NA	2,000	2,500	2,000	2,000	1,996
Televised testimony of child abuse victims	NA	NA	1,000	0	0	0	50	550	1,000	1,000	1,000	998
Weed and Seed program	NA	NA	NA	NA	NA	NA	NA	0	33,500	33,500	33,500	33,925
White Collar Crime Information Center[9]	NA	NA	NA	NA	0	1,400	3,850	3,850	5,350	7,350	9,250	9,230
Juvenile justice programs												
Block grants	NA	NA	NA	NA	NA	NA	NA	0	250,000	250,000	237,994[7]	249,450
Child abuse investigation and prosecution	NA	NA	1,500	1,500	3,000	4,500	4,500	4,500	7,000	7,000	7,000	8,481
Court appointed special advocates	NA	NA	NA	NA	4,500	6,000	6,000	6,000	7,000	9,000	10,000	11,475
Judicial child abuse training	NA	NA	500	500	500	750	750	1,000	2,000	2,000	2,000	1,996
Juvenile justice discretionary programs	21,044	22,796	22,823[5]	23,372[5]	44,640	70,600	70,600	80,100	130,850	193,394	196,910	207,452
Juvenile justice formula grants	48,361	49,255	49,735[5]	50,078	58,310	68,600	68,600	85,100	95,100	77,556	76,540	76,372
Missing Alzheimer's program	NA	NA	NA	NA	NA	NA	900	900	900	900	900	898
Missing children	3,971	7,971	8,471	8,471	6,621	6,721	5,971	5,971	12,256	17,168	19,952	22,997

TABLE 1.11

Allocation of Office of Justice programs' funds by type of justice activity, fiscal years 1990–2001[1] [CONTINUED]

In thousands of dollars

Type of budget activity	1990[2]	1991[2]	1992	1993	1994	1995	1996	1997	1998[3]	1999[3]	2000[3]	2001[4]
Violence against women programs												
Encouraging arrest policies	NA	NA	NA	NA	NA	NA	28,000	33,000	59,000	34,000	34,000	33,925
Law enforcement and prosecution grants	NA	NA	NA	NA	NA	26,000	130,000	145,000	172,000	206,750	206,750	209,717
Rural domestic violence and child abuse enforcement	NA	NA	NA	NA	NA	NA	7,000	8,000	25,000	25,000	25,000	24,945
Violence against women training programs	NA	NA	NA	NA	NA	NA	1,000	1,000	2,000	5,000	5,000	4,989
Crime Victims Fund[10]	123,250	126,750	127,968	150,000	138,534	178,891	227,707	528,942	362,891	324,038	500,000[11]	537,500[12]
Programs previously funded by OJP[13]												
Emergency assistance[14]	9,927	0	1,000	0	0	0	0	0	0	0	0	0
High intensity drug trafficking areas[15]	NA	32,024	37,110	0	0	0	0	0	0	0	0	0
Mariel Cuban[16]	4,963	4,963	4,963	2,500	0	0	0	0	0	0	0	0
Other Crime Bill programs	NA	NA	NA	NA	NA	1,500	11,900	1,950	27,750	0	0	0

[1]Detail may not add to total because of rounding.
[2]Includes effect of Gramm-Rudman-Hollings reductions.
[3]Appropriations.
[4]Includes rescission per Public Law 106–554.
[5]Reflects the total program level, which includes unused carryover earmarked by Congress for addition to appropriated amount.
[6]Includes $150 million supplemental appropriation for the Police Hiring Program.
[7]Includes rescission per Public Law 106–113.
[8]A program to aid State and local law enforcement agencies in the exchange of intelligence information.
[9]This previously was part of the Regional Information Sharing System.
[10]Represents amount deposited in previous year.
[11]Collections totaled $985.2 million, however, an obligation limitation of $500 million was placed on total collections.
[12]Collections totaled $777 million, however, an obligation limitation of $537.5 million was placed on total availability
[13]Previously funded OJP programs may still be operational for either of the following reasons: (1) the program may be operating on funds appropriated in prior fiscal years; (2) the program may be subsumed under another program that is currently funded.
[14]A program authorized to provide funds, equipment, intelligence information, and/or personnel to a requesting State in the event of a law enforcement emergency.
[15]Funds transferred from the Office of National Drug Control Policy.
[16]Refers to an appropriation to be allocated to States housing Mariel Cuban refugees in State correctional facilities.

SOURCE: "Table 1.11. Allocation of Office of Justice Programs' Funds," in *Sourcebook of Criminal Justice Statistics 2000,* U.S. Department of Justice, Bureau of Justice Statistics, Washington, DC, 2001

CHAPTER 2

TYPES OF CRIME

In 2002 the Federal Bureau of Investigation's (FBI) Uniform Crime Report (UCR) estimated that one Crime Index offense was committed every 2.7 seconds in the United States. Property crimes were committed more frequently (one every 3.0 seconds) than violent crimes (one every 22.1 seconds), down from one every 19 seconds in 1996. The Crime Clock does not imply these crimes were committed with regularity; instead it represents the relative frequency of occurrence. Note this frequency of occurrence does not take into account population increases, as does the per capita crime rate.

The FBI, in its annual *Crime in the United States* report, publishes data for serious crimes in the Crime Index. The Index includes murder, rape, robbery, aggravated assault, burglary, larceny-theft, motor vehicle theft, and arson.

Although the number of crimes in the United States in 2002 remained high, at over 11.8 million, the total of Crime Index offenses remained relatively unchanged from 2001, rising only by 0.1 percent. Violent crimes comprised 12.0 percent of all Crime Index offenses in 2002, while property crimes accounted for 88.0 percent. According to five-year trend data, as shown in Figure 2.1, the Crime Index in 2002 was 4.9 percent lower than in 1998. The Crime Index rate, which equals the number of Crime Index offenses per 100,000 inhabitants, actually registered a 10.9 percent drop from the 1998 rate. (See Figure 2.1.)

MURDER

The FBI defines murder and non-negligent manslaughter as "the willful (non-negligent) killing of one human being by another." The figures for murder do not include suicides, accidents, or justifiable homicides either by citizens or law enforcement officers. In 2002 a murder was committed every 32.4 minutes according to the UCR's Crime Clock. The murder rate was 5.6 murders for every 100,000 inhabitants. In 2002 murders were most likely to occur in July and September and least likely to occur in February.

Murder Rate Decline

The total of homicides in 2002 was 16,204, compared to 16,037 in 2001. (See Table 2.1.) Murder and non-negligent manslaughter declined by 4.5 percent from 1998 to 2002, and by 33.9 percent from 1993.

FIGURE 2.1

Crime Index offenses, 2002

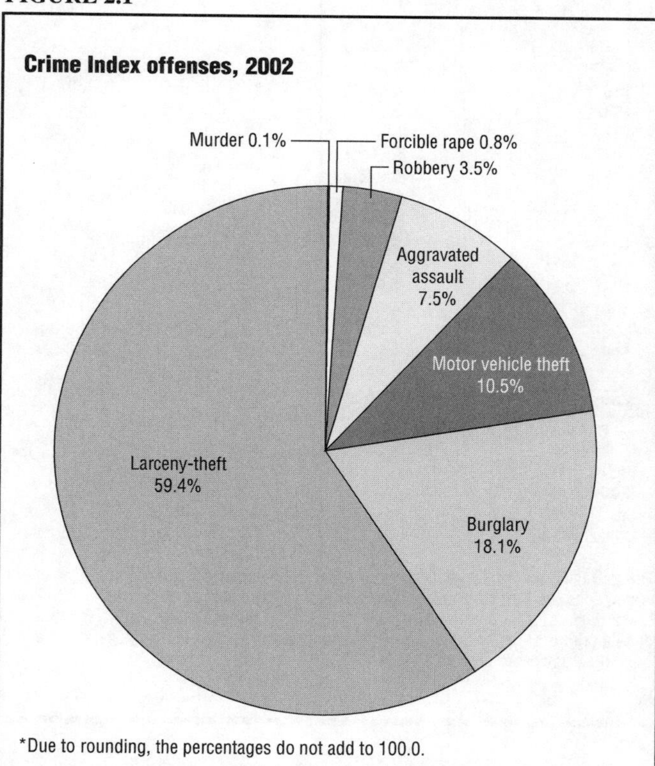

*Due to rounding, the percentages do not add to 100.0.

SOURCE: "Figure 2.3: Crime Index Offenses, Percent Distribution, 2002," in *Crime in the United States 2002,* Federal Bureau of Investigation, Washington, DC, 2003

TABLE 2.1

Index of Crime[1], 1983–2002

Population[2]	Crime Index	Modified Crime Index[3]	Violent crime[4]	Property crime[4]	Murder and non-negligent man-slaughter	Forcible rape	Robbery	Aggravated assault	Burglary	Larceny-theft	Motor vehicle theft	Arson[3]
					Number of offenses							
Population by year:												
1983-233,791,994	12,108,630		1,258,087	10,850,543	19,308	78,918	506,567	653,294	3,129,851	6,712,759	1,007,933	
1984-235,824,902	11,881,755		1,273,282	10,608,473	18,692	84,233	485,008	685,349	2,984,434	6,591,874	1,032,165	
1985-237,923,795	12,430,357		1,327,767	11,102,590	18,976	87,671	497,874	723,246	3,073,348	6,926,380	1,102,862	
1986-240,132,887	13,211,869		1,489,169	11,722,700	20,613	91,459	542,775	834,322	3,241,410	7,257,153	1,224,137	
1987-242,288,918	13,508,708		1,483,999	12,024,709	20,096	91,111	517,704	855,088	3,236,184	7,499,851	1,288,674	
1988-244,498,982	13,923,086		1,566,221	12,356,865	20,675	92,486	542,968	910,092	3,218,077	7,705,872	1,432,916	
1989-246,819,230	14,251,449		1,646,037	12,605,412	21,500	94,504	578,326	951,707	3,168,170	7,872,442	1,564,800	
1990-249,464,396	14,475,613		1,820,127	12,655,486	23,438	102,555	639,271	1,054,863	3,073,909	7,945,670	1,635,907	
1991-252,153,092	14,872,883		1,911,767	12,961,116	24,703	106,593	687,732	1,092,739	3,157,150	8,142,228	1,661,738	
1992-255,029,699	14,438,191		1,932,274	12,505,917	23,760	109,062	672,478	1,126,974	2,979,884	7,915,199	1,610,834	
1993-257,782,608	14,144,794		1,926,017	12,218,777	24,526	106,014	659,870	1,135,607	2,834,808	7,820,909	1,563,060	
1994-260,327,021	13,989,543		1,857,670	12,131,873	23,326	102,216	618,949	1,113,179	2,712,774	7,879,812	1,539,287	
1995-262,803,276	13,862,727		1,798,792	12,063,935	21,606	97,470	580,509	1,099,207	2,593,784	7,997,710	1,472,441	
1996-265,228,572	13,493,863		1,688,540	11,805,323	19,645	96,252	535,594	1,037,049	2,506,400	7,904,685	1,394,238	
1997-267,783,607	13,194,571		1,636,096	11,558,475	18,208	96,153	498,534	1,023,201	2,460,526	7,743,760	1,354,189	
1998-270,248,003	12,485,714		1,533,887	10,951,827	16,974	93,144	447,186	976,583	2,332,735	7,376,311	1,242,781	
1999-272,690,813	11,634,378		1,426,044	10,208,334	15,522	89,411	409,371	911,740	2,100,739	6,955,520	1,152,075	
2000-281,421,906	11,608,070		1,425,486	10,182,584	15,586	90,178	408,016	911,706	2,050,992	6,971,590	1,160,002	
2001-285,317,559	11,876,669		1,439,480	10,437,189	16,037	90,863	423,557	909,023	2,116,531	7,092,267	1,228,391	
2002-288,368,698	11,877,218		1,426,325	10,450,893	16,204	95,136	420,637	894,348	2,151,875	7,052,922	1,246,096	
Percent change, number of offenses:												
2002/2001	*		−0.9	+0.1	+1.0	+4.7	−0.7	−1.6	+1.7	−0.6	+1.4	
2002/1998	−4.9		−7.0	−4.6	−4.5	+2.1	−5.9	−8.4	−7.8	−4.4	+0.3	
2002/1993	−16.0		−25.9	−14.5	−33.9	−10.3	−36.3	−21.2	−24.1	−9.8	−20.3	
					Rate per 100,000 inhabitants							
Year:												
1983	5,179.2		538.1	4,641.1	8.3	33.8	216.7	279.4	1,338.7	2,871.3	431.1	
1984	5,038.4		539.9	4,498.5	7.9	35.7	205.7	290.6	1,265.5	2,795.2	437.7	
1985	5,224.5		558.1	4,666.4	8.0	36.8	209.3	304.0	1,291.7	2,911.2	463.5	
1986	5,501.9		620.1	4,881.8	8.6	38.1	226.0	347.4	1,349.8	3,022.1	509.8	
1987	5,575.5		612.5	4,963.0	8.3	37.6	213.7	352.9	1,335.7	3,095.4	531.9	
1988	5,694.5		640.6	5,054.0	8.5	37.8	222.1	372.2	1,316.2	3,151.7	586.1	
1989	5,774.0		666.9	5,107.1	8.7	38.3	234.3	385.6	1,283.6	3,189.6	634.0	
1990	5,802.7		729.6	5,073.1	9.4	41.1	256.3	422.9	1,232.2	3,185.1	655.8	
1991	5,898.4		758.2	5,140.2	9.8	42.3	272.7	433.4	1,252.1	3,229.1	659.0	
1992	5,661.4		757.7	4,903.7	9.3	42.8	263.7	441.9	1,168.4	3,103.6	631.6	
1993	5,487.1		747.1	4,740.0	9.5	41.1	256.0	440.5	1,099.7	3,033.9	606.3	
1994	5,373.8		713.6	4,660.2	9.0	39.3	237.8	427.6	1,042.1	3,026.9	591.3	
1995	5,274.9		684.5	4,590.5	8.2	37.1	220.9	418.3	987.0	3,043.2	560.3	
1996	5,087.6		636.6	4,451.0	7.4	36.3	201.9	391.0	945.0	2,980.3	525.7	
1997	4,927.3		611.0	4,316.3	6.8	35.9	186.2	382.1	918.8	2,891.8	505.7	
1998	4,620.1		567.6	4,052.5	6.3	34.5	165.5	361.4	863.2	2,729.5	459.9	
1999	4,266.5		523.0	3,743.6	5.7	32.8	150.1	334.3	770.4	2,550.7	422.5	
2000	4,124.8		506.5	3,618.3	5.5	32.0	145.0	324.0	728.8	2,477.3	412.2	
2001	4,162.6		504.5	3,658.1	5.6	31.8	148.5	318.6	741.8	2,485.7	430.5	
2002	4,118.8		494.6	3,624.1	5.6	33.0	145.9	310.1	746.2	2,445.8	432.1	
Percent change, rate per 100,000 inhabitants:												
2002/2001	−1.1		−2.0	−0.9	*	+3.6	−1.7	−2.7	+0.6	−1.6	+0.4	
2002/1998	−10.9		−12.9	−10.6	−10.5	−4.3	−11.8	−14.2	−13.5	−10.4	−6.0	
2002/1993	−24.9		−33.8	−23.5	−40.9	−19.8	−43.0	−29.6	−32.1	−19.4	−28.7	

[1]The murder and nonnegligent homicides that occurred as a result of the events of September 11, 2001, were not included in this table.
[2]Populations are Bureau of the Census provisional estimates as of July 1 for each year except 1990 and 2000 which are decennial census counts.
[3]Although arson data are included in the trend and clearance tables, sufficient data are not available to estimate totals for this offense.
[4]Violent crimes are offenses of murder, forcible rape, robbery, and aggravated assault. Property crimes are offenses of burglary, larceny-theft, and motor vehicle theft.
*Less than one-tenth of 1 percent.

SOURCE: "Table 1: Index of Crime, United States, 1983–2002," in *Crime in the United States 2002,* Federal Bureau of Investigation, Washington, DC, 2003

Murder Rate by Area

The South, the nation's most populous region, had the highest incidence of murder in 2002, accounting for 43.1 percent of all homicides in the United States. Western states were next, at 23.0 percent, followed by the Midwest at 20.4 percent, and the Northeast at 13.6 percent. (See Table 2.2.) These proportions are nearly identical to 1998 figures, when 44 percent of murders in the nation

TABLE 2.2

Index of Crime offense and population distribution, by region, 2002

Area	Population	Crime Index	Modified Crime Index[1]	Violent crime[2]	Property crime[2]	Murder and non-negligent man-slaughter	Forcible rape	Robbery	Aggravated assault	Burglary	Larceny-theft	Motor vehicle theft	Arson[1]
United States total[3]	**100.0**	**100.0**		**100.0**	**100.0**	**100.0**	**100.0**	**100.0**	**100.0**	**100.0**	**100.0**	**100.0**	
Northeast	18.8	13.2		15.8	12.8	13.6	13.5	19.2	14.6	11.5	13.2	13.1	
Midwest	22.6	21.3		19.4	21.6	20.4	25.3	19.5	18.7	20.7	22.3	18.8	
South	35.8	41.1		41.4	41.0	43.1	37.5	38.5	43.1	44.8	40.9	35.2	
West	22.8	24.4		23.4	24.6	23.0	23.7	22.8	23.7	22.9	23.6	32.9	

[1]Although arson data are included in the trend and clearance tables, sufficient data are not available to estimate totals for this offense.
[2]Violent crimes are offenses of murder, forcible rape, robbery,and aggravated assault. Property crimes are offenses of burglary, larceny-theft, and motor vehicle theft.
[3]Because of rounding, the percentages may not add to 100.0.

SOURCE: "Table 3: Index of Crime, Offense and Population Distribution by Region, 2002," in *Crime in the United States 2002,* Federal Bureau of Investigation, Washington, DC, 2003

TABLE 2.3

Murder offenders, by age, sex, and race, 2002

Age	Total	Sex			Race			
		Male	Female	Unknown	White	Black	Other	Unknown
Total	**15,813**	**10,285**	**1,108**	**4,420**	**5,356**	**5,579**	**274**	**4,604**
Percent distribution[1]	100.0	65.0	7.0	28.0	33.9	35.3	1.7	29.1
Under 18[2]	848	770	77	1	389	424	26	9
Under 22[2]	3,402	3,128	269	5	1,499	1,770	94	39
18 and over[2]	9,525	8,511	996	18	4,714	4,464	241	106
Infant (under 1)	0	0	0	0	0	0	0	0
1 to 4	1	0	1	0	0	1	0	0
5 to 8	1	1	0	0	0	1	0	0
9 to 12	26	18	7	1	7	18	0	1
13 to 16	446	401	45	0	227	198	15	6
17 to 19	1,507	1,412	92	3	648	802	42	15
20 to 24	2,916	2,656	256	4	1,265	1,547	73	31
25 to 29	1,644	1,492	150	2	769	819	37	19
30 to 34	1,120	986	132	2	573	506	27	14
35 to 39	865	749	116	0	460	385	13	7
40 to 44	638	522	115	1	367	242	21	8
45 to 49	493	425	68	0	298	172	20	3
50 to 54	311	262	44	5	195	103	7	6
55 to 59	168	150	18	0	117	41	6	4
60 to 64	83	72	11	0	59	22	2	0
65 to 69	49	41	8	0	38	9	2	0
70 to 74	45	38	6	1	32	12	0	1
75 and over	60	56	4	0	48	10	2	0
Unknown	5,440	1,004	35	4,401	253	691	7	4,489

[1]Because of rounding, the percentages may not add to 100.0.
[2]Does not include unknown ages.

SOURCE: "Table 2.6: Murder Offenders, by Age, Sex, and Race," in *Crime in the United States 2002*, Federal Bureau of Investigation, Washington, DC, 2003

occurred in the South, 22 percent occurred in Western states, 21 percent occurred in Midwestern states and 13 percent were in Northeastern states.

As seen in Table 1.2 in Chapter 1, metropolitan areas reported a murder rate in 2002 of 6.2 victims per 100,000 population, down from 6.7 victims per 100,000 persons in 1998. (As defined by the U.S. Census Bureau, a "metropolitan statistical area," or MSA, is an urbanized area including a central city of 50,000 residents or more, or a Census Bureau-defined urbanized area of at least 50,000 inhabitants and a total metropolitan population of 75,000 in New England and at least 100,000 elsewhere.) Rates for murder in 2002 in cities outside metropolitan areas were 3.2 victims per 100,000 population and in rural counties, 3.6 victims per 100,000 population.

Sex, Race, and Age

In 2002 about two-thirds of the accused murder offenders were reported to be male (65.0 percent), though in 28.0 percent of cases, the sex of the offender was not given. Of 15,813 murder offenders, 3,128 males and 269 females were under the age of 22, while 770 males and 77 females were under the age of 18. Of murder offenders in 2002 for whom race was known, 35.3 percent were black, 33.9 percent were white, and 1.7 percent were of other racial origins. The remainder were persons of unknown races. (See Table 2.3.)

The offender and the victim were usually of the same race. Of 3,582 white murder victims, 3,000 were killed by white offenders in 2002. Similarly, of 3,137 black victims of homicide, almost all (2,852) were killed by black offenders. (See Table 2.4.) Males and females were the victims of male offenders in most cases, though female murder offenders were more likely to kill males than females in 2002.

Murder Circumstances

In 2002 relatives, acquaintances, or others with personal relationships to the victims committed 75.6 percent of all murders in which the relationship of the victim to the offender was known. (Almost 43 percent of the relationships were unknown.) Of 14,054 murders in 2002, 601 wives were the victims of their husbands and 444 girlfriends were the victims of their boyfriends. Sons (239) were more likely to be murdered than were daughters (210). (See Table 2.5.) Arguments resulted in 3,730 murders in 2002, down from 4,356 in 1998. Robbery was the felony offense most likely to result in murder in 2002, as it has been since 1998. Juvenile gang killing accounted for 911 murders in 2002, up from 625 in 1998. (See Table 2.6.)

Nearly sixty-seven percent of all murders were committed with firearms in 2002. (See below for more information on firearms and crime.) Knives were used in 12.6 percent of murders; blunt instruments in 4.7 percent; per-

TABLE 2.4

Relationship between murder victim and offender, by race and sex, 2002

[Single victim/single offender]

Race of victim	Total	Race of offender: White	Black	Other	Unknown	Sex of offender: Male	Female	Unknown
White victims	3,582	3,000	483	58	41	3,169	372	41
Black victims	3,137	227	2,852	11	47	2,768	320	49
Other race victims	192	51	28	109	4	169	19	4
Unknown race	94	31	23	2	38	45	11	38

Sex of victim	Total	Race of offender: White	Black	Other	Unknown	Sex of offender: Male	Female	Unknown
Male victims	4,931	2,192	2,545	121	73	4,328	528	75
Female victims	1,980	1,086	818	57	19	1,778	183	19
Unknown sex	94	31	23	2	38	45	11	38

SOURCE: "Table 2.8: Murder Victim/Offender Relationship, by Race and Sex, 2002," in *Crime in the United States 2002,* Federal Bureau of Investigation, Washington, DC, 2003

sonal weapons (fists, feet, and the like) in 6.6 percent; and other weapons, such as poisons and explosives, in the remaining 9.3 percent. (See Table 2.7.)

Of the 9,369 murder victims killed by firearms in 2002, 661 were under the age of 18 (7 percent) and 2,358 were under 22 years of age (25 percent). Almost 50 percent of murder victims under the age of 18 and over two-thirds of those under age 22 were killed by firearms.

Between 1982 and 2001 there were 327 sniper-attack murder incidents with 379 murder victims, according to the FBI. (See Table 2.8.) In 2001 there were five sniper-attack incidents resulting in five murders, down from eight incidents in 2000 with eight victims, and much lower than the 20-year high of 47 incidents in 1988 with 55 deaths. Of the 224 offenders arrested during this period, 217 were male and seven female. Forty percent of offenders were aged 21 or under. (See Table 2.9.)

Arrests

Because murder is considered the most serious crime, it receives the most police attention and, therefore, has the highest arrest rate of all felonies. According to the 2002 UCR on murder, about 64.0 percent of murders in 2002 were cleared by arrest. The rate was somewhat lower in cities, with 62 percent of murders and non-negligent manslaughter offenses cleared by arrest in 2002. Because an arrest is made does not mean that the alleged offender is guilty or will be convicted in criminal or juvenile court.

RAPE

The FBI defines forcible rape as "the carnal knowledge of a female forcibly and against her will. Assaults or attempts to commit rape by force or threat of force are included; however, statutory rape (without force) [intercourse with a consenting minor]...and other sex offenses are excluded." Rape is a crime of violence in which the victim may suffer serious physical injury and long-term psychological pain. In 2002 95,136 forcible rapes were reported to law enforcement agencies, an increase of 4.7 percent from 2001. (See Table 2.1.) Forcible rape totals show a decrease of 10.3 percent since 1993. The rate of forcible rape in 2002 was 33.0 per 100,000 females. This represents a decline of 4.3 percent from 1998, and a 19.8 percent decline from 1993 figures, but a 3.6 percent increase over 2001 figures.

For several reasons, the statistics on rape are difficult to interpret. The crime often goes unreported. The Bureau of Justice Statistics (BJS) estimates that only about one-third of the cases of completed or attempted rape are ever reported to the police. Because their data are collected through interviews, the BJS recognizes an underreporting in its statistics as well. Homosexual rape and "date rape" (sex forced upon a woman by her escort) are not included in BJS data.

Public attitudes and legal definitions of rape are changing to encompass an ever-widening range of sexual events. These actions can include varying degrees of violence, submissiveness, and injury, but all involve women having sex against their will. (By the UCR definition, the victims of forcible rape are always female. The number of reported cases of rapes of males is so small that no statistics are available.) A majority of cases involve acquaintance rape. By the late 1990s most states also recognized marital rape, for which a husband could be charged with raping his wife. David Beatty, public policy director of the National Center for Victims of Crime, commented that acquaintance rape is far more common than stranger rape. Most experts conclude that in 80 to 85 percent of all rape cases, the victim knows the defendant.

From 1979 through 1992 the rape rate increased 23 percent. Most experts attributed at least part of the

TABLE 2.5

Murder circumstances, by relationship,* 2002

Circumstances	Total murder victims	Husband	Wife	Mother	Father	Son	Daughter	Brother	Sister	Other family	Acquain-tance	Friend	Boyfriend	Girlfriend	Neighbor	Employee	Employer	Stranger	Unknown
Total	**14,054**	**133**	**601**	**113**	**110**	**239**	**210**	**87**	**20**	**271**	**3,217**	**352**	**154**	**444**	**110**	**5**	**10**	**1,963**	**6,015**
Felony type total:	2,314	4	17	4	3	8	9	4	1	32	586	50	8	18	16	0	1	595	958
Rape	43	0	0	0	0	0	1	0	1	3	11	2	0	0	1	0	0	7	17
Robbery	1,092	0	0	0	2	0	0	2	0	13	221	10	4	1	11	0	0	396	432
Burglary	96	0	1	0	0	0	0	0	0	4	21	1	1	1	1	0	1	39	26
Larceny-theft	15	0	0	0	0	0	0	0	0	0	2	0	0	0	0	0	0	8	5
Motor vehicle theft	16	0	0	1	0	0	0	0	0	0	1	1	0	0	0	0	0	7	6
Arson	59	0	1	1	0	1	2	0	0	1	9	3	0	3	0	0	0	17	21
Prostitution and commercialized vice	8	0	0	0	0	0	0	0	0	0	3	0	0	0	0	0	0	2	3
Other sex offenses	8	0	0	0	0	1	1	0	0	0	3	0	0	2	0	0	0	0	1
Narcotic drug laws	657	0	1	0	1	0	0	1	0	1	245	22	2	2	0	0	0	67	315
Gambling	5	0	0	0	0	0	0	0	0	0	2	0	0	0	0	0	0	1	2
Other—not specified	315	4	14	2	0	6	5	1	0	10	68	11	1	9	3	0	0	51	130
Suspected felony type	67	0	0	1	0	0	0	0	0	0	6	1	0	0	0	0	0	2	57
Other than felony type total:	7,097	109	516	93	88	199	184	69	17	202	2,179	257	134	348	77	4	7	999	1,615
Romantic triangle	130	1	9	0	0	1	0	1	0	9	57	10	2	14	1	0	0	15	10
Child killed by babysitter	38	0	0	0	0	1	2	0	0	7	23	3	0	0	0	0	0	1	1
Brawl due to influence of alcohol	153	1	6	0	3	0	2	0	0	5	68	10	1	4	0	0	0	41	12
Brawl due to influence of narcotics	84	0	2	0	1	0	0	2	0	3	36	3	0	3	1	0	0	8	25
Argument over money or property	203	0	4	5	1	0	0	0	0	7	104	13	0	3	8	0	1	17	40
Other arguments	3,527	81	334	45	47	52	29	51	11	111	1,154	170	105	243	48	4	3	496	543
Gangland killings	73	0	0	0	0	0	0	0	0	0	23	0	0	0	0	0	0	20	30
Juvenile gang killings	911	0	0	0	0	0	0	0	0	1	221	0	0	0	0	0	0	200	489
Institutional killings	12	0	0	0	0	0	0	0	0	0	9	0	0	0	0	0	0	1	2
Sniper attack	11	0	1	0	0	0	0	0	0	0	0	0	0	0	0	0	0	7	3
Other—not specified	1,955	26	160	43	36	145	151	15	6	59	484	48	26	81	19	0	3	193	460
Unknown	4,576	20	68	15	19	32	17	14	2	37	446	44	12	78	17	1	2	367	3,385

*Relationship is that of victim to offender.

SOURCE: "Table 2.12: Murder Circumstances, by Relationship, 2002," in *Crime in the United States 2002,* Federal Bureau of Investigation, Washington, DC, 2003

increase in reported rape cases to a more sympathetic attitude by law enforcement authorities and a greater awareness of women's rights. After peaking in 1992, the rate steadily declined until 2002, when the rate began to climb again. (See Table 2.1.)

When and Where

In keeping with a five-year trend, rapes in 2002 occurred most frequently during the summer months of July and August. (See Table 2.10.) The rate of rape in metropolitan statistical areas in 2002 was 66.5 per 100,000 females. The rate of rape was highest in cities outside of metropolitan areas, and lower in rural counties. (See Table 1.2 in Chapter 1.) Regionally, the highest total volume of rapes (37.5 percent of all rapes) occurred in the South (the most populated region in the United States) while 13.5 percent of all forcible rapes in 2002 occurred in the Northeast. (See Table 2.2.)

Arrests

Less than half (44.5 percent) of reported forcible rapes were cleared by arrest in 2002. Of persons arrested for forcible rape, 46.1 percent were under the age of 25 and 63.4 percent were white. Juveniles (under 18) amounted to 16.7 percent of all those arrested for forcible rape in 2002.

ROBBERY

The FBI defines robbery as "the taking or attempting to take anything of value from the care, custody, or control of a person or persons by force or threat of force or violence and/or by putting the victim in fear." Robbery is a particularly threatening crime; its thousands of victims each year suffer psychological and physical trauma, and even non-victims experience anxiety from the fear of robbery. This fear can cause people to change their lives in ways destructive to social life and the sense of community, especially in urban areas.

Robbery is the only one of the seven traditional FBI Index crimes that is both a property crime and a violent crime. It shares with other crimes of property the primary motivation of acquiring money and the likelihood that the perpetrators do not know their victims. Robbery shares with other types of violent crime a relatively high probability of victim injury or death.

An estimated 420,637 robberies were reported during 2002, less than one percent fewer than in 2001. (See Table 2.1.) The number of robberies declined by 5.9 percent compared to the 1998 figures, and by 36.3 percent compared to 1993. Robbery represented 29.5 percent of the nation's violent crime in 2002.

In 2001 a bank robbery occurred on average every 52 minutes. According to Bank Crime Statistics (BCS) collected by the Violent Crimes/Fugitive Unit of the FBI, there were 8,516 bank robberies in 2001, up from 7,310 in 2000. These figures vary from those collected by the UCS, which reported 10,150 bank robberies in 2001 and 8,565 in 2000. Between 1990 and 2001 the number of bank robberies, using BCS data, has fluctuated from a high of 9,540 in 1992 to a low of 6,813 in 1999. (See Figure 2.2.) Most bank robbers between 1996 and 2000 were male (2,962 compared to 204 females) and most (831) were between 18 and 24 years old. (See Table 2.11.) Almost 58 percent of bank robberies were cleared by arrest in 2001.

TABLE 2.6

Murder circumstances, 1998–2002

Circumstances	1998	1999	2000	2001*	2002
Total	**14,209**	**13,011**	**13,230**	**14,061**	**14,054**
Felony type total:	2,510	2,215	2,229	2,364	2,314
Rape	62	47	58	61	43
Robbery	1,243	1,057	1,077	1,080	1,092
Burglary	92	81	76	80	96
Larceny-theft	17	14	23	17	15
Motor vehicle theft	15	12	25	22	16
Arson	83	66	81	71	59
Prostitution and commercialized vice	15	8	6	5	8
Other sex offenses	20	19	10	7	8
Narcotic drug laws	682	581	589	575	657
Gambling	12	17	12	3	5
Other—not specified	269	313	272	443	315
Suspected felony type	104	65	60	72	67
Other than felony type total:	7,203	6,880	6,871	7,073	7,097
Romantic triangle	187	137	122	118	130
Child killed by babysitter	23	34	30	37	38
Brawl due to influence of alcohol	211	203	188	152	153
Brawl due to influence of narcotics	117	127	99	118	84
Argument over money or property	241	213	206	198	203
Other arguments	4,115	3,471	3,589	3,618	3,527
Gangland killings	73	122	65	76	73
Juvenile gang killings	625	580	653	862	911
Institutional killings	15	13	10	8	12
Sniper attack	16	5	8	7	11
Other—not specified	1,580	1,975	1,901	1,879	1,955
Unknown	4,392	3,851	4,070	4,552	4,576

* The murder and nonnegligent homicides that occurred as a result of the events of September 11, 2001, are not included.

SOURCE: "Table 2.14: Murder Circumstances, 1998–2002," in *Crime in the United States 2002,* Federal Bureau of Investigation, Washington, DC, 2003

Rate

The robbery rate in 2002 was 145.9 per 100,000 inhabitants, a 1.7 percent decrease from 2001. The rate represents a decrease of 11.8 percent compared to 1998, and of 43.0 percent compared to 1993. (See Table 2.1.)

Robbery is largely a big-city crime. Of 420,637 total robberies reported by law enforcement agencies nationwide in 2002, some 401,140 occurred in metropolitan areas—a rate of 173.4 per 100,000 people. By comparison, the rate of robberies in cities outside metropolitan

TABLE 2.7

Murder victims, by age and weapon used, 2002

Age	Total murder victims	Weapons: Firearms	Knives or cutting instruments	Blunt objects (clubs, hammers, etc.)	Personal weapons (hands, fists, feet, etc.)[1]	Poison	Explosives	Fire	Narcotics	Strangulation	Asphyxiation	Other weapon or weapon not stated[2]
Total	**14,054**	**9,369**	**1,767**	**666**	**933**	**23**	**11**	**104**	**48**	**143**	**103**	**887**
Percent distribution[3]	100.0	66.7	12.6	4.7	6.6	0.2	0.1	0.7	0.3	1.0	0.7	6.3
Under 18[4]	1,357	661	90	52	299	5	5	21	11	16	41	156
Under 22[4]	3,398	2,358	256	94	345	6	5	29	14	23	47	221
18 and over[4]	12,406	8,568	1,646	595	607	18	6	76	36	125	58	671
Infant (under 1)	180	9	4	12	91	0	1	0	3	0	19	41
1 to 4	328	45	10	19	166	2	1	7	3	2	12	61
5 to 8	86	26	14	2	11	2	2	7	1	2	7	12
9 to 12	92	56	11	2	4	1	0	2	0	3	0	13
13 to 16	390	299	30	11	17	0	0	5	3	6	2	17
17 to 19	1,184	972	101	23	32	1	1	3	4	6	3	38
20 to 24	2,756	2,244	250	55	72	0	3	9	7	7	5	104
25 to 29	2,059	1,628	227	42	56	0	0	11	2	16	7	70
30 to 34	1,587	1,168	197	45	57	0	2	14	5	15	4	80
35 to 39	1,337	864	193	74	78	2	0	7	5	25	11	78
40 to 44	1,137	663	221	63	84	3	1	9	1	13	8	71
45 to 49	856	461	151	80	74	0	0	8	1	15	3	63
50 to 54	566	312	101	48	50	2	0	3	2	3	1	44
55 to 59	353	172	66	46	23	0	0	1	0	7	2	36
60 to 64	245	107	41	37	16	0	0	7	1	7	4	25
65 to 69	162	67	27	20	15	1	0	0	3	5	5	19
70 to 74	156	53	35	28	14	0	0	0	0	6	2	18
75 and over	289	83	57	40	46	9	0	4	6	3	4	37
Unknown	291	140	31	19	27	0	0	7	1	2	4	60

[1]Pushed is included in personal weapons.
[2]Includes drowning.
[3]Because of rounding, the percentages may not add to 100.0.
[4]Does not include unknown ages.

SOURCE: "Table 2.11: Murder Victims by Age, by Weapon, 2002," in *Crime in the United States 2002,* Federal Bureau of Investigation, Washington, DC, 2003

areas was 61.2 per 100,000 people, and the rate was 16.7 in rural counties. (See Table 1.2 in Chapter 1.)

Average Losses

The UCR for 2002 estimates that over $539 million was stolen from robbery victims in 2002. The average value of items stolen during a robbery was estimated at $1,281 per incident. Average dollar losses in 2002 ranged from $4,763 for a bank robbery to $665 for a convenience-store robbery. Nearly half (42.8 percent) of robberies occurred on the streets or highways. Robberies of commercial establishments accounted for an additional 14.6 percent and those occurring at residences, 13.5 percent. (See Table 1.8 in Chapter 1.)

The impact of robbery on its victims cannot be measured simply in terms of monetary loss. While the intention of a robber is to obtain money or property, the crime always involves the use or threat of force. Many victims suffer serious psychological and/or physical injury, sometimes even death. Firearms accounted for 42.1 percent of the weapons used in robberies in 2002. Strong-arm tactics (actual or threatened physical force) were used in 39.9 percent and knives or cutting instruments in 8.7 percent. (See Table 2.12.)

Arrests

In 2002 law authorities cleared about one-fourth (25.7 percent) of reported robbery offenses nationwide. Rural counties reported the highest clearance rate in 2002, at 41.4 percent, compared to 29.5 percent in suburban counties and 25.0 percent in cities. Of those arrested, 61.4 percent were under 25 years of age. (See Table 1.4 in Chapter 1.) Males comprised 89.7 percent of those arrested for robbery in 2002. Blacks accounted for 54.1 percent of arrestees for robbery, compared to 44.1 percent who were white. Of those cleared by arrest for robbery in 2002, 23.1 percent were juveniles under the age of 18. (See Table 1.7 in Chapter 1.)

AGGRAVATED ASSAULT

The FBI defines aggravated assault as "an unlawful attack by one person upon another for the purpose of inflicting severe or aggravated bodily injury. This type of assault is usually accompanied by the use of a weapon or by means likely to produce death or great bodily harm." In 2002 894,348 offenses of aggravated assault were reported to law enforcement agencies nationwide. The aggravated assault rate of 310.1 per 100,000 inhabitants declined by 2.7 percent from 2001. By comparison, the rate of aggravated assault has declined by 14.2 percent since 1998, and by 29.6 percent since 1993. (See Table 2.1.)

In 2002 metropolitan areas reported a rate of aggravated assault of 332.3 per 100,000 people, compared to 300.1 per 100,000 in cities outside metropolitan areas,

TABLE 2.8

Sniper-attack murder incidents, victims, and offenders, 1982–2001

Year	Number of incidents	Number of victims	Offenders*
Total	**327**	**379**	**224**
1982	12	15	8
1983	17	17	8
1984	18	37	16
1985	10	10	5
1986	9	9	4
1987	28	36	17
1988	47	55	32
1989	46	49	28
1990	40	41	24
1991	10	12	5
1992	31	33	14
1993	6	6	3
1994	2	2	5
1995	11	12	6
1996	8	8	13
1997	4	4	1
1998	10	15	15
1999	5	5	4
2000	8	8	5
2001	5	5	11

*This represents the number of instances in which the age, sex, and/or race of the offender was reported by law enforcement.

SOURCE: "Table 5.13: Sniper-Attack Murder Incidents, Victims and Offenders, 1982–2002," in *Crime in the United States 2002*, Federal Bureau of Investigation, Washington, DC, 2003

and 168.5 per 100,000 in rural counties. (See Table 1.2 in Chapter 1.) Aggravated assault was more likely to occur in the South (43.1 percent of the cases) followed by the West (23.7 percent), the Midwest (18.7 percent), and the Northeast (14.6 percent). The highest rate of aggravated assault was in July while the lowest rates were in November through February.

Weapons Used

About one-third (35.4 percent) of all aggravated assaults in 2002 were committed with weapons such as clubs or other blunt objects. Personal weapons—hands, fists, and feet—were used in 27.7 percent of the offenses, firearms in 19.0 percent, and knives or cutting instruments in 17.8 percent. By region, 21 percent of assaults were committed with firearms in Southern states, 18.0 percent in both the Midwestern and Western states, and 14.1 percent in Northeastern states. (See Table 2.13.)

Arrests

Law enforcement agencies cleared an average of 56.5 percent of the reported cases of aggravated assault in 2002. Three of every four violent crime arrests (75.8 percent) were for aggravated assault. Table 1.5 in Chapter 1 shows that offenders under the age of 18 made up 12.7 percent of all those arrested for aggravated assault. Males (79.8 percent of all offenders) were far more likely to be arrested

TABLE 2.9

Sniper-attack murder offenders, by age, sex, and race, 1982–2001

Age	Total	Sex			Race				
		Male	Female	Unknown	White	Black	American Indian/ Alaskan Native	Asian/ Pacific Islander	Unknown
Total	**224**	**217**	**7**	**0**	**117**	**94**	**2**	**2**	**9**
Under 10	0	0	0	0	0	0	0	0	0
10 to 12	1	1	0	0	1	0	0	0	0
13	5	4	1	0	5	0	0	0	0
14	2	2	0	0	1	1	0	0	0
15	8	7	1	0	5	1	0	0	2
16	6	6	0	0	3	3	0	0	0
17	7	7	0	0	2	5	0	0	0
18	15	15	0	0	7	5	1	0	2
19	20	19	1	0	7	12	0	0	1
20	17	17	0	0	5	10	0	2	0
21	9	9	0	0	1	7	0	0	1
22	15	14	1	0	5	9	1	0	0
23	6	6	0	0	5	1	0	0	0
24	12	12	0	0	8	4	0	0	0
25 to 29	36	35	1	0	19	17	0	0	0
30 to 34	17	16	1	0	13	4	0	0	0
35 to 39	11	11	0	0	7	4	0	0	0
40 to 44	6	6	0	0	6	0	0	0	0
45 to 49	6	6	0	0	5	1	0	0	0
50 to 54	5	5	0	0	3	2	0	0	0
55 to 59	1	1	0	0	1	0	0	0	0
60 to 64	2	2	0	0	1	1	0	0	0
65 and over	3	3	0	0	2	1	0	0	0
Unknown	14	13	1	0	5	6	0	0	3

SOURCE: "Table 5.19: Sniper-Attack Murder Offenders, by Age, Sex, and Race, 1982–2001," in *Crime in the United States 2002,* Federal Bureau of Investigation, Washington, DC, 2003

than females. Among those arrested for aggravated assault, 63.4 percent were white and 34.2 percent were black.

BURGLARY

The FBI defines burglary as "the unlawful entry of a structure to commit a felony or theft. The use of force to gain entry is not required to classify an offense as burglary." An estimated 2.15 million burglaries were reported in 2002, up 1.7 percent from 2001. By comparison, 2002 burglaries declined by 7.8 percent compared to the 1998 figures, and by 24.1 percent compared to the 1993 figures. (See Figure 2.3 and Table 2.1.)

In 2002 the burglary rate was 746.2 per 100,000 persons, a 0.6 percent increase from 2001. Burglary rates declined by 13.5 percent compared to the 1998 rate, and by 32.1 percent compared to the 1993 rate. (See Table 2.1.) The burglary rate in 2002 was highest in cities outside metropolitan areas (805.4 per 100,000 inhabitants), followed by metropolitan areas (768.5 per 100,000). Rural counties reported the lowest rate, at 558.2 per 100,000 population. (See Table 1.2 in Chapter 1.) The highest burglary volume was in the most populous region, the South, with 44.8 percent of total burglaries. Total burglary volume was lower in the West (22.9 percent of all burglaries) and Midwest (20.7 percent), and lowest in the Northeast (11.5 percent). (See Table 2.2.) The highest burglary rates in 2002 occurred in July, while the lowest occurred in February.

Losses

Of the 2.15 million burglaries reported in 2002, 65.8 percent were residential and 34.2 percent involved nonresidences such as stores and offices. Most residential burglaries occurred during daylight hours (61.7 percent) and nonresidential burglaries occurred at night (57.7 percent). The average value lost in burglaries was $1,549 per incident. Non-residential losses from burglary averaged $1,678, compared to $1,482 for residential burglaries. (See Table 1.8 in Chapter 1.)

These dollar amounts indicate the value of goods lost to the property owner. The burglar may collect as little as 10 cents on the dollar from the fence, the person who buys the stolen goods. A television set worth $400 might net the burglar only about $40. These statistics indicate that most burglars are commonly risking arrest for about $100 to $200.

Arrests

Law officers cleared 13.0 percent of burglaries reported to law enforcement in 2002 through arrest. In 2002 juveniles under 18 accounted for 30.4 percent of all burglary arrests and were involved in 17.3 percent of burglary offenses cleared by law enforcement agencies. The percentage of juveniles arrested for burglary is higher than the clearance rate because more than one individual may be arrested in connection with a single offense.

TABLE 2.10

Percent distribution of forcible rape, by month, 1998–2002

Month	1998	1999	2000	2001	2002
January	7.9	8.1	8.0	7.7	7.6
February	7.4	7.3	7.5	7.1	7.0
March	8.6	8.2	8.5	8.4	7.8
April	8.2	8.2	8.0	8.3	8.6
May	8.8	8.6	9.0	8.8	9.0
June	8.7	8.8	9.1	8.7	9.0
July	9.6	9.6	9.5	9.7	9.6
August	9.3	9.5	9.3	9.4	9.6
September	8.8	8.3	8.4	8.6	9.2
October	7.9	8.3	8.3	8.5	8.4
November	7.6	7.9	7.5	7.6	7.4
December	7.1	7.2	6.9	7.2	6.8

SOURCE: "Table 2.18: Forcible Rape by Month, Percent Distribution, 1998–2002," in *Crime in the United States 2002,* Federal Bureau of Investigation, Washington, DC, 2003

FIGURE 2.2

Number of bank robbery incidents reported, 1990–2001

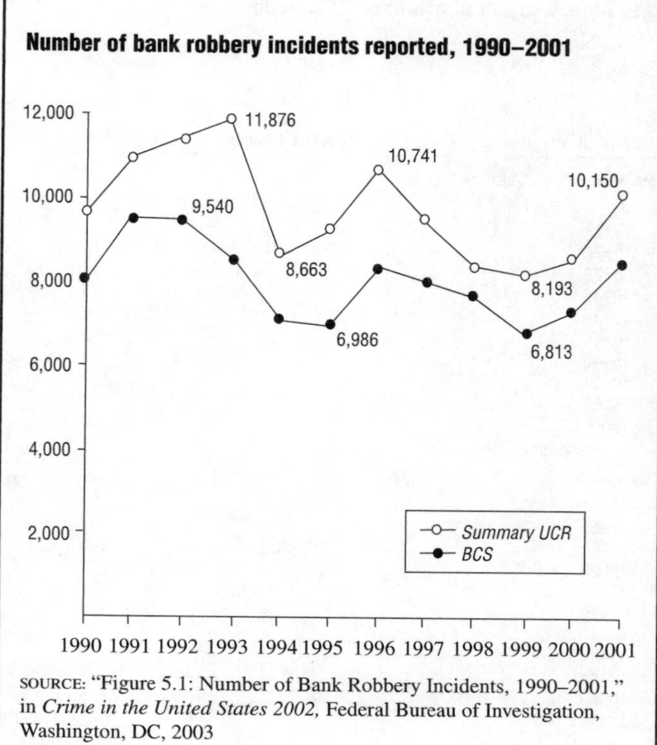

SOURCE: "Figure 5.1: Number of Bank Robbery Incidents, 1990–2001," in *Crime in the United States 2002,* Federal Bureau of Investigation, Washington, DC, 2003

Whites accounted for 70.4 percent of all persons arrested for burglary, and blacks comprised 27.5 of all such arrestees. About 86.7 percent of those arrested for burglary in 2002 were males. Arrests of juveniles for burglary in 2002 declined by 26.1 percent since 1998 and by 39.2 percent since 1993. Arrests of adults for burglary in 2002 declined by 4.2 percent since 1998 and by 24.4 percent since 1993.

LARCENY-THEFT

The FBI defines larceny-theft as "the unlawful taking, carrying, leading, or riding away of property from the possession ... of another" in which no use of force or fraud occurs. This crime category includes offenses such as shoplifting, pocket-picking, purse-snatching, thefts from motor vehicles, bicycle thefts, and so on. It does not include embezzlement, "con" games, forgery, and passing bad checks. (See Figure 2.4.)

In 2002 law enforcement agencies reported seven million larceny-theft offenses for a rate of 2,445.8 per 100,000 people. This crime category amounted to 51.9 percent of the Crime Index total arrests and 71.9 percent of all property crime arrests. The rate of larceny-theft declined by 1.6 percent from 2001, by 10.4 percent compared to 1998, and by 19.4 percent from 1993. (See Table 2.1.)

The larceny-theft rate in 2002 was 3,107.9 per 100,000 inhabitants in cities outside metropolitan areas, and 2,596.4 per 100,000 in metropolitan areas. Rural counties reported an average rate for larceny-theft of 1005.0 per 100,000 residents. The South, the most populous area of the nation, accounted for 40.9 percent of the total number of larceny-theft offenses, with the West (23.6 percent), Midwest (22.3 percent), and Northeast (13.2 percent) making up the rest. (See Table 2.2.) Larceny-theft occurred most frequently in July and August and least often in February.

Losses

The average value of property stolen (excluding motor vehicles) in 2002 was $699, and the estimated total amount stolen was $4.9 billion. The estimated loss is considered conservative because many larceny-thefts of small amounts are never reported to authorities. The average amount taken differed depending on the specific crime. For example, the average value for pickpocket offenses was $328; the average purse-snatching, $332. Shoplifting resulted in an average loss of $187. (See Table 1.8 in Chapter 1.)

Miscellaneous thefts from buildings and thefts from motor vehicles (except accessories) averaged $1,013 and $692, respectively. The average loss for bicycle theft was $257 per incident and from coin-operated machines, $250. The largest proportion of larceny was thefts from motor vehicles (except accessories), which accounted for 26.5 percent of larceny-thefts in 2002, while thefts from buildings and shoplifting accounted for 12.5 percent and 14.0 percent, respectively. Bicycle theft accounted for 3.9 percent.

Arrests

About 18.0 percent of larceny-thefts reported in 2002 were cleared. Of those arrested for larceny-theft, 29.5 percent were under 18 years of age.

Females were arrested more often for larceny-theft than for any other offense in 2002, and comprised 37.0

TABLE 2.11

Age, race, and sex of offender, 1996–2000

Sex/Age of offender	Asian/ Pacific Islander	Black	American Indian/ Alaskan Native	unknown race	White	Total
	Race of offender					
Total unknown age, sex, and race						508
Female						
12–17					8	8
18–24		26			39	65
25–29		22			20	42
30–34		13			18	31
35–39		6			8	14
40–44		2			6	8
45–49		1			5	6
50–54		2			5	7
55–59		1			4	5
over 64		1			1	2
unknown age		5		2	9	16
Total female		79		2	123	204
Male						
12–17		92		2	37	131
18–24	5	465	1	8	287	766
25–29		327		15	212	554
30–34		221		6	179	406
35–39	1	103		3	154	261
40–44		61		1	121	183
45–49		36	1	3	59	99
50–54		15		1	35	51
55–59		9		1	15	25
60–64					5	5
over 64		5			9	14
unknown age	1	262		65	139	467
Total male	7	1,596	2	105	1,252	2,962
Unknown sex						
12–17					1	1
18–24				5	5	
25–29		2		4	1	7
30–34				4	4	
40–44				1	1	
50–54		1		7		8
55–59				1	1	
over 64				1	1	
unknown age				163	4	167
Total unknown sex		3		186	6	195

SOURCE: "Table 5.11: Age, Race, and Sex of Offender, NIBRS Data, 1996–2000," in *Crime in the United States 2002,* Federal Bureau of Investigation, Washington, DC, 2003

percent of all arrestees for larceny-theft. About two-thirds (67.9 percent) of those arrested for larceny theft in 2002 were white, compared to 29.3 percent who were black.

MOTOR VEHICLE THEFT

The FBI defines motor vehicle theft as "the theft or attempted theft of a motor vehicle." In 2002 just over 1.2 million cases of auto theft were reported in the United States. The number of motor vehicle thefts increased from the previous year, up by 1.4 percent from 2001. The rate of motor vehicle thefts was 432.1 per 100,000 inhabitants, up by 0.4 percent from 2001. The 2002 rate shows a decline of 6.0 percent from 1998, and 28.7 percent from 1993. (See Table 2.1.)

The highest rate of motor vehicle theft occurred in metropolitan areas (498.6 per 100,000 inhabitants). In cities outside metropolitan areas, the motor vehicle theft rate was 207.6 per 100,000 inhabitants, while rural counties had a rate of 132.8. (See Table 1.2 in Chapter 1.)

Losses

The total value of motor vehicles stolen in 2002 was approximately $8.4 billion. The average loss per vehicle was $6,701. Many stolen cars are recovered, and insurance covers a portion of the loss for most victims. Motor vehicle thefts in 2002 occurred most often in July, and were least likely to occur in February. (See Table 2.14.)

Types of Vehicles Stolen

Nearly three-quarters of all motor vehicles reported stolen in 2002 were automobiles. The Highway Loss Data Institute lists the make and series of cars for which the most theft claims are made. In mid-2002, the most frequent passenger vehicle theft claims among 1999–2001

TABLE 2.12

Percent distribution of robberies, by region and type of weapon used, 2002

Region	Total all weapons*	Armed			Strongarm
		Firearms	Knives or cutting instruments	Other weapons	
Total	**100.0**	**42.1**	**8.7**	**9.3**	**39.9**
Northeast	100.0	34.0	10.8	8.3	46.9
Midwest	100.0	43.8	6.5	9.7	40.0
South	100.0	47.8	7.8	9.7	34.7
West	100.0	36.3	10.3	9.1	44.3

*Because of rounding, the percentages may not add to 100.0.

SOURCE: "Table 2.22: Robbery, Types of Weapons Used, by Region, Percent Distribution, 2002," in *Crime in the United States 2002,* Federal Bureau of Investigation, Washington, DC, 2003

TABLE 2.13

Aggravated assault, by region and type of weapon used, 2002

Percent distribution

Region	Total all weapons*	Firearms	Knives or cutting instruments	Other weapons (clubs, blunt objects, etc.)	Personal weapons
Total	**100.0**	**19.0**	**17.8**	**35.4**	**27.7**
Northeast	100.0	14.1	18.4	34.4	33.1
Midwest	100.0	18.0	17.2	34.7	30.1
South	100.0	21.0	19.5	37.6	21.9
West	100.0	18.0	15.2	32.6	34.3

*Because of rounding, the percentages may not add to 100.0.

SOURCE: "Table 2.24: Aggravated Assault, Types of Weapons Used, by Region, Percent Distribution, 2002," in *Crime in the United States 2002,* Federal Bureau of Investigation, Washington, DC, 2003

models were the Acura Integra, followed by the Jeep Wrangler, Jeep Cherokee 4WD, Honda Prelude, and Mitsubishi Mirage. Of passenger vehicles with the worst theft losses among 1999–2001 models, the Acura Integra ranked highest, followed by the BMW X5 4WD, Chevrolet Corvette, and the Lincoln Navigator 4WD.

Arrests

In 2002 law enforcement agencies reported that 13.8 percent of motor vehicle thefts were cleared by arrest. In many cases, the stolen vehicle was found abandoned, and no arrest was made. Young males most often committed motor vehicle theft. Males were 83.5 percent of those arrested. Some 63.8 percent of persons arrested for motor vehicle theft in 2002 were under 25 years of age, and 30.4 percent were under 18. Whites comprised 60.4 percent of those arrested and African-Americans comprised 36.5 percent.

TABLE 2.14

Motor vehicle theft by month, 1998–2002

Percent distribution

Month	1998	1999	2000	2001	2002
January	9.1	8.5	8.1	8.1	8.6
February	7.9	7.3	7.4	6.9	7.2
March	8.5	7.9	8.0	7.7	8.1
April	7.9	7.7	7.6	7.6	7.8
May	8.3	8.0	8.2	8.0	8.1
June	8.1	8.2	8.3	8.2	8.1
July	8.7	8.8	8.9	9.0	9.0
August	8.8	9.0	9.1	8.9	8.8
September	8.3	8.5	8.5	8.5	8.6
October	8.4	8.8	8.7	9.3	8.8
November	7.9	8.5	8.5	8.9	8.4
December	8.1	8.8	8.6	9.0	8.6

SOURCE: "Table 2.29: Motor Vehicle Theft by Month, Percent Distribution, 1998–2002," in *Crime in the United States 2002,* Federal Bureau of Investigation, Washington, DC, 2003

ARSON

The FBI defines arson as "any willful or malicious burning or attempt to burn, with or without intent to defraud, a dwelling house, public building, motor vehicle or aircraft, personal property of another, etc." Arson statistics have only been collected since 1979. Not included in the arson statistics are fires of suspicious or unknown origins. In 2002 66,308 arson offenses were reported by law enforcement agencies nationwide. However, because not all agencies reported arson statistics, the data for arson collected by the FBI for 2002 represents approximately 72.7 percent of the population.

Rate

The FBI reported that the rate of arson in the United States in 2002 was 32.4 offenses per 100,000 people nationwide. In cities with a population from 250,000 to 499,999, the arson rate was highest, at 68.3 per 100,000 inhabitants, while cities with 10,000 to 24,999 inhabitants had the lowest rate (20.0). Overall, cities reported an arson rate of 36.5 per 100,000 inhabitants in 2002. By comparison, suburban counties reported an arson rate of 27.0, while rural counties reported 16.6 arsons per 100,000 people.

What Is Being Burned?

In 2002 structural arson accounted for 41.3 percent of all arson offenses, or 27,373 reported incidents. Residential property accounted for 60.7 percent of all structural arsons. Mobile property comprised about one-third (33.1 percent) of all reported incidents of arson in 2002, with motor vehicles accounting for about 95 percent of all mobile property arsons. Just over one-quarter of incidents of arson were directed at property such as crops, fences, signs, timber, etc. (See Table 2.15.)

The average loss per incident in 2002 was $11,253. The overall average for all types of structures was $20,818. The average dollar loss for mobile property

FIGURE 2.3

Percent change in burglary, 1998–2002

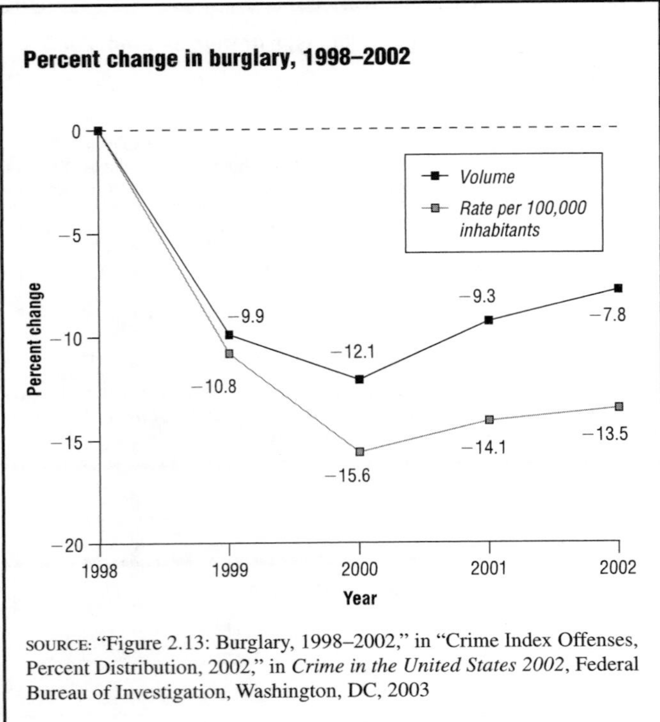

SOURCE: "Figure 2.13: Burglary, 1998–2002," in "Crime Index Offenses, Percent Distribution, 2002," in *Crime in the United States 2002*, Federal Bureau of Investigation, Washington, DC, 2003

FIGURE 2.4

Types of larceny-theft, 2002

Percent distribution*

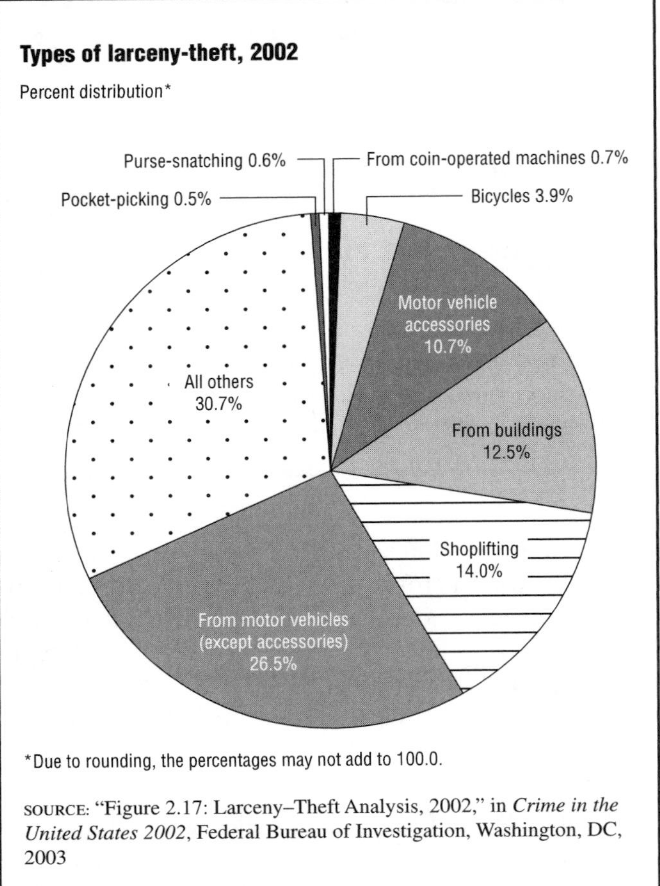

*Due to rounding, the percentages may not add to 100.0.

SOURCE: "Figure 2.17: Larceny–Theft Analysis, 2002," in *Crime in the United States 2002*, Federal Bureau of Investigation, Washington, DC, 2003

arsons was $6,073, and other property type losses averaged $2,536.

Arrests

About 16.9 percent of all reported arsons were cleared by arrest in 2002. The highest clearance rate for structural arsons and mobile property arsons was in cities with less than 10,000 inhabitants, 29.0 percent and 18.1 percent, respectively. For arsons of other property types, cities with 10,000 to 24,999 inhabitants had the highest arrest clearance rate, 25.9 percent. Cities overall had a clearance rate of 15.9 percent, while rural counties reported a 23.0 percent clearance by arrest. In 2002 juveniles under the age of 18 accounted for 43.0 percent of all arson incidents cleared by arrest. Juveniles comprised 71.8 percent of arsons of community/public structures cleared by arrest, and 21.9 percent of motor vehicle arsons cleared by arrest. Nearly half (49.4 percent) of those arrested for arson in 2002 were juveniles under the age of 18, and 67.8 percent were under the age of 25. Most persons arrested for arson in 2002 were male (84.8 percent), and 76.8 percent were white.

GUNS AND CRIME

There are enough guns in private hands to provide every adult in America with one.

—Bulletin Reports, Federal Bureau of Investigation, September 2, 1997

Based on a survey funded by a National Institute of Justice (NIJ) grant, the Police Foundation estimated that private citizens owned 192 million firearms in the United States in 1994. During the year, about 211,000 handguns and 382,000 long guns (rifles and shotguns) were stolen from the nation's homes or vehicles. Not surprisingly many stolen guns wound up in the hands of criminals.

In 2002, of the 14,054 weapons used to commit murder, 9,369 were firearms. Of those firearms, 7,176 were handguns. Among those murders in which firearms were used, 76.6 percent were handguns, 5.1 percent were rifles, 5.1 percent were shotguns, and 13.2 percent were other types of firearms or unknown. (See Table 2.16.)

Weapons Offenses and Offenders

Weapons offenses are violations of statutes or regulations that seek to control deadly weapons. Deadly weapons include firearms and their ammunition, silencers, explosives, and certain knives. From 1992 to 2002 the number of arrests for weapons offenses dropped from 129,122 to 118,148, a decline of 8.5 percent. Those under 18 years of age accounted for 25,239 of the 2002 arrests. In 2002 just over 1 percent of arrests nationwide were for weapons offenses. Of those persons arrested, 70.7 percent were white and 26.9 percent were black.

TABLE 2.15

Arson, by type of property, 2002

[12,414 agencies; 2002 estimated population 225,428,667]

Property classification	Number of offenses	Percent distribution[1]	Percent not in use	Average damage	Total clearances	Percent of offenses cleared[2]	Percent of clearances under 18
Total	**66,308**	**100.0**		**$11,253**	**11,190**	**16.9**	**42.1**
Total structure:	27,373	41.3	18.2	20,818	6,139	22.4	40.3
Single occupancy residential	11,789	17.8	19.7	18,535	2,631	22.3	31.2
Other residential	4,821	7.3	14.8	21,846	1,071	22.2	30.7
Storage	1,940	2.9	19.7	15,627	391	20.2	54.0
Industrial/manufacturing	333	0.5	22.8	71,376	62	18.6	29.0
Other commercial	2,735	4.1	15.4	45,927	485	17.7	27.6
Community/public	3,140	4.7	13.6	11,181	1,036	33.0	71.8
Other structure	2,615	3.9	24.3	11,933	463	17.7	47.1
Total mobile:	21,920	33.1		6,073	1,584	7.2	23.6
Motor vehicles	20,736	31.3		5,781	1,423	6.9	21.9
Other mobile	1,184	1.8		11,183	161	13.6	39.1
Other	17,015	25.7		2,536	3,467	20.4	53.5

[1]Because of rounding, the percentages may not add to 100.0.
[2]Includes offenses cleared by arrest or exceptional means.

SOURCE: "Table 2.32: Arson, by Type of Property, 2002," in *Crime in the United States 2002,* Federal Bureau of Investigation, Washington, DC, 2003

Crimes Committed with Firearms

From 1974 to 1993 the number of violent offenses (murders, robberies, and aggravated assaults) committed with firearms increased 78 percent. But from 1993 to 2001 the total number of violent crimes committed with firearms decreased by 63 percent.

According to *Firearm Use by Offenders* (Caroline Wolf Harlow, Ph.D., Bureau of Justice Statistics Special Report, November 2001), some 18 percent of state prisoners and 15 percent of federal prisoners in 1997 reported that they carried a firearm at the time of their offenses. Of those, 9 percent of state prisoners and 2 percent of federal prisoners in 1997 said that they fired a gun during the commission of the offense for which they were incarcerated. Most reported carrying a handgun (83 percent of state prisoners and 87 percent of federal prisoners).

Among prisoners in 1997 who reported carrying a firearm during the commission of a crime, some 23 percent of state inmates and 5 percent of federal inmates either killed or injured their victim as the result of discharging the firearm. Nonetheless, between 1993 and 1997, gunshot wounds from any type of crime declined by some 40 percent according to *Firearm Injury and Death from Crime, 1993–97,* by Marianne W. Zawitz and Kevin J. Strom (Bureau of Justice Statistics, 2000). During the same period, firearm-related homicides fell by 27 percent, from 18,300 in 1993 to 13,300 in 1997.

Crimes committed with firearms usually carry a higher penalty. About 40 percent of all state prisoners and 56 percent of all federal prisoners who used firearms were given more severe sentences. On average, state inmates who used a firearm received 18 years in prison, while those who committed similar crimes without firearms received 12 years.

TABLE 2.16

Murder victims, by weapon used, 1998–2002

Weapons	1998	1999	2000	2001[1]	2002
Total	**14,209**	**13,011**	**13,230**	**14,061**	**14,054**
Total firearms:	9,220	8,480	8,661	8,890	9,369
Handguns	7,405	6,658	6,778	6,931	7,176
Rifles	546	400	411	386	480
Shotguns	626	531	485	511	476
Other guns	16	92	53	59	74
Firearms, type not stated	627	799	934	1,003	1,163
Knives or cutting instruments	1,890	1,712	1,782	1,831	1,767
Blunt objects (clubs, hammers, etc.)	750	756	617	680	666
Personal weapons (hands, fists, feet, etc.)[2]	959	885	927	961	933
Poison	6	11	8	12	23
Explosives	10	0	9	4	11
Fire	132	133	134	109	104
Narcotics	33	26	20	37	48
Drowning	28	28	15	23	18
Strangulation	213	190	166	153	143
Asphyxiation	99	106	92	116	103
Other weapons or weapons not stated	869	684	799	1,245	869

[1]The murder and nonnegligent homicides that occurred as a result of the events of September 11, 2001, are not included.
[2]Pushed is included in personal weapons.

SOURCE: "Table 2.10: Murder Victims, by Weapon, 1998–2002," in "Crime Index Offenses, Percent Distribution, 2002," in *Crime in the United States 2002,* Federal Bureau of Investigation, Washington, DC, 2003

Firearm-Related Deaths

From 1991 to 1999 the percentage of firearm-related homicides declined from 47 percent of all firearm-related deaths to 38 percent, according to the Bureau of Justice Statistics. The reduction in the overall number of firearm-related homicides was even more dramatic, from 17,986 in 1991 to 10,828 in 1999. Though the FBI estimated that

TABLE 2.17

Justifiable homicide by private citizens,* by weapon, 1998–2002

Year	Total	Total firearms	Handguns	Rifles	Shotguns	Firearms, type not stated	Knives or cutting instruments	Other dangerous weapons	Personal weapons
1998	196	170	150	6	14	0	17	5	4
1999	192	158	137	5	10	6	18	9	7
2000	164	138	123	4	7	4	15	8	3
2001	222	183	143	10	13	17	26	6	7
2002	225	184	154	11	13	6	26	9	6

[1] The killing of a felon, during the commission of a felony, by a private citizen.

SOURCE: "Table 2.17: Justifiable Homicide by Weapon, 1998–2002: Private Citizen," in *Crime in the United States 2002,* Federal Bureau of Investigation, Washington, DC, 2003

TABLE 2.18

Justifiable homicide by law enforcement officers,* by weapon, 1998–2002

Year	Total	Total firearms	Handguns	Rifles	Shotguns	Firearms, type not stated	Knives or cutting instruments	Other dangerous weapons	Personal weapons
1998	369	367	322	15	18	12	0	0	2
1999	308	305	274	11	15	5	0	1	2
2000	309	308	274	14	13	7	0	1	0
2001	378	375	318	25	11	21	0	3	0
2002	339	335	294	18	7	16	1	3	0

* The killing of a felon by a law enforcement officer in the line of duty.

SOURCE: "Table 2.16: Justifiable Homicide by Weapon, 1998–2002: Law Enforcement," in *Crime in the United States 2002,* Federal Bureau of Investigation, Washington, DC, 2003

66 percent of the 15,517 murders in 2000 were committed with firearms, this still shows a decline, with about 10,241 homicides attributed to firearms. The National Center for Health Statistics estimated that of the other deaths caused by firearms in 1999, 57 percent were suicides, 3 percent were unintentional, and the intent in the remaining 1 percent of deaths was undetermined. The proportion of firearm-related deaths ruled to be suicides showed an increase between 1991 and 1999, rising from 48 percent to 57 percent. Although the rate of firearm-related suicides rose during that period, the overall number of such suicides declined from 18,526 in 1991 to 16,599 in 1999.

Among persons 19 years of age and younger, 59 percent (1,990) of the 3,385 firearm-related deaths in 1999 were homicides and 32 percent (1,078) were suicides. The remaining deaths were either unintentional or undetermined. Among adults 20 years of age or older, 35 percent of the 25,469 firearm-related deaths in 1999 were homicides and 61 percent were suicides.

Sources for Firearms Used in Crimes

Among prisoners in 1997 who reported carrying a firearm during their crimes, 14 percent said they bought or traded the gun from a legitimate retail outlet (store, pawn shop, flea market or gun show), a decline from the 21 percent of inmates in 1991 who reported purchasing a firearm from legitimate sources. Part of this decline may be attributed to the Brady Handgun Violence Prevention Act's requirement for criminal history checks for firearm purchases. According to the Bureau of Justice Statistics, since the law's enactment in 1994, some 689,000 of the nearly 30 million applicants for gun purchases were rejected by the FBI. Of the 7.8 million applicants for firearm permits or transfers in 2000, some 153,000 were rejected. State agencies rejected 2.5 percent of the 3.5 million criminal background checks conducted in 2000, while the FBI rejected 1.6 percent of 4.3 million checks they conducted. Friends, family, street buys, theft, and other illegal means of acquiring a gun accounted for 80 percent of firearms used in crimes.

Defensive Use of Guns

The number of justifiable homicides by private citizens (when a citizen kills a felon during the commission of a criminal offense) increased from 196 in 1998 to 225 in 2002. According to the FBI, in 2002 about 184 firearms were used in cases of justifiable homicide in the United States. Of those, most (154) were handguns. (See Table 2.17.) Among law enforcement officers, there were 339 incidents of justifiable homicide in 2002, most of which (294) involved the use of handguns. Although justifiable homicides by law enforcement officers have declined from a five-year high of 369 in 1998, there was a rise in such homicides in years 2001-2002. (See Table 2.18.)

TABLE 2.19

Workplace homicides by victim characteristics, type of event, and selected occupation and industry, 1992–2001[1]

	1992	1993	1994	1995	1996	1997	1998	1999	2000	2001[2]
Total	**1,044**	**1,074**	**1,080**	**1,036**	**927**	**860**	**714**	**651**	**677**	**639**
Victim characteristics										
Employee status										
Wage and salary workers[3]	793	786	818	823	675	632	526	485	488	470
Self-employed[4]	251	288	262	213	252	228	188	166	189	169
Sex										
Male	862	884	895	790	751	715	550	525	543	513
Female	182	190	185	246	176	145	164	126	134	126
Age										
Under 16 years	[5]	6	[5]	[5]	[5]	[5]	[5]	[5]	[5]	[5]
16 to 17 years	11	11	10	6	8	9	5	8	5	5
18 to 19 years	19	16	27	26	21	16	12	11	14	14
20 to 24 years	105	89	102	70	74	60	44	49	41	45
25 to 34 years	271	294	280	264	220	215	178	145	142	136
35 to 44 years	275	295	290	258	228	216	199	166	177	174
45 to 54 years	186	194	205	215	189	171	139	155	165	151
55 to 64 years	116	108	104	127	120	120	82	74	100	81
65 years and older	56	61	61	65	65	51	52	38	31	34
Race, ethnicity										
White	597	583	592	578	504	500	399	346	344	331
Black	192	164	210	206	171	146	128	116	118	113
Asian or Pacific Islander	105	128	129	100	105	104	74	85	84	72
American Indian, Eskimo, or Aleut	[5]	6	7	[5]	6	[5]	[5]	[5]	[5]	[5]
Other or unspecified	14	8	[5]	17	11	5	10	5	20	13
Hispanic[6]	132	185	139	130	130	101	99	95	108	106
Type of event										
Shooting	852	884	934	762	761	708	574	509	533	505
Stabbing	90	95	60	67	80	73	61	62	66	58
Hitting, kicking, beating	52	35	47	46	50	48	48	48	37	36
Other	30	48	31	153	29	26	24	26	38	38

Other Self-Protective Measures

According to *Criminal Victimization in the United States, 2001 Statistical Tables,* published by the U.S. Department of Justice, Bureau of Justice Statistics, in 70.4 percent of violent crimes, the victims offered resistance to their assailants. Only 0.9 percent used a weapon, while 9.5 percent attacked their assailant without a weapon. Eleven percent scared off or warned off their attackers and another 11 percent persuaded or appeased their attackers. Of those incidents where the victim resisted, their self-protection measure helped the situation in 67.8 percent of the cases.

WORKPLACE VIOLENCE

In 1999 the Society for Human Resource Management (SHRM) surveyed human resource professionals concerning violence in the workplace. Over half (57 percent) of those responding reported at least one violent incident between 1996 and 1999, an increase from the 48 percent of respondents who reported at least one violent incident in the workplace between 1994 and 1996.

Although violent attacks with firearms, knives, and other weapons receive the most media attention, they are rare in the workplace. Only 1 percent of the SHRM respondents reported shootings, and the same proportion reported stabbings. Verbal threats were the most frequently cited type of workplace violence (39 percent). Pushing and shoving (22 percent) and fistfights (13 percent) were the next most commonly reported incidents. Only 1 percent of respondents said that rape or sexual assault had occurred at work.

Each year the Bureau of Labor Statistics (BLS) gathers data about fatalities from job-related injuries, including homicides. According to the BLS, workplace homicides fell from 1,036 in 1995 to 639 in 2001. Firearms were used in 505 of the 2001 homicides. Males were victims (513) far more often than were females (126). (See Table 2.19.)

According to *Workplace Violence: Issues in Response,* published by the Critical Incident Response Group, National Center for the Analysis of Violent Crime, FBI Academy, Quantico, VA, there are certain factors that can "contribute to negativity and stress in the workplace, which in turn may precipitate problematic behavior." Among those factors are:

- Understaffing that leads to job overload.
- Frustrations arising from poorly defined job tasks.
- Downsizing or reorganization.
- Labor disputes and poor labor/management relations.

The Violence Prevention Center reported on the use of firearms in 65 high-profile shootings between 1963 and 2001. In 71 percent of incidents, a handgun was used, while

TABLE 2.19

Workplace homicides by victim characteristics, type of event, and selected occupation and industry, 1992–2001 [CONTINUED]

	1992	1993	1994	1995	1996	1997	1998	1999	2000	2001[2]
Major occupation										
Managerial and professional specialty occupations	185	162	149	200	184	156	132	117	141	120
Technical, sales, and administrative support jobs	353	404	426	381	332	305	239	197	235	203
Service occupations	228	212	251	216	188	181	146	156	130	171
Police and detectives	62	68	70	81	55	66	53	47	49	62
Guards	56	55	76	61	52	43	39	36	33	38
Farming, forestry, and fishing	15	11	17	20	18	10	19	19	14	11
Precision production, craft, and repair jobs	43	67	39	40	37	36	41	35	38	34
Operators, fabricators, and laborers	211	204	178	160	154	162	130	118	113	96
Major industry										
Agriculture, forestry, fishing	15	13	18	19	18	9	19	19	12	9
Construction	20	20	16	15	12	14	20	6	21	26
Manufacturing	32	46	33	44	40	43	38	26	25	32
Transportation and public utilities	117	126	118	98	76	110	69	70	65	52
Taxicabs	86	96	87	68	50	74	48	51	42	33
Wholesale trade	25	25	20	25	24	21	21	26	16	6
Retail trade	503	525	530	422	437	395	287	264	310	280
Grocery stores	166	176	196	152	146	141	95	78	111	92
Eating and drinking places	145	145	135	121	135	109	69	95	91	93
Gasoline service stations	41	53	41	36	23	34	25	17	14	16
Finance, insurance, real estate	37	35	31	53	41	28	22	34	21	20
Services	175	155	193	141	169	146	139	136	127	125
Detective and armored car services	23	32	49	27	29	21	18	17	16	21
Government[7]	104	124	104	212	100	88	94	66	78	88
Federal	11	18	12	109	11	7	16	7	6	9
State	11	20	12	17	20	19	22	11	11	10
Local	80	86	80	84	69	60	56	48	61	68

Note: These data were collected through the Census of Fatal Occupational Injuries conducted annually by the Bureau of Labor Statistics in cooperation with numerous federal, state, and local agencies. Data were compiled from various federal, state, and local administrative sources including death certificates, workers' compensation reports and claims, medical examiner reports, police reports, news reports, and reports to various regulatory agencies.

[1]Detail may not add to total because of the omission of miscellaneous categories.
[2]The workplace homicides that occurred as a result of the events of Sept. 11, 2001 are not included in this table.
[3]May include volunteers and other workers receiving compensation.
[4]Includes paid and unpaid family workers, and may include owners of incorporated businesses or members of partnerships.
[5]No data reported or data did not meet publication criteria specified by the source.
[6]Persons identified as Hispanic may be of any race; therefore detail will not add to total.
[7]Includes fatalities to workers employed by government agencies regardless of industry

SOURCE: "Table 3.135: Workplace Homicides by Victim Characteristics, Type of Event, and Selected Occupation and Industry," in *Sourcebook of Criminal Justice Statistics, 2002,* U.S. Department of Justice, Bureau of Justice Statistics, Washington, DC, 2003

a shotgun or rifle was used in the remaining 29 percent of incidents. In over half of such shootings (62 percent), the handguns were acquired legally, and in 71 percent of incidents the rifles or shotguns were legal. From 1999 to 2001 there were 25 high-profile shootings in the United States, 12 of which occurred at workplaces and seven at schools.

CHAPTER 3

VICTIMS OF CRIME

THE TRAUMA OF BEING VICTIMIZED

Becoming a crime victim can have serious consequences—outcomes the victim neither asks for nor deserves. A victim rarely expects to be victimized and seldom knows where to turn. Victims may end up in the hospital to be treated and released, or they may be confined to bed for days, weeks, or longer. Injuries may be temporary, or they may be permanent and forever change the way the victim lives. Victims may lose money or property, or they may even lose their lives—the ultimate cost for which a victim and his or her family can never be repaid.

The effects of crime are not limited to the victim. Families as well as victims may experience feelings of fear, anger, shame, self-blame, helplessness, and depression—emotions that can scar life and health for years after the event. Those who were attacked in their homes or whose homes were entered may no longer feel secure anywhere. They often blame themselves, feeling that they could have handled themselves better, or done something different to prevent being victimized.

In the aftermath of crime, when victims most need support and comfort, there is often no one available who understands. Parents or spouses may be dealing with their own feelings of anger or guilt for not being able to protect their loved ones. Friends may withdraw, not knowing what to say or do. As a result victims may lose their sense of self-esteem and no longer trust other people.

FEAR OF BECOMING A VICTIM

The fear of becoming a victim is often much greater than the likelihood of being one. Fear of crime has permeated our society so completely that it plays a daily role in our lives. In *Perceptions of Neighborhood Crime, 1995* (Carol J. DeFrances and Steven K. Smith, Washington, D.C., 1998), the Bureau of Justice Statistics (BJS) reported that about 7.3 percent of U.S. households believed that crime was a major problem in their neighborhoods.

Households in central cities (14.5 percent) were twice as likely as other households to feel that crime was a serious problem. In 1995, 19.6 percent of black central-city households identified crime as a neighborhood problem, compared to 13 percent of white central-city households.

In 2000, despite a steadily declining crime trend, 34 percent of respondents to a Gallup Poll felt that there was more crime in their area than the year before. Of those, a third lived in urban areas, 31 percent in suburban areas, and 41 percent resided in rural areas. About 34 percent of white respondents felt that crime was worse than the year before, compared to 31 percent of black respondents. Thirty-six percent of females and 32 percent of males who responded felt that there was more crime in their area than in the previous year.

THE NATIONAL CRIME VICTIMIZATION SURVEY

In 1972 the Law Enforcement Assistance Administration established the *National Crime Victimization Survey* (NCVS). The survey is an annual federal statistical study that measures the levels of victimization resulting from criminal activity in the United States. The survey was previously known as the *National Crime Survey*, but it was renamed to emphasize the measurement of victimization experienced by citizens.

Sponsored by the BJS, the survey was created because of a concern that the FBI's Uniform Crime Reports (UCR) did not fully portray the true volume of crime. The UCR provided data on crimes reported to law enforcement authorities, but it did not estimate how many crimes went unreported.

The NCVS is designed to complement the FBI's Uniform Crime Reports. It measures the levels of criminal victimization of persons and households for the crimes of rape, robbery, assault, burglary, motor vehicle theft, and larceny. Murder is not included because the NCVS data is gathered through interviews with victims. Definitions for these crimes are the same as those established in the FBI's UCR.

Many observers believe the NCVS is a better indicator of the volume of crime in the United States than the FBI statistics. Nonetheless, like all surveys, it is subject to error. The survey depends on people's memories of incidents that happened up to six months before. Many times, a victim is not sure what happened, even moments after the crime occurred.

Errors can come from other factors as well. Individuals who have been repeatedly victimized—by spousal or parental abuse, for example—may not remember individual incidents, or may remember only the most recent event. For instance, the NCVS found that a disproportionately large number of incidents are reported to have occurred at the end of the time period covered by the survey when the victim's memory was perhaps fresher. In addition, the NCVS limits the data to victims age 12 and older—an admittedly arbitrary age selection. Despite these factors, however, the BJS claims a 90 to 95 percent confidence level in the data reported in the NCVS.

The NCVS and the FBI's UCR are generally considered the primary sources of statistical information on crime in the United States. Like all reporting systems, both have their shortcomings, but each provides valuable insights into the status of crime in the United States. Over the years some significant differences have occurred in their findings. For example, the Uniform Crime Reports saw a 15 percent increase in crime from 1982 to 1991, while the NCVS reported a leveling off and, in 1990, a decrease in crime. These differences require the reader to evaluate both sets of statistics carefully, not relying solely on one or the other.

Redesigned Survey

Beginning in 1979, the NCVS underwent a thorough, decade-long redesign. The new design was expected to improve the survey's ability to measure victimization in general and particularly difficult-to-measure crimes, such as rape, sexual assault, and domestic violence. Improvements included the introduction of "short cues" or techniques to jog respondents' memories of events. Generally the redesign, as anticipated, resulted in an increased number of crimes counted by the survey. Therefore pre-1992 data cannot be directly compared to the later data.

A GENERAL DOWNTURN IN CRIME

Despite the continuing media spotlight on the high crime rate in the nation's cities, the findings from the 1996 NCVS indicated that overall crime victimization had declined from its peak in 1981. These findings support the FBI's Uniform Crime Reports, published in *Crime in the United States*.

Continuing the decline from 1997 to 1998, the rates of violent crime, personal theft, and property crime fell 6.6 percent, 18.8 percent, and 12.4 percent, respectively. Overall from 1993 to 1998 the violent victimization rate dropped 26.7 percent, the personal theft rate plummeted by 43.5 percent, and the property crime rate fell 31.8 percent. From 1998 to 2000 rates of criminal victimization (personal crimes) declined by 23.2 percent, while the overall rate for victims of property crimes dropped by 18.1 percent. (See Table 3.1.)

HOW MANY VICTIMIZATIONS IN 2002?

The figures for 2002 show a continued decline in the crime rate. In 2002 U.S. residents ages 12 and older were the victims of approximately 23 million crimes, down by almost 12 percent from the 25.9 million victimizations in 2000. About 17.5 million were property crimes. Another 5.4 million were violent crimes. Victimization rates for both violent crimes and property crimes were down for 2002, with the violent crimes rate at 23.1 per 1,000 persons, down from 27.9 in 2000, and the property crimes rate at 159 per 1,000 persons, down from 178.1 in 2000. (See Table 3.2.)

Victims of Violent Crimes

The 5.4 million violent victimizations in 2002 included 247,730 rapes/sexual assaults, 512,490 robberies, 990,110 aggravated assaults, and 3.5 million simple assaults. Attempted or threatened violent crimes accounted for 3.5 million of all crimes of violence. The NCVS reported that there were 1.1 rapes/sexual assaults and 0.3 attempted rapes for every 1,000 persons ages 12 and older. In 2002 there were 1.7 completed robberies, resulting in injury to 0.7 victims per 1,000 persons ages 12 and over. The rate for victims of aggravated assault was 4.3 per 1,000, and 15.5 for simple assaults in 2002. (See Table 3.2.)

According to the Bureau of Justice Statistics, homicide rates for all age groups showed a general decline from 1976–2000, though rates rose from 1986 to 1991 for the age groups under age 35. From 1991 to 2000 the murder rates dropped by almost half for all age groups. In 2000 persons age 18–24 were murdered at a rate higher than all other age categories. Since 1986 this age group has consistently had the highest rate of homicides. Prior to 1986 the age group from 25–30 had the highest rate. (See Figure 3.1.)

Victims of Property Crimes

In 2002 property crimes accounted for about 76 percent of all victimizations. The NCVS reported 17.5 million property crimes, including household burglaries, motor vehicle thefts, and thefts of other property. Households experienced 780,000 completed vehicle thefts, 2.5 million completed household burglaries, and 13.4 million

TABLE 3.1

Rates of criminal victimization and percent change, 1993–2000

Type of crime	Victimization rates (per 1,000 persons age 12 or older or per 1,000 households)								
						Percent change[3]			
	1993	1994	1998	1999	2000	1993–2000	1994–2000	1998–2000	1999–2000
Personal crimes[4]	52.2	54.1	37.9	33.7	29.1	-44.3%[1]	-46.2%[1]	-23.2%[1]	-13.6%[1]
Crimes of violence	49.9	51.8	36.6	32.8	27.9	-44.1[1]	-46.1[1]	-23.8[1]	-14.9[1]
Completed violence	15.0	15.4	11.6	10.1	9.0	-40.0[1]	-41.6[1]	-22.4[1]	-10.9[2]
Attempted/threatened violence	34.9	36.4	25.0	22.6	18.9	-45.8[1]	-48.1[1]	-24.4[1]	-16.4[1]
Rape/sexual assault	2.5	2.1	1.5	1.7	1.2	-52.0[1]	-42.9[1]	-20.0	-29.4[1]
Rape/attempted rape	1.6	1.4	0.9	0.9	0.6	-62.5[1]	-57.1[1]	-33.3[1]	-33.3[1]
Rape	1.0	0.7	0.5	0.6	0.4	-60.0[1]	-42.9[1]	-20.0	-33.3[2]
Attempted rape	0.7	0.7	0.4	0.3	0.2	-71.4[1]	-71.4[1]	-50.0[1]	-33.3
Sexual assault	0.8	0.6	0.6	0.8	0.5	-37.5[2]	-16.7	-16.7	-37.5[1]
Robbery	6.0	6.3	4.0	3.6	3.2	-46.7[1]	-49.2[1]	-20.0[1]	-11.1
Completed robbery	3.8	4.0	2.7	2.4	2.3	-39.5[1]	-42.5[1]	-14.8	-4.2
With injury	1.3	1.4	0.8	0.8	0.7	-46.2[1]	-50.0[1]	-12.5	-12.5
Without injury	2.5	2.6	2.0	1.5	1.6	-36.0[1]	-38.5[1]	-20.0	6.7
Attempted robbery	2.2	2.3	1.2	1.2	0.9	-59.1[1]	-60.9[1]	-25.0	-25.0
With injury	0.4	0.6	0.3	0.3	0.3	-25.0	-50.0[1]	0.0	0.0
Without injury	1.8	1.7	0.9	0.9	0.6	-66.7[1]	-64.7[1]	-33.3[1]	-33.3[1]
Assault	41.4	43.3	31.1	27.4	23.5	-43.2[1]	-45.7[1]	-24.4[1]	-14.2[1]
Aggravated	12.0	11.9	7.5	6.7	5.7	-52.5[1]	-52.1[1]	-24.0[1]	-14.9[2]
With injury	3.4	3.3	2.5	2.0	1.5	-55.9[1]	-54.5[1]	-40.0[1]	-25.0[1]
Threatened with weapon	8.6	8.6	5.1	4.7	4.2	-51.2[1]	-51.2[1]	-17.6[1]	-10.6
Simple	29.4	31.5	23.5	20.8	17.8	-39.5[1]	-43.5[1]	-24.3[1]	-14.4[1]
With minor injury	6.1	6.8	5.3	4.4	4.4	-27.9[1]	-35.3[1]	-17.0[1]	0.0
Without injury	23.3	24.7	18.2	16.3	13.4	-42.5[1]	-45.7[1]	-26.4[1]	-17.8[1]
Personal theft[5]	2.3	2.4	1.3	0.9	1.2	-47.8[1]	-50.0[1]	-7.7	33.3
Property crimes	318.9	310.2	217.4	198.0	178.1	-44.2%[1]	-42.6%[1]	-18.1%[1]	-10.1%[1]
Household burglary	58.2	56.3	38.5	34.1	31.8	-45.4[1]	-43.5[1]	-17.4[1]	-6.7
Completed	47.2	46.1	32.1	28.6	26.9	-43.0[1]	-41.6[1]	-16.2[1]	-5.9
Forcible entry	18.1	16.9	12.4	11.0	9.6	-47.0[1]	-43.2[1]	-22.6[1]	-12.7[2]
Unlawful entry without force	29.1	29.2	19.7	17.6	17.3	-40.5[1]	-40.8[1]	-12.2[1]	-1.7
Attempted forcible entry	10.9	10.2	6.4	5.5	4.9	-55.0[1]	-52.0[1]	-23.4[1]	-10.9
Motor vehicle theft	19.0	18.8	10.8	10.0	8.6	-54.7[1]	-54.3[1]	-20.4[1]	-14.0[2]
Completed	12.4	12.5	7.8	7.5	5.9	-52.4[1]	-52.8[1]	-24.4[1]	-21.3[1]
Attempted	6.6	6.3	3.0	2.4	2.7	-59.1[1]	-57.1[1]	-10.0	12.5
Theft	241.7	235.1	168.1	153.9	137.7	-43.0[1]	-41.4[1]	-18.1[1]	-10.5[1]
Completed[6]	230.1	224.3	162.1	149.0	132.0	-42.6[1]	-41.2[1]	-18.6[1]	-11.4[1]
Less than $50	98.7	93.5	58.6	53.2	43.4	-56.0[1]	-53.6[1]	-25.9[1]	-18.4[1]
$50-$249	76.1	77.0	57.8	54.0	48.9	-35.7[1]	-36.5[1]	-15.4[1]	-9.4[1]
$250 or more	41.6	41.8	35.1	31.7	29.3	-29.6[1]	-29.9[1]	-16.5[1]	-7.6
Attempted	11.6	10.8	6.0	5.0	5.7	-50.9[1]	-47.2[1]	-5.0	14.0

Note: Victimization rates may differ from those reported previously because the estimates are now based on data collected in each calendar year rather than data about events within a calendar year. Completed violent crimes include rape, sexual assault, robbery with or without injury, aggravated assault with injury, and simple assault with minor injury.
In 1993 the total population age 12 or older was 211,524,770; in 1994, 213,135,890; in 1998, 221,880,960; in 1999, 224,568,370; and in 2000, 226,804,610. The total number of households in 1993 was 99,927,410; in 1994, 100,568,060; in 1998, 105,322,920; in 1999, 107,159,550; and in 2000, 108,352,960.

[1]The difference between the indicated years is significant at the 95%-confidence level.
[2]The difference between the indicated years is significant at the 90%-confidence level.
[3]Differences in annual rates shown in each column do not take into account any changes that may have occurred during interim years.
[4]The NCVS is based on interviews with victims and therefore cannot measure murder.
[5]Includes pocket picking, purse snatching, and attempted purse snatching.
[6]Includes thefts with unknown losses.

SOURCE: Callie Marie Rennison, "Table 8. Rates of Criminal Victimization and Percent Change, 1993–2000," in *Criminal Victimization 2000: Changes 1999–2000 with Trends 1993–2000*, U.S. Department of Justice, Bureau of Justice Statistics, National Crime Victimization Survey, Washington, DC, 2001

completed thefts of other property. For every 1,000 households in the United States, 27.7 households were burglarized, down from 31.8 in 2000; 7.1 had a motor vehicle stolen, up from 5.9 in 2000; and 118.2 suffered other thefts, down from 132 in 2000.

In 2002 about 58 percent of all property crimes were thefts. Of the 13 million completed thefts, 4.1 million were thefts of less than $50. Another 4.4 million were between $50 and $249, and 3.2 million were of $250 or more. The value of the loss in the remaining thefts was unknown. (See Table 3.2.)

Reporting Crime to Police

Fewer than five of every ten violent crimes (48.5 percent) committed in 2002 were reported to the police. Women were more likely to report crimes of violence than were men. White female victims reported 50.7 percent of the violent crimes that they experienced, but white male victims reported only 44 percent. Black female victims reported 61.7 percent of the violent crimes committed against them compared to the black males rate of 48 percent. Hispanic females reported 55.5 percent of violent crimes against them,

TABLE 3.2

Number of personal and property crimes, 2002

Type of crime	Number of victimizations	Percent of all victimizations	Rate per 1,000 persons or households
All crimes	**23,036,030**	**100.0%**	**...**
Personal crimes	**5,496,810**	**23.9%**	**23.7**
Crimes of violence	5,341,410	23.2	23.1
Completed violence	1,753,090	7.6	7.6
Attempted/threatened violence	3,588,320	15.6	15.5
Rape/sexual assault	247,730	1.1	1.1
Rape/attempted rape	167,860	0.7	0.7
Rape	90,390	0.4	0.4
Attempted rape[1]	77,470	0.3	0.3
Sexual assault[2]	79,870	0.3	0.3
Robbery	512,490	2.2	2.2
Completed/property taken	385,880	1.7	1.7
With injury	169,980	0.7	0.7
Without injury	215,890	0.9	0.9
Attempted to take property	126,610	0.5	0.5
With injury	42,600	0.2	0.2
Without injury	84,020	0.4	0.4
Assault	4,581,190	19.9	19.8
Aggravated	990,110	4.3	4.3
With injury	316,260	1.4	1.4
Threatened with weapon	673,850	2.9	2.9
Simple	3,591,090	15.6	15.5
With minor injury	906,580	3.9	3.9
Without injury	2,684,510	11.7	11.6
Purse snatching/pocket picking	155,400	0.7	0.7
Completed purse snatching	55,400	0.2	0.2
Attempted purse snatching	2,140 *	0.0 *	0.0 *
Pocket picking	97,860	0.4	0.4
Total population age 12 and over	231,589,260	...	...
Property crimes	**17,539,220**	**76.1 %**	**159.0**
Household burglary	3,055,720	13.3	27.7
Completed	2,597,310	11.3	23.5
Forcible entry	1,017,660	4.4	9.2
Unlawful entry without force	1,579,650	6.9	14.3
Attempted forcible entry	458,410	2.0	4.2
Motor vehicle theft	988,760	4.3	9.0
Completed	780,630	3.4	7.1
Attempted	208,120	0.9	1.9
Theft	13,494,750	58.6	122.3
Completed	13,039,920	56.6	118.2
Less than $50	4,186,570	18.2	37.9
$50–$249	4,455,080	19.3	40.4
$250 or more	3,270,530	14.2	29.6
Amount not available	1,127,740	4.9	10.2
Attempted	454,830	2.0	4.1
Total number of households	**110,323,840**	...	...

Note: Detail may not add to total shown because of rounding.
*Estimate is based on about 10 or fewer sample cases.
Percent distribution is based on unrounded figures.
...Not applicable.
[1]Includes verbal threats of rape.
[2]Includes threats.

SOURCE: "Table 1: Personal and Property Crimes, 2002, Number, Percent Distribution, and Rate of Victimizations, by Type of Crime," in *Criminal Victimization in the United States, 2002 Statistical Tables,* U.S. Department of Justice, Office of Justice Programs, Bureau of Justice Statistics, Washington, DC, 2003

with 47 percent of Hispanic males making such reports. (See Table 3.3.)

Victims reported 40.2 percent of all the property crimes that they experienced. Motor vehicle theft was the most reported property crime, while theft of property worth less than $50 was the least reported.

FIGURE 3.1

Rate of homicide per 100,000 persons in each age category, 1976–2000

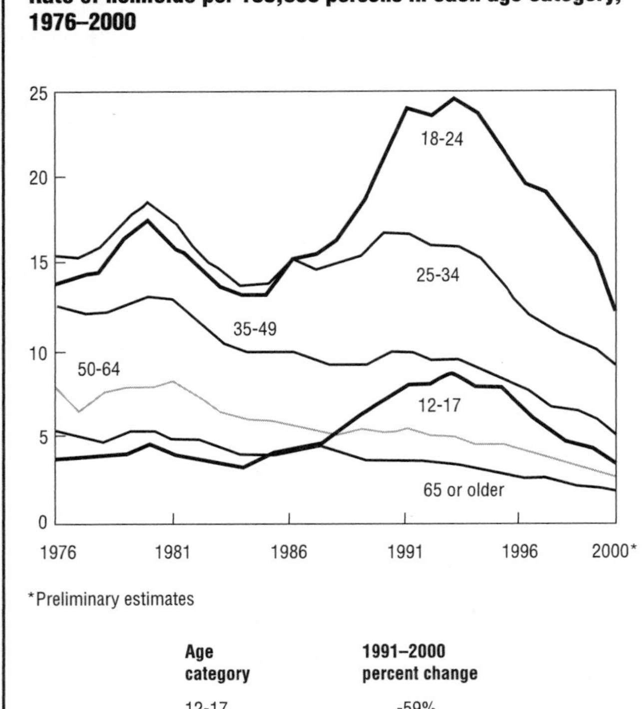

Age category	1991–2000 percent change
12-17	-59%
18-24	-50%
25-34	-47%
35-49	-52%
50-64	-53%
65 or older	-51%

SOURCE: Patsy Klaus and Callie Marie Rennison, "Rate of Homicide per 100,000 Persons in Each Age Category," in *Age Patterns in Violent Victimization, 1976–2000,* Crime Data Brief, U.S. Department of Justice, Bureau of Justice Statistics, February 2002

REASONS FOR REPORTING. BJS reports indicated several factors in reporting or not reporting a crime. For example, victims are more likely to report incidents to police if:

- Violent crimes were committed.
- The crime resulted in an injury.
- Items valued at $250 or more were stolen.
- Forcible entry occurred.

Victims of violent incidents most often cited the desire to prevent future acts of violence as a reason for reporting the crime. They also reported incidents because they thought it was the right thing to do. Victims of personal and property thefts frequently reported the incidents to enable recovery of their stolen property and to collect insurance.

Among victims who chose not to report a violent crime to the police, many indicated that the incident was private or personal in nature. In other cases, the incidents had not

TABLE 3.3

Percent of victimizations reported to police, by type of crime, gender, and race or ethnicity of victims, 2002

	Percent of all victimizations reported to the police	
Characteristic	Crimes of violence*	Property crimes
Total	**48.5 %**	**40.2 %**
Male		
White	44.0	40.2
Black	48.0	46.8
Female		
White	50.7	38.1
Black	61.7	44.7
Male		
Hispanic	47.0	37.5
Non-Hispanic	44.0	41.5
Female		
Hispanic	55.5	39.9
Non-Hispanic	52.8	39.4

Note: Excludes data on persons of "other" races.
Excludes data on persons whose ethnicity was not ascertained.
*Includes data on rape and sexual assault, not shown separately.

SOURCE: "Table 91b: Violent Crimes, 2002, Percent of Victimizations Reported to the Police, by Type of Crime and Gender and Race or Ethnicity of Victims," in *Criminal Victimization in the United States, 2002 Statistical Tables,* U.S. Department of Justice, Office of Justice Programs, Bureau of Justice Statistics, Washington, DC, 2003

been completed, the stolen property had been recovered, or the victim feared retaliation from the criminal.

CHARACTERISTICS OF VICTIMS

Gender

Males are more likely than females to become victims of violent crime. In 2002, 26.1 of every 1,000 white males were victimized by violent crime, compared to 20.9 per 1,000 white females. For black males the rate was 29.3 per 1,000, compared to 27.9 per 1,000 black females. In every category except rape/sexual assault, men were more likely than women to be victimized. (See Table 3.4.)

Age

While teenagers and young adults were more likely than older persons to become victims of violent crime, the rates for all age groups have been falling. In 2000 the rate for teenagers 12 to 15 years of age was 60.1 per 1,000; the rate for 16- to 19-year-olds was 64.4 per 1,000; and the rate for 20- to 24-year-olds was 49.5. These rates were lower than rates during the previous 17 years. (See Table 3.5.) The rates fell even lower by 2002, according to the U.S. Department of Justice. In that year the rate for those 12-15 years of age was 44.4 per 1,000; the rate for 16- to 19-year-olds was 58.2; and the rate for 20- to 24-year-olds was 47.4. Older adults were least likely to be victims of violent crimes. Individuals 50 to 64 years of age had a rate of 10.7 per 1,000, and the rate for those 65 and over was 3.4 per 1,000.

According the Office of Juvenile Justice and Delinquency Prevention (Washington, D.C.), research has shown that there can be long-term consequences to being victimized as an adolescent. When compared to adults who were not victimized as adolescents, adults who were adolescent victims were more likely to have drug problems and more likely to perpetrate violence. (See Figure 3.2.) They also committed more acts of domestic violence and were more often victims of domestic violence than adults who were not victimized as adolescents. In addition, they were almost twice as likely to become adult victims of violent crime.

Race and Ethnicity

In 2002 blacks were more likely than whites or persons of other races to be victims of most types of violent crimes. (See Table 3.3.) Hispanics experienced higher rates of violent victimization than non-Hispanics for robberies and personal theft, but lower rates in rape/sexual abuse and assaults.

For every 1,000 households in 2002, 157.6 white households, 173.7 black households, and 139.8 households of other races were victims of property crimes. The highest rate of burglaries occurred among black households (41.3 per 1,000), while the rates for white households (26 per 1,000) and households of other races (19.4 per 1,000) were considerably lower. Black households also experienced more motor vehicle thefts and general thefts. Hispanic households (17.7 per 1,000) were more than twice as likely as non-Hispanic households (8.0 per 1,000) to suffer a motor vehicle theft. (See Table 3.6.)

Income, Marital Status, and Area

INCOME. The less money that people or households earn, the more likely they are to become victims of violent crime. In 2002 the very poor (earning less than $7,500 annually) suffered violent crime at a higher rate (45.5 per 1,000 persons) than any other income group and more than double the rate for those earning $75,000 or more (19.0 per 1,000). Property crime rates for those earning less than $7,500 per year were also more elevated than those in higher income categories. (See Table 3.7.)

MARITAL STATUS. In 2002 the violent crime rate for persons who never married (43.3 per 1,000) was nearly four times higher than the rate for married people (10.6 per 1,000). The rate for divorced or separated persons (30.7 per 1,000) was almost three times higher than the rate for married people. The victimization rates for rape/sexual assault, robbery, and both kinds of assault (aggravated and simple) were significantly higher for never-married, divorced, or separated persons than for married or widowed persons. (See Table 3.8.)

REGIONS AND TYPES OF RESIDENCE. Those living in the West and in urban areas are more likely to be victimized by property crimes. In 2002, 219.9 of every 1,000

TABLE 3.4

Number of victimizations and victimization rates for persons age 12 and over, by crime type, gender, and race of victims, 2002

	Rate per 1,000 persons age 12 and over							
	Male				Female			
	White		Black		White		Black	
Type of crime	Number	Rate	Number	Rate	Number	Rate	Number	Rate
All personal crimes	**2,459,570**	**26.1**	**386,130**	**29.3**	**2,065,520**	**20.9**	**438,400**	**27.9**
Crimes of violence	2,394,330	25.4	381,780	29.0	1,998,290	20.3	423,650	27.0
Completed violence	683,120	7.2	107,160	8.1	747,390	7.6	164,040	10.4
Attempted/threatened violence	1,711,210	18.1	274,620	20.9	1,250,900	12.7	259,610	16.5
Rape/Sexual assault[1]	19,160*	0.2*	9,610*	0.7*	144,630	1.5	62,410	4.0
Robbery	235,360	2.5	75,490	5.7	135,440	1.4	42,560	2.7
Completed/property taken	173,570	1.8	60,170	4.6	101,980	1.0	38,130	2.4
With injury	76,890	0.8	25,970*	2.0*	42,920	0.4	17,810*	1.1*
Without injury	96,680	1.0	34,210	2.6	59,060	0.6	20,320*	1.3*
Attempted to take property	61,790	0.7	15,310*	1.2*	33,460	0.3	4,420*	0.3*
With injury	25,720*	0.3*	3,130*	0.2*	9,040*	0.1*	2,100*	0.1*
Without injury	36,070	0.4	12,180*	0.9*	24,430*	0.2*	2,330*	0.1*
Assault	2,139,810	22.7	296,680	22.5	1,718,230	17.4	318,690	20.3
Aggravated	485,760	5.2	98,030	7.4	302,290	3.1	94,860	6.0
With injury	145,280	1.5	19,260*	1.5*	122,620	1.2	26,710*	1.7*
Threatened with weapon	340,480	3.6	78,770	6.0	179,660	1.8	68,160	4.3
Simple	1,654,050	17.5	198,650	15.1	1,415,940	14.4	223,820	14.3
With minor injury	357,970	3.8	27,730*	2.1*	422,250	4.3	65,630	4.2
Without injury	1,296,080	13.7	170,920	13.0	993,690	10.1	158,190	10.1
Purse snatching/pocket picking	65,240	0.7	4,340*	0.3*	67,220	0.7	14,750*	0.9*
Population age 12 and over	94,313,900	...	13,164,830	...	98,643,080	...	15,706,600	...

Note: Detail may not add to total shown because of rounding.
Excludes data on persons of "other" races.
*Estimate is based on about 10 or fewer sample cases.
...Not applicable.
[1]Includes verbal threats of rape and threats of sexual assault.

SOURCE: "Table 6: Personal Crimes, 2002, Number of Victimizations and Victimization Rates for Persons Age 12 and Over, by Type of Crime and Gender and Race of Victims," in *Criminal Victimization in the United States, 2002 Statistical Tables,* U.S. Department of Justice, Office of Justice Programs, Bureau of Justice Statistics, Washington, DC, 2003

households in the West, and 215.3 per 1,000 urban households experienced property crimes. Rates in all categories of property crime in the West and in urban locations were higher than rates in other regions and locations. The lowest rates were found in rural areas (118.3 per 1,000 households), while the Northeast had the lowest rate for property crimes (117.0). (See Table 3.9.)

Victim/Offender Relationship

In 2002 strangers were often the most common perpetrators of violent crimes. Strangers accounted for 14.3 per 1,000 violent crimes for males, the largest rate for all relationship categories, but only 6.4 per 1,000 for female violent crime victims, the highest for females being persons well-known to them (7.0 per 1,000). For black victims of violent crime, 11.3 per 1,000 were committed by strangers, while the white rate for strangers was 10.2 per 1,000. For all groups of violent crime victims, relatives were least likely to be the assailants. (See Table 3.10.) Strangers were more likely to use a weapon in committing a violent crime than were persons known to the victim. Firearms were used by strangers in 11.3 percent of violent crimes, while non-strangers used a firearm only 3.2 percent of the time. (See Table 3.11.)

WHEN AND WHERE DOES VIOLENT CRIME HAPPEN?

According to the NCVS, crime happens at all times of the day and night, though particular crimes exhibit different patterns. Violent crimes occur between 6 A.M. and 6 P.M. in 52.7 percent of cases. Simple assaults occur 57.6 percent of the time during these same hours, as do 42.2 percent of aggravated assaults. Approximately two-thirds (63.2 percent) of rapes/sexual assaults occur at night. Most property crimes occur during the day, except for motor vehicle theft, which occurs 71.7 percent of the time at night.

Crime may also occur in any place. According to the NCVS, in 2002 nearly one-third (31.7 percent) of violent crime incidents occurred at or near the victim's residence. Other common locales for crime were schools (15.1 percent), commercial establishments (11.3 percent), and parking lots and garages (7.6 percent).

Victims' Activities

Most victims of crime were engaged in activities at home (26.3 percent), while 22 percent reported being involved in some form of leisure activity away from home when victim-

TABLE 3.5

Violent victimization rates by age, 1973–2000

Violent crime rate per 1,000 persons in age group

	Age of victim						
	12-15	16-19	20-24	25-34	35-49	50-64	65+
1973	81.8	81.7	87.6	52.4	38.8	17.2	9.1
1974	77.5	90.6	83.5	58.6	37.5	15.5	9.5
1975	80.3	85.7	80.9	59.5	36.9	17.8	8.3
1976	76.4	88.8	79.7	61.5	35.9	16.1	8.1
1977	83.0	90.2	86.2	63.5	35.8	16.8	8.0
1978	83.7	91.7	91.1	60.5	35.8	15.0	8.4
1979	78.5	93.4	98.4	66.3	38.2	13.6	6.2
1980	72.5	91.3	94.1	60.0	37.4	15.6	7.2
1981	86.0	90.7	93.7	65.8	41.6	17.3	8.3
1982	75.6	94.4	93.8	69.6	38.6	13.8	6.1
1983	75.4	86.3	82.0	62.2	36.5	11.9	5.9
1984	78.2	90.0	87.5	56.6	37.9	13.2	5.2
1985	79.6	89.4	82.0	56.5	35.6	13.0	4.8
1986	77.1	80.8	80.1	52.0	36.0	10.8	4.8
1987	87.2	92.4	85.5	51.9	34.7	11.4	5.2
1988	83.7	95.9	80.2	53.2	39.1	13.4	4.4
1989	92.5	98.2	78.8	52.8	37.3	10.5	4.2
1990	101.1	99.1	86.1	55.2	34.4	9.9	3.7
1991	94.5	122.6	103.6	54.3	37.2	12.5	4.0
1992	111.0	103.7	95.2	56.8	38.1	13.2	5.2
1993	115.5	114.2	91.6	56.9	42.5	15.2	5.9
1994	118.6	123.9	100.4	59.1	41.3	17.6	4.6
1995	113.1	106.6	85.8	58.5	35.7	12.9	6.4
1996	95.0	102.8	74.5	51.2	32.9	15.7	4.9
1997	87.9	96.3	68.0	47.0	32.3	14.6	4.4
1998	82.5	91.3	67.5	41.6	29.9	15.4	2.9
1999	74.5	77.6	68.7	36.4	25.2	14.4	3.9
2000	60.1	64.4	49.5	34.9	21.8	13.7	3.7

Note: Because of changes made to the victimization survey, data prior to 1992 are adjusted to make them comparable to data collected under the redesigned methodology. Estimates for 1993 and beyond are based on collection year while earlier estimates are based on data year. Due to changes in the methods used, these data differ from earlier versions.

Violent crimes included are homicide, rape, robbery, and both simple and aggravated assault.

SOURCE: "Violent Victimization Rates by Age, 1973–2000," in *Key Facts at a Glance,* U.S. Department of Justice, Bureau of Justice Statistics, Washington, DC, 2002 [Online] http://www.ojp.usdoj.gov/bjs [accessed March 18, 2004]

FIGURE 3.2

Adolescent victims and nonvictims of violence, percentage expected to experience adult problem outcomes

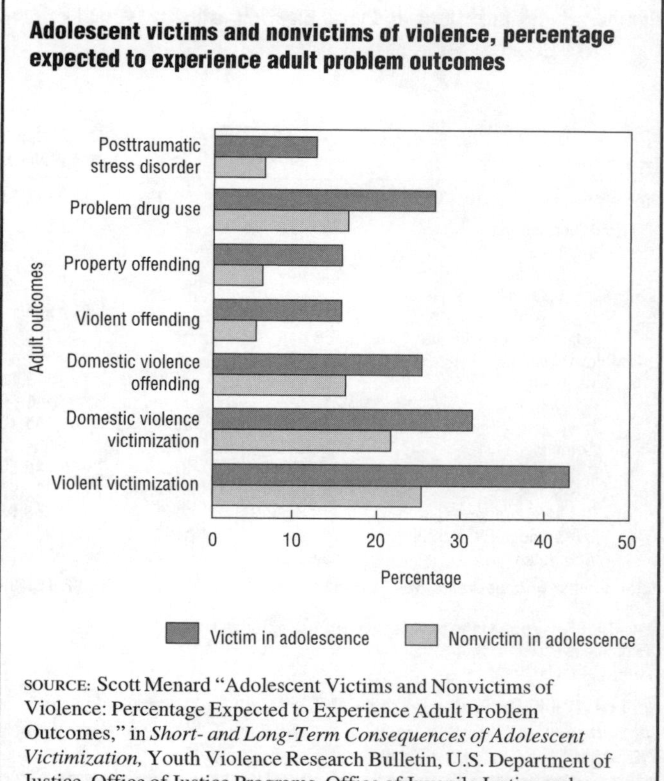

SOURCE: Scott Menard "Adolescent Victims and Nonvictims of Violence: Percentage Expected to Experience Adult Problem Outcomes," in *Short- and Long-Term Consequences of Adolescent Victimization,* Youth Violence Research Bulletin, U.S. Department of Justice, Office of Justice Programs, Office of Juvenile Justice and Delinquency Prevention, Washington, DC, February 2002

ized. Another 18.7 percent mentioned they were at work or traveling to or from work when the crime occurred; 14.2 percent reported being at school or traveling to or from school. Rapes occurred most often at home (31.8 percent) or while engaged in leisure activity away from home (30.3 percent). Robberies took place in a variety of situations:

- One in five (20.8 percent) during leisure activities
- One in five (20.2 percent) during travel
- One in four (23.7 percent) at home
- One in nine (10.8 percent) at work or while commuting to/from work

TRENDS IN VICTIMIZATION

Trends, 1973–2000

The NCVS, like the FBI's Uniform Crime Reports, found that the overall level of crime decreased from 1973 to 2000. (Although the 1993–2000 survey results cannot be directly compared to earlier statistics, adjusted data can be used to highlight trends.) More than 41 million personal and household crimes were committed in 1981. The 1981 adjusted rate of approximately 52.5 violent crimes per 1,000 persons was significantly higher than at any time before 1977. The victimization rate for violent crimes increased between 1977 and 1981 and then declined until 1986. From 1986 to 1994 the violent crime rate increased, reaching 51.8 per 1,000 in 1994. From 1994 to 2000, however, violent crime rates fell 44.1 percent, and property crime rates declined by 44.2 percent.

Property crime rates fell dramatically between 1973 (adjusted data) and 1995. After a slight increase from 1973 to 1975, the rates dropped more or less consistently through 1995. Only motor vehicle theft remained relatively stable over this period.

Violent victimizations by age dropped from 1973 to 2000. The proportion of victimizations across age groups has varied. For example, in 1973, 16- to 19-year-olds were about twice as likely to be victimized by violent crime as persons 35 to 49 years of age; this rate increased to about three times as likely by 2000. For those ages 16–19, the violent victimization rate dropped by one-fifth between 1973 and 2000. For 12- to 15-year-olds, the rate

TABLE 3.6

Number of victimizations and victimization rates by type of crime and race of head of household, 2002

	Rate per 1,000 households							
	All races		White		Black		Other	
Type of crime	Number	Rate	Number	Rate	Number	Rate	Number	Rate
Property crimes	17,539,220	159.0	14,527,440	157.6	2,434,780	173.7	576,990	139.8
Household burglary	3,055,720	27.7	2,396,810	26.0	578,880	41.3	80,030	19.4
Completed	2,597,310	23.5	2,080,340	22.6	444,040	31.7	72,930	17.7
Forcible entry	1,017,660	9.2	727,180	7.9	260,680	18.6	29,800*	7.2*
Unlawful entry without force	1,579,650	14.3	1,353,160	14.7	183,360	13.1	43,130	10.4
Attempted forcible entry	458,410	4.2	316,470	3.4	134,840	9.6	7,100*	1.7*
Motor vehicle theft	988,760	9.0	695,410	7.5	241,670	17.2	51,670	12.5
Completed	780,630	7.1	549,730	6.0	191,610	13.7	39,300	9.5
Attempted	208,120	1.9	145,690	1.6	50,060	3.6	12,380*	3.0*
Theft	13,494,750	122.3	11,435,220	124.1	1,614,240	115.2	445,290	107.9
Completed	13,039,920	118.2	11,054,970	119.9	1,556,620	111.1	428,320	103.8
Less than $50	4,186,570	37.9	3,646,500	39.6	409,720	29.2	130,360	31.6
$50–$249	4,455,080	40.4	3,717,980	40.3	598,290	42.7	138,810	33.6
$250 or more	3,270,530	29.6	2,766,820	30.0	396,330	28.3	107,390	26.0
Amount not available	1,127,740	10.2	923,680	10.0	152,290	10.9	51,760	12.5
Attempted	454,830	4.1	380,240	4.1	57,620	4.1	16,970*	4.1*
Total number of households	**110,323,840**	...	**92,182,320**	...	**14,013,850**	...	**4,127,670**	...

Note: Detail may not add to total shown because of rounding.
*Estimate is based on about 10 or fewer sample cases.
...Not applicable.

SOURCE: "Table 16: Property Crimes, 2002: Number of Victimizations and Victimization Rates by Type of Crime and Race of Head of Household," in *Criminal Victimization in the United States, 2002 Statistical Tables,* U.S. Department of Justice, Office of Justice Programs, Bureau of Justice Statistics, Washington, DC, 2003

of violent victimization dropped by one-quarter. For those ages 20–24, the rate fell over 40 percent. Rates of victimization remained within a much narrower range for those 50 to 64 years of age yet still dropped 20 percent between 1973 and 2000. (See Table 3.5.)

Trends, 1994–2000

The 2000 rates of violent victimization continued the general decline of the previous several years. From 1994 to 2000 the rate of violent crime decreased by 46.1 percent. In 1994 there were 51.8 violent victimizations per 1,000 population compared to 27.9 per 1,000 in 2000. The robbery rate fell 49.2 percent and the aggravated assault rate dropped 52.1 percent. Personal theft declined 50 percent from 1994 to 2000.

The rates of all property crime categories continued to decrease from 1994 to 2000. Motor vehicle theft showed a 52.8 percent decline. Theft rates fell 41.2 percent, continuing a steady decline that began in 1979.

COST OF VICTIMIZATION

Several different ways are available for a crime victim to consider his or her loss. Direct costs to the victim are easy to pinpoint, but indirect costs must be shared by the entire society (the expenses of the criminal justice system, for instance). In 2002 victims suffered a total economic loss of some $15.5 billion to crime. This amount refers to the actual loss of property and not to such additional expenses as medical or insurance costs. While material losses are very important, emotional costs can affect the victim for the rest of his or her life, sometimes producing radical and permanent changes in his or her lifestyle.

A National Institute of Justice Study

In *Victim Costs and Consequences: A New Look* (National Institute of Justice, Washington, D.C., 1996), Ted R. Miller, Mark A. Cohen, and Brian Wiersema estimated that from 1987 to 1990 personal crime cost $105 billion per year in medical costs, lost earnings, and public program expenses related to victim assistance. This amounts to about $425 per person (including children) in the United States. These tangible losses, however, do not account for the full impact of crime on victims. If the intangible factors of pain, suffering, reduced quality of life, and risk of death are included, victims' costs increase to an estimated $450 billion annually, or $1,800 per person.

The study excluded several crimes that also have large cost impacts, such as many forms of white-collar crime, personal fraud, and drug crimes. Also excluded were the costs of operating the nation's correctional institutions, an additional expense of approximately $40 billion annually.

VIOLENT CRIME. Violent crime, including drunk driving and arson, accounted for $426 billion of the annual total. Property crime accounted for $24 billion. Rape was considered the costliest crime, accounting for $127 billion

TABLE 3.7

Victimization rates for persons age 12 and over, by type of crime and annual family income of victims, 2002

Type of crime	Rate per 1,000 persons age 12 and over						
	Less than $7,500	$7,500–$14,999	$15,000–$24,999	$25,000–$34,999	$35,000–$49,999	$50,000–$74,999	$75,000 or more
All personal crimes	**47.2**	**32.0**	**30.8**	**27.4**	**26.0**	**19.3**	**19.7**
Crimes of violence	45.5	31.5	30.0	27.0	25.6	18.7	19.0
Completed violence	18.7	12.0	11.4	9.3	6.7	4.9	5.6
Attempted/threatened violence	26.8	19.5	18.6	17.7	18.8	13.8	13.4
Rape/Sexual assault	2.5*	3.2	2.1	1.2*	0.9*	0.2*	0.4*
Rape/Attempted rape	2.3*	2.7	1.3	0.8*	0.3*	0.1*	0.2*
Rape	0.6*	1.4*	1.0*	0.3*	0.1*	0.1*	0.1*
Attempted rape[1]	1.7*	1.3*	0.2*	0.5*	0.2*	0.0*	0.1*
Sexual assault[2]	0.3*	0.4*	0.8*	0.4*	0.6*	0.1*	0.2*
Robbery	6.3	4.1	2.9	2.9	2.2	2.1	1.0
Completed/property taken	5.0	2.4	2.4	1.9	1.9	1.5	0.8
With injury	2.4*	1.3*	1.1*	0.8*	0.5*	0.3*	0.4*
Without injury	2.7*	1.1*	1.3	1.1*	1.4	1.2	0.4*
Attempted to take property	1.3*	1.7*	0.5*	1.0*	0.3*	0.6*	0.2*
With injury	0.3*	0.9*	0.1*	0.4*	0.0*	0.2*	0.1*
Without injury	1.0*	0.8*	0.4*	0.6*	0.3*	0.4*	0.1*
Assault	36.7	24.2	25.0	22.9	22.4	16.5	17.6
Aggravated	11.2	5.8	6.1	4.1	5.2	2.5	2.8
With injury	4.2	2.4	1.8	1.5	1.3	0.5 *	0.9
Threatened with weapon	7.0	3.3	4.3	2.5	3.9	2.0	1.9
Simple	25.5	18.4	18.9	18.9	17.2	14.0	14.8
With minor injury	8.6	5.6	5.7	5.2	3.1	2.8	3.7
Without injury	16.9	12.8	13.3	13.7	14.1	11.2	11.2
Purse snatching/Pocket picking	1.7*	0.5*	0.8*	0.3*	0.4*	0.6*	0.7
Population age 12 and over	8,347,650	15,608,210	23,872,200	24,104,810	31,655,160	33,713,640	43,139,380

Note: Detail may not add to total shown because of rounding.
Excludes data on persons whose family income level was not ascertained.
*Estimate is based on about 10 or fewer sample cases.
[1]Includes verbal threats of rape.
[2]Includes threats.

SOURCE: "Table 14: Personal Crimes, 2002, Victimization Rates for Persons Age 12 and Over, by Type of Crime and Annual Family Income of Victims," in *Criminal Victimization in the United States, 2002 Statistical Tables,* U.S. Department of Justice, Office of Justice Programs, Bureau of Justice Statistics, Washington, DC, 2003

annually. Rape and sexual abuse costs represented 28.2 percent of the total costs.

The study estimated that violent crime accounts for 3 percent of all U.S. medical spending and 14 percent of injury-related medical spending. The wage losses caused by violent crime are equivalent to 1 percent of American earnings. Violent crime may also account for as much as 10 to 20 percent of expenditures for mental health care, primarily to treat victims. About half of these expenditures are for child abuse victims who are receiving treatment for abuse experienced years earlier. These estimates do not include any treatment for the perpetrators of violence.

PERSONAL CRIME. The study claimed that, by conservative estimates, personal crime reduced the average American's quality of life by 1.8 percent. Violence alone caused a 1.7 percent loss. These estimates include only costs to victimized households, ignoring the broader impact of crime-induced fear on society.

WHO PAYS THE CRIME BILL? The National Institute of Justice (NIJ) study found that crime victims and their families pay the bill for some crimes, while the public largely pays the bill for others. Insurers pay $45 billion annually due to crime, about $265 per every American adult. The federal government pays $8 billion annually for restorative and emergency services for crime victims, plus perhaps one-fourth of the $11 billion paid in health insurance payments. For arson and drunk driving, taxpayers and insurance purchasers cover almost all the tangible costs (for example, property damage and loss, medical care, police and fire services, and victim services).

Victims pay about $44 billion of the $57 billion in tangible nonservice expenses for traditional crimes of violence (murder, rape, robbery, assault, abuse, and neglect). Employers pay almost $5 billion, primarily in health insurance premiums, because of these crimes. (This estimate excludes sick leave and disability insurance costs other than workers' compensation.) Government bears the remaining costs through lost tax revenues and Medicare and Medicaid payments. Crime victim compensation accounts for 38 percent of homeowners' insurance payments and 29 percent of auto insurance payments.

TABLE 3.8

Victimization rates for persons age 12 and over, by gender and marital status of victims and type of crime, 2002

Gender and marital status	Total population	Rate per 1,000 persons age 12 and over										
		Crimes of violence	Completed violence	Attempted/ threatened violence	Rape/ Sexual assault[1]	Robbery			Assault			Purse snatching/ Pocket picking
						Total	With injury	Without injury	Total	Aggra-vated	Simple	
Male												
Never married	39,330,360	46.5	14.4	32.1	0.5*	5.3	2.2	3.1	40.7	8.8	31.9	1.3
Married	59,173,620	11.4	2.4	9.0	0.1*	0.9	0.4*	0.5	10.4	2.7	7.8	0.1*
Widowed	2,695,670	17.0	4.5*	12.5	0.0*	4.1*	1.6*	2.5*	12.9	6.8*	6.0*	0.0*
Divorced or separated	10,251,890	27.7	8.1	19.6	0.7*	4.9	2.1*	2.8	22.1	5.5	16.6	1.1*
Female												
Never married	34,699,450	39.6	14.6	25.0	4.9	2.0	0.9	1.0	32.8	5.7	27.1	0.9*
Married	58,123,160	9.7	3.1	6.7	0.3*	1.0	0.1*	0.8	8.4	1.8	6.7	0.5
Widowed	11,003,700	4.7	2.0*	2.7*	0.4*	1.4*	0.8*	0.6*	2.9	1.0*	1.9*	0.8*
Divorced or separated	14,516,310	32.9	15.2	17.7	1.3*	3.4	2.1*	1.4*	28.1	6.1	22.0	1.1*

Note: Detail may not add to total shown because of rounding.
Excludes data on persons whose marital status was not ascertained.
*Estimate is based on about 10 or fewer sample cases.
[1]Includes verbal threats of rape and threats of sexual assault.

SOURCE: "Table 12: Personal Crimes, 2002, Victimization Rates for Persons Age 12 and Over, by Gender and Marital Status of Victims and Type of Crime," in *Criminal Victimization in the United States, 2002 Statistical Tables,* U.S. Department of Justice, Office of Justice Programs, Bureau of Justice Statistics, Washington, DC, 2003

TABLE 3.9

Property crime victimization rates, by type of crime, region, and residence locality, 2002

	Rate per 1,000 households							
	All regions				Northeast			
Type of crime	All areas	Urban	Suburban	Rural	All areas	Urban	Suburban	Rural
Property crimes	**159.0**	**215.3**	**145.3**	**118.3**	**117.0**	**126.7**	**108.0**	**125.7**
Household burglary	27.7	40.5	22.4	22.6	18.4	23.2	14.0	22.7
Completed	23.5	34.1	19.1	19.5	15.0	18.8	11.3	19.3
Forcible entry	9.2	16.4	6.1	6.7	4.8	8.7	3.5	1.8*
Unlawful entry without force	14.3	17.8	12.9	12.9	10.3	10.1	7.8	17.5
Attempted forcible entry	4.2	6.4	3.4	3.0	3.4	4.3*	2.7*	3.4*
Motor vehicle theft	9.0	17.1	7.5	2.2	6.4	11.2	5.7	0.6*
Completed	7.1	13.1	6.0	2.0	5.5	9.7	4.8	0.6*
Attempted	1.9	4.0	1.4	0.3*	0.9*	1.5*	0.9*	0.0*
Theft	122.3	157.7	115.4	93.5	92.1	92.3	88.3	102.4
Completed	118.2	151.5	111.6	91.3	88.3	88.0	84.9	98.3
Less than $50	37.9	42.5	37.1	34.1	33.0	27.8	33.5	40.0
$50–$249	40.4	55.3	36.5	30.1	28.9	28.6	28.3	30.9
$250 or more	29.6	40.3	28.0	20.1	17.5	19.6	16.1	17.8
Amount not available	10.2	13.4	10.0	7.0	9.0	12.1	6.9	9.6
Attempted	4.1	6.2	3.8	2.2	3.8	4.3*	3.4	4.1*
Total number of households	**110,323,840**	**31,937,800**	**51,446,980**	**26,939,060**	**20,821,680**	**6,354,700**	**10,628,640**	**3,838,340**

	Rate per 1,000 households							
	Midwest				South			
Type of crime	All areas	Urban	Suburban	Rural	All areas	Urban	Suburban	Rural
Property crimes	**155.8**	**221.6**	**135.7**	**128.3**	**147.8**	**222.3**	**140.9**	**94.2**
Household burglary	30.7	57.1	19.4	24.4	28.2	45.3	22.2	22.3
Completed	25.9	46.9	17.1	20.4	24.1	38.8	18.4	19.9
Forcible entry	10.5	24.4	5.0	6.4	10.7	20.1	6.0	9.7
Unlawful entry without force	15.4	22.5	12.1	14.0	13.4	18.7	12.4	10.2
Attempted forcible entry	4.8	10.1	2.3*	3.9	4.1	6.6	3.8	2.4*
Motor vehicle theft	7.9	20.7	4.8	1.2*	7.9	16.0	6.4	3.3
Completed	6.0	15.5	3.9	0.9*	6.1	11.6	5.0	2.9
Attempted	1.8	5.2	1.0*	0.3*	1.8	4.4	1.4*	0.4*
Theft	117.2	143.8	111.5	102.7	111.8	161.0	112.3	68.6
Completed	113.4	137.0	108.1	100.8	108.0	155.4	107.5	67.8
Less than $50	40.3	41.1	38.9	41.5	31.9	40.5	35.5	19.1
$50–$249	38.5	50.8	35.1	33.0	37.6	58.7	35.5	22.7
$250 or more	24.9	31.3	25.2	19.0	29.7	44.8	27.3	20.2
Amount not available	9.7	13.8	8.9	7.3	8.8	11.4	9.2	5.8
Attempted	3.8	6.8	3.4	1.9*	3.8	5.6	4.8	0.8*
Total number of households	**26,238,340**	**6,822,000**	**11,482,180**	**7,934,160**	**40,202,070**	**10,310,590**	**17,922,400**	**11,969,080**

	Rate per 1,000 households			
	West			
Type of crime	All areas	Urban	Suburban	Rural
Property crimes	**219.9**	**268.3**	**196.7**	**175.0**
Household burglary	31.9	34.2	33.8	19.0
Completed	27.6	29.6	29.3	16.5
Forcible entry	9.3	11.0	10.0	1.9*
Unlawful entry without force	18.4	18.6	19.3	14.7
Attempted forcible entry	4.2	4.6	4.4	2.4*
Motor vehicle theft	14.3	19.8	13.5	2.6*
Completed	11.4	15.3	11.0	2.6*
Attempted	2.9	4.5	2.4*	0.0*
Theft	173.8	214.2	149.5	153.4
Completed	168.5	206.3	146.4	147.5
Less than $50	50.4	57.3	41.3	64.7
$50–$249	57.6	75.0	46.9	50.0
$250 or more	45.9	57.7	43.0	25.5
Amount not available	14.5	16.3	15.1	7.3*
Attempted	5.3	7.9	3.1	5.9*
Total number of households	**23,061,760**	**8,450,520**	**11,413,760**	**3,197,480**

Notes: Detail may not add to total shown because of rounding. The term "Urban" is used to denote "Central cities." The term "Suburban" is used to denote "Outside central cities." The term "Rural" is used to denote "Nonmetropolitan areas."
*Estimate is based on about 10 or fewer sample cases.

SOURCE: "Table 58: Victimization Rates by Type of Crime, Region and Locality of Residence," in *Criminal Victimization in the United States, 2002 Statistical Tables,* U.S. Department of Justice, Office of Justice Programs, Bureau of Justice Statistics, Washington, DC, 2003

TABLE 3.10

Family violence victimization rates, by victim-offender relationship, type of crime, and selected victim characteristics, 2002

		Rate per 1,000 persons age 12 and over							
		Crimes of violence[1]				Assault			
Characteristic	Total population	Relatives	Well-known	Casual acquaintances	Strangers	Relatives	Well-known	Casual acquaintances	Strangers
Gender									
Male	112,241,930	1.0	5.6	3.2	14.3	0.9	5.2	3.0	12.0
Female	119,347,330	2.8	7.0	3.2	6.4	2.5	5.9	2.7	5.2
Race									
White	192,956,980	2.0	6.0	3.2	10.2	1.8	5.4	3.0	8.7
Black	28,871,440	1.9	9.4	3.4	11.3	1.9	7.3	2.6	8.4
Other	9,760,850	0.9*	3.1	1.9*	7.5	0.9*	2.1*	1.9*	5.3
Age									
12–15	16,676,560	1.1*	15.9	8.9	16.3	1.0*	14.7	8.1	13.9
16–19	16,171,800	3.1	19.6	10.1	22.9	2.4	15.5	8.3	19.8
20–24	19,317,740	4.2	12.3	4.5	23.8	4.1	10.0	3.8	19.5
25–34	37,329,720	2.6	6.6	3.5	12.6	2.3	5.8	3.5	10.6
35–49	65,263,580	2.4	4.2	2.1	8.0	2.3	3.9	1.9	6.8
50–64	43,746,850	0.9	2.5	1.4	5.2	0.8	2.3	1.4	3.9
65 and over	33,083,000	0.2*	0.5*	0.4*	1.5	0.2*	0.4*	0.3*	1.0
Marital status[2]									
Married	117,296,790	1.3	2.0	1.0	5.6	1.3	1.7	1.0	4.9
Widowed	13,699,370	0.8*	1.9*	0.2*	3.7	0.7*	1.3*	0.2*	2.5
Divorced or separated	24,768,200	6.4	7.7	5.4	9.5	5.8	6.5	4.9	7.1
Never married	74,029,810	1.6	13.7	6.4	19.1	1.4	11.9	5.6	15.9
Family income[3]									
Less than $7,500	8,347,650	4.6	16.5	6.3	15.6	4.1	13.7	5.7	12.1
$7,500–$14,999	15,608,210	2.8	9.4	4.6	12.6	2.3	6.8	3.7	10.3
$15,000–$24,999	23,872,200	4.0	9.0	4.6	10.7	3.6	7.2	4.4	8.5
$25,000–$34,999	24,104,810	1.9	8.0	4.5	10.4	1.9	7.1	3.9	8.2
$35,000–$49,999	31,655,160	2.3	6.3	3.4	12.2	2.1	5.9	2.9	10.3
$50,000–$74,999	33,713,640	1.5	3.9	3.1	9.5	1.2	3.6	3.0	8.1
$75,000 or more	43,139,380	1.1	5.5	2.2	9.5	1.0	5.3	2.1	8.6

VICTIM SERVICES AND ASSISTANCE

Interest in assisting victims first developed in the United States as a desire for restitution (monetary compensation) to be paid to a victim by the offender. Restitution for criminal acts has a long history, dating back to biblical times. The Bible often cites money payments for injuries, and this practice continued well into the Middle Ages. Around 1100, England's Henry I began to take a part of the restitution as a charge for holding a trial and for injury inflicted on the state because a criminal act had disturbed the peace of the kingdom. Eventually assault upon an individual became considered as an assault upon society, and the king took the entire payment.

For many years, a victim was often victimized again by the very system to which he or she turned for help. In 1982 Lois Haight observed in the "Statement of the Chairman," as part of the *President's Task Force on Victims of Crime* (Washington, D.C., 1982), that somewhere along the way the system began to cater to lawyers, judges, and defendants. Meanwhile, the victim was treated with institutionalized disinterest.

The "revictimization" may begin with an insensitive police officer who questions whether a victim was really raped or whether she had enticed the rapist. The rape victim may sit alone in a hospital emergency room waiting to be treated. She may even have to pay for the rape examination herself. An assault victim may find that the hospital is more concerned with whether he or she can pay for treatment. Judges and lawyers may seem to be more involved with the accused than with the victim. In fact, victims may never know when the trial takes place. If they do take part in a trial, victims may sit all day in a bare hallway outside the courtroom, waiting to testify as a witness, and may never even be called to the witness stand.

Changing Attitudes toward Victims

Attitudes toward victims improved through the 1980s and 1990s. State and federal governments, the judicial system, and private groups grew more eager to help victims. By 1996 approximately 10,000 organizations offered services to victims of crime. These organizations included domestic violence shelters, rape crisis centers, and child abuse programs. Law enforcement agencies, hospitals, and social services agencies also provided victim services. The types of services provided include:

- Crisis intervention
- Counseling
- Emergency shelter and transportation
- Legal services

TABLE 3.10

Family violence victimization rates, by victim-offender relationship, type of crime, and selected victim characteristics, 2002 [CONTINUED]

Characteristic	Total population	Rate per 1,000 persons age 12 and over: Aggravated assault				Simple assault			
		Relatives	Well-known	Casual acquaintances	Strangers	Relatives	Well-known	Casual acquaintances	Strangers
Gender									
Male	112,241,930	0.3*	0.9	0.6	3.1	0.7	4.3	2.4	8.9
Female	119,347,330	0.5	0.9	0.3	1.2	2.0	4.9	2.5	4.0
Race									
White	192,956,980	0.4	0.8	0.5	2.0	1.4	4.6	2.5	6.7
Black	28,871,440	0.6*	1.6	0.3*	3.6	1.2	5.7	2.3	4.8
Other	9,760,850	0.0*	0.5*	0.2*	0.2*	0.9*	1.6*	1.6*	5.1
Age									
12–15	16,676,560	0.3*	1.9	0.8*	1.9	0.6*	12.8	7.3	11.9
16–19	16,171,800	0.6*	1.6*	1.6*	6.6	1.8*	14.0	6.7	13.2
20–24	19,317,740	1.4*	1.3*	0.2*	5.9	2.7	8.8	3.6	13.6
25–34	37,329,720	0.3*	1.3	0.5*	3.1	2.0	4.5	2.9	7.5
35–49	65,263,580	0.5	0.8	0.4*	1.2	1.7	3.1	1.5	5.6
50–64	43,746,850	0.0*	0.4*	0.3*	0.8	0.8	1.8	1.1	3.1
65 and over	33,083,000	0.1*	0.1*	0.0*	0.4*	0.1*	0.3*	0.3*	0.5*
Marital status[2]									
Married	117,296,790	0.2*	0.3	0.3	1.3	1.1	1.4	0.7	3.6
Widowed	13,699,370	0.3*	0.7*	0.0*	1.1*	0.4*	0.7*	0.2*	1.3*
Divorced or separated	24,768,200	1.5	1.6	0.6*	1.5	4.3	5.0	4.3	5.6
Never married	74,029,810	0.3*	1.6	0.7	4.0	1.1	10.3	4.9	12.0
Family income[3]									
Less than $7,500	8,347,650	1.8*	2.4*	1.8*	4.5	2.3 *	11.3	3.9	7.6
$7,500–$14,999	15,608,210	0.3*	1.5*	0.3*	3.3	2.0 *	5.2	3.4	7.0
$15,000–$24,999	23,872,200	0.6*	1.5	0.8*	3.1	3.1	5.6	3.6	5.3
$25,000–$34,999	24,104,810	0.3*	0.7*	0.7*	1.9	1.6	6.4	3.3	6.4
$35,000–$49,999	31,655,160	0.7*	1.2	0.5*	2.2	1.4	4.7	2.4	8.0
$50,000–$74,999	33,713,640	0.1*	0.3*	0.4*	1.6	1.1	3.3	2.6	6.5
$75,000 or more	43,139,380	0.2*	0.4*	0.4*	1.5	0.9	4.8	1.7	7.1

*Estimate is based on about 10 or fewer sample cases.
[1]Crimes of violence includes data on rape, sexual assault, and robbery, not shown separately.
[2]Excludes data on persons whose marital status was not ascertained.
[3]Excludes data on persons whose family income was not ascertained.

SOURCE: "Table 35: Family Violence, 2002: Victimization Rate by Victim-Offender Relationship, by Type of Crime and Selected Victim Characteristics," in *Criminal Victimization in the United States, 2002 Statistical Tables,* U.S. Department of Justice, Office of Justice Programs, Bureau of Justice Statistics, Washington, DC, 2003

Victim Compensation

Victim compensation is a program that pays money from a public fund to help victims with expenses incurred because of a violent crime. Margery Fry, a British magistrate and legal reformer, began advocating a victim compensation program during the 1950s. In her book *Arms of the Law* (London, 1951), Fry wondered if we have neglected restitution customs adopted by our ancestors. She noted that making up for a wrong done held wide currency in earlier societies, and that it might be wise to revisit this form of punishment. Her book and articles advocating compensation programs aroused considerable discussion in the United Kingdom and New Zealand. As a result, New Zealand's legislature passed a law permitting the government to award compensation to victims. After several years of debate, the British Parliament created an experimental program in 1964.

VICTIM COMPENSATION PROGRAMS IN THE UNITED STATES. In the United States, interest in victim compensation grew rapidly in the mid-1960s. In 1965 California became the first state to develop a victim compensation program. The idea spread across the country, with New York (1966), Hawaii (1967), Maryland (1968), Massachusetts (1968), and New Jersey (1971) soon adopting compensation programs.

By the year 2002 all 50 states, the District of Columbia, Puerto Rico, Guam, and the Virgin Islands had victim compensation programs. Most state laws include reimbursement for medical treatment and physical therapy costs, counseling fees, lost wages, funeral and burial expenses, and loss of support to dependents of homicide victims. Average maximum awards generally range from $10,000 to $25,000. Some states also require a minimum loss, most often $100, before a victim can be compensated, or a $100 deductible (amount automatically not paid for a claim).

Victim compensation normally does not cover the costs of pain and suffering, future income loss, or property loss and damage (except the loss of eyeglasses, den-

TABLE 3.11

Violent crimes by victim-offender relationship, type of crime, and weapon used, 2002

		Percent of incidents					
				Weapon used			
All incidents	Number	Total incidents Percent	No weapon used	Total	Total firearm	Hand gun	Other gun
Crimes of violence	**4,923,050**	**100 %**	**70.3 %**	**21.3 %**	**7.2%**	**6.0%**	**1.1%**
Completed violence	1,605,900	100	67.5	25.7	8.4	7.4	1.1*
Attempted/threatened violence	3,317,150	100	71.6	19.1	6.6	5.3	1.1
Rape/Sexual assault[1]	247,730	100	84.5	7.2*	4.6*	4.6*	0.0*
Robbery	458,460	100	41.3	47.0	25.6	20.5	5.1*
Completed/property taken	341,910	100	40.3	47.2	26.8	22.8	4.0*
With injury	159,120	100	48.1	39.2	11.0*	10.3*	0.7*
Without injury	182,790	100	33.6	54.2	40.5	33.7	6.9*
Attempted to take property	116,550	100	44.0	46.4	22.2*	14.0*	8.2*
With injury	39,040	100	37.3*	56.0*	17.3*	7.0*	10.3*
Without injury	77,510	100	47.4	41.6	24.7*	17.6*	7.1*
Assault	4,216,850	100	72.6	19.3	5.3	4.5	0.7*
Aggravated	848,030	100	4.0	96.0	26.5	22.4	3.5*
With injury	273,670	100	12.4	87.6	13.1	11.8	1.3*
Threatened with weapon	574,360	100	...	100.0	33.0	27.5	4.6*
Simple[2]	3,368,820	100	89.9	...	...	...	...
With minor injury	845,940	100	93.4	...	...	...	...
Without injury	2,522,890	100	88.7	...	...	...	...
Involving strangers							
Crimes of violence	2,403,050	100	59.9	28.2	11.3	9.5	1.7
Rape/Sexual assault[1]	83,930	100	70.6	13.5*	13.5 *	13.5 *	0.0*
Robbery	330,540	100	27.2	58.4	34.9	28.5	6.4*
Aggravated assault	486,100	100	2.5*	97.5	30.0	25.2	4.2*
Simple assault[2]	1,502,490	100	85.1	...	...	...	...
Involving nonstrangers							
Crimes of violence	2,520,000	100	80.1	14.6	3.2	2.7	0.5*
Rape/Sexual assault[1]	163,800	100	91.6	3.9*	0.0*	0.0*	0.0*
Robbery	127,930	100	77.6	17.6*	1.7*	0.0*	1.7*
Aggravated assault	361,940	100	6.0*	94.0	21.9	18.7	2.6*
Simple assault[2]	1,866,340	100	93.7	...	...	...	...

tures, etc., by the elderly). Compensation is paid only when other resources—private insurance or offender restitution, for example—do not cover the loss.

The federal government maintains the Crime Victims Fund, which is administered by the Office for Victims of Crime (OVC) in the U.S. Department of Justice. The Federal Victims of Crime Act of 1984 (VOCA, PL 98-473) established the fund, which administers two major formula grant programs: Victim Compensation and Victim Assistance. Like the state funds, victim compensation grants cover medical treatment and physical therapy costs, counseling fees, lost wages, funeral and burial expenses, and loss of support to dependents of homicide victims. Victim assistance funds include money for crisis intervention, counseling, emergency shelter, and criminal justice advocacy. (See below for more information on VOCA.)

Deposits into the fund come from fines, penalty assessments, and bond forfeitures collected from convicted federal criminal offenders. In 2001 legislation was passed allowing the fund to receive gifts, donations, and bequests from private entities. The federal funds from VOCA provide about 20–25 percent of the state compensation programs' total budgets through grants given to each of the states. Of every $140 awarded to a victim, $100 comes from the state and $40 comes from VOCA. Since 1985 the fund has distributed over $5.5 billion to support victim assistance and services.

Restitution Programs

Restitution programs require those who have harmed an individual to repay the victim. In the past, the criminal justice system often focused primarily on punishing the criminal, leaving victims to rely on civil court cases to regain damages. By 2000 most states permitted courts to allow restitution payments as a condition of probation and/or parole. About half of the states have laws requiring courts to order restitution or to record the reason for not doing so.

Restitution laws require that the offender be convicted before any restitution can be ordered. Most states allow a victim to claim medical expenses and property damage or loss, and most permit families of homicide victims to claim costs for loss of support. The state of Washington allows courts to determine damages for pain and suffering as well as "punitive damages" in an amount twice the victim's actual loss. In assessing damages, the courts must take into consideration the offender's ability to pay.

An offender may lose parole privileges and be imprisoned for nonpayment of restitution fees. The courts have upheld the constitutionality of incarcerating offenders for nonpayment, but the Supreme Court, in *Beardon v. Georgia*

TABLE 3.11

Violent crimes by victim-offender relationship, type of crime, and weapon used, 2002 [CONTINUED]

	Percent of incidents						
	Weapon used						
All incidents	**Gun type unknown**	**Knife**	**Sharp object**	**Blunt object**	**Other weapon**	**Weapon type unknown**	**Don't know if weapon present**
Crimes of violence	0.1 %*	4.4 %	1.0 %	3.1 %	4.0 %	1.5 %	8.5 %
Completed violence	0.0*	3.6	1.7*	5.1	5.9	1.1*	6.8
Attempted/threatened violence	0.2*	4.8	0.7*	2.1	3.1	1.7	9.3
Rape/Sexual assault[1]	0.0*	2.6*	0.0*	0.0*	0.0*	0.0*	8.4*
Robbery	0.0*	10.2	1.2*	2.3*	4.4*	3.3*	11.7
Completed/property taken	0.0*	9.9	0.6*	2.7*	3.6*	3.7*	12.5
With injury	0.0*	12.8*	1.3*	4.1*	5.4*	4.7*	12.7*
Without injury	0.0*	7.3*	0.0*	1.5*	2.0*	2.8*	12.2*
Attempted to take property	0.0*	11.3*	2.8*	1.1*	6.8*	2.2*	9.6*
With injury	0.0*	22.6*	0.0*	3.4*	6.2*	6.4*	6.7*
Without injury	0.0*	5.6*	4.2*	0.0*	7.2*	0.0*	11.1*
Assault	0.1*	3.9	1.1	3.3	4.2	1.4	8.1
Aggravated	0.6*	19.4	5.4	16.6	20.9	7.1	0.0*
With injury	0.0*	7.2*	9.1*	26.3	30.2	1.8*	0.0*
Threatened with weapon	0.9*	25.2	3.7*	12.0	16.5	9.6	0.0*
Simple[2]	...	...	...	...	...	...	10.1
With minor injury	...	...	...	...	...	...	6.6
Without injury	...	...	...	...	...	...	11.3
Involving strangers							
Crimes of violence	0.1*	5.5	1.0 *	4.2	4.0	2.1	11.8
Rape/Sexual assault[1]	0.0*	0.0*	0.0 *	0.0*	0.0*	0.0*	15.9*
Robbery	0.0*	11.9	1.6 *	0.9*	4.5*	4.6*	14.4
Aggravated assault	0.6*	19.2	4.0 *	20.3	16.5	7.5	0.0 *
Simple assault[2]	...	...	...	...	...	...	14.9
Involving nonstrangers							
Crimes of violence	0.1*	3.4	1.1*	2.0	4.1	0.9*	5.2
Rape/Sexual assault[1]	0.0*	3.9*	0.0*	0.0*	0.0*	0.0*	4.5*
Robbery	0.0*	5.8*	0.0*	6.1*	4.0*	0.0*	4.8*
Aggravated assault	0.6*	19.7	7.4*	11.6	26.8	6.6*	0.0*
Simple assault[2]	...	...	...	...	...	...	6.3

Note: Responses for weapons used are tallied once, based upon a hierarchy. In previous editions, multiple responses for weapons were tallied.
*Estimate is based on about 10 or fewer sample cases.
...Not applicable.
[1]Includes verbal threats of rape and threats of sexual assault.
[2]Simple assault, by definition, does not involve the use of a weapon.

SOURCE: "Table 66: Percent of Incidents, by Victim-Offender Relationship, Type of Crime and Weapons Use," in *Criminal Victimization in the United States, 2002 Statistical Tables,* U.S. Department of Justice, Office of Justice Programs, Bureau of Justice Statistics, Washington, DC, 2003

(461 US 660, 1983), ruled that an offender could not be sent to prison for nonpayment if he or she had made a good-faith effort to pay and could not. Such an action would violate the Fourteenth Amendment. In most cases the offender must prove his inability to make the payments. When offenders prove that they cannot pay, the courts can reduce the amount, change the schedule of payments, or suspend payment.

Besides threatening offenders with imprisonment, some jurisdictions have other methods of collection. They can garnishee wages (take the payment amount from wages before the employee receives his salary) or attach (not allow a person to use) the offender's assets (bank accounts, stocks, bonds) until he or she pays the restitution. Some jurisdictions can even sell the offender's home.

Civil Suits

A victim can sue in civil court for damages without the offender having been found guilty of criminal charges. Victims often follow this route because it is easier to win civil cases. In a criminal case, a jury or judge can find an alleged offender guilty only if the proof is "beyond a reasonable doubt." In a civil case, the burden of proof requires merely a "preponderance of the evidence" against the accused. One still has to prove a crime was committed, that there were damages, and that the accused is liable to pay for those damages. Even when victims win a civil suit, they often have trouble collecting.

VICTIMS' RIGHTS

State Laws

Victims' rights include the right to attend criminal proceedings, to be notified of proceedings such as parole hearings, and to be free from harassment. The victims' rights movement became active through the 1980s and 1990s. While the movement did not seek to reduce the rights of the accused, it wanted the system to acknowledge that victims also have rights. As a result of this movement, by 2000 almost every state (46) had enacted a "Victims' Bill of Rights," and by 2002, 32 states had passed constitutional amendments for victims' rights.

Recent Federal Action

In addition to re-authorizing some $3.3 billion in funding for the Violence Against Women Act, other Federal legislation signed into law from 1999 to 2000 addressed the needs of crime victims.

The Child Abuse Prevention and Enforcement Act (H.R. 764, signed into law March 10, 2000) increased funding for child abuse prevention and victim assistance programs, while the Strengthening Abuse and Neglect Courts Act of 2000 (S. 2272, signed into law on October 17, 2000) provided $25 million in grants to state and local agencies to reduce the backlog of cases and improve efficiency in abuse and neglect courts.

The Insurance Discrimination Provision of the Financial Services Modernization Act (S. 900, signed into law on November 2, 1999) prohibits insurance companies from terminating coverage or raising premiums of victims of domestic violence. The Protecting Seniors from Fraud Act (S. 3164, signed into law on November 22, 2000) authorized $5 million over five years to reduce crime and fraud against the elderly, while Kristen's Act (H.R. 2780, signed into law on November 9, 2000) authorized funding to help organizations find missing adults in cases where foul play is suspected or when the adult suffers from diminished mental capacity.

The Victims of Trafficking and Violence Protection Act (H.R. 3244, signed into law on October 28, 2000) reauthorized the funding of rehabilitation and shelter programs for victims of international trafficking and created new laws criminalizing forms of human trafficking such as slavery, involuntary servitude, peonage, or forced labor. This includes people who are coerced into sexual or other labor by violence, threat of violence, confiscation of legal documents, and other methods. Prison terms for all slavery violations were increased by 10 to 20 years, and life imprisonment was added for violations involving the death, kidnapping, or sexual abuse of the victim. The law also allows the President to withhold financial aid from governments that do not comply with minimum standards to eliminate such trafficking.

In February 2002 the Interagency Task Force to Combat and Monitor Trafficking in Persons, a Cabinet-level organization, was established. This Task Force is headed by the Secretary of State. In December 2002 President George W. Bush issued the National Security Presidential Directive on Trafficking in Persons, which mandated cooperation among federal agencies to assist victims of trafficking and investigate and prosecute traffickers. As of 2003, identified victims of trafficking are provided by the Department of Health and Human Services with financial support, medical care, and counseling.

Victims' Participation at Sentencing

Every state allows courts to consider or ask for information from victims concerning the impact of the offense on their lives. Forty-eight states permit victim input at sentencing. Forty-two of these states allow written victim-impact statements (detailing the effect the crime has on the victim or, in the case of murder, on the victim's family). The Child Protection Restoration and Penalties Enhancement Act of 1990 (PL 101-647) permits child victims of federal crimes to present statements commensurate with their age, including drawings. While most impact statements are used at sentencing and parole hearings, victims often have input at bail hearings, pretrial release hearings, and plea-bargaining hearings.

The state legislatures have been quicker to agree on victims' rights legislation than the federal government. California's Proposition Eight, the state's "Victims' Bill of Rights," includes Penal Code Section 1191.1, which states:

> The victim or next of kin has the right to appear, personally or by counsel, at the sentencing proceeding and to reasonably express his or her views concerning the crime, the person responsible, and the need for restitution. The court, in imposing sentence, shall consider the statements of victims and next of kin ... and shall state on the record its conclusion concerning whether the person would pose a threat to public safety if granted probation....

Edwin Villamoare and Virginia V. Neto, in *Victim Appearances at Sentencing Hearings Under the California Victims' Bill of Rights* (National Institute of Justice, Washington, D.C., 1987), found that in California there was little effect on the criminal justice system or sentencing when victims appeared at the sentencing proceedings. The victims, rather than wanting to participate in their cases, were generally more concerned with knowing what was going on with their cases. About 80 percent of the victims interviewed indicated that just the existence of the right to participate was most important, not whether they actually made use of that right. Most victims seemed only to want somebody to understand their situation and recognize their rights as victims.

PAYNE V. TENNESSEE. In 1991 the United States Supreme Court, in *Payne v. Tennessee* (501 US 808), ruled that the family of a murder victim could provide victim-impact evidence during the sentencing portion of the trial.

Pervis Payne was convicted of two counts of first-degree murder for killing Charisse Christopher and her two-year-old daughter, and one count of assault with intent to commit murder for attempting to kill her three-year-old son, Nicholas. In arguing for the death penalty, the prosecutor had presented statements from the victims' family. He stated that while there was nothing the jury could do for Charisse Christopher and her daughter, there was something that could be done for Nicholas.

In the *Payne* opinion, written by Chief Justice William Rehnquist, the Supreme Court majority overturned its earlier decisions in two similar cases, *Booth v. Maryland* (482 US 496, 1987) and *South Carolina v. Gather* (490 US 805, 1989). In these two cases the Court held that under the Eighth Amendment ("cruel and unusual punishment shall not be inflicted") a jury could not consider a victim-impact statement in a capital case (one punishable by death). The Supreme Court had found in *Booth* that

> The capital defendant must be treated as a 'uniquely individual human being' and, therefore, the Constitution requires the jury to make an individualized determination as to whether the defendant should be executed based on the character of the individual and the circumstances of the crime.

In *Payne*, the majority found that a victim-impact statement in no way limited the defendant's right to plead his or her case, adding that "victim's impact evidence is simply another form or method of informing the sentencing authority about the specific harm caused by the crime in question, evidence of a general type long considered by sentencing authorities." The High Court concluded that prohibiting victim-impact statements unfairly weighted the case in favor of the defendant.

Justices John Paul Stevens and Thurgood Marshall, with Justice Harry Blackmun joining, dissented. Fearing that the Court was overturning constitutional liberties, Justice Stevens wrote,

> Until today our capital punishment jurisprudence has required that any decision to impose the death penalty be based solely on evidence that tends to inform the jury about the character of the offense and the character of the defendant. Evidence that serves no purpose other than to appeal to the sympathies or emotions of the juror has never been considered admissible.

According to Stevens the majority had obviously been moved by an argument that had strong political appeal but no proper place in a reasoned judicial argument.

Witnessing Executions

As noted in *FYI: Rights of Survivors of Homicide* (1999), a publication of the National Center for Victims of Crime (NCVC), various states have statutes allowing victims' family members to be present at executions. As of December 1998 at least 13 states had statutes allowing immediate family members of victims to witness executions: Alabama, Arkansas, California, Delaware, Kentucky, Louisiana, Mississippi, Nevada, Ohio, Oklahoma, South Carolina, Tennessee, and Washington. Other states, though they do not have formal statutes, have informal policies permitting victims' families to view executions: Florida, Illinois, Montana, North Carolina, Pennsylvania, Texas, Utah, and Virginia. Most states limit the viewing to immediate family members and may limit the total number of viewers.

In Delaware in January of 1996 two sons of a victim watched the hanging of their father's murderer. In 1997 relatives of victims murdered in three different states watched the execution of an Ohio man, Michael Lee Lockart. In February of 1998 family members of the two murder victims of Texan Karla Faye Tucker witnessed her execution by lethal injection. These family members declared that seeing the execution helped put closure to their tragedy. Other witnesses to such executions, however, report that they have yet to find closure.

Just how many victims' immediate family members (over age 18) can be present at executions varies from state to state, depending on the statutes in place. In most states, the number is limited. Some states allow only a few to attend, while others set no limits. Accommodating those family members wishing to be present becomes complicated when executions involve notorious criminals, especially mass murderers.

Such was the case of Timothy McVeigh, who was sentenced to death for bombing the Alfred P. Murrah Federal Building in Oklahoma City on April 19, 1995, killing 168 people and injuring many others. Prior to McVeigh's execution, set for June 11, 2001, more than 250 survivors and victims' relatives asked to witness the execution. In order to accommodate so many, a lottery was established to select 10 victims/family members to watch the sentence performed. Others wishing to see the execution were able to watch the event in a federal prison in Oklahoma City on closed-circuit television.

FEDERAL ACTIONS

The Federal Victim and Witness Protection Act of 1982

In 1982 Congress enacted the Federal Victim and Witness Protection Act, a bill designed to protect and assist victims and witnesses of federal crimes. The law permits victim-impact statements in sentencing hearings to provide judges with information concerning financial, psychological, or physical harm suffered by victims. The law also provides for restitution for victims and prevents victims and/or witnesses from being intimidated by threatening verbal harassment. The law establishes penalties for acts of retaliation by defendants against those who testify against them.

Victims who provide addresses and telephone numbers are to be notified of major events in the criminal proceedings, including the arrest of the accused, the times of any court appearances at which the victim may appear, the release or detention of the accused, and the victim's opportunities to address the sentencing court. The guidelines also recommend that federal officials consult victims and witnesses to obtain their views on such procedures as proposed dismissals and plea negotiations. Officials must not disclose the names and addresses of victims and witnesses.

Federal Victims of Crime Act (VOCA)

In 1984 Congress passed the Federal Victims of Crime Act (VOCA, PL 98-473), which committed the federal government to promote state and local victim support and compensation programs. The act established the Crime Victims Fund (see above). Two significant changes were made in the VOCA in 1988. To be eligible for federal funds, the 1998 amendments required that state programs must also include compensation for survivors of victims of drunk driving and domestic violence. These two groups had previously been excluded from compensation.

The Comprehensive Crime Control Act of 1990

In 1990 President George Bush signed the Comprehensive Crime Control Act (PL 101-647) that covered many aspects of crime control, including protection for victims of child abuse, penalties for Savings and Loan fraud, and mandatory death penalties. Included in the law is the Victims' Rights and Restitution Act of 1990, which secures victims of federal crimes the right to be treated with fairness and respect, reasonably protected from the accused, notified of court proceedings, afforded an opportunity to meet with a federal prosecutor, and provided with restitution. The act also bars criminals and convicted drunken drivers from declaring bankruptcy to avoid paying restitution.

The Compensation and Assistance to Victims of Terrorism or Mass Violence Act (1996)

In spring of 1996 Congress amended the VOCA (Justice for Victims of Terrorism Act of 1996, PL 104-132). The act authorized compensation for citizens victimized by terrorist acts, both at home and abroad. The law allows the director of the Victims Crime Fund (see above) to make supplemental grants to states to assist residents who are victims of terrorism.

After the terrorist attacks on the United States of September 11, 2001, the October 2001 USA Patriot Act authorized the transfer of emergency supplemental appropriation funding into the Emergency Reserve account to assist victims of the attacks. On April 22, 2002, the OVC announced that it had awarded $40 million to offer mental health counseling for victims of the September 11 attacks, their families, and crisis responders who helped victims of the attacks. The grants included funds to compensate victims for counseling services and to support state and local programs that offer various forms of counseling.

The Air Transportation Safety and System Stabilization Act

On September 22, 2001, the 107th Congress enacted Public Law 107-42, "The Air Transportation Safety and System Stabilization Act." In addition to requiring the federal government to compensate the air carriers for losses incurred as a result of the September 11th attacks, the Act established the "September 11th Victim Compensation Fund of 2001." The fund provides compensation to victims of the attacks who elect not to join in litigation (lawsuits) seeking additional money. The fund compensates any individual who was physically injured, or the families and beneficiaries of victims killed, as a result of the terrorist-related aircraft crashes of September 11th, 2001. The amount of non-economic loss compensation includes a $250,000 non-economic award for each deceased victim as well as $100,000 for the spouse and each dependent of a deceased victim. Although life insurance pay-outs, pensions and retirement accounts may be deducted from the final amount, the Department of Justice stated that it would be very rare that a claimant would receive less than $250,000.

CHAPTER 4
HATE CRIMES AND TERRORISM IN THE UNITED STATES

Crimes committed by hate groups or offenders and those committed by terrorist groups are often very similar, both in method and in effect. For example, a person acting from a motive of religious bias might use an incendiary device (one that causes fire, such as a Molotov cocktail) to burn down a mosque, church, or synagogue. A terrorist group might use the same type of device to burn down a government building. In both cases the results are property damage, intimidation, and possibly even the deaths of or injuries to innocent people.

The primary difference between these types of crime is the motive behind the act. While there are no single, comprehensive definitions for hate crimes and terrorism, the Federal Bureau of Investigation (FBI) uses these working definitions:

- Hate crime (also known as bias crime) is a criminal offense committed against a person, property, or society that is motivated, in whole or in part, by the offender's bias against a race, religion, ethnic/national-origin group, or sexual-orientation group.
- Terrorism is the unlawful use of force or violence against persons or property to intimidate or coerce a government, the civilian population, or any segment thereof, committed to further political or social objectives.

HATE AND TERRORIST GROUPS

The Southern Poverty Law Center (SPLC), a civil-rights advocacy group, reported that 751 hate groups were active in the United States in 2003, up 6 percent from 708 in 2002 and an increase of 64 percent from the 1990 figure of 457. The SPLC categorizes these groups as Ku Klux Klan (with 158 active groups in 2003), Neo-Nazi (149), Racist Skinhead (39), Christian Identity (31), Black Separatist (136), and Neo-Confederate (91). In addition, there were 147 other hate groups that espoused a mixture of beliefs and doctrines. The large rise in Black Separatist groups (from 82 in 2002 to 136 in 2003) made up much of the gain in active hate groups. The SPLC states that many of these groups may have already been in existence, but their counting methods of these groups improved. (The SPLC makes clear that organizations it considers to be hate groups are not necessarily involved in or advocate violent or criminal activity.)

Klan groups are generally related to the Ku Klux Klan in racist ideology if not in organization. The Klan militantly advocates white supremacy. Neo-Nazi groups also generally embrace white-supremacy doctrines. Not all Skinheads are racist or belong to an organized group; only Skinhead groups espousing racial hate doctrines are included in the list. Christian Identity groups are basically racist, anti-Semitic religious organizations opposed to anything they view as a threat to their faith, particularly Jewish people. Black Separatists are ideological groups that support or promote racially based hate and the separation of the races.

Through the 1990s hate groups increasingly used computer technology to spread their doctrines. In 2003, according to the SPLC, there were 497 hate sites on the Internet, a 12 percent increase from 443 in 2002. The nature of Internet sites and their establishment is such that a single individual may post a Web site and appear to be a large organization.

Militia Groups

Members of the militia movement believe it is imperative they prepare to defend themselves against the federal government and other assumed enemies. On weekends many militias practice military maneuvers to defend themselves against federal troops. They practice survival skills so they can outlast an occupation. Others refuse to pay taxes or appear in court. They frequently resist arrest. Many are members of the Identity religion, a sect that believes whites are God's chosen people and that the federal government is satanic and must be fought as a religious obligation. Many fear the influence of public schools and choose to home-school their children.

While militias have been active in the United States for over a generation, it was the bombing of the Alfred P. Murrah Federal Building in Oklahoma City on April 19, 1995, a crime attributed to Timothy McVeigh and Terry Nichols, both thought to be militia members, that made most Americans aware of their activities. Law enforcement authorities believe that militias are a growing threat to the American people. They fear the paranoid and xenophobic (fearing or hating strangers or foreigners) tendencies of many of these groups will lead to more violence and destruction.

Militia members generally describe themselves as patriots trying to save the nation from an enemy unrecognized by most other Americans. This enemy might be the so-called "New World Order," a unified world government, usually aligned with the United Nations. The North American Free Trade Agreement on Tariffs and Trade (NAFTA) and the General Agreement on Tariffs and Trade (GATT) are also considered evidence of efforts to create a one-world government.

Other perceived enemies include African-Americans and Jews, who threaten what the groups consider essential American values. Many recognized racist organizations, such as the Ku Klux Klan, also espouse anti-government rhetoric. In fact many anti-Semitic groups consider the United States a Zionist Occupied Government (ZOG), with Jews occupying and controlling the government and media. Other militias believe themselves the only true Christians and refer to Biblical scripture to justify their beliefs and actions.

Some groups include members who are neither racist nor anti-Semitic, but who believe the federal government is dangerous to individual freedom. Most militia groups consider the federal government an enemy whose goal is to take away individual rights and/or draw the United States into a world government. Therefore, in order to save national sovereignty, they must destroy the federal government.

Militia leaders and members point to the Brady Handgun Violence Prevention Act of 1993 (PL 103-159), commonly known as the Brady Bill, as evidence of the government's attempts to limit individual rights. The Brady Bill requires a waiting period to purchase handguns. Militias also cite governmental blunders in 1992 at Ruby Ridge, Idaho, where authorities shot and killed the son and the wife of militia leader Randy Weaver, and in 1993 at the Branch Davidian compound outside Waco, Texas, which contributed to the deaths by fire of dozens of cult members. These events are accepted as evidence of the continuing federal government campaign to destroy individual freedoms. The federal government's environmental policy is seen as a further attempt to restrict individual freedoms.

HATE CRIME LEGISLATION

Federal Laws

In 1990 Congress passed the Hate Crime Statistics Act (PL 101-275), which required the attorney general to "acquire data ... about crimes that manifest evidence of prejudice based on race, religion, sexual orientation or ethnicity" and to publish a summary of the data. The Hate Crimes Statistics Act was amended by the Violent Crime and Law Enforcement Act of 1994 (PL 103-322) to include bias-motivated acts against disabled persons. Further amendments in the Church Arsons Prevention Act of 1996 (PL 104-155) directed the FBI to track bias-related church arsons as a permanent part of its duties. In 1990 only 11 states reported information on hate crimes. By 2002, 12,073 law enforcement agencies reported their data.

State Laws

According to data released by the Anti-Defamation League (ADL) in 2003, four states—Arkansas, Indiana, South Carolina, and Wyoming—had no laws that assigned criminal penalties to hate crimes. In one of these states, Arkansas, hate crimes are considered civil matters, not criminal offenses. In Wyoming, there are no laws specifying whether hate crimes require civil actions or criminal penalties. Forty-six states assign enhanced penalties to hate crimes, meaning the penalty for a crime is increased if the prosecutor is able to prove the attack was hate-motivated. Most states and the District of Columbia have statutes specifically addressing vandalism of places of worship and cemeteries. Thirty states and the District of Columbia included crimes motivated by sexual-orientation bias in their definitions of hate crimes.

The constitutionality of these laws has been challenged on the grounds they punish free thought. In 1992 the U.S. Supreme Court, in *R.A.V. v. City of St. Paul* (112 S.Ct. 2538), found a Minnesota law outlawing certain "fighting words" unconstitutional. In this case, the defendant had burned a cross "inside the fenced yard of a black family." The Court ruled that

> Although there is an important governmental interest in protecting the exercise of the black resident's right to occupy a dwelling free from intimidation, we cannot say that, under the circumstances before us, the government interest is unrelated to the suppression of free expression.

A law limiting pure speech or symbolic speech can only be upheld if it meets the "clear and present danger" standard of *Brandenburg v. Ohio* (395 U.S. 444, 1969). This standard means that speech may be outlawed if it incites or produces "imminent lawless action."

In June 1993, however, the Supreme Court, in *Mitchell v. Wisconsin* (113 S.Ct. 2194), upheld laws that impose harsher prison sentences and greater fines for criminals who are motivated by bigotry. The Court found that such statutes as the Wisconsin law do not illegally restrict free speech and are not so general as to restrict constitutional behavior.

HATE CRIME OFFENSES

Hate crimes are criminal offenses motivated by the offender's personal prejudice or bias. The FBI includes hate crimes in its Uniform Crime Reporting program. Its first reports to include hate-crime data were *Crime in the United States: 1996* (1997), and *Hate Crime Statistics: 1996* (Clarksburg, West Virginia, no date). In the 1994 Violent Crime and Law Enforcement Act, Congress added hate-motivated crimes against disabled persons to the list of bias crimes. The FBI began collecting data on crimes against persons with disabilities on January 1, 1997.

Data on hate crimes are incomplete because many incidents go unreported or cannot be verified as hate crimes. Some victims do not report hate crimes due to fear that the criminal justice system is biased against the group to which the victim belongs and that law enforcement authorities will not be responsive. Many attacks against homosexuals are not reported because the victims do not want to reveal their sexuality to others. In addition, proving that an offender acted from bias can be a long, tedious process, requiring much investigation. Until a law enforcement investigator can find enough evidence in a particular case to be sure the offender's actions came, at least in part, from bias, the crime is not counted as a hate crime.

Hate Crimes in 2002

According to the FBI, the number of hate crimes reported to the authorities fluctuated from 7,684 in 1993 to 5,852 in 1994 to 8,759 reported incidents in 1996. In 1998, 7,755 incidents were reported; by 2000 that number had increased to 8,152 incidents. In 2002 the number dropped to 7,462 hate crime incidents reported to the FBI. Racial bias motivated 49.7 percent of the hate crimes in 2002; religious bias, 17.8 percent; sexual-orientation bias, 16.6 percent; and ethnic bias, 15.2 percent. (See Figure 4.1.) Among the specific bias types, anti-black incidents accounted for the largest number of single-bias incidents (2,486), followed by 931 anti-Jewish incidents and 1,219 anti-gay and anti-lesbian incidents. (See Table 4.1.)

A hate crime may have more than one victim and multiple offenders. To tabulate hate-crime data, the FBI counts one offense for each victim of a crime against persons and one offense for each distinct act of crime against property and crime against society. Therefore, more offenses (8,832) and victims (9,222) were reported than incidents (7,462) in 2002.

FIGURE 4.1

Bias-motivated offenses, 2002

Percent distribution,* 2002

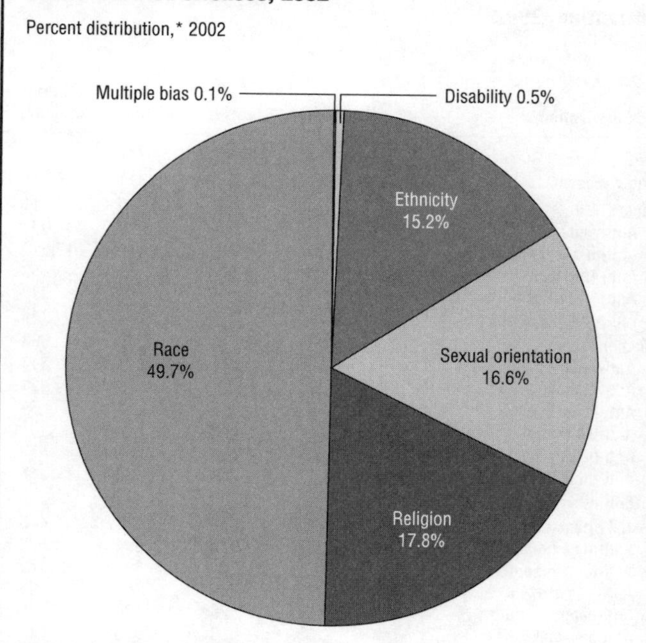

*Due to rounding, the percentages may not add to 100.0.

SOURCE: "Figure 2.19: Bias–Motivated Offenses, 2002," in *Crime in the United States 2002*, Federal Bureau of Investigation, Washington, DC, 2003

In 2002 some 7,459 incidents of single-bias hate crime occurred. A single-bias incident is a hate crime in which one type of offense (such as assault) is committed as the result of one bias-motivation (such as anti-black sentiment). Individuals were victims of 3,135 racial incidents, 1,140 sexual-orientation incidents, and 979 ethnicity/national-origin incidents. Additional single-bias incidents targeted institutions, government agencies, and religious organizations. (See Table 4.2.)

Kinds of Crime Motivated by Hate

Hate crimes are categorized in three ways: crimes against persons, crimes against property, and crimes against society. In 2002 about 67.5 percent of hate offenses were crimes against persons. Of the 5,960 hate crimes against persons, over half (3,105) were acts of intimidation, while 2,826 were assaults (1,791 simple assaults and 1,035 aggravated assaults). (See Table 4.3.)

About one-third (2,823) of hate crimes in 2002 were property crimes, a decrease from 2,905 in 1998. Most property crimes (2,347) were acts of destruction, damage, and/or vandalism. Less than 1 percent (49) of all hate crimes were crimes against society.

In the wake of the events of September 11, 2001, a surge in attacks against people of Arab descent and Muslims in general was reported, including incidents of fire

TABLE 4.1

Hate crime incidents, offenses, and known offenders, by bias motivation, 2002

Bias motivation	Incidents	Offenses	Victims[1]	Known offenders[2]
Total	**7,462**	**8,832**	**9,222**	**7,314**
Single-bias incidents	7,459	8,825	9,211	7,311
Race:	3,642	4,393	4,580	4,011
Anti-white	719	888	910	1,064
Anti-black	2,486	2,967	3,076	2,510
Anti-American Indian/Alaskan Native	62	68	72	52
Anti-Asian/Pacific Islander	217	268	280	242
Anti-multiple races, group	158	202	242	143
Religion:	1,426	1,576	1,659	568
Anti-Jewish	931	1,039	1,084	317
Anti-Catholic	53	58	71	21
Anti-Protestant	55	57	58	34
Anti-Islamic	155	170	174	103
Anti-other religion	198	217	237	73
Anti-multiple religions, group	31	32	32	18
Anti-atheism/agnosticism/etc.	3	3	3	2
Sexual orientation:	1,244	1,464	1,513	1,438
Anti-male homosexual	825	957	984	1,022
Anti-female homosexual	172	207	221	172
Anti-homosexual	222	259	267	225
Anti-heterosexual	10	26	26	6
Anti-bisexual	15	15	15	13
Ethnicity/national origin:	1,102	1,345	1,409	1,247
Anti-hispanic	480	601	639	656
Anti-other ethnicity/national origin	622	744	770	591
Disability:	45	47	50	47
Anti-physical	20	20	20	21
Anti-mental	25	27	30	26
Multiple-bias incidents[3]	3	7	11	3

[1]The term *victim* may refer to a person, business, institution, or society as a whole.
[2]The term *known offender* does not imply that the identity of the suspect is known, but only that an attribute of the suspect is identified, which distinguishes him/her from an unknown offender.
[3]A multiple-bias incident only occurs when two or more offense types are committed in a single incident. In a situation when there is more than one offense type, the agency can indicate a different bias type for each offense. In the case of a single offense type, only one bias type can be indicated.

SOURCE: "Table 2.33: Number of Incidents, Offenses, Victims, and Known Offenders, by Bias Motivation, 2002," in *Crime in the United States 2002*, Federal Bureau of Investigation, Washington, DC, 2003

bombings, shootings, and other acts of violence. In 2000 there were only 33 reported incidents of anti-Islamic hate crimes. In the four months following the attacks, more than 250 incidents against Muslims, Arabs, and South Asians were reported. Some 70 persons were charged on the state and local levels with hate crimes directed at Arab or Muslim Americans as a result of the September 11 terrorist attacks. As of February 2002 the FBI had initiated 318 hate crime investigations involving Americans of Arab, Muslim, and Sikh heritage.

Hate-Motivated Murders

The most severe hate-motivated crime against a person is murder. In 2002, 11 bias-motivated murders were reported to the FBI, less than 1 percent of all hate offenses. By their very nature, however, murders motivated by hate or bias are the most horrible and unforgettable to society. The nation was shocked and outraged by the brutal killing of a black man, James Byrd, Jr., near the small town of Jasper, Texas, in June 1998. Two white men convicted in the murder, John William King and Lawrence Russell Brewer, were suspected of ties to white supremacy organizations. A third man, Shawn Allen Berry, was also convicted. These men beat and kicked Byrd and then chained him to the back of a pickup truck and dragged him until his body was torn apart.

To "help" the town, the Ku Klux Klan came to Jasper, stating that they were there to protect whites from blacks. The Black Muslims and the New Black Panthers came to protect blacks from whites. Fortunately, law enforcement officers and the townspeople of Jasper were able to prevent further violence. The townspeople repeatedly expressed their sorrow at the murder and begged outsiders to go away and let them try to cope with the crime and its aftermath. The Byrd family issued a written statement asking the public not to use the murder as an excuse for more hatred and retribution. They asked that Americans view the incident as a wake-up call, and that it lead to a time of self-examination and reflection.

Despite the publicity the Byrd case received, the pleas of his family seem to have had little effect on national hate crime murder statistics. Each year, equally shocking cases of hate-motivated murders occur. Buford Furrow Jr., a man with links to a white supremacist group, killed a Filipino-American postal worker after opening fire on a Jewish day care center in Los Angeles, California, in August of 1999. In March 2000 in Wilkinsburg, Pennsylvania, Ronald Taylor, an African-American, shot five white men, killing three of them. One month later, five people, including a Jewish woman, an Indian, two Asians, and one African-American, were killed in Pittsburgh, Pennsylvania, when Richard Scott Baumhammers, an immigration lawyer, went on a shooting rampage in April 2000. Also in 2000, in a crime similar to the killing of Byrd in Texas, two teenaged boys beat an African-American gay man and then ran over him with a car repeatedly until he was dead. In Texas, Byrd's death did lead to the passage of the James Byrd Jr. Hate Crimes Act on May 11, 2001. The bill intensifies penalties for crimes motivated by the victim's race, religion, sex, disability, sexual orientation, age, or national origin.

Another famous case of racially motivated murder came to a close after almost 30 years on May 22, 2002. On that day, Bobby Frank Cherry, 71, a former Ku Klux Klan member, was convicted of four counts of murder stemming from the 1963 bombing of the 16th Street Baptist Church in Birmingham, Alabama. Four girls were killed—three were 14 years of age and one was 11 years old. Cherry, who had been trained in demolition in the Army, claimed during the trial that he could not have planted the bomb the night before the attack because he

TABLE 4.2

Hate crime incidents by victim type and bias motivation, 2002

Bias motivation	Total incidents	Victim type: Individual	Business/ financial institution	Government	Religious organization	Society/ public	Other/ unknown/ multiple
Total	**7,462**	**6,122**	**266**	**165**	**183**	**205**	**521**
Single-bias incidents	**7,459**	**6,120**	**266**	**165**	**183**	**205**	**520**
Race	3,642	3,135	122	90	13	113	169
Religion	1,426	828	99	41	165	60	233
Sexual orientation	1,244	1,140	12	22	1	12	57
Ethnicity/national origin	1,102	979	31	11	4	17	60
Disability	45	38	2	1	0	3	1
Multiple-bias incidents*	**3**	**2**	**0**	**0**	**0**	**0**	**1**

*A multiple-bias occurs only when two or more offense types are committed in a single incident. In the case of a single offense type, only one bias can be indicated.

SOURCE: "Table 8: Hate Crime Incidents by Victim Type by Bias Motivation, 2002," in *Hate Crime Statistics 2002,* Federal Bureau of Investigation, Washington, DC, 2003

was at home watching wrestling on TV with his cancer-stricken wife. Prosecutors were able to show that not only was there no wrestling on TV that night, but that Cherry's wife was not diagnosed with cancer until two years after the bombing. Thomas E. Blanton, Cherry's surviving accomplice in the bombing, was convicted in 2001 and sentenced to life in prison. A third accomplice, Robert Chambliss, was convicted in 1977 and later died in prison.

Where Do Hate Crimes Occur?

Of bias incidents in 2002, most (2,198) occurred at the victim's home, compared to 1,490 on highways, streets, roads, and alleys. School and college locations accounted for 789 hate crimes, 461 occurred in parking lots and garages, and 284 occurred in places of worship. (See Table 4.4.)

Who Commits Hate Crimes?

Hate crimes may be committed by an individual, a group of individuals, or an organization with a bias against certain races, religions, or societal groups. The ADL states that perpetrators of hate crimes fall into three groups: mission-oriented, reactive, and thrill-seeking.

The mission-oriented perpetrator may or may not be a member of an extremist organization, but always acts from an ideology of bigotry seeking to rid the world of what that individual or group considers evil. This type of perpetrator is the least common type of offender.

Another type of hate-crime perpetrator is the "reactive offender." This type of offender feels that he or she is retaliating against some perceived imminent harm, threat, or danger from the victim, and sees the race, ethnicity, religion, or lifestyle of the victim as responsible for the perpetrator's own problems in life. The offense is usually opportunistic (based on spur-of-the-moment impulses). Frequently, alcohol or drug use is a factor. The reactive offender is the most common type of perpetrator.

TABLE 4.3

Hate crime incidents, offenses, and known offenders, by type of offense, 2002

Offense type	Incidents[1]	Offenses	Victims[2]	Known offenders[3]
Total	**7,462**	**8,832**	**9,222**	**7,314**
Crimes against persons:	4,784	5,960	5,960	6,090
Murder and nonnegligent manslaughter	11	11	11	15
Forcible rape	8	8	8	16
Aggravated assault	800	1,035	1,035	1,498
Simple assault	1,473	1,791	1,791	2,436
Intimidation	2,484	3,105	3,105	2,117
Other[4]	8	10	10	8
Crimes against property:	2,823	2,823	3,213	1,423
Robbery	131	131	179	269
Burglary	131	131	163	86
Larceny-theft	151	151	157	95
Motor vehicle theft	9	9	9	3
Arson	38	38	47	27
Destruction/damage/ vandalism	2,347	2,347	2,642	927
Other[4]	16	16	16	16
Crimes against society[4]	49	49	49	61

[1]The actual number of incidents is 7,462. However, the column figures will not add to the total because incidents may include more than one offense type, and these are counted in each appropriate offense type category.
[2]The term *victim* may refer to a person, business, institution, or society as a whole.
[3]The term *known offender* does not imply that the identity of the suspect is known, but only that an attribute of the suspect is identified, which distinguishes him/her from an unknown offender. The actual number of known offenders is 7,314. However, the column figures will not add to the total because some offenders are responsible for more than one offense type, and they are, therefore, counted more than once in this table.
[4]Includes additional offenses collected in NIBRS.

SOURCE: "Table 2.34: Number of Offenses, Victims, and Known Offenders, by Offense Type, 2002," in *Crime in the United States 2002,* Federal Bureau of Investigation, Washington, DC, 2003

TABLE 4.4

Hate crime incidents by bias motivation and location, 2002

Location	Total incidents	Bias motivation: Race	Religion	Sexual orientation	Ethnicity/national origin	Disability	Multiple-bias incidents*
Total	**7,462**	**3,642**	**1,426**	**1,244**	**1,102**	**45**	**3**
Air/bus/train terminal	63	38	8	10	5	2	0
Bank/savings and loan	19	9	4	4	2	0	0
Bar/night club	128	63	5	42	18	0	0
Church/synagogue/temple	284	28	241	4	10	1	0
Commercial office building	200	83	48	18	48	3	0
Construction site	19	11	2	2	4	0	0
Convenience store	114	38	9	17	49	1	0
Department/discount store	58	37	11	6	4	0	0
Drug store/doctor's office/hospital	51	24	10	8	9	0	0
Field/woods	69	43	6	10	10	0	0
Government/public building	82	38	20	9	14	1	0
Grocery/supermarket	51	22	10	7	12	0	0
Highway/road/alley/street	1,490	855	117	309	200	9	0
Hotel/motel/etc.	55	26	10	10	9	0	0
Jail/prison	42	26	2	4	10	0	0
Lake/waterway	12	5	1	3	3	0	0
Liquor store	14	4	1	1	8	0	0
Parking lot/garage	461	277	62	68	52	2	0
Rental storage facility	9	4	2	0	1	2	0
Residence/home	2,198	1,092	373	383	338	9	3
Restaurant	166	74	14	29	48	1	0
School/college	789	402	149	167	66	5	0
Service/gas station	78	39	13	7	18	1	0
Specialty store (TV, fur, etc.)	93	38	24	6	25	0	0
Other/unknown	915	365	284	120	138	8	0
Multiple locations	2	1	0	0	1	0	0

*A multiple-bias occurs only when two or more offense types are committed in a single incident. In the case of a single offense type, only one bias can be indicated.

SOURCE: "Table 10: Hate Crime Incidents by Bias Motivation, by Location," in *Hate Crime Statistics, 2002,* Federal Bureau of Investigation, Washington, DC, 2003

In 1997 the Leadership Conference Education Fund (LCEF), a civil-rights advocacy group, published *Cause for Concern: Hate Crimes in America* (Washington, D.C.). Surprisingly, the LCEF found that "youthful thrill-seekers" were also responsible for a large number of hate crimes.

In 2002 whites committed 3,712 of all hate crimes (about 42 percent), blacks were responsible for 1,082 (12 percent), and the offender was unknown in about 34 percent of all cases. Racial acts by whites against blacks accounted for 1,689 hate crimes, the largest percentage of all racial incidents. Of the 639 racially motivated attacks by blacks, 497 were directed against whites. (See Table 4.5.)

The Burning of Houses of Worship

A rash of church arsons in the early 1990s—53 black churches were burned between 1990 and June 1996, 23 of them in 1996 alone—created a wave of national concern, and motivated the federal government to commit new resources to investigate the fires. In June 1996 the National Church Arson Task Force (NCATF) was formed to coordinate the efforts of federal, state, and local law enforcement. The FBI and the Bureau of Alcohol, Tobacco, and Firearms (ATF) worked with local and state law officers to investigate church arsons. Other federal groups also pitched in to help rebuild houses of worship and ease community tensions.

From January 1995 to mid-August 2000, the NCATF investigated 945 arsons and bombings of houses of worship. Almost 33 percent were black churches (310). Over 67 percent were other houses of worship. Of the 486 arsons that occurred in the South, 43.8 percent were aimed at black places of worship. (See Figure 4.2.)

ARRESTS. From 1995 through August 2000, law enforcement officers made arrests in 36.2 percent of 945 investigations of arsons of houses of worship. Investigations in 61.8 percent of cases were still pending. (See Figure 4.3.) Of the 342 suspects arrested, 136 were arrested for attacks on black houses of worship and 290 for acts against nonblack places of worship.

RACE, AGE, AND SEX OF ARRESTEES. For all of the arsons, over 80 percent of arrestees were white, while

TABLE 4.5

Hate crime offenses by known offender's race and bias motivation, 2002

Bias motivation	Total offenses	Known offender's race: White	Black	American Indian/Alaskan Native	Asian/Pacific Islander	Multiple races, group	Unknown race	Unknown offender
Total	**8,832**	**3,712**	**1,082**	**46**	**61**	**218**	**651**	**3,062**
Single-bias incidents	**8,825**	**3,710**	**1,082**	**46**	**61**	**218**	**648**	**3,060**
Race:	**4,393**	**2,040**	**639**	**29**	**38**	**127**	**344**	**1,176**
Anti-white	888	130	497	8	11	34	71	137
Anti-black	2,967	1,689	84	14	26	72	217	865
Anti-American Indian/Alaskan Native	68	31	1	2	0	1	9	24
Anti-Asian/Pacific Islander	268	104	38	4	1	15	22	84
Anti-multiple races, group	202	86	19	1	0	5	25	66
Religion:	**1,576**	**327**	**46**	**1**	**8**	**13**	**138**	**1,043**
Anti-Jewish	1,039	179	15	1	4	5	98	737
Anti-Catholic	58	10	1	0	2	1	3	41
Anti-Protestant	57	17	3	0	0	0	7	30
Anti-Islamic	170	59	19	0	1	7	9	75
Anti-other religion	217	50	6	0	1	0	17	143
Anti-multiple religions, group	32	11	1	0	0	0	4	16
Anti-atheism/agnosticism/etc.	3	1	1	0	0	0	0	1
Sexual orientation:	**1,464**	**679**	**210**	**8**	**6**	**46**	**88**	**427**
Anti-male homosexual	957	458	151	4	5	30	50	259
Anti-female homosexual	207	94	25	2	0	7	12	67
Anti-homosexual	259	118	29	2	1	8	25	76
Anti-heterosexual	26	6	0	0	0	0	1	19
Anti-bisexual	15	3	5	0	0	1	0	6
Ethnicity/national origin:	**1,345**	**647**	**178**	**8**	**9**	**29**	**73**	**401**
Anti-Hispanic	601	323	111	0	0	5	25	137
Anti-other ethnicity/national origin	744	324	67	8	9	24	48	264
Disability:	**47**	**17**	**9**	**0**	**0**	**3**	**5**	**13**
Anti-physical	20	9	6	0	0	0	2	3
Anti-mental	27	8	3	0	0	3	3	10
Multiple-bias incidents*	**7**	**2**	**0**	**0**	**0**	**0**	**3**	**2**

*A multiple-bias incident occurs only when two or more offense types are committed in a single incident. In a situation where there is more than one offense type, the agency can indicate a different bias for each offense. In the case of a single offense type, only one bias can be indicated.

SOURCE: "Table 5: Hate Crime Offenses by Known Offender's Race, by Bias Motivation," in *Hate Crime Statistics, 2002,* Federal Bureau of Investigation, Washington, DC, 2003

15.1 percent of those arrested were African-American and 3 percent were Hispanic. Of attacks on black churches, 62.5 percent of arrestees were Caucasian, 36.8 percent were African-American, and less than 1 percent were Hispanic. For all other houses of worship, almost 90 percent of those arrested were Caucasian, while 5.2 percent were African-American, 4.1 percent were Hispanic, and one percent were Asian. (See Figure 4.4.)

Males (91.9 percent) ages 14 to 24 (58.2 percent) were the most likely group to be arrested for church arsons and bombings. Only 8.1 percent of those arrested were females. Only 27.6 percent of arrestees were older than age 24. Some 14.2 percent of arrestees (61) were between the ages of six and 13. (See Figure 4.5.)

TERRORISM

While no single definition of terrorism is available, the FBI uses the following definitions in its annual report (*Terrorism in the United States, 1999,*Washington, D.C., 2001):

- Domestic terrorism involves groups or individuals who are based and operating entirely within the United States and Puerto Rico without foreign direction. Their acts are directed at elements of the U.S. government or population.

- International terrorism is the unlawful use of force or violence by a group or individual with some connection to a foreign power, or whose acts cross international boundaries. Their aim is to intimidate or coerce a government, the civilian population, or any segment of these to achieve a political or social objective.

From 1980 to 1999 (the latest date for which the FBI had information) the FBI recorded 327 incidents, or suspected incidents of terrorism in the United States, that killed 205 people and injured 2,037. Of the 327 incidents,

FIGURE 4.2

Arson, bombing, and attempted bombing investigations by type of church, January 1, 1995–August 15, 2000

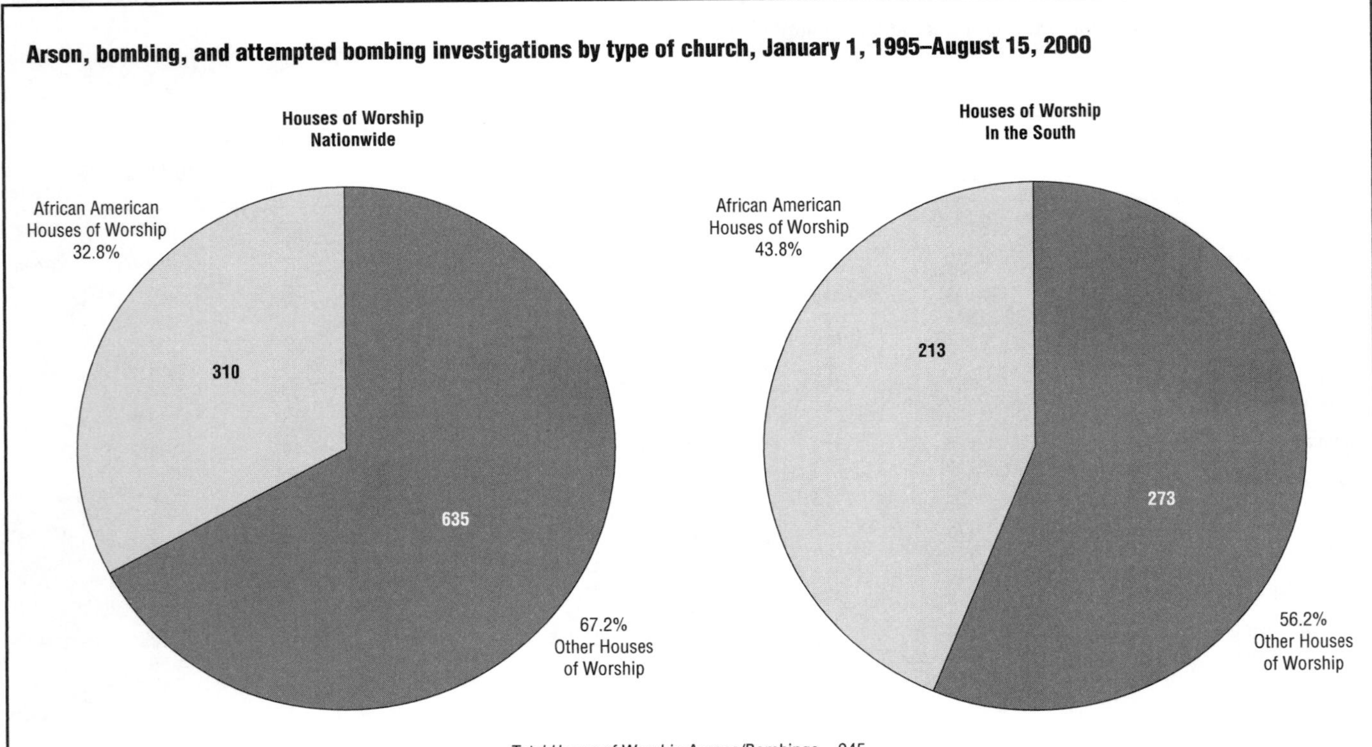

SOURCE: "Chart A: Breakdown of Arson/Bombing/Attempted Bombing Investigations, January 1, 1995–August 15, 2000," *National Church Arson Task Force—Fourth Year Report*, Bureau of Alcohol, Tobacco and Firearms, Washington, DC, 2000 [Online] http://www.atf.treas.gov/pub/gen_pub/report2000/index.htm [accessed April 12, 2004]

239 were attributed to domestic terrorists and 88 were international. During the same time period, 130 planned acts of terrorism were prevented by U.S. law enforcement agencies. Of those, 88 were planned by domestic groups or individuals and 47 by international groups or individuals.

According to the FBI, while the overall number of terrorist incidents declined from 1990 to 1999 when compared to the previous ten years, the attacks resulted in greater destruction and numbers of casualties. Of the 60 terrorist attacks between 1990 and 1999, 182 people were killed and nearly 2,000 were injured. By comparison, from 1980 to 1989, there were more than four times as many attacks (267), but the death toll was only 23, with 105 injuries.

Incidents of Domestic Terrorism

On April 19, 1995, one of the most deadly acts of domestic terrorism occurred in Oklahoma City when a two-ton truck bomb exploded just outside the Alfred P. Murrah federal building, killing 168 people and injuring 518. Because a day-care center was in the building very near the site of the explosion, many of the victims were children. Federal authorities later arrested Timothy McVeigh for the crime. McVeigh, who was rumored to be associated with an anti-government militia group, was convicted and executed in 2001.

While the toll in lives and property damage was much lower than in the Oklahoma City bombing, the Olympic Games bombing of 1996 created international alarm. In July of 1996, during the Olympic Summer Games in Atlanta, a nail-packed pipe bomb exploded in a large common area. One person was killed and more than 100 injured. Authorities believed the perpetrator may have been affiliated with a so-called Christian Identity group, many of whom see the Olympic Games as part of a satanic New World Order.

Shortly after the attack, suspicion centered on a security guard at Centennial Park, where the blast occurred. He was later cleared and given an official apology. In May of 1998 the FBI added Eric Robert Rudolph to its Top Ten Most Wanted list, seeking him for questioning about the Olympics bombing and two others that followed. Rudolph was also charged with bombing the New Woman All Women Health Care Center (Birmingham, Alabama) in January of 1998. In that blast, an off-duty police officer was killed and a nurse was seriously injured. Rudolph eluded authorities for five years, but was captured in Murphy, North Carolina, on May 31, 2003.

In January of 1998 Theodore Kaczynski was sentenced to life imprisonment with no possibility of parole for his actions as the "Unabomber." Over a 17-year period

FIGURE 4.3

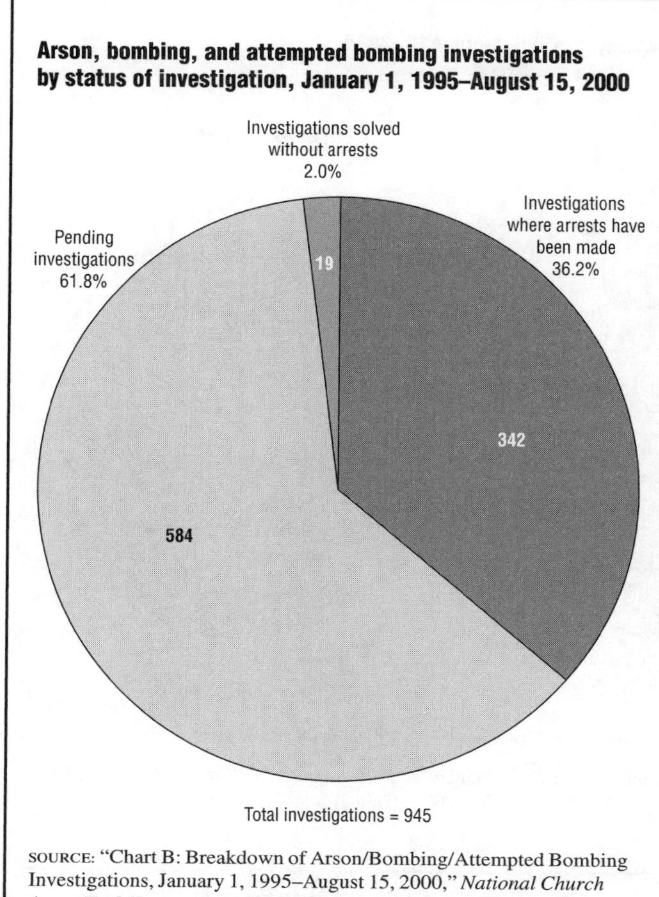

SOURCE: "Chart B: Breakdown of Arson/Bombing/Attempted Bombing Investigations, January 1, 1995–August 15, 2000," *National Church Arson Task Force—Fourth Year Report*, Bureau of Alcohol, Tobacco and Firearms, Washington, DC, 2000 [Online] http://www.atf.treas.gov/pub/gen_pub/report2000/index.htm [accessed April 12, 2004]

Kaczynski committed 16 bombings in several states. Although he claimed the bombings (usually letter bombs) were directed against the federal government, the victims were generally not directly related to government. Three people were killed and 23 persons injured in the attacks. The manhunt for Kaczynski was one of the longest, most difficult cases in U.S. history, involving hundreds of federal and state law enforcement agents.

Kaczynski was not apprehended until his 56-page "manifesto" was published in *The New York Times* and *The Washington Post* newspapers. His brother, David, read the document and recognized the words as his brother's. Contacting the FBI, David shared his fears that his brother Theodore was the Unabomber. This tip led to the subsequent capture of Theodore, who later pleaded guilty at his trial and received a sentence of life imprisonment without the possibility of parole.

On September 25, 2001, a letter postmarked September 20 from St. Petersburg, Florida, containing a white powdery substance, was handled by an assistant to NBC News anchorman Tom Brokaw. After complaining of a rash, the assistant consulted a physician and tested positive for exposure to the anthrax bacterium (*bacillus anthracis*), an infectious agent which, if inhaled into the lungs, can lead to death. Over the next two months, envelopes testing positive for anthrax were received by various news organizations in the United States and by government offices, including the offices of Senate Majority Leader Tom Daschle and of New York Governor George Pataki. As a result of exposure to anthrax sent via the U.S. mail, five people died, including two postal workers who handled letters carrying the anthrax spores. Hundreds more who were exposed were placed on antibiotics as a preventative measure. Despite an intensive investigation by the FBI and other law enforcement agencies, no arrests in the case had been made as of May 2004.

In a spree that began on May 3, 2002, 18 pipe bombs were found in rural mailboxes in Illinois, Iowa, Nebraska, Colorado, and Texas, injuring five people. Four days after the first bomb exploded, the FBI arrested 21-year-old college student Luke J. Helder in connection with the bombings. Helder was charged by federal prosecutors in Iowa with using an explosive device to maliciously destroy property affecting interstate commerce and with using a destructive device to commit a crime of violence, punishable by up to life imprisonment. The pipe bombs, some of which did not detonate, were accompanied by letters warning of excessive government control over individual behavior.

On February 3, 2004, traces of ricin, a white powdery poison that can be deadly if inhaled or ingested, were found on a letter-opening machine in the mailroom of Senate Majority Leader Bill Frist. All three Senate office buildings were quickly closed, and about 50 Senate workers were put under quarantine; they also took precautionary decontamination showers. No illnesses were reported in the incident. The FBI subsequently reported that in November of 2003 a letter containing ricin, mailed from Chattanooga, Tennessee, and addressed to the White House, was intercepted at a mail sorting facility in the Washington area. The letter was signed "Fallen Angel." The same name appeared in an October, 2003, letter left at the Greenville, South Carolina, post office. This letter contained a metal vial filled with ricin. The two letters complained about recent trucking regulations requiring additional rest for interstate drivers. The FBI was investigating to see if the three incidents were related.

Eco-terrorism

Since the late 1970s some extremist environmental and animal rights groups have turned increasingly to criminal violence to promote their ideas and attack their perceived enemies. Eco-terrorism is the name given to these fringe actions. The FBI has defined eco-terrorism as "the use or threatened use of violence of a criminal nature against innocent victims or property by an environmentally-

FIGURE 4.4

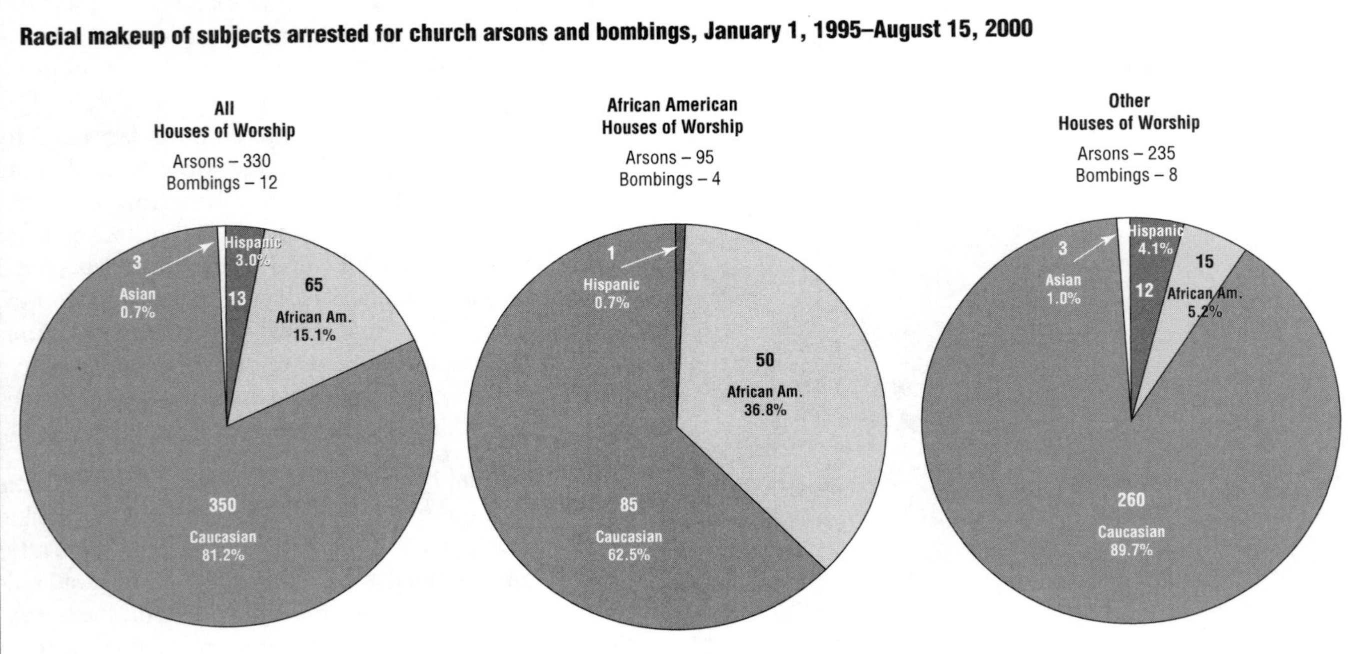

Note: Five (5) additional Caucasian subjects arrested for arson/bombing of an African American House of Worship and a non-African American House of Worship

SOURCE: "Chart C: Racial Makeup of Subjects Arrested for Church Arsons/Bombings Nationwide, January 1, 1995–August 15, 2000," *National Church Arson Task Force—Fourth Year Report*, Bureau of Alcohol, Tobacco and Firearms, Washington, DC, 2000 [Online] http://www.atf.treas.gov/pub/gen_pub/report2000/index.htm [accessed April 12, 2004]

oriented, subnational group for environmental-political reasons, or aimed at an audience beyond the target, often of a symbolic nature." Corporate and university research laboratories, furriers, fast food restaurants, real estate developers, automobile dealers, logging companies, and medical-supply firms have been among their most frequent targets. Most prominent among these eco-terrorists have been the underground Earth Liberation Front (ELF) and the related Animal Liberation Front (ALF), which have committed some 600 criminal acts since 1996, according to the FBI. Their actions—including arson, vandalism, and bombings—resulted in some $43 million in damages between 1996 and 2002, while in 2003 alone, eco-terrorist damage estimates attributed to ELF and ALF surpassed $50 million. The FBI reports that there have been over $200 million in damages from all eco-terrorist incidents since the late 1980s.

The most damaging practice of the Earth Liberation Front has been arson using incendiary devices equipped with timing mechanisms. On October 19, 1998, ELF burned eight structures at a Vail, Colorado, ski resort, which resulted in $12 million in damages. In August 2002 the group burned a U.S. Forest Service Station in Irvine, Pennsylvania, resulting in over $700,000 in damage and the loss of valuable research files. In the most destructive act of eco-terrorism in U.S. history, ELF burned down a newly-built San Diego, California, 5-story apartment complex in August 2003, causing some $50 million in damage. The following month, they burned four San Diego homes under construction for an estimated $1 million in damages. In addition, the group has vandalized sport utility vehicle (SUV) dealerships in Pennsylvania, California, and New Mexico, resulting in over $2.5 million in damages.

The Animal Liberation Front has also taken credit for a number of violent acts across the country, ranging from vandalism to arson. In November of 1997, ALF staged an arson attack on a Bureau of Land Management wild horse corral in Burns, OR, destroying the complex and causing $450,000 in damages. In June of 1998 another arson attack occurred at the U.S. Department of Agriculture Animal Damage Control Building near Olympia, Washington, causing over $2 million in damages. ALF has also taken responsibility for the firebombing of a McDonald's restaurant in Tucson, AZ, on September 11, 2001, that caused some $500,000 in damages. In a statement made before the U.S. Senate in May of 2001, FBI director Louis J. Freeh labeled the Animal Liberation Front "one of the most active extremist elements in the United States."

Other animal rights groups using violence to promote their ideas include the Animal Liberation Brigade—Revolutionary Cells, which set off two small bombs at the

FIGURE 4.5

Subjects arrested for church arsons and bombings by age and gender, January 1, 1995–August 15, 2000

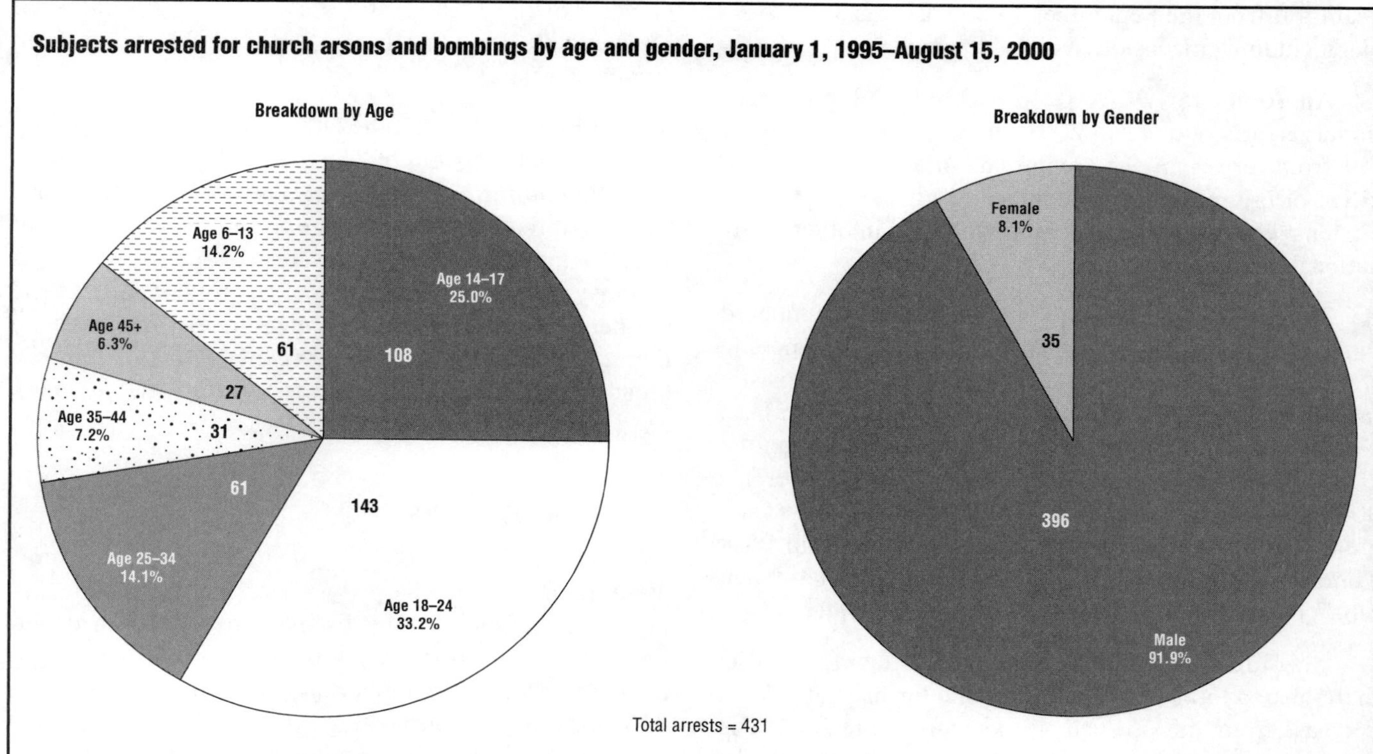

SOURCE: "Chart D: Demographic Information on Subjects Arrested for Church Arsons/Bombings Nationwide, January 1, 1995–August 15, 2000," *National Church Arson Task Force—Fourth Year Report*, Bureau of Alcohol, Tobacco and Firearms, Washington, DC, 2000 [Online] http://www.atf.treas.gov/pub/gen_pub/report2000/index.htm [accessed April 12, 2004]

Emeryville, California, headquarters of the Chiron Corp., a biotechnology company, in August of 2003. On September 26, 2003, the same group set off a bomb at Shaklee Corp. in Pleasanton, California.

Incidents of International Terrorism

In 1993 the World Trade Center in New York, a symbol of American financial wealth and power, was the target of international terrorists, who detonated a bomb in the subterranean parking garage, killing six people and injuring 1,000. On September 11, 2001, the World Trade Center's two 110-story office towers were once again the target of a Muslim terrorist group. At 7:59 A.M., American Airlines Flight 11 departed Logan International Airport in Boston bound for Los Angeles. Forty-six minutes later, at 8:45 A.M., the aircraft, diverted by hijackers, crashed into the North Tower of the World Trade Center. At 9:02 A.M., United Airlines Flight 175, also bound for Los Angeles from Boston and also diverted by hijackers, crashed into the South Tower of the World Trade Center. Both towers collapsed shortly thereafter, killing not only thousands of office workers and facility personnel trapped inside, but more than 300 firefighters and rescue workers helping to evacuate them.

By 9:45 A.M., two more domestic airlines had been commandeered by hijackers and crashed. American Airlines Flight 77 crashed into the Pentagon, a symbol of American military power, killing over 100 people who were in that section of the building at the time. United Airlines Flight 93 crashed in a field on the outskirts of Pittsburgh, Pennsylvania, the result of an attempt by some passengers to wrestle control of the aircraft from the hijackers. There were no survivors on any of the flights. The 19 hijackers were associated with the al-Qaeda group. Al-Qaeda's leader, Osama Bin Laden, went into hiding after the United States launched attacks on al-Qaeda's bases in Afghanistan in October, 2001.

The September 11 attacks were the worst acts of international terrorism on U.S. soil in the history of the United States. When the official cleanup and recovery efforts ended with a final ceremony on May 30, 2002, the New York City Office of Emergency Management gave the final tolls for the destruction caused by the attacks in that city. Of the 2,823 people killed in the World Trade Center, only 1,102 victims had been identified. An estimated 3.1 million hours of labor were spent on cleanup and 108,342 truckloads, over 1.8 million tons, of debris had been removed.

In addition to all those killed in New York, 64 passengers and crew from Flight 77 and 125 military and civilian personnel from the Pentagon were killed. All 44 passengers and crew on Flight 93 also died in the crash. The total death toll from the September 11 attacks was 3,056 people, including citizens of 78 different countries.

Approximately 3,370 people were killed in international terrorist attacks in 2001, the highest annual death toll from terrorism ever recorded. In addition to those killed or injured in the September 11 attacks, eight U.S. citizens were killed and 15 were wounded in other international terrorist attacks in 2001.

The casualties inflicted in 2001 far outnumbered those of 2000 or any previous year. In 2000, 409 people were killed worldwide in acts of international terrorism, including only 23 U.S. citizens, of whom 17 were U.S. Navy sailors. The sailors were killed in an attack on the USS Cole in the port of Aden, Yemen, on October 12, 2000. Other U.S. fatalities in 2000 included Carlos Caceres, an aid worker killed by a militia-led mob in West Timor, and Kurt Erich Schork, a journalist killed when rebels in Sierra Leone shot down a U.N. helicopter.

According to the U.S. State Department, in 2002 there were a total of 199 international terrorist attacks, a decrease from the 355 such attacks recorded in 2001. The number of casualties as the result of these attacks decreased. In 2002, 30 U.S. citizens were killed as the result of international terrorist attacks. The number of anti-U.S. attacks in 2002 was 77, a decrease of 65 percent from 2001's total of 219.

One of the most widely reported murders of a U.S. citizen by international terrorists happened early in 2002. On January 23, 2002, *Wall Street Journal* reporter Daniel Pearl was abducted in Pakistan while on his way to interview a Muslim fundamentalist leader. A month later the FBI confirmed that it had received a videotape containing "indisputable" confirmation that Pearl, 38, had been killed by his captors. Pearl's killing resulted in the arrest of several people believed to have been involved with the crime, including the alleged ringleader of the group, Ahmed Omar Saeed Sheikh, who had ties to radical Muslim extremist groups in the region. Pearl's wife, Mariane, who was pregnant at the time of his abduction, gave birth to their son in May 2002.

Aftermath of the Attacks

As a result of the September 11 attacks, the Office of Homeland Security was established by Presidential Executive Order to coordinate federal, state, and local anti-terrorism efforts. Governor Tom Ridge of Pennsylvania was appointed to head the Office, the focus of which is on the detection and prevention of future terrorist attacks, as well as incident management and response and recovery in the event of an attack. In addition, the Homeland Security Council was established to advise the President on all aspects of homeland security. Council members include the Vice President and Attorney General of the United States as well as Secretaries of Defense, Health and Human Services, Transportation, and the Treasury.

On March 12, 2002, the Office of Homeland Security implemented a system of Threat Conditions as a way of providing uniform advisories of possible terrorist threats. The five threat-conditions range from Low (a low risk of terrorist attack) to Severe (a severe risk of terrorist attacks that may necessitate the closing of government offices and the deployment of emergency personnel). Intermediate threat conditions are Guarded (general risk of terrorist attacks), Elevated (significant risk of terrorist attacks), and High (high risk of terrorist attacks).

ANTHRAX HOAXES

As of December 20, 2001, the FBI reported that some 40 individuals were charged with staging anthrax hoaxes in the weeks following the discovery of anthrax-laced letters sent to the nation's capitol and to various news organizations. Between October and November 2001, some 750 hoax letters purporting to contain anthrax were received by organizations worldwide, resulting in the closures of U.S. Postal Service offices, schools, and other organizations.

Some 550 anthrax hoax letters were sent to abortion and family planning clinics nationwide. Of those, 300 were received on October 15, 2001—the same day that an anthrax-tainted letter was discovered in the offices of U.S. Senator Tom Daschle. On November 7, 2001, another 250 such letters were received by various family clinics and advocacy groups nationwide. Some of the letters were labeled "Time Sensitive—Urgent Security Notice Enclosed," while others were sent with return addresses fraudulently ascribed to the Planned Parenthood Federation of America or the National Abortion Federation. On December 5, 2001, Clayton Lee Waagner, 44, was arrested near Cincinnati, Ohio, in connection with both waves of anthrax hoax letters sent to abortion and family planning clinics. Waagner, who had escaped from an Illinois jail in February 2001 while awaiting sentencing for weapons possession and auto theft, was convicted in December 2003 on 51 charges, including extortion, mailing threatening communication, and threatening use of a weapon of mass destruction.

Others arrested for various anthrax hoaxes across the United States included a Los Angeles City fire captain charged with mailing threatening communication to his ex-wife, a former U.S. Postal Service worker who allegedly sent mail labeled "Anthrax Inclosed" [*sic*], a former Social Security Administration employee who threatened to use anthrax to "resolve" a dispute regarding his disability payments, and a U.S. Capitol Police Officer.

The police officer allegedly placed an anonymous note in a Capitol Police station as a joke on November 7, 2001. The note read: "PLEASE INHALE. YES. THIS COULD BE? CALL YOUR DOCTOR FOR FLU-SMPTOMS. THIS IS A CAPITOL POLICE TRAINING EXCERCISE! I HOPE YOU PASS."

In a press release dated December 20, 2001, FBI Director Robert S. Mueller warned that the FBI "will continue to vigorously investigate and arrest those individuals who commit these crimes." Penalties for such offenses carry a maximum of five years imprisonment and a fine of up to $250,000.

CHAPTER 5

JUVENILE CRIME

JUVENILE ARRESTS

According to the Office of Juvenile Justice and Delinquency Prevention (OJJDP), a branch of the U.S. Department of Justice, an estimated 2.27 million juveniles (people under the age of 18) were arrested in 2001. This number represents a decrease of 20 percent from 1997 to 2001 and of 4 percent from 2000 to 2001. Most of the juveniles who were arrested were males, and were 15 or older. The only categories of crime in which juveniles under 15 accounted for the majority of arrests were arson (64 percent) and for sex offenses other than forcible rape and prostitution (54 percent). They also accounted for about 40 percent of arrests in the categories of non-aggravated assault, forcible rape, burglary, larceny-theft, and vandalism. Arrest rates for female juvenile offenders in 2001 were highest for prostitution and commercialized vice (69 percent of all juvenile arrests for these crimes), running away (59 percent), embezzlement (44 percent), larceny-theft (39 percent) and offenses against family and children (37 percent). (See Table 5.1.)

Males are arrested more often than females. In 2002, 72 percent of arrested juveniles were male, and 28 percent were female. The ratio of juvenile male to female arrests was even higher for violent crime: 82 percent in 2002 were male, and 18 percent were female.

From 1993 to 2002 female juvenile arrests increased by 6.4 percent. For such violent crimes as murder and robbery from 1993 to 2002, female juvenile arrests decreased. For forcible rape, however, female juvenile arrests increased by 45.8 percent. During the same period female juvenile arrests for drug abuse violations increased 120 percent, embezzlement arrests increased 76.2 percent, and offenses against the family and children increased by 54.9 percent. (See Table 1.6 in Chapter 1.)

In 2001 juveniles comprised 15.4 percent of all Violent Crime Index arrests in the United States, a decrease from the 1997 rate of 17.2 percent, and 30.4 percent of all Property Crime Index arrests, a decrease from the 1997 rate of 34.8 percent. Juveniles accounted for 49.5 percent of arson arrests, 38.9 percent of arrests for vandalism, 32.7 percent of motor vehicle thefts, and 23.6 percent of all robberies in the United States in 2001. (See Table 5.2.) In 2002 those under 18 years old comprised 16.5 percent (1.6 million) of all arrests in the U.S., 14.9 percent (66,508) of violent crime arrests, and 29.8 percent (349,000) of property crime arrests. (See Table 1.4 in Chapter 1.)

Police have a variety of options when dealing with juvenile offenders. In 2002 some 18 percent of all juvenile cases were handled within the police department and the offenders released. Seven percent were referred to criminal or adult court, while 72.8 percent were referred to juvenile court. Rural counties were more likely to refer cases to criminal or adult court (11.5 percent), while suburban counties were more likely to refer cases to juvenile court (74.1 percent). Cities with populations over 250,000 were more likely to handle cases within the police department (20.1 percent) or refer them to juvenile court (76.3 percent), while few referrals were made to criminal or adult court (1.9 percent). (See Table 5.3.)

Violent Crimes

The rate of juvenile arrests for violent crimes increased dramatically in the late 1980s and early 1990s, peaking in 1994 at over 500 per 100,000 youths ages 10 through 17. Between 1994 and 2001 juvenile arrests for Violent Crime Index offenses declined by 44 percent to a rate of 296 arrests for every 100,000 persons 10 to 17 years of age. (See Figure 5.1.) For juveniles 15 to 17 years of age, the Violent Crime Index arrest rate declined by 46 percent between 1994 and 2001, compared to a 24 percent decline for adults 18 to 24 years of age, a 30 percent drop for arrestees 25 to 29 years old, and a 22 percent decline for adult arrestees 30 to 39 years of age. (See Figure 5.2.)

TABLE 5.1

Estimated number of juvenile arrests, 2001

Most serious offense	Number of juvenile arrests	Percent of total juvenile arrests: Female	Percent of total juvenile arrests: Under age 15	Percent change: 1992–2001	Percent change: 1997–2001	Percent change: 2000–2001
Total	**2,273,500**	**28%**	**32%**	**−3%**	**−20%**	**−4%**
Crime Index total	587,900	29	37	−31	−28	−5
Violent Crime Index	96,500	18	33	−21	−21	−2
Murder and nonnegligent manslaughter	1,400	10	12	−62	−47	−2
Forcible rape	4,600	1	38	−24	−14	−1
Robbery	25,600	9	24	−32	−35	−4
Aggravated assault	64,900	23	37	−14	−13	−1
Property Crime Index	491,400	31	38	−32	−29	−6
Burglary	90,300	12	38	−40	−30	−6
Larceny-theft	343,600	39	39	−27	−30	−6
Motor vehicle theft	48,200	17	25	−51	−26	−2
Arson	9,300	12	64	−7	−9	8
Nonindex						
Other assaults	239,000	32	43	30	−2	2
Forgery and counterfeiting	5,800	36	11	−27	−26	−8
Fraud	8,900	33	16	−5	−18	−9
Embezzlement	1,800	44	7	152	24	−10
Stolen property (buying, receiving, possessing)	26,800	17	27	−45	−37	−6
Vandalism	105,300	13	44	−29	−22	−7
Weapons (carrying, possessing, etc.)	37,500	11	34	−35	−26	0
Prostitution and commercialized vice	1,400	69	15	−8	−5	15
Sex offenses (except forcible rape and prostitution)	18,000	8	54	−10	6	1
Drug abuse violations	202,500	15	17	121	−7	0
Gambling	1,400	3	13	−53	−47	−17
Offenses against the family and children	9,600	37	37	109	−11	6
Driving under the influence	20,300	18	5	35	5	−3
Liquor law violations	138,100	32	10	21	−9	−11
Drunkenness	20,400	21	13	4	−21	−10
Disorderly conduct	171,700	30	40	34	−21	1
Vagrancy	2,300	19	25	−37	−24	−10
All other offenses (except traffic)	397,200	26	28	27	−13	−3
Suspicion	1,300	36	33	−53	−42	9
Curfew and loitering	142,900	31	28	34	−29	−13
Runaways	133,300	59	38	−25	−30	−6

SOURCE: "Estimated Number of Juvenile Arrests, 2001," in *Statistical Briefing Book,* U.S. Department of Justice, Office of Justice Programs, Office of Juvenile Justice and Delinquency Prevention, Washington, DC, 2003 [Online] http://ojjdp.ncjrs.org/ojstatbb/crime/qa05101.asp?qaDate=20030531 [accessed April 10, 2004]

Over the past few years the largest decline in juvenile violent crime arrests was in the murder rate. Arrests of juveniles for murder peaked in 1993. Between 1993 and 2001, the juvenile arrest rate for murder had dropped almost 70 percent, reaching its lowest level in 20 years and erasing the more than 50 percent rise in juvenile murders from 1986 to 1993. (See Figure 5.3.) Juveniles were arrested in 10 percent of all murders committed in 2001.

Juvenile arrest rates for forcible rape, robbery, and aggravated assault also declined from their peak levels in the early- to mid-1990s. From 1980 to 1991, the juvenile arrest rate for forcible rape increased by 44 percent. By 2001, the rate had fallen to a level 13 percent lower than in 1980. (See Figure 5.4.) By 2001 juvenile arrest rates for robbery fell 59 percent from the peak years of 1994–1995. (See Figure 5.5.) The juvenile arrest rate for aggravated assault fell by 33 percent between 1994 and 2001. However, the 2001 rate was still 37 percent higher than it was in 1980. (See Figure 5.6.)

Property Crimes

From 1980 to 1994, juvenile arrests for Property Crime Index offenses were relatively stable for persons 10 to 17 years of age. From 1994 to 2001 the juvenile Property Crime Index arrest rates declined by 41 percent, to a 20-year low. (See Figure 5.7.) Consistent with a 20-year trend, in 2001, Property Crime Index arrest rates were higher for 16-year-olds than any other age group. Adults ages 30 to 49 comprised the only age group to register a higher arrest rate in 2001 than it had in 1980. (See Figure 5.8.)

Between 1992 and 2001, the juvenile arrest rate for burglary declined 40 percent. (See Figure 5.9.) Compared to 1980, when 230,500 juveniles were arrested for burglary, 2001 saw only 90,300 juveniles arrested for the same

TABLE 5.2

Percent of all arrests involving persons under age 18, 1997–2001

	1997	1998	1999	2000	2001
Total crimes	**18.6%**	**17.9%**	**17.2%**	**16.9%**	**16.6%**
Violent Crime Index	**17.2%**	**16.6%**	**16.1%**	**15.8%**	**15.4%**
Murder/nonnegligent manslaughter	13.6%	11.9%	9.5%	9.3%	10.2%
Forcible rape	17.1%	17.2%	17.0%	16.4%	16.8%
Robbery	29.8%	26.9%	25.4%	25.3%	23.6%
Aggravated assault	14.2%	14.3%	14.2%	13.9%	13.6%
Property Crime Index	**34.8%**	**33.0%**	**32.3%**	**32.0%**	**30.4%**
Burglary	36.8%	35.1%	33.5%	33.0%	31.0%
Larceny-theft	33.5%	31.9%	31.4%	31.2%	29.6%
Motor vehicle theft	39.9%	35.9%	35.3%	34.3%	32.7%
Arson	50.0%	52.1%	53.6%	52.8%	49.5%
Nonindex					
Other assaults	17.3%	17.8%	18.0%	18.0%	18.2%
Forgery and counterfeiting	7.1%	6.2%	6.4%	5.9%	5.1%
Fraud	2.7%	2.9%	3.5%	3.1%	2.8%
Embezzlement	7.8%	9.1%	9.8%	10.3%	9.1%
Stolen property	25.4%	24.5%	23.5%	23.4%	22.0%
Vandalism	42.9%	42.2%	41.9%	40.6%	38.9%
Weapons	23.9%	23.7%	24.2%	23.6%	22.6%
Prostitution/commercialized vice	1.4%	1.5%	1.4%	1.5%	1.8%
Sex offenses (other)	18.2%	17.0%	17.7%	18.6%	19.7%
Drug abuse violations	13.9%	13.2%	12.7%	12.9%	12.8%
Gambling	16.5%	12.5%	11.9%	14.0%	12.9%
Offenses against family	6.5%	7.0%	6.6%	6.4%	6.7%
Driving under influence	1.3%	1.5%	1.5%	1.4%	1.4%
Liquor laws	24.9%	25.0%	24.2%	23.3%	22.6%
Drunkenness	3.3%	3.5%	3.2%	3.4%	3.3%
Disorderly conduct	26.5%	26.4%	26.9%	25.9%	27.6%
Vagrancy	10.9%	9.6%	7.9%	9.3%	8.2%
All other offenses	12.0%	11.8%	11.4%	11.2%	11.0%
Suspicion	25.3%	25.3%	23.5%	21.1%	31.7%
Curfew and loitering	100.0%	100.0%	100.0%	100.0%	100.0%
Runaways	100.0%	100.0%	100.0%	100.0%	100.0%
Population ages 10 to 17	**30,707,300**	**30,962,500**	**31,278,200**	**32,570,500**	**32,967,900**

SOURCE: H. Snyder, C. Puzzanchera, and W. Kang, "Percent of All Arrests Involving Persons under Age 18 in the United States," "Easy Access to FBI Arrest Statistics 1994–2001," in *Statistical Briefing Book,* U.S. Department of Justice, Office of Justice Programs, Office of Juvenile Justice and Delinquency Prevention, Washington, DC, 2003 [Online] http://ojjdp.ncjrs.org/ojstatbb/ezaucr [accessed April 10, 2004]

offense. After remaining relatively constant between 1980 and 1992, by 2001 the juvenile arrest rate for larceny-theft had declined by 21 percent. Females accounted for 39 percent of all juvenile arrests for larceny-theft in 2001. (See Figure 5.10.) Between 1983 and 1990, the juvenile arrest rate for motor vehicle theft rose by 138 percent. Then, between 1990 and 2001, that rate declined by 57 percent, leaving it virtually the same as the 20-year low in 1983. (See Figure 5.11.) After rising by 55 percent from 1987 to 1994, juvenile arson arrests declined by 30 percent between 1994 and 2000. In 2001 the rate increased slightly. (See Figure 5.12.)

Drug Abuse Violations

After remaining within a limited range from 1980 to 1993, the juvenile arrest rate for drug abuse violations rose by 77 percent between 1993 and 1997. By 2001 the rate was down by 16 percent from its 1997 levels but still far above pre-1993 levels. (See Figure 5.13.) Between 1992 and 2001, juvenile arrests for drug abuse violations rose by 121 percent.

Race and Ethnicity

As in adult arrest rates, minorities are disproportionately represented in juvenile arrests. While black youths comprise roughly 15 percent of the total juvenile population, of some 1.5 million juvenile arrests in 2001, 410,668 (26.4 percent) of those arrested were black and 1.1 million (70.9 percent) were white. The overall rate of arrest for black youths between 1980 and 2000 rose by 10 percent, compared to a rise of 6 percent for whites and 2 percent for American Indians during the same time period.

In 1994 Violent Crime Index arrest rates peaked for both black and white juveniles. By 2001, rates declined by 56 percent for black juveniles and 33 percent for white juveniles arrested for violent Crime Index Offenses. The American Indian Violent Crime Index arrest rate peaked in 1995 and fell by 28 percent by 2001. For Asians, the rate peaked in 1996 and fell by 45 percent by 2001. (See Figure 5.14.) In 2001 arrest rates for Property Crime Index offenses were 47 percent below 1980 levels for black juveniles and 40 percent below for white juveniles. Arrests of Asian juveniles for Property Crime Index offenses were less than half the 1980 levels, while American Indians saw a drop of 34 percent. (See Figure 5.15.) In 2001 the rate of arrests of blacks and whites did not show as much disparity for property crimes as for violent

TABLE 5.3

Police disposition of juvenile offenders taken into custody, 2002

Population group	Total[1]	Handled within department and released	Referred to juvenile court jurisdiction	Referred to welfare agency	Referred to other police agency	Referred to criminal or adult court
Total agencies: 6,073 agencies; population 130,229,927						
Number	**732,282**	**132,825**	**532,940**	**4,779**	**10,183**	**51,555**
Percent[2]	**100.0**	**18.1**	**72.8**	**0.7**	**1.4**	**7.0**
Total cities: 4,577 cities; population 92,489,061						
Number	**611,897**	**115,191**	**444,336**	**3,956**	**7,901**	**40,513**
Percent[2]	**100.0**	**18.8**	**72.6**	**0.6**	**1.3**	**6.6**
Group I						
32 cities, 250,000 and over; population 23,601,703						
Number	122,767	24,627	93,612	525	1,638	2,365
Percent[2]	100.0	20.1	76.3	0.4	1.3	1.9
Group II						
88 cities, 100,000 to 249,999; population 13,193,782						
Number	81,448	13,344	61,791	636	1,143	4,534
Percent[2]	100.0	16.4	75.9	0.8	1.4	5.6
Group III						
235 cities, 50,000 to 99,999; population 16,120,073						
Number	111,816	26,075	78,439	533	1,822	4,947
Percent[2]	100.0	23.3	70.2	0.5	1.6	4.4
Group IV						
405 cities, 25,000 to 49,999; population 14,310,637						
Number	94,913	17,183	68,483	1,187	1,769	6,291
Percent[2]	100.0	18.1	72.2	1.3	1.9	6.6
Group V						
Number	105,574	18,232	74,556	553	670	11,563
Percent[2]	100.0	17.3	70.6	0.5	0.6	11.0
Group VI						
2,921 cities, under 10,000; population 10,925,901						
Number	95,379	15,730	67,455	522	859	10,813
Percent[2]	100.0	16.5	70.7	0.5	0.9	11.3
Suburban counties						
568 agencies; population 25,198,464						
Number	86,648	13,068	64,180	478	1,745	7,177
Percent[2]	100.0	15.1	74.1	0.6	2.0	8.3
Rural counties						
928 agencies; population 12,542,402						
Number	33,737	4,566	24,424	345	537	3,865
Percent[2]	100.0	13.5	72.4	1.0	1.6	11.5
Suburban area[3]						
3,286 agencies; population 62,227,924						
Number	321,746	60,621	227,447	1,826	3,557	28,295
Percent[2]	100.0	18.8	70.7	0.6	1.1	8.8

[1]Includes all offenses except traffic and neglect cases.
[2]Because of rounding, the percentages may not add to 100.0.
[3]Suburban area includes law enforcement agencies in cities with less than 50,000 inhabitants and county law enforcement agencies that are within a Metropolitan Statistical Area. Suburban area excludes all metropolitan agencies associated with a central city. The agencies associated with suburban areas also appear in other groups within this table.

SOURCE: "Table 68: Police Disposition of Juvenile Offenders Taken into Custody, 2002," in *Crime in the United States 2002,* Federal Bureau of Investigation, Washington, DC, 2003

crimes (1.9 and 3.6, respectively), though still noticeably disproportionate in both categories. Between 1980 and 2001 the juvenile arrest rate for all crimes by race showed a general decline. The total juvenile arrest rate for blacks fell by 5 percent, the rate for whites fell 10 percent, and the rate for Asians fell 19 percent. The total rate for black juveniles peaked in 1995 and fell by 38 percent by 2001. (See Figure 5.16.)

Gender

Although the juvenile arrest rate for all crimes rose for both females and males from 1983 to 1997, the increase for females was 72 percent compared to 30 percent for males. By 2001, the arrest rate for male juveniles was below its 1983 levels, while the rate for females remained 38 percent higher than in 1983. (See Figure 5.17.) By 2001, Juvenile Violent Crime Index arrests had declined from their 1994 peak to a rate for females of 112 arrests per 100,000 persons 10 to 17 years of age, and a rate for males of 471. This violent crime rate for female juveniles of 112 per 100,000 was still 59 percent above where it had stood in 1980 (70 per 100,000), while the rate for males was 20 percent below its 1980 level (587 per 100,000). Despite these shifts, in 2001 the violent crime index arrest rate for juvenile males remained more than four times that for female juveniles. (See Figure

FIGURE 5.1

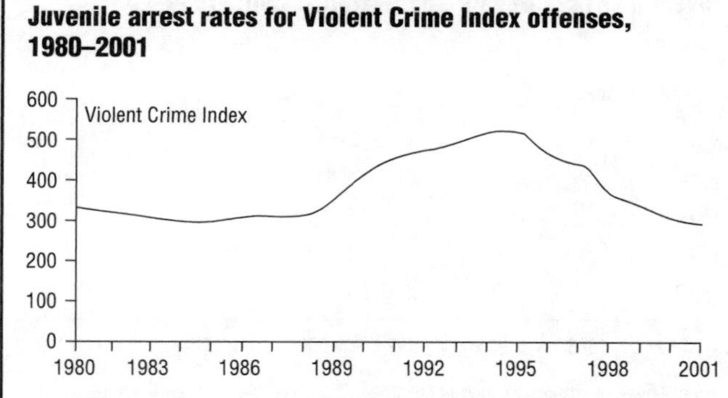

Juvenile arrest rates for Violent Crime Index offenses, 1980–2001

Note: Rates are arrests of persons ages 10–17 per 100,000 persons ages 10–17 in the resident population. The Violent Crime Index includes the offenses of murder and nonnegligent manslaughter, forcible rape, robbery, and aggravated assault.

SOURCE: "Juvenile Arrest Rates for Violent Crime Index Offenses, 1980–2001," in *Statistical Briefing Book,* U.S. Department of Justice, Office of Justice Programs, Office of Juvenile Justice and Delinquency Prevention, Washington, DC, 2003 [Online] http://ojjdp.ncjrs.org/ojstatbb/crime/JAR_Display.asp?ID=qa0520120030531 [accessed April 10, 2004]

FIGURE 5.2

Age-specific violent crime arrest rates per 100,000 population, 1980, 1994, and 2001

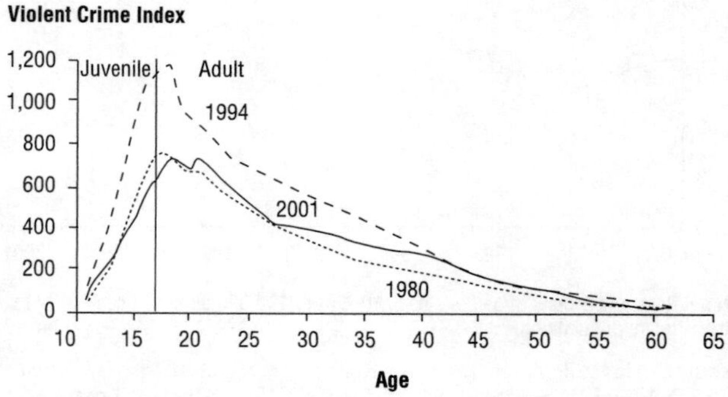

Violent Crime Index

Juvenile
Adult
1994
2001
1980

Age

Note: The Violent Crime Index includes the offenses of murder and nonnegligent manslaughter, forcible rape, robbery, and aggravated assault.

SOURCE: "Age-Specific Violent Crime Arrest Rates, 1980, 1994, and 2001," in *Statistical Briefing Book,* U.S. Department of Justice, Office of Justice Programs, Office of Juvenile Justice and Delinquency Prevention, Washington, DC, 2003 [Online] http://ojjdp.ncjrs.org/ojstatbb/crime/qa05301.asp?qaDate=20030531 [accessed April 10, 2004]

FIGURE 5.3

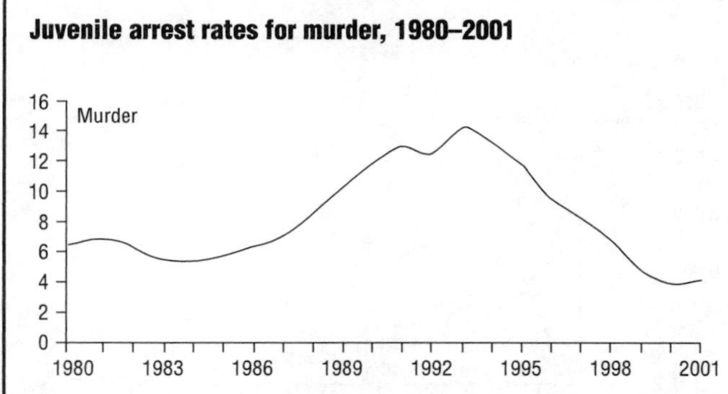

Juvenile arrest rates for murder, 1980–2001

Note: Rates are arrests of persons ages 10–17 per 100,000 persons ages 10–17 in the resident population.

SOURCE: "Juvenile Arrest Rates for Murder, 1980–2001," in *Statistical Briefing Book,* U.S. Department of Justice, Office of Justice Programs, Office of Juvenile Justice and Delinquency Prevention, Washington, DC, 2003 [Online] http://ojjdp.ncjrs.org/ojstatbb/crime/JAR_Display.asp?ID=qa0520220030531 [accessed April 10, 2004]

FIGURE 5.4

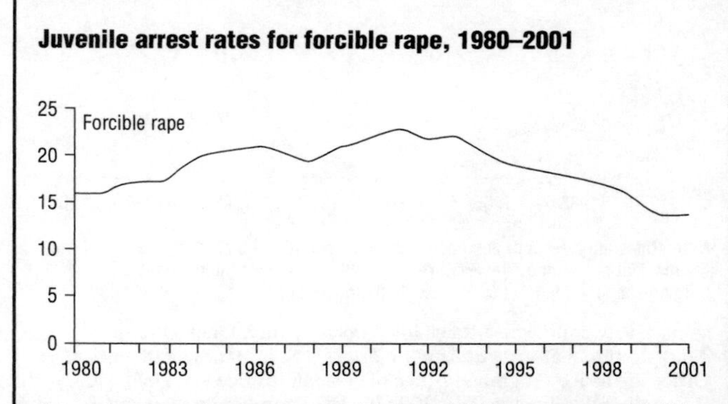

Juvenile arrest rates for forcible rape, 1980–2001

Note: Rates are arrests of persons ages 10–17 per 100,000 persons ages 10–17 in the resident population.

SOURCE: "Juvenile Arrest Rates for Forcible Rape, 1980–2001," in *Statistical Briefing Book,* U.S. Department of Justice, Office of Justice Programs, Office of Juvenile Justice and Delinquency Prevention, Washington, DC, 2003 [Online] http://ojjdp.ncjrs.org/ojstatbb/crim/JAR_Display.asp?ID=qa0520320030531 [accessed April 10, 2004]

5.18.) For Property Crime Index offenses, the rate of arrest for female juveniles fell by 26 percent from 1996 to 2001. Between 1991 and 2001, the number of male juveniles arrested for Property Crime offenses decreased by 51 percent. (See Figure 5.19.)

THE CRIMES—COURT STATISTICS

The OJJDP publishes statistics on juvenile court cases (*Juvenile Court Statistics, 1999,* Washington, D.C., 2003) and on juvenile cases sent for trial in adult criminal court. The OJJDP categorizes juvenile crimes in two ways:

- Delinquency offenses—acts that are illegal regardless of the age of the perpetrator
- Status offenses—acts that are illegal only for minors, such as truancy, running away, or curfew violations

Juvenile courts handled 1.6 million delinquency cases in 2000, some 9 percent less than in 1996 but 43 percent higher than the level of caseloads in 1985. (See Table 5.4.) A case can include more than one charge. For example, a youth brought on three different robbery charges at the

FIGURE 5.5

Juvenile arrest rates for robbery, 1980–2001

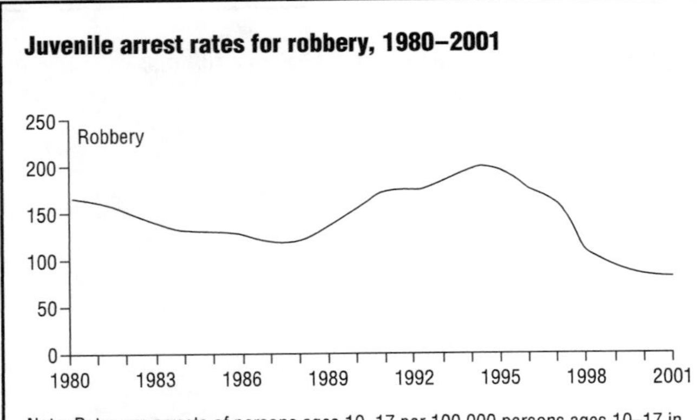

Note: Rates are arrests of persons ages 10–17 per 100,000 persons ages 10–17 in the resident population.

SOURCE: "Juvenile Arrest Rates for Robbery, 1980–2001," in *Statistical Briefing Book,* U.S. Department of Justice, Office of Justice Programs, Office of Juvenile Justice and Delinquency Prevention, Washington, DC, 2003 [Online] http://ojjdp.ncjrs.org/ojstatbb/crime/JAR_Display.asp?ID=qa0520420030531 [accessed April 10, 2004]

FIGURE 5.6

Juvenile arrest rates for aggravated assault, 1980–2001

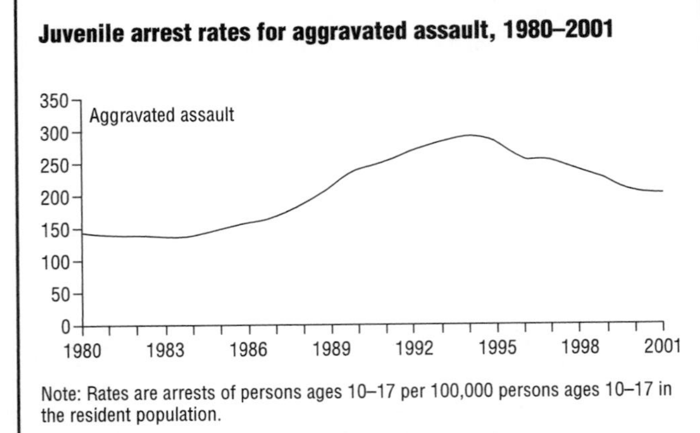

Note: Rates are arrests of persons ages 10–17 per 100,000 persons ages 10–17 in the resident population.

SOURCE: "Juvenile Arrest Rates for Aggravated Assault, 1980–2001," in *Statistical Briefing Book,* U.S. Department of Justice, Office of Justice Programs, Office of Juvenile Justice and Delinquency Prevention, Washington, DC, 2003 [Online] http://ojjdp.ncjrs.org/ojstatbb/crime/JAR_Display.asp?ID=qa0520520030531 [accessed April 10, 2004]

FIGURE 5.7

Juvenile arrest rates for Property Crime Index offenses, 1980–2001

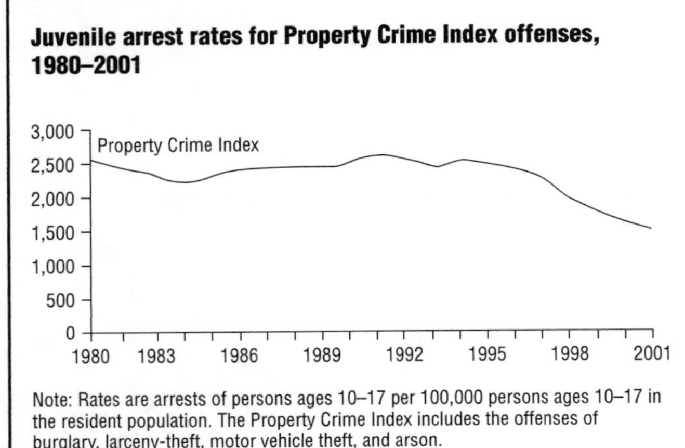

Note: Rates are arrests of persons ages 10–17 per 100,000 persons ages 10–17 in the resident population. The Property Crime Index includes the offenses of burglary, larceny-theft, motor vehicle theft, and arson.

SOURCE: "Juvenile Arrest Rates for Property Crime Index Offenses, 1980–2001," in *Statistical Briefing Book,* U.S. Department of Justice, Office of Justice Programs, Office of Juvenile Justice and Delinquency Prevention, Washington, DC, 2003 [Online] http://ojjdp.ncjrs.org/ojstatbb/crime/JAR_Display.asp?ID=qa0520620030531 [accessed April 10, 2004]

FIGURE 5.8

Age-specific Property Crime Index arrest rates, per 100,000 population, 1980, 1994, and 2001

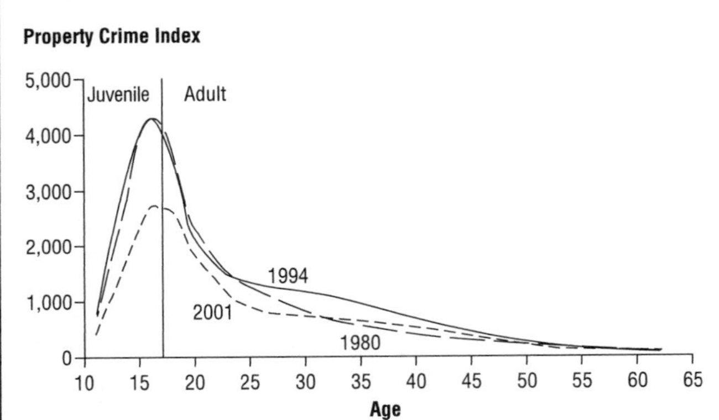

Note: The Property Crime Index includes the offenses of burglary, larceny-theft, motor vehicle theft, and arson.

SOURCE: "Age-Specific Property Crime Index Arrest Rates, 1980, 1994, and 2001," in *Statistical Briefing Book* U.S. Department of Justice, Office of Justice Programs, Office of Juvenile Justice and Delinquency Prevention, Washington, DC, 2003 [Online] http://ojjdp.ncjrs.org/ojstatbb/crime/qa05305.asp?qaDate=20030531 [accessed April 10, 2004]

same time is counted as one case. Since 1960 the juvenile court caseload increased over 400 percent, from 1,100 delinquency cases on a given day in 1960 to 4,500 in 2000. (See Figure 5.20.)

Juvenile courts take delinquency cases referred by law enforcement agencies, social service agencies, schools, parents, probation officers, or victims. In 2000 law enforcement agencies referred 84 percent of delinquency cases to juvenile court. Property offenses were referred to juvenile court most frequently, followed by person offenses, drug offenses, and public order offenses. (See Figure 5.21.) Of all juveniles taken into custody for delinquency by law enforcement agencies in 2000, over 66 percent were referred to juvenile court jurisdiction, 33 percent were handled in the police department and released, and 1 percent of juveniles arrested were referred directly to criminal (adult) court. Table 5.5 shows juvenile court processing for a typical 1,000 delinquency cases in 2000.

In 2000 property offenses made up about 41 percent of delinquency cases, with the most frequent charge being larceny-theft, which accounted for 18.5 percent of all delinquency cases handled in 2000. About 23 percent of delinquency cases involved an offense against persons.

FIGURE 5.9

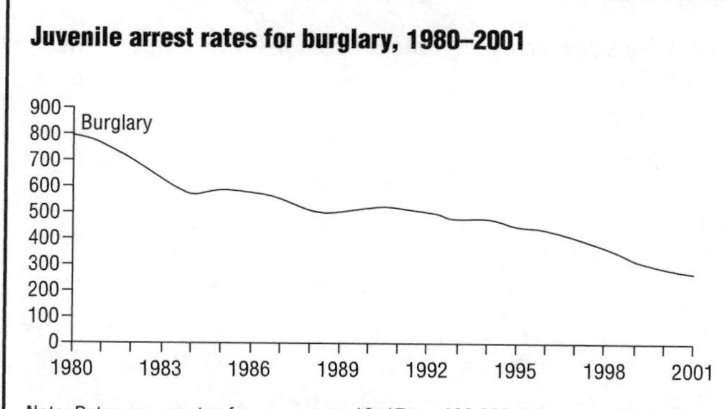

Note: Rates are arrests of persons ages 10–17 per 100,000 persons ages 10–17 in the resident population.

SOURCE: "Juvenile Arrest Rates for Burglary, 1980–2001," in *Statistical Briefing Book,* U.S. Department of Justice, Office of Justice Programs, Office of Juvenile Justice and Delinquency Prevention, Washington, DC, 2003 [Online] http://ojjdp.ncjrs.org/ojstatbb/crime/JAR_Display.asp?ID=qa0520720030531 [accessed April 10, 2004]

FIGURE 5.10

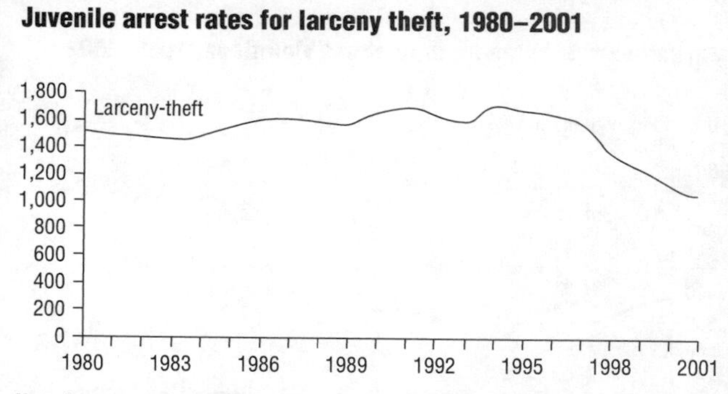

Note: Rates are arrests of persons ages 10–17 per 100,000 persons ages 10–17 in the resident population.

SOURCE: "Juvenile Arrest Rates for Larceny-Theft, 1980–2001," in *Statistical Briefing Book,* U.S. Department of Justice, Office of Justice Programs, Office of Juvenile Justice and Delinquency Prevention, Washington, DC, 2003 [Online] http://ojjdp.ncjrs.org/ojstatbb/crime/JAR_Display.asp?ID=qa0520820030531 [accessed April 10, 2004]

FIGURE 5.11

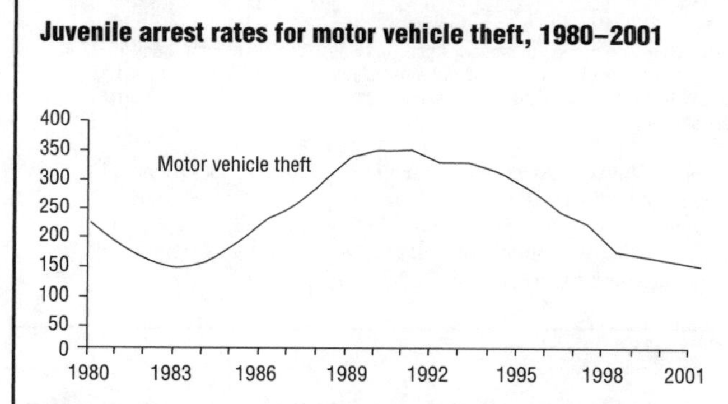

Note: Rates are arrests of persons ages 10–17 per 100,000 persons ages 10–17 in the resident population.

SOURCE: "Juvenile Arrest Rates for Motor Vehicle Theft, 1980–2001," in *Statistical Briefing Book,* U.S. Department of Justice, Office of Justice Programs, Office of Juvenile Justice and Delinquency Prevention, Washington, DC, 2003 [Online] http://ojjdp.ncjrs.org/ojstatbb/crime/JAR_Display.asp?ID=qa0520920030531 [accessed April 10, 2004]

FIGURE 5.12

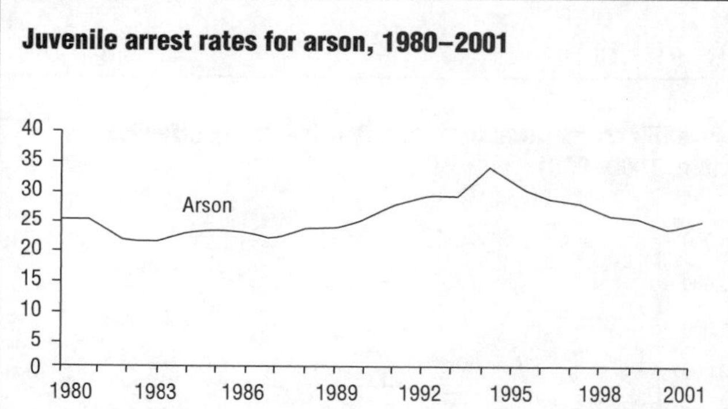

Note: Rates are arrests of persons ages 10–17 per 100,000 persons ages 10–17 in the resident population.

SOURCE: "Juvenile Arrest Rates for Arson, 1980–2001," in *Statistical Briefing Book,* U.S. Department of Justice, Office of Justice Programs, Office of Juvenile Justice and Delinquency Prevention, Washington, DC, 2003 [Online] http://ojjdp.ncjrs.org/ojstatbb/crime/JAR_Display.asp?ID=qa0521020030531 [accessed April 10, 2004]

Public order offenses, such as disorderly conduct, weapons offenses, and liquor law violations, amounted to 24 percent. Drug law violations made up 11.8 percent of total cases, a 22 percent decrease since 1996.

While the number of delinquency cases rose 43 percent from 1985 to 2000, the increases varied by offense. Violent sex offenses, other than forcible rape, increased by 160 percent. Weapons violations increased 175 percent. Liquor law violations rose 103 percent, and nonviolent sex offenses were up 94 percent.

Age

In 2000 delinquency case rates in juvenile court for drug use and public order offenses increased with the age of the juvenile, while case rates for property crimes peaked with juveniles 16 years of age. (See Figure 5.22.) Seventeen-year-olds had a much higher increase in case rates than did younger persons. Their case rate increase for drug offenses was three times the rate of 13-year-olds, while for property and person offenses, it was about twice as much for each.

Detention

A juvenile court may place youths in a detention facility during court processing. Detention may be needed either to protect the community from the juvenile, to protect the juvenile, or both. Also, detention is sometimes necessary to ensure a youth's appearance at scheduled hearings or evaluations.

FIGURE 5.13

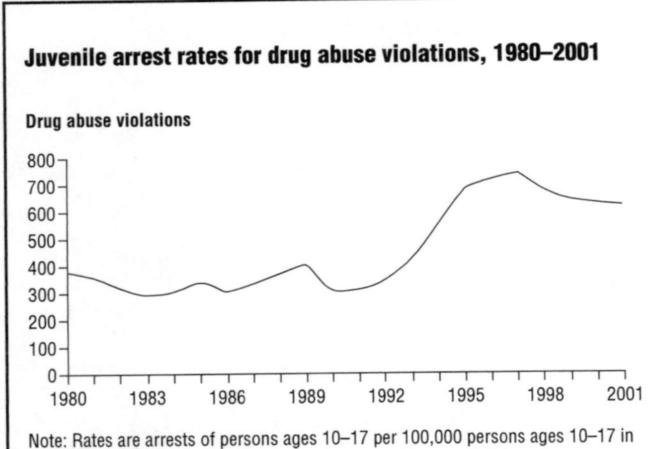

Note: Rates are arrests of persons ages 10–17 per 100,000 persons ages 10–17 in the resident population.

SOURCE: "Juvenile Arrest Rates for Drug Abuse Violations, 1980–2001," in *Statistical Briefing Book* U.S. Department of Justice, Office of Justice Programs, Office of Juvenile Justice and Delinquency Prevention, Washington, DC, 2003 [Online] http://ojjdp.ncjrs.org/ojstatbb/crime/JAR_Display.asp?ID=qa05214200305 31 [accessed April 10, 2004]

FIGURE 5.15

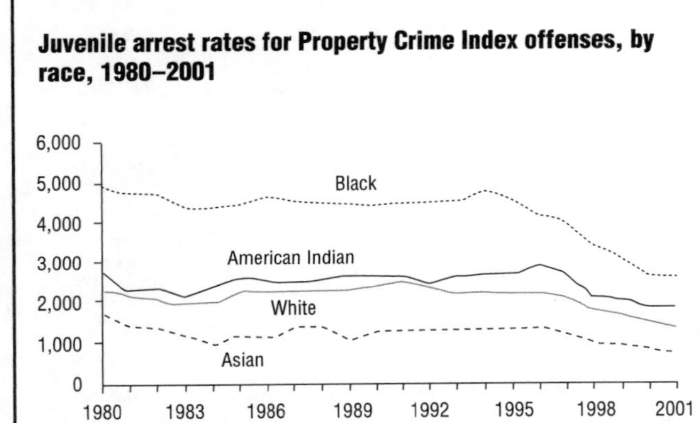

Note: Rates are arrests of persons ages 10–17 per 100,000 persons ages 10–17 in the resident population. Persons of Hispanic ethnicity may be of any race, i.e., white, black, American Indian, or Asian. Arrests of Hispanics are not reported separately.

SOURCE: "Juvenile Arrest Rates for Property Crime Index Offenses by Race, 1980–2001," in *Statistical Briefing Book,* U.S. Department of Justice, Office of Justice Programs, Office of Juvenile Justice and Delinquency Prevention, Washington, DC, 2003 [Online] http://ojjdp.ncjrs.org/ojstatbb/crime/JAR_Display.asp?ID=qa05266200305 31 [accessed April 10, 2004]

In 1999 youths were held in detention facilities at some point between referral to court intake and case disposition (final outcome of court processing) in 20 percent of all delinquency cases disposed. Property offense cases were the least likely to involve detention (16 percent), and those involving drugs, person offenses, and public order (23 percent each) were the most likely to result in detention.

Between 1990 and 1999 the number of juveniles detained in drug cases increased by 62 percent. Those

FIGURE 5.14

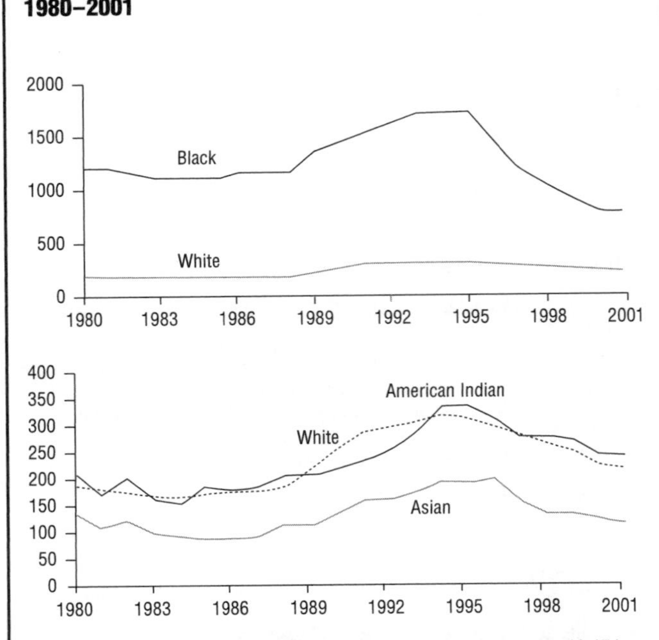

Note: Rates are arrests of persons ages 10-17 per 100,000 persons ages 10-17 in the resident population. Persons of Hispanic ethnicity may be of any race, i.e., white, black, American Indian, or Asian. Arrests of Hispanics are not reported separately.

SOURCE: "Juvenile Arrest Rates for Violent Crime Index Offenses by Race, 1980–2001," in *Statistical Briefing Book,* U.S. Department of Justice, Office of Justice Programs, Office of Juvenile Justice and Delinquency Prevention, Washington, DC, 2003 [Online] http://ojjdp.ncjrs.org/ojstatbb/crime [accessed March 19, 2004]

detained in person offense cases grew by 32 percent. Overall detained delinquency cases increased by 11 percent, adding to the problems of housing detained juveniles.

Male juveniles charged with a delinquency offense were more likely than females to be held in a secure facility while awaiting the disposition of their cases. In 1999, 21 percent of male juveniles and 16 percent of female juveniles were detained. This represents a 4 percent increase in male juvenile detainees from 1990 to 1999. The number of female juveniles detained increased by 50 percent. African-American juveniles were detained in 25 percent of delinquency cases, compared to 18 percent of whites in 1999.

Case Processing

No nationwide uniform procedure exists for processing juvenile cases, but cases do follow similar paths. An intake department first screens cases. The intake department can be the court itself, a state department of social services, or a prosecutor's office. The intake officer may decide that the case will be dismissed for lack of evidence, handled formally (petitioned), or resolved informally (non-petitioned). Formal processing can include

FIGURE 5.16

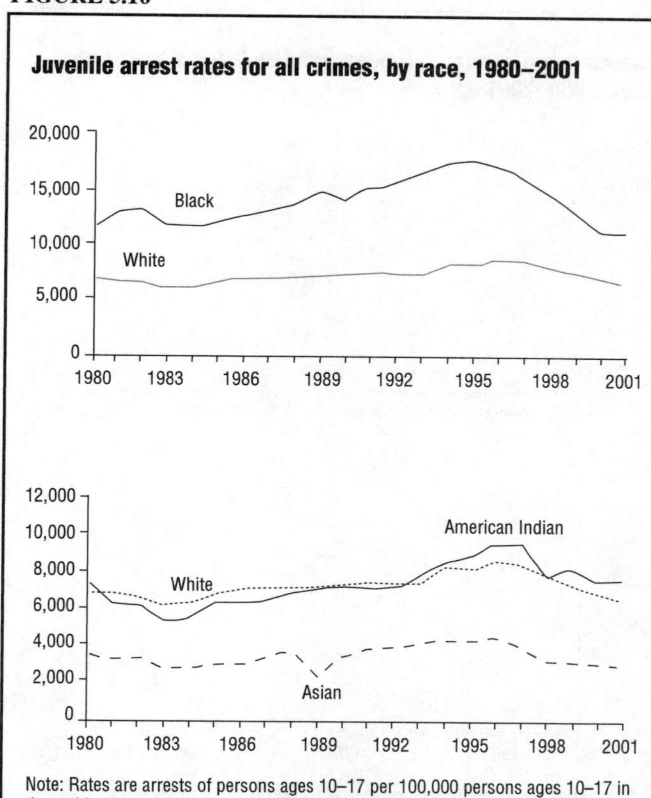

Note: Rates are arrests of persons ages 10–17 per 100,000 persons ages 10–17 in the resident population. Persons of Hispanic ethnicity may be of any race, i.e., white, black, American Indian, or Asian. Arrests of Hispanics are not reported separately.

SOURCE: "Juvenile Arrest Rates for All Crimes by Race, 1980–2001," in *Statistical Briefing Book,* U.S. Department of Justice, Office of Justice Programs, Office of Juvenile Justice and Delinquency Prevention, Washington, DC, 2003 [Online] http://ojjdp.ncjrs.org/ojstatbb/crime/JAR_Display.asp?ID=qa0526020030531 [accessed April 10, 2004]

FIGURE 5.17

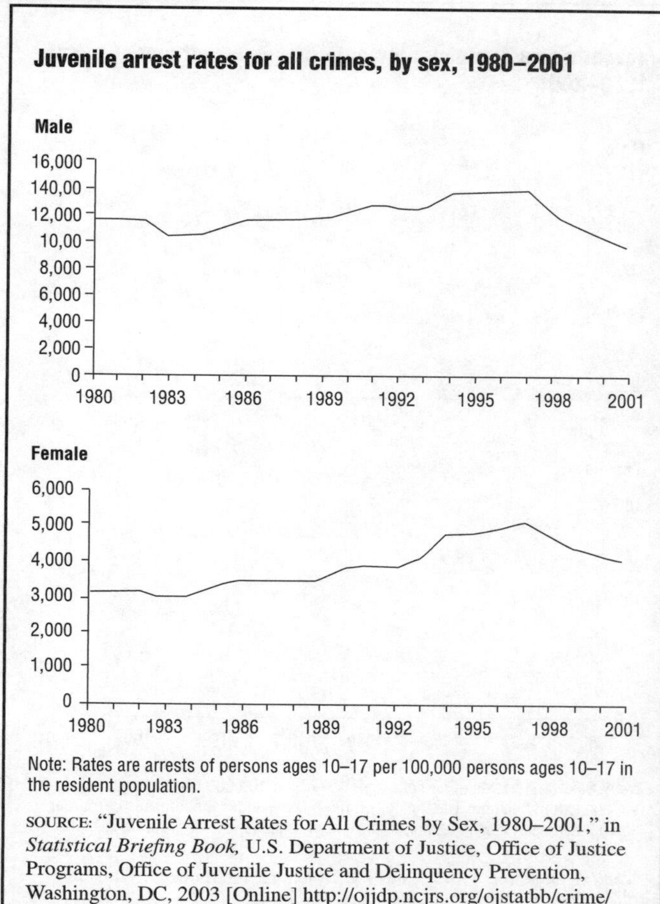

Note: Rates are arrests of persons ages 10–17 per 100,000 persons ages 10–17 in the resident population.

SOURCE: "Juvenile Arrest Rates for All Crimes by Sex, 1980–2001," in *Statistical Briefing Book,* U.S. Department of Justice, Office of Justice Programs, Office of Juvenile Justice and Delinquency Prevention, Washington, DC, 2003 [Online] http://ojjdp.ncjrs.org/ojstatbb/crime/JAR_Display.asp?ID=qa0523020030531 [accessed April 10, 2004]

placement outside the home, probation, a trial in juvenile court, or transfer to an adult court. Informal processing may consist of referral to a social services agency, a fine, some form of restitution, or informal probation. Both formal and informal processing can result in dismissal of the charges and release of the juvenile. Table 5.5 shows the processing of juvenile delinquency cases in 2000.

In 2000, 39 percent of delinquency cases were either adjudicated or waived to criminal court, up from 38 percent in 1999. (See Figure 5.23.) Some 58 percent of all delinquency cases were formally processed in 2000. Of the formally processed delinquency cases in 2000, 66 percent resulted in a finding of delinquency (the equivalent of a verdict of guilty in adult criminal court). About one percent of delinquency cases in 2000 resulted in a waiver (or transfer) of the juvenile to adult criminal court.

Between 1985 and 2000 the number of adjudicated delinquency cases resulting in formal probation rose 108 percent, those resulting in residential placement rose 49 percent, and those resulting in other sanctions, such as community service or restitution, rose by 84 percent. The number of cases dismissed (about 3 percent of the total) remained about the same for the entire time period. (See Figure 5.24.)

PROSECUTING MINORS AS ADULTS

Many people believe that some crimes are so terrible that the courts should focus on the type of offense and not the age of the accused. From 1987 to 1993, there was a dramatic 65 percent increase in the rate of arrests of juveniles for murder. The homicides were overwhelmingly concentrated among black teenagers in the nation's largest cities. Rates of other violent crimes, like rape, robbery, and aggravated assault, also increased during this time. Most experts believe the increases were related to an upsurge in violent gangs selling crack cocaine and lax controls on access to handguns during this time.

Politicians responded to voter outrage at the increase in violent crime among juveniles and several high-profile murders involving juveniles. By the year 2000 all 50 states and the District of Columbia had one or more laws permitting the transfer of youths to criminal courts to be tried as adults. Many states have also expanded these laws in order to make

FIGURE 5.18

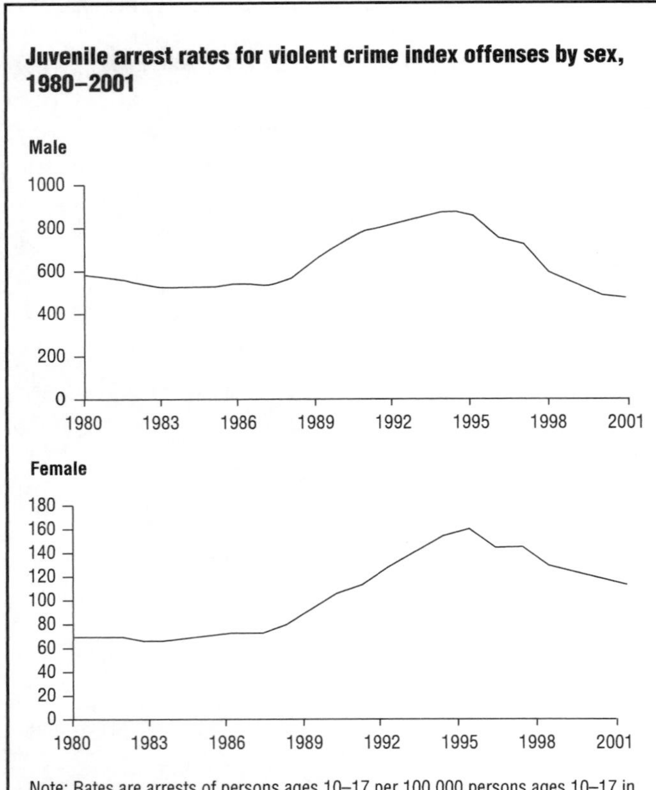

Juvenile arrest rates for violent crime index offenses by sex, 1980–2001

Note: Rates are arrests of persons ages 10–17 per 100,000 persons ages 10–17 in the resident population. The Violent Crime Index includes the offenses of murder and nonnegligent manslaughter, forcible rape, robbery, and aggravated assault.

SOURCE: "Juvenile Arrest Rates for Violent Crime Index Offenses by Sex, 1980–2001," in *Statistical Briefing Book,* U.S. Department of Justice, Office of Justice Programs, Office of Juvenile Justice and Delinquency Prevention, Washington, DC, 2003 [Online] http://ojjdp.ncjrs.org/ojstatbb/crime [accessed March 19, 2004]

FIGURE 5.19

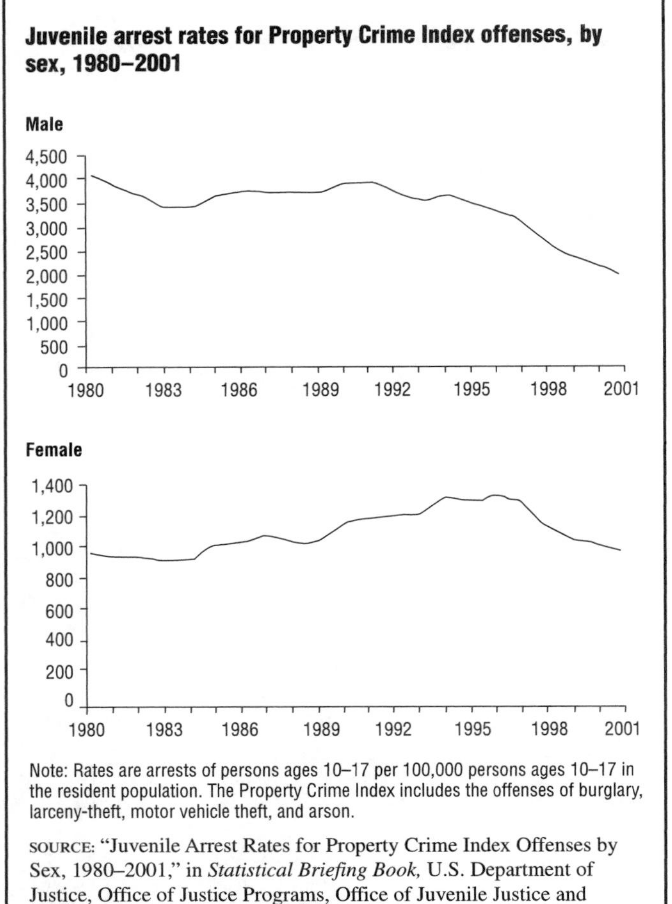

Juvenile arrest rates for Property Crime Index offenses, by sex, 1980–2001

Note: Rates are arrests of persons ages 10–17 per 100,000 persons ages 10–17 in the resident population. The Property Crime Index includes the offenses of burglary, larceny-theft, motor vehicle theft, and arson.

SOURCE: "Juvenile Arrest Rates for Property Crime Index Offenses by Sex, 1980–2001," in *Statistical Briefing Book,* U.S. Department of Justice, Office of Justice Programs, Office of Juvenile Justice and Delinquency Prevention, Washington, DC, 2003 [Online] http://ojjdp.ncjrs.org/ojstatbb/crime/JAR_Display.asp?ID=qa05236200305 31 [accessed April 10, 2004]

it easier to prosecute juveniles as adults. For example, a 1995 Missouri law removed the minimum age limit, which had been 14, for trying children as adults in cases involving drug dealing, murder, rape, robbery, and first-degree assault. The law also permits children 12 years old to be prosecuted as adults for other crimes. A Texas law allows children as young as 10 to be sentenced to up to 40 years' incarceration. In Idaho, criminal courts have jurisdiction over juveniles arrested for carrying concealed weapons on school property.

The number of cases transferred from juvenile to adult courts increased 47 percent between 1987 and 1996, from 6,800 to 10,000. However, despite increasing numbers, the proportion of transferred cases overall remained fairly constant in the 1990s. In 1992, 1.4 percent of all formally processed delinquency cases were transferred to criminal (adult) court. In 2000, 1 percent of all formally processed delinquency cases were waived to adult court.

Does the Practice Make a Difference?

Because the murder rate by juveniles consistently declined from 1992 to 2001, dropping about 62 percent (to 1,400 murders in 2001), some public officials believe that efforts to curb crime by trying children as adults has worked. Other experts attribute the decline in the murder rate to big-city police crackdowns on illegal guns, expanded after-school crime prevention programs, and the decline of crack cocaine and violent gangs.

A Florida study suggested that juveniles tried in adult courts were likely to be rearrested more quickly and more often than juveniles who went through the juvenile court system ("The Transfer of Juveniles to Criminal Court: Does It Make A Difference?" *Crime and Delinquency,* April 1996). The study compared the rearrest rates of juveniles transferred to criminal court to a matched sample (similar crimes, past court experience, age, gender, and race) of those retained in the juvenile system. Thirty percent of transferred youths were rearrested, compared to only 19 percent of the nontransferred ones. Transferred youths who were rearrested had committed a new offense within 135 days of release, compared to 227 days for youths processed in juvenile courts.

TABLE 5.4

Delinquency cases handled by juvenile courts, 1985–2000

Most serious offense	Number of cases	Percent change			
		1985–2000	1991–2000	1996–2000	1999–2000
Total delinquency	**1,633,300**	**43%**	**16%**	**−9%**	**−2%**
Person offenses	375,600	107	35	−1	−3
Criminal homicide	1,700	22	−25	−37	−7
Forcible rape	4,700	36	−32	−39	−16
Robbery	22,600	7	−15	−25	11
Aggravated assault	51,200	−8	−29	−41	−12
Simple assault	255,800	43	−23	−36	−5
Other violent sex offenses	12,500	160	79	15	−1
Other person offenses	27,200	96	42	20	9
Property offenses	668,600	165	32	35	−15
Burglary	108,600	−3	−21	−23	−4
Larceny-theft	303,200	−10	−26	−26	−4
Motor vehicle theft	38,300	−23	−30	−25	−3
Arson	8,300	−7	−21	−27	−5
Vandalism	106,800	3	−46	−29	−3
Trespassing	49,400	22	14	−7	−2
Stolen property offenses	25,200	26	−5	−13	−3
Other property offenses	28,900	−7	−17	−25	−15
Drug law violations	194,200	−8	−15	−22	−4
Public order offenses	395,000	61	−9	−7	9
Obstruction of justice	179,200	164	197	5	2
Disorderly conduct	90,200	106	79	11	2
Weapons offenses	37,500	175	142	20	5
Liquor law violations	27,000	103	54	0	1
Nonviolent sex offenses	14,900	94	12	−15	−6
Other public order offenses	46,200	50	126	110	37
Violent crime index[1]	80,100	12	31	23	8
Property crime index[2]	458,300	47	46	−4	−11

[1]Includes criminal homicide, forcible rape, robbery, and aggravated assault.
[2]Includes burglary, larceny-theft, moter vehicle theft, and arson.

SOURCE: "Deliquency Cases, 2000," in *Statistical Briefing Book,* U.S. Department of Justice, Office of Justice Programs, Office of Juvenile Justice and Delinquency Prevention, Washington, DC, 2003 [Online] http://ojjdp.ncjrs.org/ojstatbb/court/qa06201 .asp?qaDate=20030811 [accessed April 10, 2004]

Some of the inherent problems in transferring juveniles to adult court are discussed in the book *Youth on Trial: A Developmental Perspective of Juvenile Justice,* edited by Thomas Grisso and Robert G. Schwartz (University of Chicago Press, Chicago, IL, 2000). According to the research presented in the book, juveniles find it more difficult than adults to make "knowing and intelligent" decisions at many junctures in the criminal justice process. Problems arise in particular in the waiving of Miranda rights, which allow the juvenile to remain silent and talk to a lawyer before responding to questions posed by law enforcement officers. The waiving of these rights can lead to much more serious consequences in adult court than in juvenile proceedings. As the book points out, "questions must be raised regarding the juvenile's judgment, decision-making capacity, and impulse control as they relate to criminal culpability" in adult proceedings. Researchers and experts in child development emphasize the need to understand an adolescent's intellectual, social, and emotional development before deciding if a youth can be held blameworthy as an adult for a particular criminal offense.

STATUS OFFENSE CASES

Status offenses are law violations for which an adult cannot be prosecuted (runaway, truancy, alcohol possession, ungovernability cases, etc.). From 1990 to 1999, according to the Office of Juvenile Justice and Delinquency Prevention publication *Juvenile Court Statistics 1999* (2003), liquor law violations accounted for 42 percent of status offense cases for 17-year-olds, followed by runaway cases at 10 percent, and ungovernability (also known as incorrigibility) cases at 9 percent.

In many communities, social service agencies rather than juvenile courts have responsibility for accused status offenders. National estimates of informally handled status offense cases are not calculated because of differences in screening procedures. The statistics, therefore, focus on formally handled (petitioned) status offense cases.

Age, Sex, and Race

Children over 16 accounted for three-fourths of all liquor law violations from 1990 to 1999. Persons under the

FIGURE 5.20

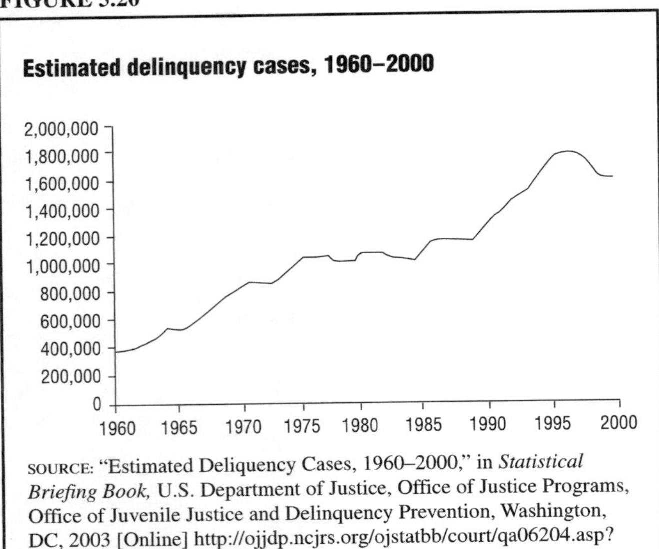

SOURCE: "Estimated Deliquency Cases, 1960–2000," in *Statistical Briefing Book,* U.S. Department of Justice, Office of Justice Programs, Office of Juvenile Justice and Delinquency Prevention, Washington, DC, 2003 [Online] http://ojjdp.ncjrs.org/ojstatbb/court/qa06204.asp?qaDate=20030811 [accessed April 10, 2004]

FIGURE 5.21

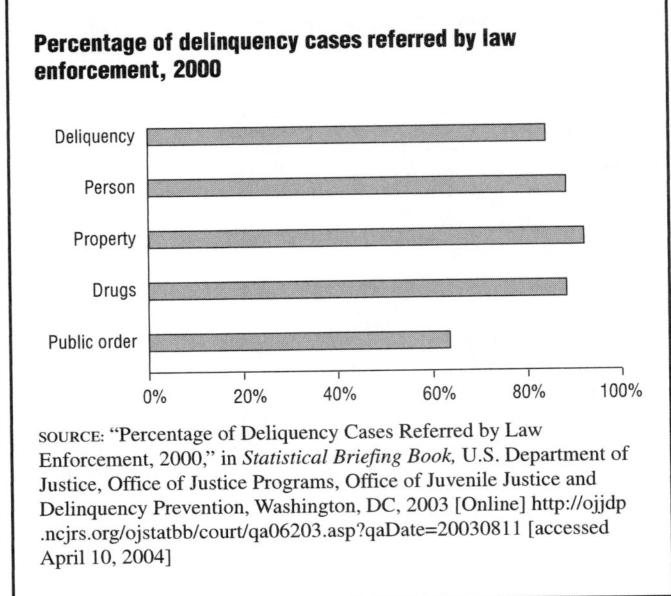

SOURCE: "Percentage of Deliquency Cases Referred by Law Enforcement, 2000," in *Statistical Briefing Book,* U.S. Department of Justice, Office of Justice Programs, Office of Juvenile Justice and Delinquency Prevention, Washington, DC, 2003 [Online] http://ojjdp.ncjrs.org/ojstatbb/court/qa06203.asp?qaDate=20030811 [accessed April 10, 2004]

FIGURE 5.22

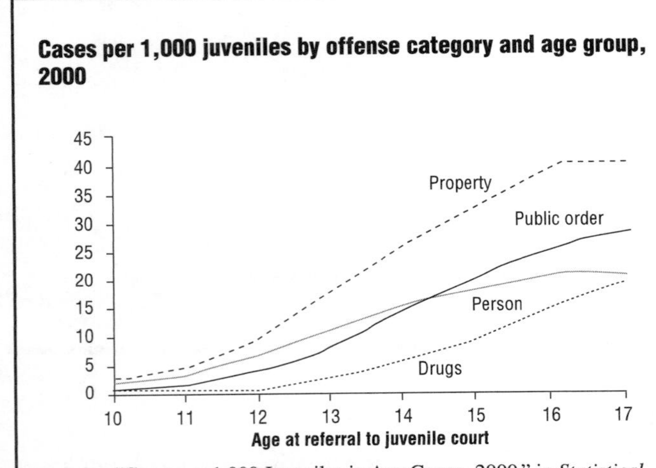

SOURCE: "Cases per 1,000 Juveniles in Age Group, 2000," in *Statistical Briefing Book,* U.S. Department of Justice, Office of Justice Programs, Office of Juvenile Justice and Delinquency Prevention, Washington, DC, 2003 [Online] http://ojjdp.ncjrs.org/ojstatbb/court/qa06202.asp?qaDate=20030811 [accessed April 10, 2004]

age of 15 made up two-thirds of all the runaway cases during the same period. Truancy was most common among 15-year-olds (30 percent of the cases), as were runaway cases (28 percent), and ungovernability cases (25 percent).

Between 1990 and 1999 females accounted for a larger proportion of petitioned status offense cases than in delinquency cases. The offense profiles of male and female status offense cases reflect the relatively high male involvement in liquor law violations (70 percent) and the higher female involvement in runaway cases (61 percent). Males accounted for 55 percent of all ungovernability cases and 54 percent of all truancy cases.

Between 1990 and 1999 white youths were held in 74 percent of runaway, 71 percent of truancy, and 72 percent of ungovernability cases, and in 90 percent of all status liquor law violation cases. Compared with their representation in the general population, white youths were overrepresented in liquor law violation cases and under-represented in the other three categories. Blacks accounted for 22 percent of runaway, 25 percent of truancy, and 26 percent of ungovernability cases. (Nearly all youth of Hispanic ethnicity are included in the white racial category.)

Detention and Case Processing

The handling of status crimes has changed considerably since the mid-1980s. The Juvenile Justice and Delinquency Prevention Act of 1974 (PL 93-415) offered substantial federal funds to states that tried to reduce the detention of status offenders. The primary responsibility for status offenders was often transferred from the juvenile courts to child welfare agencies. As a result, the character of the juvenile courts' activities changed.

Prior to this change many juvenile detention centers contained a substantial number of young people whose only "crime" was that their parents could no longer control them. By not routinely institutionalizing these adolescents, the courts demonstrated that the youths were seen as deserving the same rights as adults. A logical extension of this has been that children accused of violent crimes are also now being treated legally as if they were adults.

Those involved in petitioned status offense cases are rarely held in detention. From 1990 to 1999 only 12 percent of runaway cases were detained, 2 percent of truancy cases, and 7 percent of ungovernability and liquor law cases, respectively. Males were more often detained than were

TABLE 5.5

Juvenile court processing of a typical 1,000 delinquency cases, 2000

Total delinquency
1,633,300 estimated cases

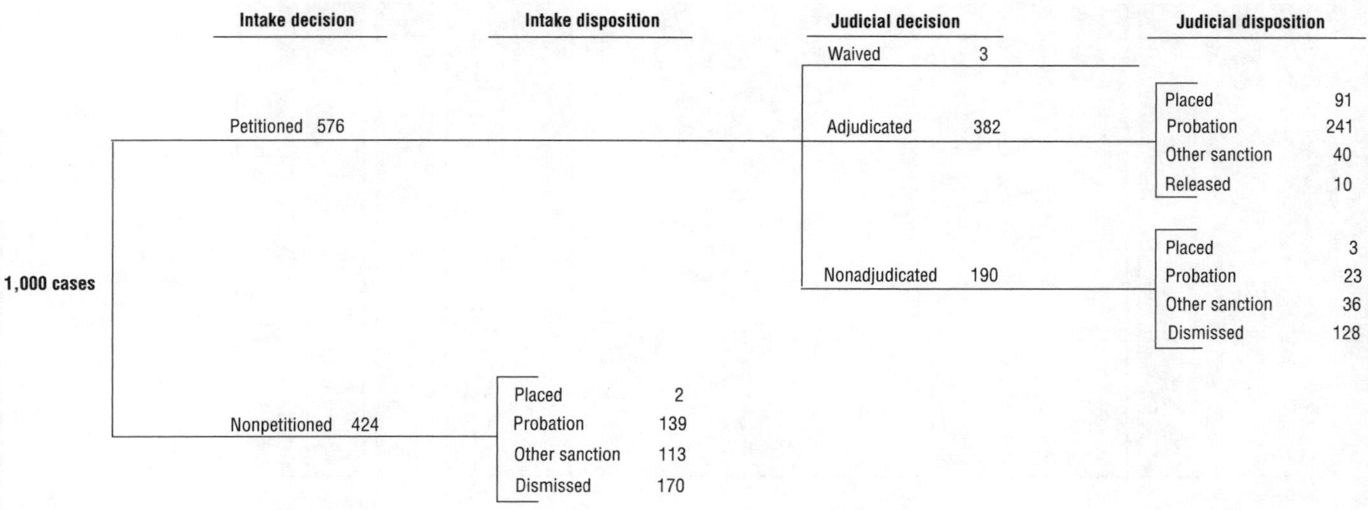

Detail may not add to total because of rounding.

SOURCE: "Juvenile Court Processing for a Typical 1,000 Delinquency Cases, 2000," in *Statistical Briefing Book,* U.S. Department of Justice, Office of Justice Programs, Office of Juvenile Justice and Delinquency Prevention, Washington, DC, 2003 [Online] http://ojjdp.ncjrs.org/ojstatbb/court/JCSCF_Display.asp [accessed April 10, 2004]

females. Males composed 60 percent of runaway, 54 percent of truancy, 55 percent of ungovernability, and 57 percent of liquor law cases held for detention. Whites made up 65 percent of all runaway cases held for detention, 71 percent of truancy cases, 72 percent of ungovernability cases, and 69 percent of liquor law cases held for detention.

According to the Office of Juvenile Justice and Delinquency Prevention, over half of the petitioned status offense cases from 1990 to 1999 resulted in adjudication (ruling in a court). For whites 47 percent of runaway, 60 percent of truancy, 62 percent of ungovernability, and 58 percent of liquor law cases were adjudicated. For blacks the numbers were similar: 44 percent of runaway, 63 percent of truancy, 60 percent of ungovernability, and 50 percent of liquor law cases resulted in adjudication. Males were more likely to receive adjudication in liquor law cases (60 percent) than were females (55 percent). For all groups runaway cases were least likely to result in adjudication. Of the cases adjudicated, 57 percent of runaway cases received probation, 78 percent of truancy cases, 65 percent of ungovernability cases, and 58 percent of liquor law cases. Other dispositions include placement outside of their homes, such as in a detention home or boot camp, and other sanctions, such as restitution or community service.

HOLDING PARENTS RESPONSIBLE

For many decades, civil liability laws held parents at least partly responsible for damages caused by their children. Also, child welfare law included actions against those who contributed to the delinquency of a minor. By the 1990s, in response to rising juvenile crime rates, communities and states passed stronger laws about parental responsibility. Several states have enacted laws making parents criminally responsible for their children's crimes.

For example, in California, parents can be prosecuted for "gross negligence"—failing to supervise their children adequately. If convicted, they can receive a sentence of up to one year in jail and a $2,500 fine. A Louisiana law allows parents to be fined up to $1,000 and imprisoned for up to six months if found guilty of "improper supervision of a minor" (for example, the child is associating with drug dealers, members of a street gang, or convicted felons).

In 1995 Judge Wayne Creech of Family Court in Columbia, South Carolina, ordered a 15-year-old girl chained to her mother for one month. The girl had a history of shoplifting and truancy. In May of 1996 a Michigan jury convicted the parents of a 16-year-old of a criminal misdemeanor for failing to control his behavior. The teenager had broken the law more than once, and his parents claimed that he intimidated them to prevent their interference. Nonetheless the judge fined them $100 each and ordered them to pay court costs of $1,000. Critics of this type of parental liability state that victims are just looking for someone to blame and that U.S. law usually holds people responsible for crimes only if they actively participate. They believe that if standard rules of Ameri-

FIGURE 5.23

Trend in the handling of delinquency cases, 1985–2000

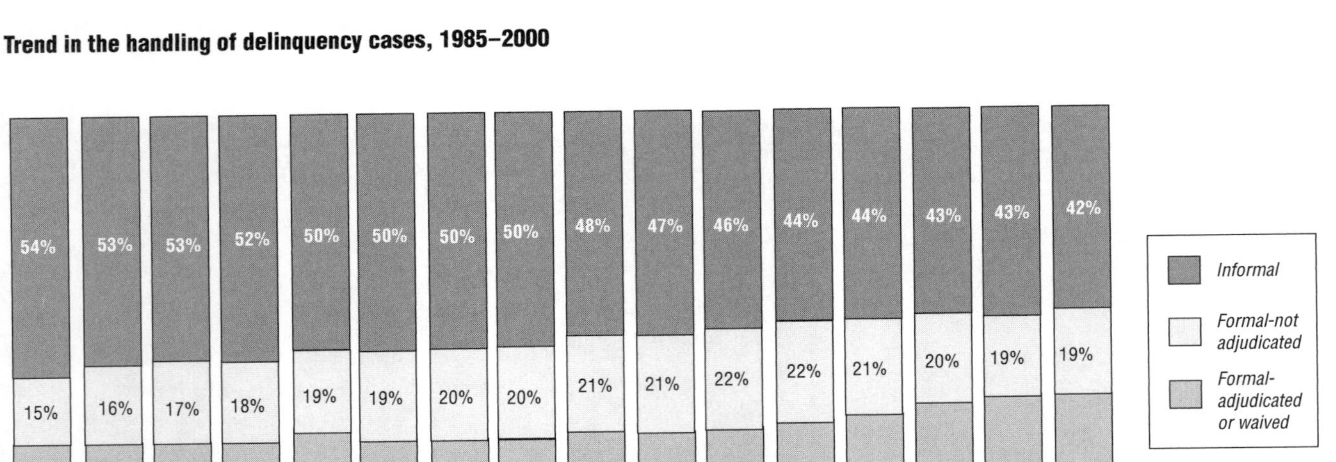

Detail may not total 100% because of rounding

SOURCE: "Manner of Handling Profile for Deliquency Cases, 1985–2000," in *Statistical Briefing Book,* U.S. Department of Justice, Office of Justice Programs, Office of Juvenile Justice and Delinquency Prevention, Washington, DC, 2003 [Online] http://ojjdp.ncjrs.org/ojstatbb/court/qa06402.asp?qaDate=20030811 [accessed April 10, 2004]

can law are practiced, the prosecutor of a case should have to prove that the parents intended to participate in a crime in order to be found guilty.

Many states require that parents pay for costs or program fees related to juvenile courts or corrections. For example, Idaho, Indiana, and New Hampshire passed laws in 1995 making parents pay for the care of their children confined in juvenile facilities. In Alaska, Arizona, Idaho, New Hampshire, North Dakota, and Virginia, parents are responsible for victim restitution. Some states, such as Rhode Island and Texas, require parents to participate with their children in counseling or education programs and at adjudicatory (court) hearings. Based on preliminary findings, involvement of parents in their child's case processing can be effective in deterring repeat offenses.

CURFEWS

Curfews for young people have existed off and on since the 1890s, when curfews were enacted to curb crime among immigrant youths. States and cities tend to pass curfew ordinances when citizens perceive a need to maintain more control over juveniles. Because of the rising juvenile crime rates in the late 1980s and early 1990s, more than 1,000 jurisdictions across the United States imposed youth curfews. Most curfew laws restrict juveniles to their homes or property between the hours of 11 P.M. and 6 A.M. weekdays, allowing them to stay out later on weekends. The laws allow exceptions for young people going to and from school, church events, or work and for those who have a family emergency or are accompanied by their parents.

Critics of curfew ordinances argue that they violate the constitutional rights of children and parents. First, Fourth, Ninth, and Fourteenth Amendment rights, they argue, are endangered by curfew laws—especially the rights of free speech and association, privacy, and equal protection. The critics also argue that no studies have proven the effectiveness of curfew laws. In 1994 the Supreme Court let stand a lower court ruling (*Qutb v. Bartlett,* F.3rd 488, 62 LW 2343, Rev. 1994) that a Dallas, Texas, curfew law was constitutional.

Are Curfews Successful in Reducing Crime?

Although no statistical studies have concentrated on the effectiveness of curfews, many cities reported declines in juvenile crime and victimization after establishing curfews. John Pionke, a U.S. Conference of Mayors researcher, noted in 1997 that a number of cities showed a 30 to 50 percent decline in juvenile crime over a period of a year after instituting curfews. The Dallas Police Department recorded an 18 percent decline in juvenile victimization and a 15 percent decline in juvenile arrests during curfew hours. New Orleans, Louisiana and Long Beach, California also reported significant decreases. However,

FIGURE 5.24

Adjudicated delinquency cases by disposition, 1985–2000

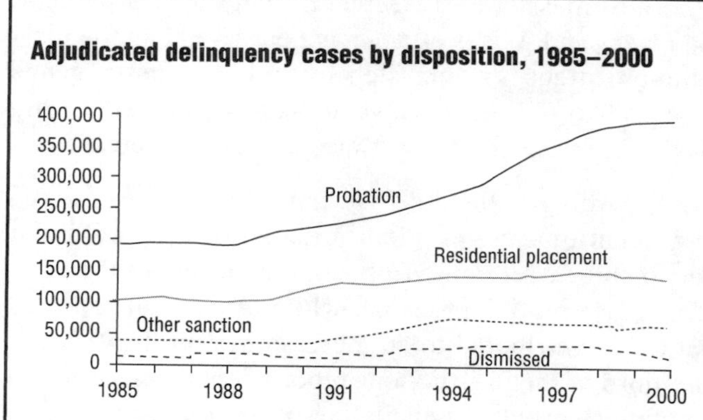

Note: Cases are categorized according to their most severe disposition.

SOURCE: "Adjudicated Delinquency Cases by Disposition, 1985–2000," in *Statistical Briefing Book,* U.S. Department of Justice, Office of Justice Programs, Office of Juvenile Justice and Delinquency Prevention, Washington, DC, 2003 [Online] http://ojjdp.ncjrs.org/ojstatbb/court/qa06501.asp?qaDate=20030811 [accessed April 10, 2004]

Long Beach and several other cities found that, to some extent, the crime rates had been "displaced"—that is, more juvenile crime was occurring in the non-curfew hours. Some observers argue that reduction figures are politically motivated by city officials to justify the curfew and that more studies of the information are needed.

To be successful, curfews need sustained enforcement and community support and involvement. Other factors for success include creating recreational, educational, and job opportunities for juveniles, building anti-drug and anti-gang programs, and providing hotlines for community questions or problems.

YOUTH GANGS

Although gangs have been a part of American life since the early eighteenth century, modern street gangs pose a greater threat to public safety and order than ever before. Many gangs originated as social clubs. In the early twentieth century, most street gangs were small groups who engaged in delinquent acts or minor crimes, such as fighting with other gangs. By the late twentieth century, however, they were frequently involved in violence, intimidation, and the illegal trafficking of drugs and weapons. An increasing number supported themselves by the sale of crack cocaine, heroin, and other illegal drugs, and had easy access to high-powered guns and rifles.

What Is a Gang?

A gang can be defined as a group of persons with a unique name and identifiable marks or symbols who claim a territory or turf, associate on a regular basis, and often engage in criminal or antisocial behavior. For gangs whose primary activities include violence and drugs, the FBI uses the term "violent street gang/drug enterprise." These gangs are, in fact, organized criminal conspiracies and can be prosecuted under the federal organized crime statutes. The National Youth Gang Center (NYGC) defines a "youth gang" as a group of youths, ages 10 to 22, who can be classified by local law enforcement agencies as a gang. Law enforcement officials prefer the term "street gang" because it includes both adults and juveniles and indicates where the majority of the gang's activities take place.

The Growth of Youth Gangs

According to the Office of Juvenile Justice and Delinquency Prevention, during the 1970s about 1 percent of all U.S. cities reported having youth gang problems. Cities reporting these problems were referred to as gang cities. By 2001, some 3,000 jurisdictions across the U.S. reported gang activities. The biggest growth in gang cities occurred during the 1980s and 1990s, when gangs increased in numbers by 281 percent. Between 1995 and 1998, gang activity was reported in some 1,550 cities and 450 counties where it had previously gone unreported. In 2001 youth gangs were active in 100 percent of cities with populations of 250,000 or more, 85 percent of cities with a population between 100,000 and 249,999, 65 percent of cities with a population between 50,000 and 99,999; 44 percent of cities with a population between 25,000 and 49,999, and 35 percent of suburban counties.

The National Youth Gang Survey

Since 1996, the National Youth Gang Center has conducted the *National Youth Gang Survey* (NYGS), an annual survey of all police and sheriff's departments serving cities and counties with populations of 25,000 or greater. In addition, the NYGS surveys a random sampling of law enforcement agencies serving rural localities with populations between 2,500 and 25,000. Respondents are asked to report information about youth gangs in their jurisdiction, excluding motorcycle gangs, hate or ideology-based groups, prison gangs and adult gangs.

Over 24,000 gangs were active in the United States in 2001. Although this represents an overall decline of 5 percent from 1999 levels, 42 percent of cities with populations of over 25,000 reported an increase in the number of gang members. Ninety-five percent of cities reporting gang activity in 2001 also reported gang activity in previous survey years. Over 90 percent of gang members are male, although some youth gangs were reported to have female members. The racial and ethnic composition of gangs changed little over the period of 1996 to 2000, with survey respondents reporting that 47 percent of gang members were Hispanic, 31 percent were black, 13 percent were white, and 7 percent were Asian.

GANGS AND VIOLENT CRIME. At least one gang-related homicide from 1999 to 2000 was reported in 91 percent of cities with populations over 250,000, 64 percent of cities with populations between 100,000 and 200,000, 55 percent of cities with populations between 50,000 and 100,000, and 32 percent of cities with between 25,000 and 50,000 residents. Los Angeles and Chicago accounted for a total of 698 gang-related murders in 2001. This number is more than the total of 637 gang-related murders reported in 130 other cities with a population of 100,000 or more. Fifty-nine percent of all Los Angeles murders and 53 percent of all Chicago murders are gang-related.

Types of Gangs and Activities

The 1995 National Assessment of Gangs study asked prosecutors to indicate the types of gangs operating within their jurisdiction. The study also asked whether or not members of those gangs were involved in drugs or in committing violent crimes. For gangs identified as drug traffickers, the study asked what types of drugs were involved.

Among respondents reporting gang problems, most jurisdictions reported the presence of local black gangs. These gangs originated in that jurisdiction, rather than migrating from California (Crips or Bloods). The second most-prevalent gang types in large jurisdictions were Hispanic gangs, followed closely by motorcycle gangs.

In large jurisdictions 50 percent of prosecutors reported the presence of Crips and Bloods, with 90 percent involved in violent crimes and 92 percent involved in drug trafficking. The survey data did not reveal whether local Crips and Bloods had any continuing connection with the Los Angeles gangs. Studies indicate that the names and colors often persist long after dropping any real Los Angeles connection. Caribbean-based gangs were virtually always reportedly involved in drug trafficking. These gangs dealt mainly in cocaine (more than 96 percent).

Asian gangs were more frequently reported to be involved in violent crimes than in drug trafficking. Prosecutors reported the presence of Asian gangs in 52 percent of large jurisdictions but in only 14 percent of small jurisdictions.

Since the early 1990s youth gangs have begun to appear in Native American communities. The National Youth Gang Center published the *2000 Survey of Youth Gangs in Indian Country* in 2000. The survey defined an Indian community as being composed of American Indian, Alaska Native, or Aleut persons who live within an Indian reservation, pueblo, rancheria, or village and who comprise a federally recognized tribe or community. Some 300 federally recognized tribal communities participated in the survey. Twenty-three percent of Indian communities reported youth gang activity during 2000. Most reported that their youth gang problem first began in the early 1990s. The survey showed that 80 percent of gang members were male. Seventy-eight percent were either American Indian, Alaska Native, or Aleut, with Hispanic/Latinos making up 12 percent, Caucasians 7 percent, and blacks and Asians at 2 percent each. Among the most common offenses committed by Indian country gangs were graffiti (47 percent), vandalism (40 percent), drug sales (22 percent), and aggravated assault (15 percent).

According to the *2001 National Youth Gang Survey* 63 percent of gang-problem jurisdictions reported that gang members returning from confinement contributed to an increase in violent crime, while 68 percent reported that they contributed to an increase in drug-trafficking. One-third of the jurisdictions reported that there were no community programs available to assist gang members returning from confinement, while 35 percent could not provide information regarding such programs.

Two Studies of Big City Gangs

Two 1995 studies, one funded by the National Institute of Justice (NIJ) and one by the OJJDP, interviewed 50 gang members in each of four communities: Aurora, Colorado; Denver, Colorado; Broward County, Florida; and Cleveland, Ohio. As a control group, 50 youths in each area from the at-risk population who were not gang members were also interviewed. The results of the one-time, confidential interviews showed that gang members were significantly more involved in crime than nonmembers.

According to Dr. C. Ronald Huff (Ohio State University), the principal investigator in the NIJ study, 58 percent of the Colorado and Florida gang members and 45 percent of the Cleveland gang members said they had personally stolen cars. In comparison, control group youths reported much lower car thefts (Colorado and Florida, 12.5 percent; Cleveland, 4 percent). Forty percent of the Cleveland gang members reported participating in a drive-by shooting, compared to only 2 percent of the control group. About 64 percent of the Colorado and Florida gang members stated that members of their gangs had committed homicide, while only 6.5 percent of nonmembers said that their friends had killed someone.

Gang members were also much more likely than nonmembers to own guns. More than 90 percent of gang members in the study communities reported that their peers had carried concealed weapons; more than 80 percent stated that members had taken guns to school. Of the control groups, about half said friends had carried a concealed weapon, and one-third reported friends had taken guns to school.

Gang members were more involved than at-risk nonmembers in drug trafficking. More than 70 percent of gang members reported selling drugs, while only 6 to 9 percent of youths in the control groups said they had sold drugs.

Young Juveniles

In "Early Precursors of Gang Membership: A Study of Seattle Youth" (*Juvenile Justice Bulletin*, Office of

Juvenile Justice and Delinquency Prevention, December 2001), Karl G. Hill, Christina Lui, and J. David Hawkins reported on the results of a study in Seattle, Washington, in which fifth-graders were tracked through the age of 18. Of 808 study participants, 124 joined a gang between the ages of 13 and 18. About 69 percent of those belonged to a gang for less than one year, and less than 1 percent of study participants who joined a gang at age 13 were still in a gang at 18 years of age.

According the report, study participants who remained in the gang for several years "were the most behaviorally and socially maladjusted children," often exhibiting "early signs of violent externalizing such as aggression and hyperactivity." Also, study participants who associated with antisocial peers were more than twice as likely to remain in a gang for more than one year. Among the risk factors identified as contributing to gang involvement were learning disabilities, availability of marijuana, low academic achievement, other neighborhood youth in trouble, and youths living with one parent along with other unrelated adults.

JUVENILES AND GUNS

Schools and neighborhoods can be dangerous places for many young Americans. Knives, revolvers, and even shotguns turn up in searches of school lockers. News reports describe incidents of children being shot on playgrounds or of youths firing rifles as they cruise the streets in cars. The use of deadly weapons in violent incidents has increased fear among citizens of all ages.

According to Stuart Greenbaum, a public safety specialist, guns had become readily available to juveniles by the 1980s. In fact, Greenbaum believes that guns are the weapons of choice for youth ("Kids and Guns: From Playgrounds to Battlegrounds," *Juvenile Justice*, vol. 3, no. 2, September 1997). The juvenile arrest rate for weapons law violations increased over 100 percent between 1987 and 1993. Between 1993 and 2001, that rate fell by 49 percent, returning to approximately the same level as in 1987. (See Figure 5.25.)

FIGURE 5.25

Juvenile arrest rates for weapons law violations, 1980–2001

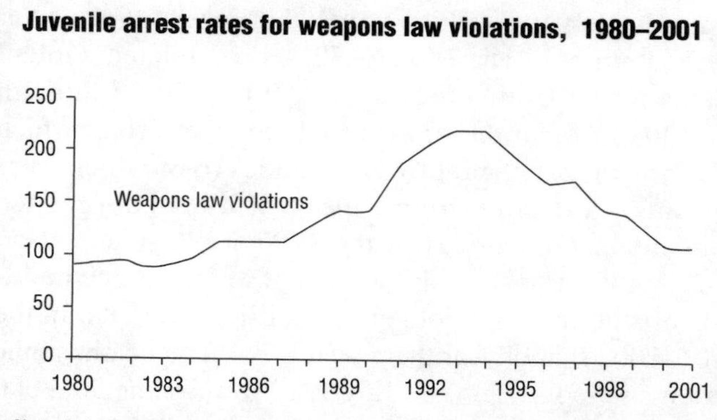

Note: Rates are arrests of persons ages 10–17 per 100,000 persons ages 10–17 in the resident population.

SOURCE: "Juvenile Arrest Rates for Weapons Law Violations, 1980–2001," in *Statistical Briefing Book*, U.S. Department of Justice, Office of Justice Programs, Office of Juvenile Justice and Delinquency Prevention, Washington, DC, 2003 [Online] http://ojjdp.ncjrs.org/ojstatbb/crime/JAR_Display.asp?ID=qa0521320030531 [accessed April 10, 2004]

From 1983 to 1994 gun homicides by juveniles tripled while homicides involving other types of weapons decreased. From 1993 to 2001, however, homicides by youth declined by 70 percent, primarily those involving firearms. Gun suicides also increased in the 1980s and early 1990s. From 1980 to 1994 the suicide rate for persons ages 15 to 19 grew 29 percent; firearms-related suicides accounted for 96 percent of the increase. The risk of suicide is estimated to be five times greater in households where guns are present. Beginning in 1995, the number of firearm-related suicides for persons 19 years of age or younger gradually declined, from 1,450 to 1,078 in 1999. Still, due to the overall decline in all firearm-related deaths during those years (from 5,285 to 3,385), the percentage of firearm-related suicides for persons under 19 rose from 27 percent of all firearm-related deaths in 1995 to 33 percent in 1998, then dropped off slightly to 32 percent in 1999.

According to the U.S. Bureau of Alcohol, Tobacco, and Firearms (ATF), juveniles and youth are more likely than adults to use handguns and semiautomatic weapons in crimes. In 1996 the ATF began the Youth Crime Gun Interdiction, a pilot program in 17 cities throughout the nation aimed at reducing youth violence involving firearms. The cities in the program send information on all "crime guns" to the ATF's National Tracing Center.

In 1997 the ATF announced that four of ten handguns confiscated by law enforcement officers during 1996 were collected from persons ages 24 and under. Handguns accounted for 80 percent of the firearms taken from youths and juveniles, compared to 70 percent of guns taken from adults. Six of ten of the handguns confiscated from youths and juveniles were semiautomatic pistols. Most of the guns involved in youth crimes had been obtained from illegal firearms traffickers. About 25 percent of the crime guns wound up in illegal firearms sellers' hands, often as a result of household burglary, within three years of the guns' original legitimate sale through retail channels. This "fast time to crime" indicated the ease with which a criminal can fence a stolen gun, and the pervasiveness of the illegal firearms market.

SCHOOL CRIME

As reported in *Indicators of School Crime and Safety 2003* (jointly published by the Bureau of Justice Statistics and the National Center for Education Statistics, 2004), in 2001 students 12 to 18 years of age were the victims of approximately two million nonfatal crimes of violence or theft at school. There were 32 school-related violent deaths in the United States from July 1, 1999 through June 30, 2000. Of those, 24 were homicides (16 of which were students) and eight were suicides (6 of which were students), a decline from a peak of 49 school-related homicides and suicides in the 1995–1996 school year. This number translates into a rate of less than one homicide or suicide at school per one million students. In the 2001–2002 school year there were 17 violent deaths in the nation's schools. Between July 1, 1992 and June 30, 2000 there were 390 school-associated violent deaths in elementary and secondary schools. Of this number 234 were homicides and 43 were suicides of school-aged youth. During this same period some 24,000 youths aged five to 19 years old were victims of homicide and over 16,000 committed suicide away from school. In each of the years surveyed, students were 70 times more likely to be the victim of a homicide away from school than at school.

Despite the relative safety of schools, in the five years between 1997 and 2002, several school shootings received national media attention.

- March 5, 2001: Two were killed and 13 wounded at Santee High School in Santana, California when a student opened fire from a school bathroom.
- February 29, 2000: A six-year-old student was killed at Theo J. Buell Elementary School near Flint, Michigan, by a fellow student (also six years old) who brought a handgun to school.
- April 20, 1999: Twelve students and a teacher were fatally shot at Columbine High School in Littleton, Colorado, by students Eric Harris, 18, and Dylan Klebold, 17, who eventually killed themselves after their hour-long rampage.
- May 21, 1998: Two students were killed and 25 were wounded at Thurston High School in Springfield, Oregon, by student Kip Kinkel, who also murdered his parents.
- December 1, 1997: Three students were killed and five were wounded as they participated in a prayer circle at Heath High School in West Paducah, Kentucky.
- October 1, 1997: Two students were killed and seven were wounded by student Luke Woodham, 16, who had earlier killed his mother.

According to the *Youth Risk Behavior Surveillance—United States, 2001* (Centers for Disease Control and Prevention, 2002), a self-report survey of high school students, 5.7 percent of students reported carrying a gun on at least one day in the thirty days prior to the survey. Overall, male students were significantly more likely than females to carry a gun (10.3 percent compared with 1.3 percent). A total of 17.4 percent of students nationwide reported carrying some type of weapon, such as a gun, knife or club, on at least one day prior to the survey. In 2001, 29.3 percent of males and 6.2 percent of females reported carrying a weapon on school property. Black female students (8.6 percent) were more likely than white female students (5.1 percent) to have carried a weapon in school, while white male students (31.3 percent) were more likely than black male students (22.4 percent) to have carried a weapon in school.

The percentage of secondary school students who reported feeling unsafe at school decreased from 1995 to 1999, with the percentage between 1999 and 2001 remaining unchanged, according to *Indicators of School Crime and Safety: 2003*. The percentage of all secondary school students who reported carrying a weapon dropped from 12 percent in 1993 to just 6 percent in 2001. In 2001 5 percent of secondary school students reported avoiding one or more places at school, a decrease from 9 percent in 1995. Twelve percent reported that in the previous six months, someone at school had used a derogatory word against them related to their race, religion, ethnicity, gender, or sexual orientation. Some 36 percent reported seeing hate-related graffiti at school.

Nonfatal School Crimes

In 2001 some 161,000 students ages 12 to 18 were victims of nonfatal serious violent crimes (rape, sexual assault, robbery, and aggravated assault). When simple assault was factored in, the number of school-related victimizations increased significantly, to about 764,000 in 2001. The violent victimization rate for students at school was 28 crimes per 1,000 students in 2001, a drop from 71 crimes per 1,000 students in 1992.

There were no significant differences in the rates of victimization for students at urban and suburban schools in 2001, although students in urban schools were more likely than suburban students to be victimized away from school. Students between the ages of 12 and 14 were more likely to be victims of school-related crime than were older students 15 through 18 years of age. Older students were more likely to be victimized away from school than were younger students.

Crimes against Teachers

Teachers are also subject to violence in the schools, either committed by students or by those from outside the school. Some 1.3 million nonfatal crimes at school between 1997 and 2001 were committed against teachers. About one-fourth of those (473,000) were violent crimes, including rape, sexual assault, robbery, and aggravated or simple assault. Thefts accounted for the remaining

817,000 nonfatal crimes against teachers. During this period there were about 48,000 serious violent crimes (about 10 percent of the violent crimes reported), resulting in a rate of victimization of 21 violent crimes per 1,000 teachers, and two serious violent crimes per 1,000 teachers.

Senior and junior high school teachers were more likely to be victimized by violent crimes (usually simple assault) and experienced a higher incidence of theft than elementary school teachers. Male teachers were victimized at a rate of 39 violent crimes per 1,000 teachers, compared to a rate of 16 for female teachers. Teachers in urban schools were victimized at a rate of 28 violent crimes per 1,000 teachers, compared to a rate of 16 in suburban schools and 13 in rural areas. Teachers in urban areas were also more likely to be victims of theft (42 thefts per 1,000 teachers) than were those in rural areas (26 thefts per 1,000 teachers).

JUVENILES IN CUSTODY

According to the *Census of Juveniles in Residential Placement Databook* (U.S. Department of Justice, Office of Juvenile and Delinquency Prevention, 2002), on October 27, 1999, some 108,931 juveniles were confined in residential custody facilities in the United States. Residential placements include both public and private detention, correctional, and shelter facilities. Of the 104,237 delinquents (criminal offenders) in residential placement on that date, 31,817 had been involved in property offenses, 38,005 in violent offenses, and 9,882 in drug offenses. There were also 4,694 status offenders in residential placement.

CHAPTER 6
SENTENCING AND CORRECTIONS

SENTENCING AND TIME SERVED

In 2000 state and federal courts convicted some 984,000 adults of felonies, according to the Bureau of Justice Statistics (BJS). Of those, 924,700 were adults convicted in state courts and 59,123 were convicted in federal jurisdictions. Some 68 percent of convicted felons were sentenced to a period of incarceration in 2000. Of those, 40 percent went to state prisons and 28 percent to local jails. Those in jails were usually confined for less than one year.

In 2000 the average felony sentence imposed by state courts was 36 months in prison. On average, violent offenders served the most time (66 months), compared to averages of 27 months for property offenses, 30 months for drug offenses, and 25 months for weapons offenses. (See Table 6.1.)

TABLE 6.1

Length of felony sentences imposed by state courts, 2000

Most serious conviction offense	Average maximum sentence length (in months) for felons sentenced to:			
	Incarceration			
	Total	Prison	Jail	Probation
All offenses	36 mo	55 mo	6 mo	38 mo
Violent offenses	66 mo	91 mo	7 mo	44 mo
Property offenses	27 mo	42 mo	6 mo	38 mo
Drug offenses	30 mo	47 mo	6 mo	36 mo
Weapons offenses	25 mo	38 mo	7 mo	36 mo
Other offenses	22 mo	38 mo	6 mo	40 mo

Note: Means exclude sentences to death or to life in prison. Sentence length data were available for 852,616 incarceration and probation sentences.

SOURCE: "Lengths of Felony Sentences Imposed by State Courts, 2000," in "Criminal Sentencing Statistics," U.S. Department of Justice, Bureau of Justice Statistics, Washington, DC, December 10, 2003 [Online] http://www.ojp.usdoj.gov/bjs/sent.htm [accessed March 8, 2004]

The length of a prison sentence was almost always longer than the time actually served by a convicted felon in 2000. In state prisons, the actual time served was about 55 percent of the overall sentence. Most states (but not the federal system) have parole boards that determine when a prisoner will be paroled (released from prison). In the federal system and in most states, prisoners can earn time credits for good behavior ("good time") to shorten their time in prison.

"Three Strikes" Laws

As of 2004, 26 states and the federal government had "Three Strikes" laws, which require repeat criminals to serve enhanced prison terms if they are convicted of three violent felonies. Most of these laws were enacted during the 1990s in response to a significant rise in crime, particularly violent crime, during the first half of the decade. The consequence of these laws was a rise in the prison population, along with its attendant costs.

Opponents of Three Strikes laws argue that the laws demand even more prisons to house prisoners for longer periods. Also, reducing the possibility of parole results in more and more elderly prisoners, who are statistically much less likely to commit crimes than younger prisoners, and who have increasing health-care needs. By the year 2000 many states that had passed Three Strikes laws were wondering how to pay for more prisons and longer incarcerations.

Since 2000 several states have loosened their mandatory minimum sentencing laws or taken other measures to reduce their prison populations. For example, in 2001 Mississippi adopted an early-release provision for nonviolent offenders, and states such as California, Texas, North Carolina, Connecticut, Idaho, and Arkansas have passed legislation mandating the diversion of nonviolent drug offenders to community-based treatment programs.

On April 1, 2002, the United States Supreme Court agreed to consider whether California's Three Strikes law,

FIGURE 6.1

Capital punishment: Persons executed, 1930–2002

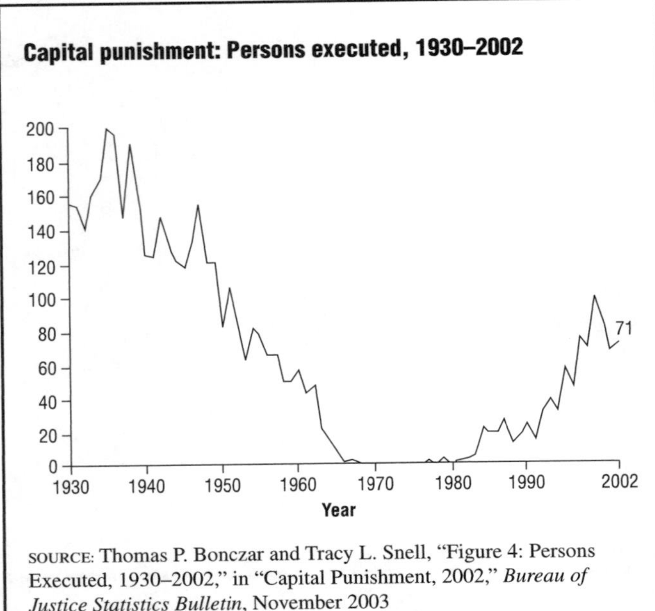

SOURCE: Thomas P. Bonczar and Tracy L. Snell, "Figure 4: Persons Executed, 1930–2002," in "Capital Punishment, 2002," *Bureau of Justice Statistics Bulletin*, November 2003

FIGURE 6.2

Persons under death sentence, 1953–2002

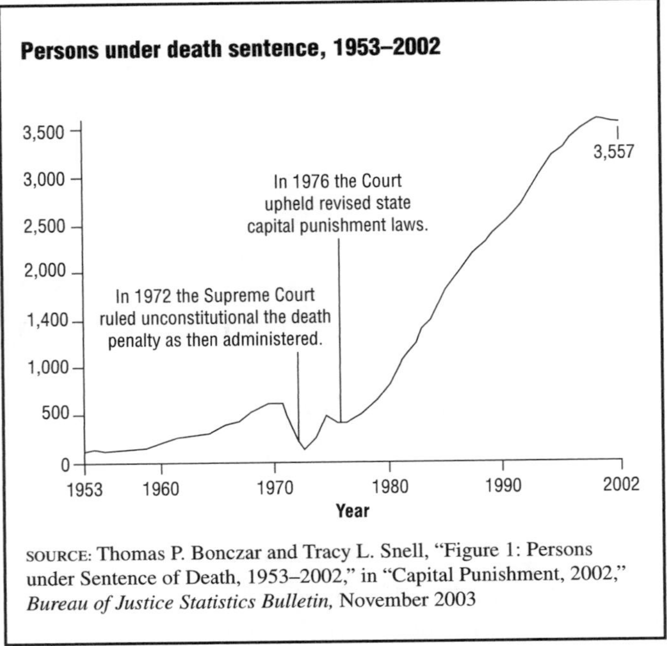

SOURCE: Thomas P. Bonczar and Tracy L. Snell, "Figure 1: Persons under Sentence of Death, 1953–2002," in "Capital Punishment, 2002," *Bureau of Justice Statistics Bulletin*, November 2003

considered to be one of the toughest in the country, violates the Eighth Amendment's ban against cruel and unusual punishment. Over half (57 percent) of California prisoners sentenced under the Three Strikes law were convicted of nonviolent third-strike felonies, including drug possession and petty theft, and are serving mandatory sentences of 25 years to life without the possibility of parole. In March 2003 the Supreme Court, in a five–four decision, upheld the right of states to impose lengthy sentences on repeat felony offenders, regardless of the relative seriousness of the "third-strike" felony.

THE DEATH PENALTY

Executions in the United States had been dropping for decades since their height of some 200 a year in the late 1930s. By the 1960s capital punishment was seldom used at all. (See Figure 6.1.) In 1972 the U.S. Supreme Court ruled the death penalty unconstitutional as it was then administered by the states. But in 1976 the Court approved revised capital punishment laws. Since that time, the number of persons under sentence of death has risen from less than 500 to over 3,500. (See Figure 6.2.)

Thirty-eight states and the federal government had laws sanctioning the death penalty in 2004. Of those, 37 states and the federal government allowed the use of lethal injection, and one state (Nebraska) required electrocution as the means of execution. The states that authorized the death penalty by lethal injection were: Alabama, Arizona, Arkansas, California, Colorado, Connecticut, Delaware, Florida, Georgia, Idaho, Illinois, Indiana, Kansas, Kentucky, Louisiana, Maryland, Mississippi, Missouri, Montana, Nevada, New Hampshire, New Jersey, New Mexico, New York, North Carolina, Ohio, Oklahoma, Oregon, Pennsylvania, South Carolina, South Dakota, Tennessee, Texas, Utah, Virginia, Washington, and Wyoming. Although New York law authorizes the use of lethal injection, in June 2004 the state's highest court ruled that the state's sentencing laws were unconstitutional and instructed the state legislature to revise sentencing laws or death penalty sentences in New York would be invalid. In addition to lethal injection, ten states permit the use of electrocution, five states allow the use of the gas chamber, and three states permit the use of a firing squad. New Hampshire and Washington permit hanging as a means of execution. In April 2004, 3,487 inmates were on death row in the United States.

According to the Bureau of Justice Statistics, of the 3,557 prisoners under sentence of death at the end of 2002, 98.6 percent were male and 1.4 percent were female. Slightly more than half (54.2 percent) were white, 43.6 percent were African-American, and 2.2 percent of prisoners under death sentence were of other races, including 27 who were self-identified as American Indian and 33 who identified themselves as Asian. Over half of death row inmates (51.8 percent) had dropped out of school by the 11th grade, while 38.5 percent were high school graduates or had completed the GED equivalency, and 9.7 percent had attended college. Some 54.3 percent of death row prisoners had never married, compared to 22.1 percent who were married and 20.8 percent who were divorced or separated. (See Table 6.2.) In 2002, 71 people (69 men and two women) were executed in the United States. Of those, 53 were white and 18 were African-American. Lethal injection was used in 70 of the executions in 2002, while electrocution was used in one execution.

TABLE 6.2

Demographic characteristics of prisoners under death sentence, 1953–2002

Characteristic	Prisoners under sentence of death, 2002 Yearend	Admissions	Removals
Total number under sentence of death	**3,557**	**159**	**179**
Gender			
Male	98.6%	96.9%	97.2%
Female	1.4	3.1	2.8
Race			
White	54.3%	52.2%	67.0%
Black	43.7	45.9	31.8
All other races*	2.0	1.9	1.2
Hispanic origin			
Hispanic	11.5%	14.9%	9.5%
Non-Hispanic	88.5	85.1	90.5
Education			
8th grade or less	14.7%	21.4%	14.5%
9th-11th grade	37.1	34.9	36.2
High school graduate/GED	38.5	37.3	36.2
Any college	9.7	6.3	13.1
Median	11th	11th	11th
Marital status			
Married	22.1%	25.8%	23.9%
Divorced/separated	20.8	16.7	22.0
Widowed	2.8	6.8	3.1
Never married	54.3	50.7	50.9

Note: Calculations are based on those cases for which data were reported. Missing data by category were as follows:

	Yearend	Admissions	Removals
Hispanic origin	399	38	21
Education	511	33	27
Marital status	342	27	20

*At yearend 2001, other races consisted of 27 American Indians, 32 Asians, and 12 self-identified Hispanics. During 2002, 2 Asians and 1 American Indian were admitted; and 1 Asian and 1 American Indian were removed.

SOURCE: Thomas P. Bonczar and Tracy L. Snell, "Table 5: Demographic Characteristics of Prisoners under Sentence of Death, 2002," in "Capital Punishment, 2002," *Bureau of Justice Statistics Bulletin,* November 2003

Most prisoners on death row at the end of 2002 were repeat offenders, with 59.5 percent having prior felony convictions. However, of those, only 7.8 percent had prior homicide convictions. Some 15.6 percent of death row inmates committed their capital offense while on parole, 9.4 percent while on probation, and 6.7 percent while there were other charges pending against them. Fifty-four percent of death row inmates at year end, 2002, reported that they had no pending legal status at the time of their capital offense.

According to "Capital Punishment 2002" by Thomas P. Bonczar and Tracy L. Snell (*Bureau of Justice Statistics Bulletin,* November 2003), between 1977 and 2002 some 6,532 persons were under the sentence of death in the United States. Of those, some 12.5 percent (820) were executed and 38.8 percent either died of natural causes or had their death sentences lifted and received other dispositions. During that time period, 66.3 percent of the 820 executions occurred in five states—Texas (289), Virginia (87), Missouri (59), Oklahoma (55), and Florida (54). In 2002, 33 executions were carried out in Texas, accounting for 46.4 percent of the 71 executions carried out in the United States.

Proponents of the Death Penalty

Some supporters of the death penalty, as a deterrent, look back to 1966 when there was a virtual moratorium on execution at the state level and the murder rate began to increase (by 1980 it was more than twice the 1963 rate). Along with this trend, there was an upswing in the number of felony murders as compared to crimes of passion. By the mid-1990s, when the number of executions had increased, the murder rate dropped again (as it did in the 1930s, when both homicides and executions were at their highest point in national history). Even though the absence of capital punishment does not alone cause murder rates to rise, supporters say, it still plays a major role. Further, they argue, no other punishment can substitute for execution as a deterrent because even life sentences often end early in parole or pardon. Recidivism can occur after release; and innocent victims outnumber prisoners wrongfully executed.

A second reason frequently cited for support of the death penalty is its function as retribution. This satisfies an emotional need for victims' loved ones, meets the demands of certain moral codes, and contributes to a sort of social cohesiveness (by allowing law-abiding persons to band together and show their support of shared values). Those who feel that punishment should be "proportional" argue that nothing less than the murderer's own death fits the crime of homicide.

Death penalty proponents do not believe that execution methods used in civilized nations like the United States are barbaric. They also point to capital punishment's continuation in most of the Western world until the 1950s and the support it has even today in European countries where it has been abolished. They contend that the Eighth Amendment's prohibition against cruel and unusual punishment does not extend to execution and was never intended to be interpreted that way. In *Furman v. Georgia* (1976), the U.S. Supreme Court found only that the death penalty was used fairly. Plus, they add, the American legal system includes an appeals process, which can stretch on for years after the imposition of a death sentence. Out of 453 prisoners on death row in Texas, for example, only 33 were executed in 2002. Advocates for the death penalty further argue that more capital cases are overturned because of judicial error than due to defendants' innocence.

Troubling Questions

Studies done by the Gallup Poll in 2000 show that though the death penalty is still supported by the majority of Americans (66 percent), support has dropped since its peak in 1994 (80 percent). In the same poll, some 91 percent of respondents said they believed that in the past 20 years at least one person sentenced to death was innocent. These opinions probably have something to do with publicity surrounding several death penalty convictions being overturned due to newly obtained DNA evidence. Other issues, such as erroneous eyewitness accounts, false confessions and testimony, and police or prosecutorial misconduct, have called into question the fairness of capital punishment trials and sentencing of death row inmates.

In Oklahoma in 2001 the discovery of the possible false testimony of state witness forensic chemist, Joyce Gilchrist, left dozens of cases in question. In September 2001 the Department of Justice released a study that documented that race and geography play a role in who is sentenced to death, echoing the findings of several other independent studies across the nation. In Texas, lawyers of 43 inmates who received the death penalty were later sanctioned for misconduct or even disbarred, according to the *Chicago Tribune*. According to the American Civil Liberties Union (ACLU), nationally there was a 68 percent rate of serious error in death penalty trials.

Because of questions brought about by these cases, several states that allowed the death penalty imposed moratoriums on executions until studies were completed. In Illinois in 2000 Republican Governor George Ryan declared a moratorium after 13 inmates on death row were found innocent within a few months. He put together a commission to review the state's system and offer suggestions for improvements. In April of 2002, 85 changes, including reducing the number of capital crimes, videotaping police interrogations, forbidding capital punishment in cases where the conviction is based solely on the testimony of a single eyewitness, and increasing competent counsel protections, were recommended by the commission. In January 2003 Governor Ryan commuted the sentences of all death row inmates in Illinois to prison time. In May 2002 Democratic Governor Parris Glendening of Maryland, also declared a moratorium until a study could be completed by the University of Maryland in September 2002, and the state legislature had time to review the results.

According to The Innocence Project, a nonprofit legal clinic at the Benjamin N. Cardozo School of Law, from the reinstatement of the death penalty in 1976, until June 24, 2002, 108 people on death row had been exonerated from the crimes for which they had been sentenced to death. The American Bar Association asked for a moratorium on the death penalty in 1997. In 2001 Senators Russell Feingold (D-WI) and Jesse Jackson Jr. (D-IL), proposed the "National Death Penalty Moratorium Act of 2001" (S. 233), calling for a moratorium on the federal death penalty and a federal independent commission on problems within the system.

The Execution of Mentally Retarded Criminals

On June 20, 2002, the United States Supreme Court ruled in favor of Virginia death row inmate Daryl Renard Atkins, who is mentally retarded, and declared that the execution of mentally retarded individuals is unconstitutional. The court, in a 6–3 vote, held that such executions constituted a violation of the Eighth Amendment's ban against cruel and unusual punishment. Until this ruling, some 20 states allowed the execution of mentally retarded persons who were convicted of capital crimes.

In writing for the majority of the court, Justice John Paul Stevens held, "This consensus unquestionably reflects widespread judgment about the relative culpability of mentally retarded offenders, and the relationship between mental retardation and the penological purpose served by the death penalty.... Their deficiencies do not warrant an exemption from criminal sanctions, but they do diminish their personal culpability."

In their dissent, Chief Justice William Rehnquist and Justices Antonin Scalia and Clarence Thomas expressed the view that the court went too far in its ruling, which effectively opens the door for inmates with IQs of 70 or less to appeal their death sentences.

Juries Must Decide

In 1972 a U.S. Supreme Court ruling about the constitutionality of capital punishment brought the nation's executions to a halt. The court's decision on *Furman v. Georgia* stated that state death penalty statutes lacked standards and gave too much discretion to individual judges and to juries. After states addressed some of the issues troubling the court, including mandatory death sentences for some crimes, the court ruled in 1976, in *Gregg v. Georgia*, that the death penalty was constitutional.

This decision did not address individual states' laws about who determined sentencing for capital offenses. However, on June 24, 2002, the U.S. Supreme Court ruled that juries, not judges, must make the final determination to impose the death penalty in a capital case. The ruling, written by Justice Ruth Bader Ginsburg, held that a sentence imposed by a judge violates a defendant's constitutional right to a trial by jury. Joining Justice Ginsburg were Justices John Paul Stevens, Antonin Scalia, Anthony M. Kennedy, David H. Souter, and Clarence Thomas. Justice Stephen Breyer agreed with the majority in a separate opinion. Justice Sandra Day O'Connor wrote the dissenting opinion and was joined by Chief Justice William H. Rehnquist.

The seven to two ruling, which involved the case of an Arizona death row inmate, overturns at least 150 death penalty sentences (not the guilty verdicts) and could potentially affect over 800 death sentences nationwide. The ruling affects all cases in Arizona, Idaho, and Montana, where a single judge was allowed to decide whether to impose the death penalty. The cases will have to be reconsidered in six other states: Colorado and Nebraska, where panels of judges made sentencing decisions, and Florida,

TABLE 6.3

Prisoners under jurisdiction of state or federal correctional authorities, by region and jurisdiction, year end 2001–02

Region and jurisdiction	Total 12/31/02	Total 06/30/02	Total 12/31/01	Percent change 12/31/01–12/31/02	Percent change 6/30/02–12/31/02
U.S. total	**1,440,655**	**1,423,095**	**1,404,032**	**2.6%**	**1.2%**
Federal	163,528	161,681	156,993	4.2	1.1
State	1,277,127	1,261,414	1,247,039	2.4	1.2
Northeast	175,907	175,118	172,599	1.9%	0.5%
Connecticut[1]	20,720	20,243	19,196	7.9	2.4
Maine	1,900	1,841	1,704	11.5	3.2
Massachusetts	10,329	10,620	10,588	−2.4	−2.7
New Hampshire	2,451	2,476	2,392	2.5	−1.0
New Jersey	27,891	28,054	28,142	−0.9	−0.6
New York	67,065	67,131	67,533	−0.7	−0.1
Pennsylvania	40,168	39,275	38,062	5.5	2.3
Rhode Island[1]	3,520	3,694	3,241	8.6	−4.7
Vermont[1]	1,863	1,784	1,741	7.0	4.4
Midwest	245,303	243,876	240,679	1.9%	0.6%
Illinois	42,693	43,142	44,348	−3.7	−1.0
Indiana	21,611	21,425	20,966	3.1	0.9
Iowa[2]	8,398	8,172	7,962	5.5	2.8
Kansas	8,935	8,758	8,577	4.2	2.0
Michigan	50,591	49,961	48,849	3.6	1.3
Minnesota	7,129	6,958	6,606	7.9	2.5
Missouri	30,099	30,034	28,757	4.7	0.2
Nebraska	4,058	4,031	3,937	3.1	0.7
North Dakota	1,112	1,168	1,111	0.1	−4.8
Ohio	45,646	45,349	45,281	0.8	0.7
South Dakota	2,898	2,900	2,790	3.9	−0.1
Wisconsin	22,133	21,978	21,495	3.0	0.7

TABLE 6.3

Prisoners under jurisdiction of state or federal correctional authorities, by region and jurisdiction, year end 2001–02 [CONTINUED]

Region and jurisdiction	Total 12/31/02	Total 06/30/02	Total 12/31/01	Percent change 12/31/01–12/31/02	Percent change 6/30/02–12/31/02
South	574,174	564,592	560,352	2.5%	1.7%
Alabama	27,947	27,495	26,741	4.5	1.6
Arkansas	13,090	12,655	12,594	3.9	3.4
Delaware[1]	6,778	6,957	7,003	−3.2	−2.6
Florida[2]	75,210	73,553	72,404	3.9	2.3
Georgia[2]	47,445	46,417	45,937	3.3	2.2
Kentucky	15,933	16,172	15,424	3.3	−1.5
Louisiana	35,736	36,171	35,810	−0.2	−1.2
Maryland	24,162	24,329	23,752	1.7	−0.7
Mississippi	22,705	22,001	21,460	5.8	3.2
North Carolina	32,803	32,755	32,253	1.7	0.1
Oklahoma	23,385	23,435	22,780	2.7	−0.2
South Carolina	23,715	23,017	22,576	5.0	3.0
Tennessee	24,989	24,277	23,671	5.6	2.9
Texas	162,003	158,131	162,070	0.0	2.4
Virginia	33,729	32,739	31,662	6.5	3.0
West Virginia	4,544	4,488	4,215	7.8	1.2
West	281,743	277,828	273,409	3.0%	1.4%
Alaska[1]	4,398	4,205	4,571	−3.8	4.6
Arizona[2]	29,359	29,103	27,710	6.0	0.9
California	162,317	160,315	159,444	1.8	1.2
Colorado	18,833	18,320	17,448	7.9	2.8
Hawaii[1]	5,423	5,541	5,431	−0.1	−2.1
Idaho	6,204	5,802	5,984	3.7	6.9
Montana	3,290	3,515	3,328	−1.1	−6.4
Nevada	10,478	10,426	10,233	2.4	0.5
New Mexico	5,989	5,875	5,668	5.7	1.9
Oregon	12,086	11,812	11,410	5.9	2.3
Utah	5,567	5,353	5,339	4.3	4.0
Washington	16,062	15,829	15,159	6.0	1.5
Wyoming	1,737	1,732	1,684	3.1	0.3

Note: As of December 31, 2001, the transfer of responsibility for sentenced felons from the District of Columbia to the Federal Bureau of Prisons was completed. The District of Columbia no longer operates a prison system and has been excluded from NPS.
[1]Prisons and jails form one integrated system. Data include total jail and prison population.
[2]Population figures are based on custody counts.

SOURCE: Paige M. Harrison and Allen J. Beck, Table 3: "Prisoners under the Jurisdiction of State or Federal Correctional Authorities, by Region and Jurisdiction, Yearend 2001 to 2002," in "Prisoners in 2002," *Bureau of Justice Statistics Bulletin,* July 2003

Alabama, Indiana, and Delaware, where a jury can recommend a sentence of death, but a judge ultimately decided on the penalty. The Supreme Court did not decide how the ruling would affect each state. It is possible that the death row inmates' sentences could be commuted to life in prison, or that the inmates could be resentenced, facing the death penalty sentence again.

CORRECTIONS IN THE UNITED STATES

In 2002 about 6.7 million Americans, or about 3.1 percent of the adult population of the United States, were under some form of correction supervision (prison, jail, probation, and parole). According to the Bureau of Justice Statistics, by December 31, 2001, over two million persons (2,166,260) were incarcerated in federal, state, and local correctional facilities in the United States. Of those, about two-thirds (1,440,655) were in federal or state custody, while some 665,475 were held in local jails. Most prisoners in federal and state prisons are incarcerated in the South (574,174), the most populous region of the nation, followed by the West (281,743), the Midwest (245,303), and the Northeast (175,907). (See Table 6.3.) The other 4.5 million people under some form of correction supervision were either on probation or paroled. Probation and parole consist of court ordered community supervision of convicted offenders by law enforcement agencies, though probation is usually given in place of incarceration and parole is obtained after a period of incarceration. Both usually require the offender to follow specific rules of conduct while in the community.

According to the Bureau of Justice Statistics, in 2002 there were 3,437 sentenced African-American male inmates per 100,000 African-American males in the United States, compared to 1,176 sentenced Hispanic male inmates per 100,000 Hispanic males and 450 white male inmates per 100,000 white males. African-American males in their twenties and thirties had much higher rates of incarceration compared to other ethnic and age groups. Of the 1.29 million offenders in local jails or prison in 2002, some 442,300 (34 percent) were black males between the ages of 20 and 39. In terms of the general population, 10.4 percent of all African-American non-Hispanic males from 25 to 29 years of age were in prison or jail in 2002, compared to 2.4 percent of Hispanic males, and 1.2 percent of white males in the same age group.

TABLE 6.4

Number of sentenced inmates in federal prisons, by most serious offense, 1995, 2000, and 2001

	Number of sentenced inmates in federal prisons			Percent change,	Percent of total growth,
Offense	**1995**	**2000**	**2001**	**1995–2001**	**1995–2001**
Total	88,658	131,739	142,766	61.0%	100.0%
Violent offenses	11,409	13,740	16,117	41.3%	8.7%
Homicide[1]	1,068	1,363	2,364	121.3	2.4
Robbery	8,377	9,712	10,218	22.0	3.4
Other violent	1,964	2,665	3,535	80.0	2.9
Property offenses	7,842	10,135	10,664	36.0%	5.2%
Burglary	177	462	642	262.7	0.9
Fraud	5,823	7,506	7,617	30.8	3.3
Other property	1,842	2,167	2,405	30.6	1.0
Drug offenses	52,782	74,276	78,501	48.7%	47.5%
Public-order offenses	15,655	32,325	36,443	132.8%	38.4%
Immigration	3,420	13,676	15,012	338.9	21.4
Weapons	7,446	10,822	12,539	68.4	9.4
Other public-order	4,789	7,827	8,892	85.7	7.6
Other/unknown[2]	970	1,263	1,041	7.3%	0.1%

Note: All data are from the BJS Federal justice database. Data are for September 30 and based on sentenced inmates, regardless of sentence length.
[1]Includes murder, nonnegligent manslaughter, and negligent manslaughter.
[2]Includes offenses not classifiable.

SOURCE: Paige M. Harrison and Allen J. Beck, "Table 18: Number of Sentenced Inmates in Federal Prisons by Most Serious Offense, 1995, 2000, and 2001," in "Prisoners in 2002," *Bureau of Justice Statistics Bulletin,* July 2003

Prisons and Jails—How Do They Differ?

The terms "prison" and "jail" are frequently used interchangeably. Jails, however, are generally city or county institutions while prisons are usually state or federal institutions. Jails are used to confine adults serving short sentences (generally one year or less) or persons awaiting trial or other legal disposition. Prisons, on the other hand, house convicted criminals sentenced to lengthy terms.

The Growth in the Incarceration Rate

From 1980 to 2000 there were increases among all four groups of adult correctional populations in the United States, with the incarceration rate tripling. The number of prisoners on death row increased over five times, from 692 to 3,593, in that 20-year period. As of 2002, the incarceration rate was 476 per 100,000 U.S. residents, an increase from 411 per 100,000 residents in 1995. Annually, between 1995 and 2001, the incarcerated population grew an average of 3.6 percent. In 2002 the growth rate dropped to 2.6 percent.

The United States has a larger share of its population in prison, on parole, or on probation than any other nation. Marc Mauer, in *Comparative International Rates of Incarceration: An Examination of Causes and Trends* (The Sentencing Project, Washington, D.C., 2003), compared prison populations and practices around the world. Statistics provided by the Sentencing Project show that in 2002, the incarceration rate (including prisoners, parolees, and probationers) in Russia was 628 per 100,000 persons, while the U.S. rate was 702 per 100,000 persons. The next closest country was South Africa, with an incarceration rate of 400, followed by the United Kingdom (139), Spain (125), Canada (116), and Australia (112).

According to the Bureau of Justice Statistics, drug offenders (246,100) make up the largest percentage of the U.S. federal prison population. In 2001 they constituted 55 percent of the federal prison population, down from 60 percent in 1995. Immigration violators account for 10 percent of the federal prison population, an increase of 339 percent since 1995. (See Table 6.4.) Male prisoners (93.6 percent) far outnumbered female prisoners (6.4 percent) in 2002. (See Table 6.5.)

JAIL INMATES

Inmates may be in jails for a variety of reasons:

- They may be individuals waiting for arraignment, trial, conviction, and/or sentencing, or they may be probation, parole, and bail bond violators.
- Juveniles may be temporarily jailed to wait for transfer to juvenile facilities.
- Mentally ill persons are often held in jails pending transfer to mental health facilities.

Table 6.6 lists these and other reasons for holding inmates in jails.

Jails are a generally neglected part of the corrections system. They frequently fail to meet minimum standards

TABLE 6.5

Number of sentenced prisoners under state or federal jurisdiction, by gender, race, Hispanic origin, and age, 2002

	Number of sentenced prisoners							
	Males				Females			
	Total[1]	White[2]	Black[2]	Hispanic	Total[1]	White[2]	Black[2]	Hispanic
Total	**1,291,326**	**436,800**	**586,700**	**235,000**	**89,044**	**35,400**	**36,000**	**15,000**
18–19	36,400	8,800	17,300	8,400	1,300	700	500	200
20–24	218,300	59,400	105,400	47,400	8,900	3,700	3,100	2,100
25–29	248,400	70,700	123,000	49,300	15,900	5,500	6,500	3,000
30–34	245,700	83,900	111,400	46,200	22,100	8,500	9,200	3,600
35–39	220,600	79,400	102,500	34,200	19,400	7,800	8,300	2,900
40–44	150,200	56,300	64,600	25,300	10,700	4,100	4,700	1,400
45–54	127,300	55,800	48,500	18,800	8,400	3,700	3,000	1,400
55 or older	38,900	21,500	10,800	4,800	1,900	1,200	500	200

Note: Based on custody counts from National Prisoners Statistics and updated from jurisdiction counts by gender at yearend. Estimates by age derived from the Surveys of Inmates in State and Federal Correctional facilities, 1997. Estimates were rounded to the nearest 100.
[1]Includes American Indians, Alaska Natives, Asians, Native Hawaiians, and other Pacific Islanders.
[2]Excludes Hispanics.

SOURCE: Paige M. Harrison and Allen J. Beck, "Table 13: Number of Sentenced Prisoners under State and Federal Jurisdiction by Gender, Race, Hispanic Origin, and Age, 2002," in "Prisoners in 2002," *Bureau of Justice Statistics Bulletin,* July 2003

for space, care, and staffing and have to mix a wide range of inmates—hardened criminals awaiting trial, those with serious mental problems or addictions, drunks disturbing the peace, and those who are not yet convicted (and may never be). Because the stay in jail is usually brief, medical care, recreation, and opportunities for work or activity are frequently minimal.

Population in the Nation's Jails

Department of Justice statisticians Paige M. Harrison and Jennifer C. Karberg report on the U.S. jail population in "Prison and Jail Inmates at Midyear 2002" (Bureau of Justice Statistics, Washington, D.C., April 2003). At midyear 2002, 737,912 persons were under some form of jail supervision, either confined in jails or supervised outside jail facilities, up from 702,044 in 2001. Of those, 665,475 were being held in jail, while the remaining persons were in jail-supervised programs such as electronic monitoring or community service or other work programs.

For the year ending June 26, 2002, the average daily jail population was 652,082, up from 618,319 in 2000 and 509,828 in 1995. Between 1995 and 2002 the average daily population of female jail inmates rose from 51,300 to 76,817, while the male population increased from 448,000 to 581,441. Proportionally the number of female inmates grew from 10 percent of the jail inmate population to 11.7 percent, and the number of males decreased from 90 percent to 88.3 percent.

Minority groups accounted for a majority (54.5 percent) of local jail inmates in 2002. Non-Hispanic whites made up 43.8 percent of the jail population; non-Hispanic African-Americans, 39.8 percent; and Hispanics, 14.7 percent. Other races (Asian Americans, Pacific Islanders, American Indians, and Alaska Natives) accounted for 1.6 percent. Among non-Hispanic African-Americans, the jail incarceration rate (740 per 100,000) was more than five times that of non-Hispanic whites (147 per 100,000) and almost three times the rate of Hispanics (256 per 100,000).

TABLE 6.6

Characteristics of jails

- receive individuals pending arraignment and hold them awaiting trial, conviction, or sentencing
- readmit probation, parole, and bailbond violators and absconders
- temporarily detain juveniles pending transfer to juvenile authorities
- hold mentally ill persons pending their movement to appropriate health facilities
- hold individuals for the military, for protective custody, for contempt, and for the courts as witnesses
- release convicted inmates to the community upon completion of sentence
- transfer inmates to Federal, State, or other authorities
- house inmates for Federal, State, or other authorities because of crowding of their facilities
- relinquish custody of temporary detainees to juvenile and medical authorities
- sometimes operate community-based programs as alternatives to incarceration
- hold inmates sentenced to short terms (generally under 1 year).

SOURCE: Allen J. Beck and Jennifer Karberg, "Jails," in *Prison and Jail Inmates at Midyear 2000*, U.S. Department of Justice, Bureau of Justice Statistics, Washington, DC, 2001

Most juveniles in correctional custody were housed in juvenile facilities. However, at midyear 2002 an estimated 7,248 persons under age 18 were kept in adult jails, most having been tried as adults or awaiting trial as adults in criminal court.

The Growing Jail Population

From 1995 to 2002 the number of jail inmates grew from 507,044 to 665,475, a rise in the jail incarceration rate from 193 to 231 jail inmates per 100,000 U.S. residents. In June 2002 jails housed 33 percent of all incarcerated prisoners, the same as at midyear 2001. Since jail sentences

TABLE 6.7

Prisoners under age 18 in state and private adult correctional facilities, by type of facility, security level, and region, June 30, 2000

		All facilities			Type of facility: Confinement facilities			Type of facility: Community-based facilities		
	Total	Maximum*	Medium	Minimum/ low	Maximum*	Medium	Minimum/ low	Maximum	Medium	Minimum/ low
Total	**4,095**	**2,008**	**1,582**	**505**	**2,008**	**1,490**	**444**	**X**	**92**	**61**
State	3,927	2,007	1,441	479	2,007	1,427	437	X	14	42
Private	168	1	141	26	1	63	7	X	78	19
Region										
Northeast	760	461	233	66	461	231	66	X	2	0
Midwest	699	244	225	230	244	234	197	X	1	33
South	2,150	1,132	819	199	1,132	730	175	X	89	24
West	486	171	305	10	171	305	6	X	0	4

Note: As of June 30, 2000, there were no persons under age 18 in federal facilities. Age information was not available for 1,471 state inmates.
*Includes facilities with the security designations super maximum, close, or high.

SOURCE: "Table 6.33: Prisoners under Age 18 in State and Private Adult Correctional Facilities, by Type of Facility, Security Level, and Region, United States, June 30, 2000," in *Sourcebook of Criminal Justice Statistics 2002,* U.S. Department of Justice, Bureau of Justice Statistics,Washington, DC, 2003

remained stable at about seven months, the dramatic growth of the local jail population seemed more related to the increased number of arrests than to longer sentences. In June 2002 jails were about 93 percent occupied.

STATE AND FEDERAL PRISONS

Persons convicted of murder, burglary, or larceny/ theft are most likely to be sent to a state prison. If the crime is a federal offense or was committed outside a state jurisdiction, the offender can be sentenced to a federal prison. Federal offenses include crimes that

- Are committed against a federal institution (bank, post office, or federally insured credit union) or a federal officer (FBI, Drug Enforcement Administration, or U.S. Treasury agent).
- Are committed on the high seas, on government reservations or territories, or in other areas under federal jurisdiction, such as Washington, D.C.
- Involve crossing state lines (kidnapping or transporting stolen automobiles, for example).
- Involve interstate crime, such as telephone or mail fraud.

Prison Population

The BJS regularly surveys the nation's correctional facilities. The 2002 survey counted 2,166,260 prisoners. State and federal prisons housed two-thirds (1,440,655) of all persons incarcerated in the United States with the other third in local jails. Of those held in prisons, state prisons housed over 88.6 percent (1,277,127), while federal prisons held about 11.4 percent (163,528). These figures show a 2.5 percent increase in the state prison population and a 5.8 percent increase in the federal prison population over the previous year. (See Table 6.3.) As of June 30, 2000, there were 4,095 inmates under the age of 18 in state (3,927) and private adult (168) correctional facilities. More than half of these inmates (2,150) were incarcerated in the South, followed by the Northeast (760), the Midwest (699), and the West (486). (See Table 6.7.)

TABLE 6.8

Number of persons held in state or federal prisons or in local jails, 1995–2002

	Total inmates in custody	Prisoners in custody on December 31: Federal	Prisoners in custody on December 31: State	Inmates in jail on June 30	Incarceration rate[1]
1995	1,585,586	89,538	989,004	507,044	601
1996	1,646,020	95,088	1,032,440	518,492	618
1997	1,743,643	101,755	1,074,809	567,079	648
1998	1,816,931	110,793	1,113,676	592,462	669
1999[2]	1,893,115	125,682	1,161,490	605,943	691
2000[3]	1,937,482	133,921	1,176,269	621,149	684
2001[3]	1,961,247	143,337	1,180,155	631,240	685
2002[3]	2,033,331	151,618	1,209,640	665,475	701
Percent change, 2001–2002	3.7%	5.8%	2.5%	5.4%	
Average annual increase, 1995–2002	3.6%	7.8%	2.9%	4.0%	

Note: Counts include all inmates held in public and private adult correctional facilities.
[1]Number of prison and jail inmates per 100,000 U.S. residents at yearend.
[2]In 1999, 15 states expanded their reporting criteria to include inmates held in privately operated correctional facilities. For comparisons with previous years, the state count 1,137,544 and the total count 1,869,169 should be used.
[3]Total counts include federal inmates in nonsecure, privately operated facilities (6,598 in 2002, 6,515 in 2001 and 6,143 in 2000).

SOURCE: Paige M. Harrison and Allen J. Beck, "Table 1: Number of Persons Held in State or Federal Prisons or in Local Jails, 1995–2002," in "Prisoners in 2002," *Bureau of Justice Statistics Bulletin,* July 2003

The rate of prisoners per 100,000 population has risen steadily while there has been a decline in the overall crime rate. Since 1995 the incarceration rate has risen from 601 per 100,000 to 701 per 100,000 in 2002. One in every 143 U.S. residents was incarcerated in a federal or state prison or a local jail in 2002. (See Table 6.8.)

In 2002 Maine had the highest yearly increase in the number of prisoners (11.5 percent), while Alaska saw the

TABLE 6.9

Estimated number of sentenced prisoners under state jurisdiction, by offense, gender, race, and Hispanic origin, 2001

Offense	All	Male	Female	White	Black	Hispanic
Total	**1,208,700**	**1,132,500**	**76,200**	**424,200**	**548,800**	**205,300**
Violent offenses	596,100	571,700	24,400	208,100	267,800	102,600
Murder[1]	159,200	150,700	8,500	51,500	77,100	27,800
Manslaughter	16,900	15,000	1,900	6,300	6,300	3,500
Rape	30,900	30,600	300	15,100	11,700	2,700
Other sexual assault	87,600	86,600	1,000	50,700	21,300	12,600
Robbery	155,300	150,100	5,200	34,100	91,100	26,200
Assault	118,800	113,100	5,600	38,700	50,300	25,300
Other violent	27,400	25,500	1,900	11,700	10,000	4,700
Property offenses	233,000	213,100	20,000	101,800	92,300	32,500
Burglary	104,700	101,300	3,400	45,700	41,200	14,700
Larceny	45,500	39,600	5,800	17,400	20,300	6,100
Motor vehicle theft	18,000	17,300	700	6,900	6,700	4,200
Fraud	33,700	25,400	8,300	17,100	13,000	3,100
Other property	31,100	29,500	1,600	14,700	11,100	4,500
Drug offenses	246,100	222,900	23,200	57,300	139,700	47,000
Public-order offenses[2]	129,900	121,600	8,300	56,000	47,300	22,300
Other/unspecified[3]	3,600	3,200	400	900	1,700	800

Note: Data are for inmates with a sentence of more than 1 year under the jurisdiction of state correctional authorities.
[1]Includes nonnegligent manslaughter.
[2]Includes weapons, drunk driving, court offenses, commercialized vice, morals and decency charges, liquor law violations, and other public-order offenses.
[3]Includes juvenile offenses and unspecified felonies.

SOURCE: Paige M. Harrison and Allen J. Beck, "Table 15: Estimated Number of Sentenced Prisoners Under State Jurisdiction, by Offense, Gender, Race, and Hispanic Origin, 2001," in "Prisoners in 2002," *Bureau of Justice Statistics Bulletin,* July 2003

largest decrease (3.8 percent). The two states with the most prisoners were also the country's largest: California (162,317) and Texas (162,003). By region, the West saw the highest increase in prisoners (3 percent), followed by the South (2.5 percent), with the Midwest and Northeast at 1.9 percent respectively. The South, the nation's most populous region, had the most prisoners overall (574,174), followed by the West (281,743), the Midwest (245,303), and the Northeast (175,907).

CHARACTERISTICS OF PRISONERS

Gender

In 2002 women accounted for a total of 89,044 prisoners under state (76,200) and federal (12,844) correctional authorities. Of females in state prisons in 2001, 24,400 (32 percent) were convicted of violent offenses, 23,200 (30.4 percent) on drug offenses, and 20,000 (26.2 percent) on property offenses. (See Table 6.9.) From 1995 to 2001 the number of females in state prisons increased for violent offenses by 48.6 percent, for property offenses by 22.3 percent, and for drug offenses by 12.8 percent. (See Table 6.10.) Since 1995 the average annual percentage increase of female prisoners (5.2 percent) has outpaced that of male prisoners (3.5 percent). (See Table 6.11.)

In 2002 men accounted for a total of 1,291,326 prisoners under state (1,132,500) and federal (158,826) correctional authorities. Of males in state prisons in 2001, 571,700 (50.4 percent) were convicted of violent offenses, 222,900 (19.6 percent) on drug offenses, and 213,100 (18.8 percent) on property offenses. From 1995 to 2001 the number of males in state prisons increased for violent offenses by 63.9 percent, for public-order offenses by 20.8 percent, and for drug offenses by 15.2 percent. In 2002 the rate of sentenced male prisoners (912 per 100,000 males in the resident population) was significantly higher than the rate for sentenced females (61 per 100,000 females).

TABLE 6.10

Growth of sentenced prison population under state jurisdiction, by gender and offense, 1995–2001

	All prisoners		Male prisoners		Female prisoners	
Offense	Increase, 1995–2001	Percent of total	Increase, 1995–2001	Percent of total	Increase, 1995–2001	Percent of total
Total	**207,300**	**100%**	**189,300**	**100%**	**18,100**	**100%**
Violent	130,800	63.1	121,300	63.9	8,700	48.6
Property	3,600	1.7	−200	—	4,000	22.3
Drug	30,600	14.8	28,900	15.2	2,300	12.8
Public-order	42,400	20.4	39,500	20.8	2,900	16.2

SOURCE: Paige M. Harrison and Allen J. Beck, "Table 16: Partitioning by Gender and Offense, the Growth of the Sentenced Prison Population under State Jurisdiction, 1995–2001," in "Prisoners in 2002," *Bureau of Justice Statistics Bulletin,* July 2003

Race and Ethnicity

According to "Prisons in 2002," between 1995 and 2002, there were only slight changes in the percentages of federal or state prisoners by race and ethnicity. In 1995

TABLE 6.11

Prisoners under jurisdiction of state or federal correctional authorities, by gender, year end 1995, 2001, and 2002

	Men	Women
All inmates		
2002	1,343,164	97,491
2001	1,313,053	92,979
1995	1,057,406	68,468
Percent change, 2001–2002	2.4%	4.9%
Average annual 1995–2002	3.5	5.2
Sentenced to more than 1 year		
2002	1,291,326	89,044
2001	1,260,033	85,184
Percent change, 2001–2002	2.5%	4.5%
Incarceration rate*		
2002	906	60
1995	789	47

*The number of prisoners with sentences of more than 1 year per 100,000 residents on December 31.

SOURCE: Paige M. Harrison and Allen J. Beck, "Table 5: Prisoners under the Jurisdiction of State or Federal Correctional Authorities by Gender, 1995, 2001, and 2002," in "Prisoners in 2002," *Bureau of Justice Statistics Bulletin,* July 2003

white inmates made up 33.5 percent of all state and federal prisoners, while blacks were 45.7 percent, and Hispanics were 17.6 percent. In 2002 white inmates were 34.2 percent of the prison population, blacks were 45.1 percent, and Hispanics were 18.1 percent. Of the 1,291,326 male prisoners under state or federal correctional authority in 2002, black males made up 45.4 (586,700) percent of the total, white males 33.8 percent (436,800), and Hispanic males 18.1 percent (235,000). Of the 89,044 female prisoners, black females made up 40.4 percent (36,000) of the total, white females 39.7 percent (35,400), and Hispanic females 16.8 percent (15,000).

Offenses

Of the four offense categories (violent, property, drug, and public-order), the largest growth in state prisoners from 1995 to 2001 was among violent offenders. Of the 207,300 additional prisoners in state prisons during this period, violent offenders made up 63.1 percent (130,800). Public-order offenders were 20.4 percent (42,400) of the increase, drug offenders 14.8 percent (30,600), and property offenders 1.7 percent (3,600). (See Table 6.10.)

Among the 90,700 additional white inmates in state prison from 1995 to 2001, violent offenders made up 58.7 percent of the total, public-order offenders were 20 percent (18,000), and drug offenders were 17.9 percent (16,200). The black inmate population in state prisons grew during this period by 83,200. Violent offenders made up 56.9 percent of the increase (47,400), drug offenders 22.9 percent (19,100), and public-order offenders 20.2 percent

TABLE 6.12

Growth of sentenced prison population under state jurisdiction, by race, Hispanic origin, and offense, 1995–2001

	White prisoners		Black prisoners		Hispanic prisoners	
Offense	Increase, 1995–2001	Percent of total	Increase, 1995–2001	Percent of total	Increase, 1995–2001	Percent of total
Total	**90,700**	**100%**	**83,200**	**100%**	**35,300**	**100%**
Violent	53,100	58.7	47,400	56.9	29,900	81.5
Property	3,000	3.3	0	—	−100	—
Drug	16,200	17.9	19,100	22.9	−1,400	—
Public-order	18,000	20	16,800	20.2	6,800	18.5

SOURCE: Paige M. Harrison and Allen J. Beck, "Table 17: Partitioning by Race, Hispanic Origin, and Offense, the Growth of the Sentenced Prison Population under State Jurisdiction, 1995–2001," in "Prisoners in 2002," *Bureau of Justice Statistics Bulletin,* July 2003

(16,800). Of the additional 35,300 Hispanic inmates in state prison from 1995 to 2001, violent offenders were 81.5 percent of the total (29,900) and public-order offenders were 18.5 percent (6,800). (See Table 6.12.)

Between 1995 to 2001 the number of incarcerated violent offenders in federal prisons rose from 11,409 to 16,117, an increase of 41.3 percent. Federal inmates sentenced for property offenses in this period increased by 36 percent, from 7,842 to 10,664. The number of drug offenders in federal prisons rose from 52,782 in 1995 to 78,501 in 2001, an increase of 48.7 percent. The number of public order offenders in federal prisons increased by 132.8 percent, from 15,655 to 36,443.

Many inmates were in possession of a firearm during the offense for which they are currently serving time in prison, according to *Firearm Use by Offenders* (U.S. Department of Justice, Office of Justice Programs, Bureau of Justice Statistics, November 2001). In 1997, among inmates in federal prisons, 15.5 percent of males and 6.2 percent of females carried a firearm during their current offense. Of male inmates in state prisons, 19.1 percent had carried a firearm compared to 7.3 percent of female inmates. Younger inmates were more likely to have carried a firearm when committing their current offense: 35.5 percent of state prisoners 20 years old or younger and 23 percent of federal prisoners in the same age group. (See Table 6.13.)

Mental Health

In 2000, 10 percent of all state inmates were receiving psychotropic medications, and one in eight state prisoners were in some type of mental health therapy or counseling, according to the Bureau of Justice Statistics. Some 217,420 prisoners were confined in 155 state facilities specializing in psychiatric confinement.

Of state prison inmates, 22.1 percent of females confined to female-only facilities were receiving psychotropic medication as of mid-year 2000, compared to 8.7 percent

TABLE 6.13

Possession of a firearm during current offense, by selected characteristics for state and federal prison inmates, 1997

	Prison inmates			
	State		Federal	
Selected characteristic	Number	Percent who possessed a firearm during current offense	Number	Percent who possessed a firearm during current offense
Gender				
Male	972,572	19.1%	81,102	15.5%
Female	64,669	7.3	6,364	6.2
Race/Hispanic origin				
White	346,188	14.8%	25,977	16.7%
Black	482,302	21.1	33,100	17.7
Hispanic	176,089	17.6	24,040	8.1
Other	32,662	19.3	4,349	17.9
Age				
20 or younger	61,663	35.5%	935	23.0%
21–24	143,533	26.8	6,865	18.6
25–34	396,166	16.5	31,970	15.5
35–44	305,765	13.3	26,636	12.8
45–54	100,133	17.4	14,393	15.3
55 or older	29,980	21.7	6,667	13.0
Educational attainment				
Some high school or less	445,479	16.8%	25,642	13.9%
GED	260,743	23.6	17,150	19.2
High school diploma	190,805	16.7	21,292	14.5
Some college	110,122	16.5	15,233	15.1
College graduate	27,649	12.1	7,963	8.3
Citizenship				
United States	983,876	18.5%	71,307	16.9%
Latin America	47,257	14.5	14,638	5.7
Other	4,609	22.0	1,376	2.4
Military service				
Served	129,913	16.4%	12,746	17.2%
Did not serve	907,142	18.6	74,676	14.4

SOURCE: Caroline Wolf Harlow, "Table 5: Possession of a Firearm During Current Offense, by Selected Characteristics for State and Federal Prison Inmates, 1997," in "Firearm Use by Offenders," *Bureau of Justice Statistics Bulletin,* November 2001

of male state prisoners in male-only facilities. Of state prisoners confined to facilities housing both males and females, 15.2 percent of inmates were receiving psychotropic medication as of June 30, 2000. Inmates in female-only facilities were also more likely to receive therapy or counseling in 2000 (27.1 percent), compared to inmates in male-only facilities (11.9 percent), and in institutions that housed both males and females (14.3 percent). (See Table 6.14.)

Education

Compared to the general population, federal and state prisoners have a lower level of educational attainment. In 1997, according to the Bureau of Justice Statistics, 18.4 percent of the general population 18 years or older had not completed high school. Inmates in state prisons had a rate of 39.7 percent, more than double the rate for the general population, while those in federal prisons had a rate of 26.5 percent. In the general population, 33.2 percent attained a high school diploma as their highest level of education. Among inmates in federal prisons the rate was 27 percent and in state prisons 20.5 percent. Prisoners were more likely than the general population to have earned a General Educational Development (GED) certificate, a test which indicates the same level of attainment as a high school graduate: 28.5 percent of state prisoners had a GED, while 22.7 percent of federal prisoners had a GED. In the general population, 26.4 percent went beyond high school to attend college but did not attain a degree. Among state prisoners 9 percent attended college, while 15.8 percent of federal prisoners had attended college. Twenty-two percent of the general population were college graduates, while only 8.1 percent of federal prisoners and 2.4 percent of state prisoners had college degrees. (See Table 6.15.)

About nine out of 10 state prisons offer inmates an educational program. All federal prisons offer educational programs of some kind. The most common programs available are secondary education, offered by 98.7 percent of federal prisons, basic adult education (97.4 percent), and vocational training programs (93.5 percent). Among state prisons 91.2 percent have an educational program. The most common programs are secondary education, offered by 83.6 percent of state prisons, basic adult education (80.4 percent), and vocational training programs (55.7 percent). (See Table 6.16.) About 52 percent of state prisoners and 57 percent of federal prisoners have taken a class while in prison.

PROBATION AND PAROLE

At the end of 2002 nearly 4.74 million adults were on probation or parole in the United States, up from 3.2 million at the end of 1990. The total number of probationers in 2002 was 3,995,165. Fifty percent were convicted of felonies, 49 percent of misdemeanors, and 1 percent of other types of infractions. Twenty-four percent of probationers had drug law violations as their most serious offense. (See Table 6.17.)

Of probationers in 2002, 23 percent were female, compared to 21 percent in 1995. Whites comprised 55 percent of probationers in 2002, a slight increase from 53 percent in 1995, while blacks accounted for 31 percent of probationers, the same percentage as in 1995. In 2002 probationers of Hispanic origin represented 12 percent of all probationers, down from 14 percent in 1995.

In 2002, 753,141 adults were on parole. Almost all offenders on parole (96 percent) had served a felony sentence of one year or more. More than half of parolees in 2002 received mandatory release from prison as the result of a sentencing statute (requirement) or because of good-time provisions. Thirty-nine percent received parole as the result of a decision by a state parole board, 59 percent fewer than in 1990. Fourteen percent of all parolees in 2002 were women, up from 10 percent in 1995. Thirty-nine percent of adult parolees were white, 42 percent were black, with Hispanics making up 18 percent of parolees. (See Table 6.18.)

TABLE 6.14

Inmates receiving mental health treatment in state confinement facilities, by facility characteristic, June 30, 2000

	Number of inmates receiving —					
	24-hour mental health care		Therapy/ counseling		Psychotropic medications	
Facility characteristic	Number	Percent	Number	Percent	Number	Percent
Total[1]	16,986	1.8%	122,376	12.9%	95,114	9.8%
Facility operation						
Public	16,270	1.8%	116,296	13.0%	90,721	10.0%
Private	716	1.3	6,080	10.8	4,393	7.7
Authority to house						
Males only	13,064	1.5%	100,371	11.9%	74,736	8.7%
Females only	830	1.5	14,744	27.1	12,119	22.1
Both	3,092	5.9	7,261	14.3	8,259	15.2
Security level						
Maximum/high	6,928	2.4%	44,637	14.9%	35,069	11.5%
Medium	9,608	1.8	65,726	12.6	52,208	9.8
Minimum/low	448	0.4	11,593	9.3	7,355	5.8
Facility size[2]						
1,500 or more	6,298	1.4%	59,970	12.8%	45,283	9.3%
750-1,499	5,140	1.6	41,953	13.0	31,816	9.9
250-749	4,582	3.5	16,831	13.4	14,866	11.6
100-249	888	3.3	3,309	12.4	2,867	10.9
Fewer than 100	78	2.3	313	11.0	282	8.8

[1]Excludes inmates in mental health treatment in Florida for whom only statewide totals were reported.
[2]Based on the average daily population between July 1, 1999, and June 30, 2000.

SOURCE: Allen J. Beck and Laura M. Maruschak, Table 4: "Inmates Receiving Mental Health Treatment in State Confinement Facilities, by Facility Characteristic, June 30, 2000," in *Bureau of Justice Statistics Special Report: Mental Health Treatment in State Prisons, 2000,* U.S. Department of Justice, Office of Justice Programs, Washington, DC, July 2001

TABLE 6.15

Educational attainment of state and federal prison inmates, 1997 and 1991; local jail inmates, 1996 and 1989; probationers, 1995; and the general population, 1997

	Prison inmates							
	State		Federal		Local jail inmates			
Educational attainment	1997	1991	1997	1991	1996	1989	Proba- tioners	General population
8th grade or less	14.2%	14.3%	12.0%	11.0%	13.1%	15.6%	8.4%	7.2%
Some high school	25.5	26.9	14.5	12.3	33.4	38.2	22.2	11.2
GED*	28.5	24.6	22.7	22.6	14.1	9.2	11.0	...
High school diploma	20.5	21.8	27.0	25.9	25.9	24.0	34.8	33.2
Postsecondary/some college	9.0	10.1	15.8	18.8	10.3	10.3	18.8	26.4
College graduate or more	2.4	2.3	8.1	9.3	3.2	2.8	4.8	22.0
Number	1,055,495	706,173	88,705	53,677	503,599	393,111	2,029,866	192,352,084

Note: Probationers have been excluded from the general population. General population includes the noninstitutional population 18 or older. Detail may not add to 100% due to rounding.
*General Educational Development certificate.
...Not available in the Current Population Survey.

SOURCE: Caroline Wolf Harlow, "Table 1: Educational Attainment for State and Federal Prison Inmates, 1997 and 1991, Local Jail Inmates, 1996 and1989, Probationers, 1995, and the General Population, 1997," in "Education and Correctional Populations," *Bureau of Justice Statistics Bulletin,* January 2003

Federal Clemency

The U.S. president is authorized under the constitution to grant pardons and commutations to those convicted of federal crimes. The U.S. Pardon Attorney evaluates all applications, investigates the cases, and makes recommendations. A pardon occurs after an individual has served his sentence and allows that person to regain any civil rights and trade or professional licenses he or she may have lost due to being a felon. A commutation reduces the prison time of an individual now serving his or her sentence. Between 1953 and 2002 there have been 5,275 pardons granted and 585 commutations. (See Table 6.19.)

RECIDIVISM

The recidivism rate measures the degree to which inmates return to criminal behavior after their release from prison. In "Recidivism of Prisoners Released in 1994" (Bureau of Justice Statistics Special Report, June 2002), authors Patrick A. Langan, Ph.D., and David J. Levin, Ph.D., released the findings of a study that tracked

TABLE 6.16

Educational programs offered in state, federal, and private prisons, 2000 and 1995, and in local jails, 1999

Educational programs	State prisons		Federal prisons		Private prisons		Local jails
	2000	1995	2000	1995	2000	1995	1999
With an education program	91.2%	88.0%	100.0%	100.0%	87.6%	71.8%	60.3%
Basic adult education	80.4	76.0	97.4	92.0	61.6	40.0	24.7
Secondary education	83.6	80.3	98.7	100.0	70.7	51.8	54.8
College courses	26.7	31.4	80.5	68.8	27.3	18.2	3.4
Special education	39.6	33.4	59.7	34.8	21.9	27.3	10.8
Vocational training	55.7	54.5	93.5	73.2	44.2	25.5	6.5
Study release programs	7.7	9.3	6.5	5.4	28.9	32.7	9.3
Without an education program	8.8	12.0	0.0	0.0	12.4	28.2	39.7
Number of facilities	1,307	1,278	*	*	242	110	2,819

Note: Detail may not add to total because facilities may have more than one educational program.
*Changed definitions prevent meaningful comparisons of the numbers of federal facilities, 1995 and 2000.

SOURCE: Caroline Wolf Harlow, "Table 3: Educational Programs Offered in State, Federal, and Private Prisons, 2000 and 1995, and Local Jails, 1999," in "Education and Correctional Populations," *Bureau of Justice Statistics Bulletin,* January, 2003

272,111 former inmates three years after their release from prison in 15 states—Arizona, California, Delaware, Florida, Illinois, Maryland, Michigan, Minnesota, New Jersey, New York, North Carolina, Ohio, Oregon, Texas, and Virginia. Of prisoners tracked, over two-thirds (67.5 percent) were rearrested for a new offense during the three years after their release from prison. Of the 272,111 prisoners released in 1994, 46.9 percent were convicted of a new crime, and 25.4 percent were sentenced to prison for the new offense. Almost 52 percent of the 272,111 were back in prison, whether for a new crime or a technical violation of their release.

By offense, the highest rate of rearrest was for motor vehicle theft (78.8 percent), followed by selling stolen property (77.4 percent), larceny (74.6 percent), burglary (74 percent), and robbery (70.2 percent). The sale, use or possession of illegal weapons also accounted for an arrest rate of 70.2 percent. The lowest rates of rearrest in the three years following release from prison in 1994 were for homicide (40.7 percent), sexual assault other than rape (41.4 percent), rape (46 percent), and driving under the influence (51.5 percent).

Male prisoners released in 1994 were more likely to be rearrested (68.4 percent) than females (57.6 percent). African-Americans were more likely to be rearrested (72.9 percent) than were Hispanics (64.6 percent) and whites (62.7 percent). Inmates ages 25 to 29 (22.8 percent) and 30 to 34 (22.7 percent) were most likely to be rearrested, while inmates 45 years of age or older (7.5 percent) were least likely to re-offend in the three years after release from state prison. Of the 211,111 former inmates released in 1994, 7.6 percent were rearrested in a state other than the one that released them.

Arrest history made a difference in recidivism; the more arrests the prisoner had prior to release, the more likely the prisoner's rearrest. Of those with one arrest prior to their release, 41 percent were rearrested. About 47 percent of those with two prior arrests, 55 percent of those with three earlier arrests, and 82 percent of those with more than fifteen prior arrests (18 percent of all released prisoners) were rearrested within a three-year period.

Of 2002 parolees 45 percent successfully met the terms of their supervision, while 41 percent returned to prison either because of a parole violation or a new criminal offense. For those on probation in 2002, 14 percent returned to prison, a decrease from 21 percent in 1995.

WHAT IS THE SOLUTION?

Is prison the answer to crime? Is prison supposed to punish, or is it supposed to rehabilitate? It is certainly the primary method the government uses to show that it takes crime seriously and will not let it go unpunished. It keeps dangerously violent criminals off the street, which has very likely contributed somewhat to the drop in crime during the 1990s.

Prisoners are often considered society's failures, people—mostly men—who have failed in their relationships with their families, schools, and jobs. They suffer disproportionately from physical, drug, and alcohol abuse. They may have low self-esteem and exhibit hostility towards others, especially those in authority. Prisoners bring their own society into prison, which usually revolves around drugs, smuggling, extortion, predatory sexual behavior, and violence.

Many penologists (persons who study prison management and the reformation of criminals) believe that locking up greater numbers of offenders reduces the rate of crime. Mandatory sentencing and habitual-offender laws give longer sentences to those who have broken the law. If criminals are in prison, they are not on the streets committing crimes. Some experts believe longer sentences have acted as a deterrent and played a major role in the recent decline in criminal activity.

TABLE 6.17

Characteristics of adults on probation, 1995, 2000, and 2002

Characteristic of adults on probation	1995	2000	2002
Total	**100%**	**100%**	**100%**
Gender			
Male	79%	78%	77%
Female	21	22	23
Race			
White	53%	54%	55%
Black	31	31	31
Hispanic	14	13	12
American Indian/Alaska Native	1	1	1
Asian/Pacific Islander[1]	--	1	1
Status of probation			
Direct imposition	48%	56%	60%
Split sentence	15	11	9
Sentence suspended	26	25	22
Imposition suspended	6	7	9
Other	4	1	1
Status of supervision			
Active	79%	76%	75%
Inactive	8	9	10
Absconded	9	9	11
Supervised out of state	2	3	2
Other	2	3	2
Type of offense			
Felony	54%	52%	50%
Misdemeanor	44	46	49
Other infractions	2	2	1
Most serious offense			
Sexual assault	**	**	2%
Domestic violence	**	**	7
Other assault	**	**	10
Burglary	**	**	8
Larceny/theft	**	**	13
Fraud	**	**	5
Drug law violations	**	24	24
Driving while intoxicated	16	18	17
Minor traffic offenses	**	6	6
Other	84	52	8
Adults entering probation			
Without incarceration	72%	79%	83%
With incarceration	13	16	14
Other types	15	5	2
Adults leaving probation			
Successful completions	62%	60%	62%
Returned to incarceration	21	15	14
With new sentence	5	3	3
With the same sentence	13	8	6
Unknown	3	4	4
Absconder[2]	**	3	3
Other unsuccessful[2]	**	11	13
Death	1	1	--
Other	16	11	9

Note: For every characteristic there were persons of unknown status or type. Detail may not sum to total because of rounding.
**Not available.
-- Less than 0.5%.
[1]Includes Native Hawaiians.
[2]In 1995 absconder and other unsucessful were reported among "other".

SOURCE: Lauren E. Glaze, "Table 4: Characteristics of Adults on Probation, 1995, 2000, and 2002," in "Probation and Parole in the United States, 2002," *Bureau of Justice Statistics Bulletin,* August 2003

TABLE 6.18

Characteristics of adults on parole, 1995, 2000, and 2002

Characteristic	1995	2000	2002
Total	**100%**	**100%**	**100%**
Gender			
Male	90%	88%	86%
Female	10	12	14
Race			
White	34%	38%	39%
Black	45	40	42
Hispanic	21	21	18
American Indian/Alaska Native	1	1	1
Asian/Pacific Islander[1]	--	--	--
Status of supervision			
Active	78%	83%	82%
Inactive	11	4	4
Absconded	6	7	8
Supervised out of state	4	5	5
Other	--	1	2
Sentence length			
Less than 1 year	6%	3%	4%
1 year or more	94	97	96
Type of offense			
Violent	**	**	24%
Property	**	**	26
Drug	**	**	40
Other	**	**	10
Adults entering parole			
Discretionary parole	50%	37%	39%
Mandatory parole	45	54	52
Reinstatement	4	6	7
Other	2	2	2
Adults leaving parole			
Successful completion	45%	43%	45%
Returned to incarceration	41	42	41
With new sentence	12	11	11
Other	29	31	30
Absconder[2]	**	9	9
Other unsuccessful[2]	**	2	2
Transferred	2	1	1
Death	1	1	1
Other	10	2	1

Note: For every characteristic there were persons of unknown status or type. Detail may not sum to total because of rounding.
-- Less than 0.5%.
**Not available.
[1]Includes Native Hawaiians.
[2]In 1995 absconder and "other unsuccessful" statuses were reported among "other."

SOURCE: Lauren E. Glaze, "Table 7: Characteristics of Adults on Parole, 1995, 2000, and 2002," in "Probation and Parole in the United States, 2002," *Bureau of Justice Statistics Bulletin,* August 2003

Others disagree. In "Reforming Sentencing and Corrections for Just Punishment and Public Safety," (*Sentencing and Corrections*, National Institute of Justice, No. 4, September 1999), authors Michael E. Smith and Walter J. Dickey reported on hearings by the Wisconsin Governor's Task Force on Sentencing and Corrections conducted in 1996, which focused on a Milwaukee neighborhood where public safety "was in serious disrepair." According to the police testimony at the hearings, at a certain high crime corner some "94 drug arrests were made within a 3-month period.... Despite the two-year prison terms routinely handed down by the sentencing judges (for drug offenses), the drug market continued to thrive at the intersection, pos-

TABLE 6.19

Executive clemency applications for federal offenses received, disposed of, and pending in Office of U.S. Pardon Attorney, fiscal years 1953–2002

TABLE 6.19

Executive clemency applications for federal offenses received, disposed of, and pending in Office of U.S. Pardon Attorney, fiscal years 1953–2002 [CONTINUED]

Fiscal year	Pending from previous fiscal year	Received	Granted		Denied
			Pardons	Commutations	
1953	543[1]	599	97	8	356
1954	681	461	55	7	348
1955	732	662	59	4	684
1956	647	585	192	9	568
1957	463	585	232	4	443
1958	369	406	98	6	302
1959	369	434	117	2	286
1960	398	437	149	5	244
1961	437[1]	481	226	18	266
1962	408	595	166	16	315
1963	506	592	133	45	233
1964	687	921	315	73	437
1965	783	1,008	195	80	569
1966	947	865	364	81	726
1967	641	863	222	23	520
1968	739	749	13	3	415
1969	1,057[1]	724	0	0	505
1970	1,276	459	82	14	698
1971	941	454	157	16	648
1972	574	516	235	20	410
1973	425	485	202	5	341
1974	362	426	187	8	337
1975	256	610	147	9	325
1976	385	742	106	11	442
1977	568[1]	738	129	8	301
1978	868	641	162	3	836
1979	508	710	143	10	448
1980	617	523	155	11	498
1981	474[1]	547	76	7	259
1982	679	462	83	3	547
1983	508	447	91	2	306
1984	556	447	37	5	326
1985	635	407	32	3	279
1986	728	362	55	0	290
1987	745	410	23	0	311
1988	824	384	38	0	497
1989	673[1]	373	41	1	392
1990	616	354	0	0	289
1991	681	318	29	0	681
1992	289	379	0	0	192
1993	476[1]	868	36	2	251
1994	1,048	808	0	0	785
1995	1,071	612	53	3	588
1996	1,039	512	0	0	371
1997	1,174	685	0	0	555
1998	1,304	608	21	0	378
1999	1,512	1,009	34	14	601
2000[2]	1,872	1,388	70	6	1,027
2001[3]	2,153	1,169	218	40	160
2002	3,320	1,248	0	0	1,985

Note: Article II, Section 2 of the U.S. Constitution authorizes the president to grant executive clemency for federal criminal offenses. The U.S. pardon attorney, in consultation with the attorney general's office, receives and reviews all petitions for executive clemency, initiates the necessary investigations, and prepares the recommendations of the attorney general to the president. Clemency may be a reprieve, remission of fine or restitution, commutation, or pardon. A "pardon," which is generally considered only after sentence completion, restores basic civil rights and may aid in the reinstatement of professional or trade licenses that may have been lost as a result of the conviction. A "commutation" is a reduction of sentence. Commutations include remission of fines. Petitions denied also include those that are closed administratively. Cases in which multiple forms of relief were granted are counted in only one category. The figures presented in this table do not include clemency actions on draft resisters, or military deserters and absentees during the Vietnam war era.

[1]In inaugural years, these figures are for the outgoing administration.

[2]In addition to the six commutations, President Clinton granted one reprieve of an execution date during fiscal year 2000.

[3]In addition to the 40 commutations, President Clinton granted 1 reprieve of an execution date during fiscal year 2001.

SOURCE: "Table 5.73: Executive Clemency Applications for Federal Offenses Received, Disposed of, and Pending in the Office of the U.S. Pardon Attorney, Fiscal Years 1953–2002," in *Sourcebook of Criminal Justice Statistics 2002,* U.S. Department of Justice, Bureau of Justice Statistics, Washington, DC, 2003

ing risks to the safety of all who lived nearby or had to pass through on their way to work or school." According to the testimony, the incarceration of some 100 drug-offense felons "did not increase the public safety at the street corner."

As an alternative to incarceration, programs advocating restorative and community justice are based on principles that address the needs of victims, communities and offenders. As reported by Leena Kurki in "Incorporating Restorative and Community Justice Into American Sentencing and Corrections" (*Sentencing and Corrections,* National Institute of Justice, No. 3, September 1999), the basic principles of restorative justice are that crime involves disruptions in a three-dimensional relationship of victim, offender, and community; that because crime harms the victim and the community, the primary goals should be to repair that harm by healing the victim and community; that the victim, community, and offender should all participate in determining the response to crime; and that case disposition should be based primarily on the victim's and the community's needs.

One example of restorative justice is Victim-Offender Mediation, in which offenders meet with the victim(s) of their crime. These meetings, facilitated by a mediator, focus on the effects of the crime on the life of the victim and on the community at large. A restitution agreement is reached between the offender and the victim. Another example of restorative justice is Family Group Conferencing, which involves the meeting of the victim and the offender plus family, friends, co-workers and teachers of the victim and offender. According to Kurki, family group conferencing originated in New Zealand, where it became part of the juvenile justice system in 1989. As of 1999, about 30 percent of juvenile offenders in New Zealand were sent to family group conferencing instead of to juvenile court.

A Rand Corporation report, *Diverting Children from a Life of Crime: Measuring Costs and Benefits* (1996), found that programs helping children avoid crime were more cost-effective than imprisoning repeat offenders for long periods. The study concluded that a state government could prevent 157 crimes annually by investing $1 million in parent-training programs. They could prevent another 258 crimes by investing $1 million in graduation incentive programs. On the other hand, spending $1 million in constructing and operating new prisons for long-term prisoners would prevent only 60 crimes a year. A cost-benefit comparison seems to favor spending on early crime intervention rather than on construction of prisons.

CHAPTER 7

WHITE-COLLAR CRIME

A DEFINITION

The *Dictionary of Criminal Justice Data Terminology* (Bureau of Justice Statistics) defines white-collar crime as "nonviolent crime for financial gain committed by means of deception by persons . . . having professional status or specialized technical skills."

The following is a list of the specific crimes that the Bureau of Justice includes in white-collar crime:

- Counterfeiting is the manufacture or attempted manufacture of a copy of a negotiable instrument (coins, currency, securities, stamps, and official seals) with value set by law or possession of such a copy without authorization and with intent to defraud (cheat).
- Embezzlement is the misappropriation (dishonest use) or illegal disposal of property trusted to an individual with intent to defraud the legal owner or intended beneficiary (someone benefiting). Embezzlement differs from fraud in that it involves a breach (violation) of trust that previously existed between the victim and the offender.
- Forgery is the alteration of something written by another or writing something that claims to be either the act of another or to have been done at a time or place other than was, in fact, the case.
- Fraud is the intentional misrepresentation of fact to unlawfully deprive a person of his or her property or legal rights without damage or threatened or actual injury to persons.
- White-collar regulatory offenses is the violation of federal regulations and laws other than those listed above, including import and export (not including drug offenses), antitrust, transportation, food and drug, labor and agricultural offenses.

HOW MANY CRIMES?

Although the above crimes are not part of the Crime Index total, the FBI keeps statistics on forgery and counterfeiting, fraud, and embezzlement. According to *The Measurement of White-Collar Crime Using Uniform Crime Reporting (UCR) Data* (U.S. Department of Justice, Federal Bureau of Investigation, Criminal Justice Information Services Division, Washington, DC, 2002), from 1997 through 1999, some 3.8 percent of all criminal offenses reported to the FBI were white-collar crime, for a total of 5.9 million offenses. Fraud offenses comprised most of the white-collar crimes reported to the FBI between 1997 and 1999, followed by forgery and counterfeiting, embezzlement, and bribery. Between 1993 and 2002 arrests for forgery and counterfeiting increased by 8.3 percent, arrests for embezzlement rose by 49.4 percent, and arrests for fraud dropped by 10.4 percent. Despite the low percentage of white-collar crime out of all crimes, it is speculated that white-collar crime can cost far more than street crimes due to the large financial losses incurred by corporate crimes against the government, environment, and society as a whole.

As defined by the FBI, fraud is a somewhat broad category that includes the following offenses: false pretenses, swindles, confidence games, credit card/ATM fraud, impersonation, welfare fraud, and wire fraud. Between 1997 and 1999, there were a reported 61,230 false pretenses/swindle/confidence game offenses, followed by 23,308 credit card/ATM offenses, and 8,689 fraud incidents that involved impersonation. Welfare fraud and wire fraud accounted for 1,289 and 984 reported offenses, respectively, between 1997 and 1999. The FBI reports that between April 1, 1996 and September 30, 2003, they received 268,536 Suspicious Activity Reports (SAR) from banks for crimes involving check fraud, check kiting, and counterfeit checks and negotiable instruments.

WHITE-COLLAR CRIME ARRESTS

In 1929 the FBI introduced the Uniform Crime Reporting (UCR) system to collect information about crimes reported to the police. In 1982 a study of the UCR was completed and a recommendation was made to redesign the system to provide more comprehensive and detailed crime statistics. This resulted in a five-year program to update the system to become the National Incident-Based Reporting System (NIBRS), which collects data on each reported crime incident. The system currently reports on cases of homicide, forcible rape, robbery, aggravated assault, burglary, larceny-theft, motor vehicle theft, and arson. Some information about offenses, victims, offenders, and reported arrests for 21 additional crime categories is included. The NIBRS system also provides information on 46 different crimes and 11 lesser offenses, including white-collar crimes.

Under the UCR system, white-collar offenses that are measured only include fraud, forgery/counterfeiting, embezzlement, and a category for "all other crimes." The latter category does not differentiate white-collar crimes from other crimes in this category. The only information available for each of the categories is arrest information, which includes the age, sex, and race of the arrestee. Because the NIBRS system is still in transition, with some agencies still using the UCR system, the data about other white-collar crimes available from NIBRS in 1997–1999 are not representative of all agencies in the nation.

According to *The Measurement of White-Collar Crime Using Uniform Crime Reporting (UCR) Data,* the rate of arrest for white-collar crimes in 1997–1999 varied by offense. For fraud offenses (reported most often), the arrest rate was 131.5 arrests per 100,000 inhabitants, while embezzlement had the lowest arrest rate, at 6.5 per 100,000 inhabitants.

WHITE-COLLAR CRIME OFFENDERS AND VICTIMS

White-collar crime offenders were usually male, with the exception of embezzlers. Between 1997 and 1999 white-collar crimes were largely perpetrated by whites, who represented 70 percent or more of offenders across all categories of white-collar crime.

According to the FBI, between 1997 and 1999, businesses, financial institutions, and government and religious organizations were more likely to be the victims of fraud, counterfeiting, and embezzlement, while individuals were more likely to be the victims of bribery. There were some 143 incidents of bribery against individuals between 1997 and 1999 according to the FBI, compared to 36 against government organizations and 16 against businesses.

IDENTITY THEFT

The incidence of identity theft has risen significantly since 1999, making it one of the fastest-growing and most difficult to prevent types of crime. Thieves steal personal information from victims, such as their social security, driver's license, credit card, or other identification numbers, and then set up new bank or credit card accounts or otherwise misrepresent themselves as their victims to fraudulently obtain money. There is no central office keeping track of identity theft. There are, however, several different federal agencies—including the Federal Trade Commission (FTC) and the Social Security Administration's Office of the Inspector General—and three private consumer reporting agencies which compile figures.

The FTC was required by the Identity Theft Act to form the FTC Identity Theft Hotline and Data Clearinghouse in 1999 to track incidents of this type of crime. In 1999 there were 445 calls per week to the Hotline. By June of 2001 the number of callers to the hotline had increased to 1,800 per week, a rise of about 400 percent. Total identity theft complaints received by the FTC rose from 86,212 in 2001 to 214,905 in 2003, an increase of about 150 percent in two years. Identity theft is the most common consumer fraud crime reported to the FTC, accounting for 42 percent of all such crimes.

In 2003 personal information stolen from identity theft victims was used to set up new or misuse existing credit card accounts in 33 percent of the cases. Other identity theft crimes include unauthorized use of telephone, utility, and other communications services (21 percent), bank fraud (17 percent), and employment-related fraud (11 percent). (See Table 7.1.) By 2003, 8 percent of victims reported an identity theft that resulted in the forging of a government document, such as a driver's license or social security card. About 19 percent of victims reported that they had experienced more than one type of identity theft. This accounts for the reported percentages exceeding 100 percent.

In 2003 28 percent of identity theft victims were between 18 and 29 years old, 25 percent were 30 to 39 years old, and 21 percent were from 40 to 49 years old. Those under the age of 18 and over 60 were the least likely to be targets of identity theft. (See Figure 7.1.)

According to the FTC, about 21 percent of callers to the Identity Theft Hotline reported having a personal relationship with the suspected offender. Nearly 10 percent of identity theft victims reported a family member as the suspect. Roommates and co-habitants were identified as suspects by less than three percent of callers.

Most callers to the Identity Theft Hotline stated that they did not know how their identities were stolen, and most did not discover the theft until one year after their personal information began to be misused. Victims of identity theft were sometimes unable to obtain credit or financial services, telecommunication services, or utility

TABLE 7.1

How victims' information is misused in identity fraud cases, January 1–December 31, 2003

Theft subtypes	Percent of all victims
Credit card fraud: 33%	
New accounts	19.2%
Existing accounts	12.0
Unspecified	1.4
Phone or utilities fraud: 21%	
Wireless—new	10.4%
Telephone—new	5.6
Utilities—new	3.8
Unauthorized charges to existing accounts	0.6
Unspecified	0.8
Bank fraud: 17%	
Existing accounts	8.2%
Electronic fund transfer	4.8
New accounts	3.8
Unspecified	0.5
Employment-related fraud: 11%	
Employment-Related Fraud	11.1%
Attempted identity theft: 8%	
Attempted identity theft	8.0%
Government documents or benefits fraud: 8%	
Fraudulent tax return	3.7%
Driver's license issued/forged	2.3
Government benefits applied/received	1.3
Social Security card issued/forged	0.4
Other government docs issued/forged	0.4
Unspecified	<0.1
Loan fraud: 6%	
Business/personal/student loan	2.3%
Auto loan/lease	2.0
Real estate loan	1.0
Unspecified	0.3
Other identity theft fraud: 19%	
Other	11.6%
Illegal/criminal	2.1
Medical	1.8
Internet/e-mail	1.7
Apartment/house rented	0.9
Bankruptcy	0.3
Insurance	0.3
Property rental fraud	0.2
Child support	0.2
Securities/other investments	0.2
Magazines	0.1

*Percentages are based on the 214,905 total victims reporting. Percentages add to more than 100 because approximately 19% of victims reported experiencing more than one type of identity theft. All victims reported experiencing at least one type of identity theft.

SOURCE: "How Victims' Information Is Misused, January 1–December 31, 2003," in *National and State Trends in Fraud and Identity Theft January–December 2003,* Federal Trade Commission, Washington, DC, January 22, 2004

services as the result of credit problems arising from the identity theft.

The Social Security Administration (SSA) reports that in 1998 some 11,000 complaints were received about misuse of social security numbers. In 2001 the number of complaints had risen to about 65,000. An SSA review concluded that about 81 percent of these incidents of misuse involved identity theft.

Identity theft is also used by illegal aliens. Each year thousands of aliens are stopped at the border for attempting to enter the country by using counterfeit or fraudulently obtained identity documents. The Immigration and Naturalization Service (INS) reports that 99,171 fraudulent documents were seized by their inspectors in 1998, with 114,023 being seized in 2001. The most common documents are border crossing cards and alien registration cards. To counter this trend, the Enhanced Border Security and Visa Entry Reform Act of 2002 called for all U.S. travel and entry documents to be machine-readable and contain biometric identifying information.

CORPORATE CRIME

Tracking white-collar crime, and especially corporate crime, is generally much more complicated than tracking other crimes. There often is no one single offender or one victim to report the crime. White-collar crime is often based on establishing trust between the victim and the offender before any crime is committed. Building trust expands the time frame of the crime, permitting repeated victimizations of an unsuspecting victim.

Different types of ethical violations linked to corporate crime include misrepresentation in advertising, deceptive packaging, the lack of social responsibility in television commercials, the sale of harmful and unsafe products, the sale of virtually worthless products, polluting the environment, kickbacks and payoffs, unethical influences on government, unethical competitive practices, personal gain for management, unethical treatment of workers, stealing of trade secrets, and the victimization of local communities by corporations.

Corporate crime is nothing new. In the article "Schemers and Scams: A Brief History of Bad Business" (*Fortune,* March 18, 2002), a brief chronology of corporate malfeasance is given, including some of the more well-known corporate crimes of the past 15 years:

- In 1989 Charles Keating was convicted of fraudulently marketing junk bonds, which led to the collapse of Lincoln Savings and Loan. The cost to taxpayers for the bank's failure was estimated at $3.4 billion. Keating served five years of a twelve-year prison sentence.
- In 1997 Columbia/HCA insurance company was the target of the largest-ever federal investigation into

FIGURE 7.1

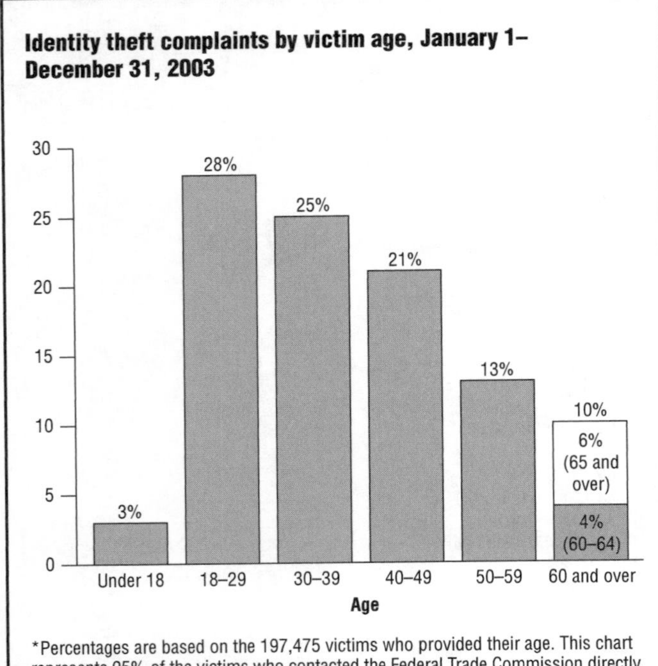

SOURCE: "Identity Theft Complaints by Victim Age, January 1–December 31, 2003," in *National and State Trends in Fraud and Identity Theft January–December 2003*, Federal Trade Commission, Washington, DC, January 22, 2004

health-care scams. An $840 million Medicare-fraud settlement was agreed to in 2000.

- In 1998 Al Dunlap, nicknamed "Chainsaw Al" in the press after taking over companies and reducing costs by firing people, was fired from Sunbeam for illicitly manufacturing earnings. He overstated revenues, booking sales, for example, on grills neither paid for nor shipped.
- In 2001 Al Taubman, former chairman of Sotheby's auction house, was convicted of conspiracy for price-fixing at Sotheby's and Christie's auction houses.

In November 1998, 46 states collectively settled lawsuits they had brought against cigarette manufacturers to recoup the tobacco-related costs of health care paid out by state Medicaid agencies. Although the sale of tobacco products was legal, the states alleged that tobacco firms knew of the highly addictive nature of smoking yet deliberately concealed their research findings from the general public for decades while promoting tobacco use. According to the terms of the settlement, the tobacco industry agreed to pay out some $206 billion over 25 years. The states of Florida, Texas, Minnesota and Mississippi settled their lawsuits separately for some $40 billion over 25 years.

Between 2001 and 2002 there were a number of verdicts in cases brought against tobacco companies, some of them resulting in million-dollar jury awards. In March 2002 an Oregon jury found Phillip Morris liable for a smoker's death and ordered the company to pay $150 million in punitive damages. In June 2001 a California jury awarded former smoker Richard Boeken $3 billion in punitive damages, later reduced to $100 million. Also in June of 2001 a New York jury found the U.S. tobacco industry liable for "unfair and deceptive business practices" and awarded some $17.8 million to Empire Blue Cross and Blue Shield of New York for the health costs of smoking-related illnesses.

A Different Type of Crime

Corporate crime can cost billions of dollars, but because these losses are frequently spread out over so many uninformed victims, it usually does not create the same initial public impact as, for example, an armed robbery of a few hundred dollars. There often is no single person to take the blame. Corporations can be so complex and powerful that the rules of justice applied to individuals are often applied differently to business. A board of directors is not imprisoned for a corporate wrongdoing; instead, the corporation may be fined.

Despite their potential to do extensive damage, corporate crimes are not regarded with the same fear as "street crime." Personal attacks are far more frightening, even to persons who have never been physically assaulted, than the seemingly remote possibility of dying a slow death due to air pollution, or buying defective tires, or using a poorly tested drug. On the other hand, someone who has had a considerable part, or perhaps all, of their savings stolen as the result of fraud or embezzlement can face a painfully insecure future because they may no longer have the money intended to support their later years. Nonetheless, except in certain spectacular cases that receive extensive media coverage such as the savings and loan fraud of the 1980s, the consequences of corporate misbehavior are generally ignored.

Corporate Espionage

Many corporations are becoming concerned about the potential espionage activities of competing corporations. In a computerized global economy where a competitor's advantage can mean life or death for a company, trade secrets, copyrighted information, patents, and trademarks become very important. Most major companies have developed sophisticated security systems to protect their secrets. Stealing classified corporate information has become a major issue for national governments. In a 2001 report by the U.S. General Accounting Office (GAO), it was reported that the American Society for Industrial Security, which surveys Fortune 500 companies, estimated that potential losses to American businesses from theft of proprietary information were $45 billion in 2000.

Many governments have begun to use their national intelligence organizations to protect local companies from espionage by foreign companies or governments. In the United States, the Economic Espionage Act of 1996 (PL 104-294) made it a federal crime to steal trade secrets for another country.

STEALING FROM THE DEPARTMENT OF DEFENSE

The U.S. Department of Defense has a long history of lax control of its ordering and payment procedures, a serious problem in a department that spent an estimated $304 billion in 2003 and is expected to spend $314 billion in 2004 (GPO Access, March 24, 2004 [Online] http://www.gpoaccess.gov/usbudget/fy00/guide02.html [Accessed 12 July 2004]). The U.S. Department of Justice is continually looking for instances in which contractors have defrauded the government. Normally, these investigations end in agreement by the defrauding company to pay a fine.

In March of 1998 the U.S. Department of Justice announced that Unisys Corporation and Lockheed Martin Corporation would pay $3.2 million to settle allegations they had sold spare parts at inflated prices to the Department of Commerce for the NEXRAD Doppler Radar System. During the same month, the Pall Aeropower Corporation agreed to pay $2.2 million to settle allegations that it defrauded the United States by overcharging the Department of the Army for air filters for the AH-1 "Cobra" helicopter. The government also alleged that Pall had defrauded the Department of Defense on other contracts, but the settlement dismissed all allegations.

On March 30, 1998, the U.S. Department of Justice announced that Alliant Techsystems, Inc., and Hercules, Inc., had agreed to pay $4.5 million to settle allegations they illegally overcharged the Navy for labor costs on contracts implementing the Intermediate-Range Nuclear Forces (INF) Treaty. According to the complaint, "Managers at Alliant and Hercules regularly directed their employees to mischarge labor time to a number of military contracts even though management knew the employees did not devote as much time to the contract as was charged to the government." On April 23, 1998, the Justice Department reported that M/A-COM, Inc., a division of AMP Incorporated, agreed to pay $3 million to settle claims that it failed to perform some required tests on electronic components.

FALSIFYING CORPORATE DATA

The Securities and Exchange Commission (SEC) reported that falsifying corporate data, especially on financial statements, increased in the 1990s. The falsified reports included statements inflating sales, hiding ownership of the corporation, and embezzlement. In July 2003 President George W. Bush created the Corporate Fraud Task Force to oversee investigation and prosecution of crimes involving corporate fraud.

The collapse of the Enron corporation was one of the most glaring examples of corporate crime and falsification of corporate data in recent history. Enron was founded in 1985 in Houston as an oil pipeline company. As electrical power markets were deregulated in the late-1990s, Enron expanded and became an energy broker trading in electricity and other energy commodities. In effect, Enron became the middleman between power suppliers and power consumers. However, instead of simply brokering energy deals, Enron devised increasingly complex contracts with buyers and sellers that allowed Enron to profit from the difference in the selling price and the buying price of commodities such as electricity. In order to service these contracts, which were becoming increasingly speculative due to the instability of unregulated electricity prices, Enron executives created a number of so-called "partnerships"—in effect, "paper" companies whose sole function was to hide debt and make Enron appear to be much more profitable than it actually was.

On December 2, 2001, Enron filed for bankruptcy protection, listing some $13.1 billion in liabilities and $24.7 billion in assets—$38 billion less than the assets listed only two months earlier. As a result, thousands of Enron employees lost their jobs. Perhaps worse, many Enron employees—who had been encouraged by company executives to invest monies from their 401k retirement plans in Enron stock—had their retirement savings reduced to almost nothing as a result of the precipitous decline in value of Enron stock. The stock dropped from $34 dollars a share on October 16, 2001, to pennies per share as of December 2, 2001. Most chilling, Enron executives, who themselves reaped millions in profits from Enron stock, barred employees from cashing in their stock in late October when it still had some value.

According to internal emails and other inter-office communications, warnings were given to Enron executives and to its accounting firm, Arthur Andersen, that Enron was heading for financial disaster as early as a year before Enron declared bankruptcy. The beginning of the end occurred on October 16, 2001, when Enron announced a $638 billion loss for the third quarter. As a result, the value of Enron's stockholders' equity was reduced by $1.2 billion. On November 8, 2001, Enron announced that it had overstated its earnings for the past four years by as much as $585 million. It also owed some $3 billion in obligations—to be paid in company stock—to various partnerships Enron had created to offset its rising debt. By November 28, 2001, Enron's debt instruments were downgraded to junk bond status, making it impossible for Enron to forestall its collapse by borrowing more money to service its debt.

In the wake of Enron's collapse, some 10 committees in the U.S. Senate and House of Representatives began to investigate whether Enron defrauded investors by deliberately concealing financial information. The shredding of financial and inter-office documents by both Enron and its accounting firm, Arthur Andersen, was also under investigation. Meanwhile, numerous lawsuits were filed against Enron, Arthur Andersen, and former Enron executives including former Chairman Kenneth L. Lay and former CEO, Jeffrey Skilling. Former Enron Vice Chairman, Clifford Baxter, was found shot to death in his car on January 15, 2002, in an apparent suicide. News reports linked Baxter's death to his despondency over his role in the Enron scandal. Enron treasurer Ben Glisan, Jr., was convicted on conspiracy charges to commit wire and securities fraud. He was sentenced to five years in prison on September 10, 2003. Jeffrey Skilling turned himself in to authorities on February 19, 2004 to face nearly three dozen criminal charges.

On June 15, 2002, a New York jury found accounting firm Arthur Andersen guilty of obstructing justice in connection with the Enron collapse. After a six-week trial and 10 days of jury deliberations, Arthur Andersen was convicted of destroying Enron documents during an ongoing federal investigation of the company's accounting practices. During the trial, executives of Arthur Andersen testified that the documents were destroyed as the result of customary housekeeping duties, not as a means to prevent federal investigators from seeing them. As a result of the verdict, Andersen faced a fine of $500,000 and a term of probation of up to five years. In the aftermath of the Enron scandal, the 89-year-old accounting firm laid off some 7,000 employees and lost more than 650 of its 2,300 clients.

Other recent examples of alleged falsification of corporate data include the filing for bankruptcy in January 2002 of Global Crossing, a telecommunications company. In February 2002 the Securities and Exchange Commission (SEC) opened an investigation into Global Crossing and its auditor—again, the accounting firm of Arthur Andersen—for questionable accounting practices.

L. Dennis Kozlowski, the former chief executive of Tyco International Ltd., was indicted in June 2002 by a New York grand jury on charges of evading more than $1 million in sales taxes on at least six paintings valued at some $13 million. According to the indictment, Kozlowski allegedly directed New York gallery employees to ship empty cartons to the Tyco corporate headquarters in New Hampshire, where Tyco employees were instructed to sign for the "shipments." The paintings, New York's case claims, eventually ended up in Kozlowski's Manhattan apartment for his own personal use. Kozlowski is accused of trying to evade the New York City taxes that would have been owed on paintings purchased by someone in-state (paintings purchased from out-of-state are not subject to these taxes). On June 26, 2002, the Manhattan district attorney added a charge of evidence-tampering to the other charges against Kozlowski, claiming that he removed a shipping invoice from a crate of documents before it was sent to the district attorney's office. All told, Kozlowski faced 12 felony charges and one misdemeanor charge. Kozlowski's trial ended April 3, 2004 in a mistrial.

In July 2002 John Rigas, his two sons, and two other executives of the Adelphia Communications Corporation, one of the nation's largest cable television companies, were charged with wire fraud, bank fraud, and securities fraud for failing to disclose billions of dollars worth of company debt. Their deception defrauded investors, creditors, and the general public by making them believe the company was in better financial health than it was. The deception ran from 1999 to May 2002.

On November 4, 2003, Richard Scrushy, former CEO of HealthSouth, the nation's largest provider of outpatient surgery, rehabilitative healthcare services, and diagnostic imaging, surrendered to FBI agents. He faced an 85-count indictment for allegedly inflating company earnings by some $2.7 billion and falsifying financial statements to hide the fraud. He also was charged with taking some $267 million in company funds for himself. Scrushy is one of 16 HealthSouth executives under indictment for fraud.

According to *Fortune Magazine* (March 18, 2002), between 1992 and 2001, the Securities and Exchange Commission (SEC) filed criminal charges in 609 cases involving stock fraud or other corporate crime. Of the 609 referrals, U.S. attorneys prosecuted 187 defendants. Of those, 147 defendants were found guilty and 87 went to jail or prison. From 1997 to 2000 the SEC filed some 3,000 civil cases. Of those, 39.1 percent involved securities offerings violations, followed by 16.3 percent for insider trading, 12.2 percent for stock manipulation, 11.5 percent for financial disclosure violations, and 3.1 percent for fraud against consumers. The remaining civil cases brought by the SEC were either for contempt or for other causes of action.

BANK FRAUD

The FBI investigates incidents of financial institution fraud (FIF), including insider fraud, check fraud, mortgage and loan fraud, and financial institution failures. According to the *Financial Institution Fraud and Failure Report, Fiscal Year 2003* (U.S. Department of Justice, Federal Bureau of Investigation, Washington, DC, 2003), in the early 1990s the FBI was heavily involved in investigating savings and loan failures due to insider fraud. In 1992 there were 758 financial institution failure investigations, the highest recorded. This number dropped throughout the 1990s and in 2003 only 67 cases were under investigation.

According to U.S. Department of Justice figures, the number of convictions in FIF cases declined from 1999, when 2,878 convictions were reported, to 2002, with

TABLE 7.2

Financial institution fraud and failure matters handled by the U.S. Department of Justice, 1986–2002

	Cases pending		Convictions[1]		Indictments	Dollar amounts (in millions)			Failed financial institutions under investigation at end of fiscal year
	Total	Major cases[2]	Total	Major cases[2]		Recovered	Restitution	Fine	
1986	7,286	2,948	1,957	533	X	X	X	X	202
1987	7,622	3,393	2,309	740	X	X	X	X	282
1988	7,385	3,446	2,197	851	X	X	X	X	357
1989	7,819	3,605	2,174	791	X	X	X	X	404
1990	7,613	3,672	2,461	1,043	X	X	X	X	530
1991	8,678	4,336	2,559	986	2,784	$59.4	$490.7	$7.8	670
1992	9,772	5,071	2,751	1,136	3,064	67.1	402.7	14.6	740
1993	10,088	5,405	3,233	1,407	3,446	89.6	1,333.5	10.5	651
1994	9,286	4,926	2,926	1,348	2,867	240.6	865.0	10.4	531
1995	8,641	4,413	2,616	1,298	2,880	185.1	1,139.9	16.8	395
1996	8,574	4,070	2,510	1,255	2,630	67.2	359.1	442.7	247
1997	8,512	3,859	2,551	1,342	2,437	41.2	537.1	25.7	200
1998	8,577	3,709	2,613	1,207	2,691	62.4	491.0	5.5	142
1999	8,799	3,855	2,878	1,488	2,869	114.5	834.3	77.8	129
2000	8,638	4,081	2,783	1,394	2,877	48.5	589.0	8.0	99
2001	8,184	4,383	2,702	1,363	2,738	45.8	754.2	15.2	97
2002	7,305	4,287	2,397	1,328	2,471	28.2	1,983.8	7.6	71

Note: Financial institutions include banks, savings and loans, and credit unions.
[1]Includes pre-trial diversions.
[2]A major case is defined as a case involving a failed financial institution, or where the amount of reported loss or exposure i s $100,000 or more.

SOURCE: "Table 3.151: Financial Institution Fraud and Failure Matters Handled by the U.S. Department of Justice," in *Sourcebook of Criminal Justice Statistics 2002*, U.S. Department of Justice, Bureau of Justice Statistics, Washington, DC, 2003

2,397 convictions. Almost $2 billion in restitution was reported in 2002, more than double the amount for 2001. (See Table 7.2.)

With the decline of insider fraud cases, the FBI has turned its investigations to external fraud schemes involving criminals seeking to defraud financial institutions. In 2003 the FBI reported 5,869 FIF cases under investigation, some 4,000 of which were classified as major cases (loss exceeding $100,000).

FRAUD AGAINST INSURANCE COMPANIES

Annually, thousands of cases are reported involving acts of fraud against insurance companies, such as faking a death to collect life insurance, setting fire to a house to collect property insurance, or claiming injuries not actually suffered. According to "A Statistical Study of State Insurance Fraud Bureaus: A Quantitative Analysis, 1995 to 2000" (Coalition Against Insurance Fraud, May 2001), insurance fraud bureaus in 41 states received nearly 89,000 referrals involving insurance fraud in 2000, up by 5 percent from 1999. There were 21,000 more cases of fraud reported to insurance fraud bureaus in 2000 than in 1995. Four states—New York, California, New Jersey, and Florida—accounted for 73 percent of all referrals. Referrals may come from insurance companies, consumers, and government and law enforcement agencies.

In 2000 insurance fraud bureaus referred some 3,998 cases of insurance fraud for prosecution, resulting in 2,123 criminal convictions nationwide. Florida reported 386 criminal convictions for insurance fraud in 2000, followed by New York (318), Pennsylvania (276), Arizona (137), and New Jersey (90). In 2000 there were some 1,100 civil actions initiated by insurance bureaus for insurance fraud. This was down somewhat from the 1,200 civil actions brought by insurance bureaus in 1999. Still, the number of civil actions brought by insurance bureaus in 2000 was more than triple the 344 civil actions brought in 1995.

In 2002 the United States Postal Inspection Service (USPIS) arrested three Kentucky men for defrauding insurance companies out of some $13 million. They fraudulently issued life insurance policies to people suffering from AIDS. To dupe the insurance companies into insuring the AIDS victims, they arranged for the blood of healthy people to be submitted for testing instead of the blood of the actual applicants.

In March 2004 one of the largest insurance frauds of recent times was unearthed in southern California. Following a 15-month investigation by the FBI, dozens of outpatient-surgery clinics were charged with performing unnecessary surgeries on patients and then overcharging their insurance companies. The patients themselves were part of the fraud, being recruited to have surgeries performed with the promise of a share of the insurance money. Some $300 million reportedly was stolen.

FRAUD BY INSURANCE COMPANIES

In addition to the criminal attempts to swindle insurance companies, insurance companies sometimes defraud their customers. On April 30, 2001, a final settlement was reached in the class action brought against Principal Mutual Life Insurance Company by some 960,000 current and former life insurance policy holders who alleged that they were misled by false and misleading marketing materials when they purchased their policies.

In January of 2002 a preliminary settlement of $59 million was announced in a class action lawsuit brought by automobile policyholders in Georgia against Allstate Insurance Company. Policyholders alleged that Allstate failed to provide payment for the loss of an automobile's market value after an accident when paying for the repair costs of automobiles involved in accidents. Also in January 2002 a final settlement of almost $5.6 million was approved in the class action suit brought by parties in 27 states against United Services Automobile Association (USAA). As in the Allstate action, automobile policyholders alleged that USAA failed to compensate them for the loss of value of vehicles after an accident.

SECURITIES FRAUD

There are many laws regulating the securities markets—which include the New York Stock Exchange (NYSE) and the National Association of Securities Dealers Automated Quotation (NASDAQ)—and the corporations who sell "securities" on the markets. These regulations require corporations to be honest with their investors about the corporations, and stockbrokers to be forthcoming with their clients.

Despite these rules, both the corporate officials who release information about their companies and the stockbrokers who help people invest in securities may knowingly lie to or hide information from consumers in order to raise the stock level of a company for their own profit. Corporations may commit this type of fraud by releasing false information to the financial markets through news releases, quarterly and annual reports, SEC filings, market analyst conference calls, proxy statements, and prospectuses. Brokers may commit this type of fraud by failure to follow clients' instructions when directed, misrepresentation or omission of information, unsuitable recommendations or investments, unauthorized trades, and excessive trading (churning). Since brokerage analysts' recommendations to clients may affect the fees earned by the firms' investment banking operations, it may be profitable for the analysts to play up the value of certain stocks.

The Stanford Law School Securities Class Action Clearinghouse, in cooperation with Cornerstone Research, tracks the number of securities class action filings. In 2002 the number filed was 225, an increase of over 200 percent from the 1996 number of 108. Of these 225 filings, 113 were against firms traded on the New York Stock Exchange and 85 were against companies traded on NASDAQ. There were 53 filings in New York, 43 in California, and 22 in Delaware. Companies in the communications industry were most often filed against (58), followed by those in the noncyclical consumer industry (47) and finance (33). The most common allegations made were misrepresentation in financial documents and false forward-looking statements.

In addition to the traditional securities class action filings, two new types of securities class filings have been introduced. "IPO Allocation" filings allege misconduct in the allocation of Initial Public Offering (IPO) stock, that is, stock for companies going public for the first time. In 2001 there were 312 IPO Allocation filings recorded. In 2002 "Analyst" filings were introduced. These filings allege that investment banks or individual securities analysts at such banks issued biased research reports or ratings on companies. These reports were not based on factual information and did not disclose conflicts of interest. Numbers for Analyst filings have not yet been tracked by the Clearinghouse.

In May 2002 the stock brokerage company Merrill Lynch agreed to settle a case brought against it by the New York Attorney General Eliot Spitzer, for allegedly hyping certain stocks publicly in order to gain banking business while privately criticizing the stocks to others. The settlement amount agreed to by Merrill Lynch was $100 million. In addition to the monetary sum, Merrill Lynch must now include a warning on its stock recommendations to advise investors that it may be doing business with the companies whose stock it is rating.

Oil and Gas Investment Frauds

While many oil and gas investments are legitimate, this area is well-known for fraudulent offers. Oil- and gas-well deals are sometimes offered by "boiler rooms," or fly-by-night operations that consist of nothing more than bare office space and a dozen or so desks and telephones. Boiler room operators employ telephone solicitors trained to use high-pressure sales tactics. These con artists make repeated unsolicited telephone calls in which they follow a carefully scripted sales pitch that guarantees high profits. Some swindlers surround themselves with the trappings of legitimacy, including professionally designed color brochures.

In a fraudulent oil and gas scheme, scam artists promoting the investment often offer limited partnership interests to prospective investors who live outside the state where the well is located and outside the state the scam artists are calling from. This distance reduces chances for an investor to visit the site of a well or what may be nonexistent company headquarters.

Individuals subjected to a high-pressure sales pitch in an unsolicited telephone call should watch for the following tip-offs that they may be dealing with a swindler:

- The oil well investment "can't miss."
- Very little risk is involved.
- The promoter has hit oil or gas on every other well previously drilled.
- A lot of oil or gas has been found in an adjacent field.
- A large reputable oil company is already operating near the company's leased property, or planning to do so.
- A decision must be made immediately to invest in order to assure the purchase of one of the few interests remaining unsold.
- The deal is only available to a few lucky and specially chosen investors.
- The salesperson has personally invested in the venture himself.
- A tip from a reputable geologist has given the company a unique opportunity to make this venture a success.

One can reduce the risk of being swindled by being suspicious of any deal that promises a fantastic return at little risk.

TELEMARKETING FRAUD

Telemarketing is a form of direct marketing in which representatives from companies call consumers or other businesses in order to sell their goods and services. Telemarketing services may also be tied in with other forms of direct marketing such as print, radio, or television marketing. For example, an advertisement on the television may request the viewer to call a toll-free number. The overwhelming majority of telemarketing operations are legitimate and trustworthy.

The National Fraud Information Center (NFIC) is a project of the National Consumers League, a nonprofit organization founded in 1992. The NFIC considers itself "a vital resource for consumers and law enforcement agencies in the fight against telemarketing fraud." The National Fraud Information Center reported the following swindles as the top 10 telemarketing frauds for 2003.

- Credit Card Offers (23 percent). Individuals who would normally have difficulty getting a credit card are offered the chance to do so for a fee paid up front. Often, the credit card is never issued. (Average loss: $233)
- Prizes/Sweepstakes (21 percent). Prize awards, often phony, are offered in exchange for a certain amount of money paid up front. (Average loss: $3,031)
- Work at Home Plans (10 percent). The swindler offers expensive kits to launch work-at-home businesses, such as envelope stuffing, that seldom generate much, if any, income. (Average loss: $392)
- Magazines (7 percent). Bogus magazine subscriptions are offered for an up-front fee. (Average loss: $110)
- Advance Fee Loans (6 percent). Similar to credit card scams, for an up-front fee, loans that seldom materialize are offered to individuals who would normally not qualify for a loan through a legitimate lender. (Average loss: $1,662)
- Lotteries/Lottery Clubs (5 percent). Individuals are told they have won, or are offered assistance to win, a lottery, often based in a foreign country. (Average loss: $5,127)
- Buyers Clubs (4 percent). Membership to non-existent buyers clubs that purport to offer deeply discounted prices are offered for an up-front fee. (Average loss: $225)
- Travel/Vacations (2 percent). Offers of free or discounted travel are offered but not delivered. (Average loss: $571)
- Telephone Slamming (2 percent). Telephone customers are tricked into switching their telephone companies, often without knowing that they have agreed to the change. (Average loss: $103)
- Business Opportunities/Franchises (2 percent). Opportunities to start a new business, guaranteed to be an easy moneymaker, are offered for a fee. (Average loss: $5,376)

Characteristics of Telemarketing Fraud Schemes

The USPIS investigates and enforces over 200 federal statutes related to crimes against the U.S. Mail, the Postal Service, and its employees. It investigates any crime that uses the U.S. Mail to further a scheme, no matter where it originated: via phone, mail, or Internet. The USPIS offers a list of guidelines that can help prevent a person from being victimized by a fraudulent telemarketing scheme. This list can be applied to any type of offer, not just telemarketing offers.

- *The offer sounds too good to be true.* An unbelievable-sounding deal probably is not legitimate.
- *High-pressure sales tactics.* A swindler often refuses to take no for an answer; he has a sensible-sounding answer for your every hesitation, inquiry, or objection.
- *Insistence on an immediate decision.* Swindlers often say you must make a decision "right now," and they usually give a reason, like, "The offer will expire soon."
- *You are one of just a few people eligible for the offer.* Don't believe it. Swindlers often target hundreds of thousands—and sometimes millions—of solicitations to consumers across the nation.

- *Your credit card number is requested for verification.* Do not provide your credit card number (or even just its expiration date) if you are not making a purchase, even if you are asked for it for "identification" or "verification" purposes, or to prove "eligibility" for the offer. If you give your card number, the swindler may make unauthorized charges to your account, even if you decide not to buy anything. Once that is done, it may be very hard to get your money back.
- *You are urged to provide money quickly.* A crook may try to impress upon you the urgency of making an immediate decision by offering to send a delivery service to your home or office to pick up your check. This may be to get your money before you have a chance to think carefully about the offer and change your mind, or to avoid the possibility of mail fraud charges in the future.
- *There is no risk.* All investments have some risk, except for U.S. Government obligations. And if you are dealing with a swindler, any "money-back guarantee" he or she makes will simply not be honored.
- *You are given no detailed written information.* If you must send money or provide a credit card number before the telemarketer gives you the details in writing, be skeptical. Do not accept excuses such as, "It's such a new offer we don't have any written materials yet," or "You'll get written information after you pay."
- *You are asked to trust the telemarketer.* A swindler, unable to get you to take the bait with all of his other gimmicks, may ask you to "trust" him. Be careful about trusting a stranger you talk to on the phone.
- *You are told you have won a prize, but you must pay for something before you can receive it.* This payment can either be a requirement to purchase a minimum order of cleaning supplies or vitamins, or it can be a shipping/handling charge or a processing fee. Do not deal with a promoter who uses this tactic.

Recent Telemarketing Fraud Arrests

In 2002 the USPIS closed 40 illegal telemarketing operations. Among those companies shut down was a firm in Philadelphia which targeted businesses, offering lighting and maintenance supplies over the phone. The firm would then charge exorbitant amounts for the delivered products. The operators were doing $9.3 million in yearly business at the time they were arrested. Another case involved three Canadians who were arrested by the USPIS for calling elderly Americans claiming the victims had won Cadillacs, if they would pay upfront transportation, tax, and license fees. Some 100 victims lost an estimated $250,000 in the scheme.

On November 17, 2003, Canadians Philip Arcand and his wife, Roberta Galway, were sentenced to 10 years in prison for telemarketing fraud. Their scheme involved calling unsuspecting Americans and offering protection against credit card fraud. Their program would supposedly protect consumers from unwanted charges on their credit cards if their cards were stolen by thieves. To institute the service, the victim was asked to give out his credit card number to purchase it. Later, outrageous charges would appear on the victim's card, whether or not they had agreed to take the "protection" service. In all, some $12 million was stolen from consumers.

MAIL CRIME

The USPIS investigates a number of crimes involving the nation's mail, including mail fraud, mail theft, and the mailing of controlled substances. Between the years 1981 and 2002, arrests for mail fraud rose from 1,100 to 1,634 respectively, an increase of about 48.5 percent. The peak arrests for mail fraud (1,965) occurred in 1993. In 2002 the USPIS was also responsible for 5,858 arrests for mail theft, which includes the theft or possession of stolen mail, down from 6,364 arrests in 2001. The mailing of controlled substances such as narcotics, steroids, and drug paraphernalia accounted for 1,385 arrests by the USPIS in 2002, down from 1,662 arrests in 2001. Other crimes investigated by the USPIS in 2002 included the use of counterfeit postage, money orders, child exploitation (child pornography), and the mailing of obscene matter and sexually oriented advertisements.

Mail fraud can involve a number of different crimes against businesses, consumers, and government in which the U.S. mail system has been used. During 2002 the USPIS arrested the chief financial officer of a Minnesota company who embezzled over $14 million by approving checks to brokerage accounts he secretly controlled and using company money to buy merchandise he later resold for his own profit. In a fraud that took in $60 million, a Massachusetts firm offered to help novice inventors develop and market their ideas, charging rates of $4,000 to $12,000 for the service. Some 34,000 people were taken in by the scheme. The company head was arrested by the USPIS and sentenced to eight years in prison. In a fraud aimed at the government of New York, two owners of a construction company were charged with fraudulently obtaining $40 million by misleading the state's minority business enterprise program about the true owners of subcontractor companies.

COMPUTER CRIME

Types of Computer Crime

By the 1990s computer-assisted crime had become a major element of white-collar crime. Like corporate crime, computer crime often goes unrecorded. The National Institute of Justice defines three different types of computer crimes:

- Computer abuse is a broad range of intentional acts that may or may not be specifically prohibited by criminal statutes. Any intentional act involving knowledge of computer use or technology...if one or more perpetrators made or could have made gain and/or one or more victims suffered or could have suffered loss.

- Computer fraud is any crime in which a person uses the computer either directly or as a vehicle for deliberate misrepresentation or deception, usually to cover up embezzlement or theft of money, goods, services, or information.

- Computer crime is any violation of a computer crime law.

Computer crime is faceless and bloodless, and the financial gain can be huge. A common computer crime involves tampering with accounting and banking records, especially through electronic funds transfers. These electronic funds transfers, or wire transfers, are cash management systems that allow the customer electronic access to an account, automatic teller machines, and internal banking procedures, including on-line teller terminals and computerized check processing.

Computers and their technology (printers, modems, computer bulletin boards, e-mail) are used for credit card fraud, counterfeiting, bank embezzlement, theft of secret documents, vandalism, and other illegal activities. Experts place the annual value of computer crime at anywhere from $550 million to $5 billion a year. Even the larger figure may be underestimated, because many victims try to hide the crime. Few companies want to admit their computer security has been breached and their confidential files or accounts are vulnerable. No centralized databank exists for computer crime statistics. Computer crimes are often counted under other categories such as fraud and embezzlement.

The first state computer crime law took effect in Florida in 1978. An Arizona law took effect two months later. Other states soon followed, and by 2000, Vermont was the only state without a specific computer crime provision.

In 1986 Congress passed the Computer Fraud and Abuse Act (PL 99-474) that makes it illegal to perpetrate fraud on a computer. The Computer Abuse Amendments of 1994 (PL 103-322) make it a federal crime "through means of a computer used in interstate commerce of communication...[to] damage, or cause damage to, a computer, computer system, network, information, data, or program...with reckless disregard" for the consequences of those actions to the computer owner. This law refers to someone who maliciously destroys or changes computer records or knowingly distributes a virus that shuts down a computer system. A virus program is one that resides inside another program, activated by some predetermined code to create havoc in the host computer. Virus programs can be transmitted either through the sharing of disks and programs or through electronic mail.

Computer giant Microsoft teamed with the FBI, Secret Service, and Interpol in November 2003 to announce the Anti-Virus Reward Program. Under the program, Microsoft will pay the monetary rewards for information leading to the arrest and conviction of anyone responsible for launching malicious viruses and worms on the Internet. The first two rewards were for information leading to the arrest and conviction of those responsible for the MSBlast.A worm and the Sobig virus.

CORPORATIONS AND COMPUTER CRIME. The Computer Security Institute in San Francisco, California, conducted "The 2003 Computer Crime and Security Survey" with the participation of the FBI's San Francisco Computer Intrusion Squad. The study found that of 530 computer security practitioners from major U.S. corporations, government agencies, financial and medical institutions, and universities, some 56 percent had detected computer security breaches within the last 12 months. Three-quarters of respondents stated that their institution had suffered financial losses due to computer breaches. Financial losses of $201 million were reported by nearly half of the respondents due to breaches in their computer security.

According to the survey, the most serious financial losses resulted from the theft of proprietary information, with respondents reporting total losses of over $70 million. Denial of service, resulting in a total loss of $65 million, was the next most expensive security breach. Still, despite these significant financial losses, only 30 percent of respondents reported the computer intrusions to law enforcement. In part, this low level of reporting of computer crime to law enforcement may have to do with an unwillingness to reveal the proprietary nature of the information breached.

Survey respondents reported various types of attacks on or unauthorized uses of their computer systems. Eighty percent of respondents stated they had detected employee abuse of Internet access privileges, such as downloading pornography or pirating software. Eighty-two percent reported the detection of computer viruses, while 15 percent reported financial fraud, up from only 3 percent in 2000.

HOLDING A COMPANY HOSTAGE. For a company, the most feared type of computer crime involves the sabotage or threatened sabotage of the company's computer system. It is almost impossible to determine how often this happens since very few companies ever report the incidents.

Most American companies of any size have become totally dependent on their computers. Management is generally unaware of how computers work and are fully dependent on their systems administrator or the person responsible for keeping the computers running. In fact, in many companies, the systems administrator might be considered the most powerful person in the company, although his or her salary and title might not indicate it. While the computer system might have a sophisticated security system, these are often only a hindrance to an experienced systems analyst.

In the computer age, several new scenarios of employee threats have generated increasing concern. A disgruntled employee might want to take revenge on the company. A systems administrator responsible for the running of the company computer system might feel unappreciated. A discontented employee might create a "logic bomb" that explodes a month after he or she has left and destroys most of the company records, bringing the company's operations to a complete halt. An unhappy or overly ambitious systems administrator might walk into the company president's office and inform her that he wants a huge bonus or the computer system will cease to exist the next morning. The company cannot fire him or her for fear he or she will carry out the threat. They cannot hurriedly bring in a replacement because, by the time he or she could understand what had been done, the system could be destroyed.

Experts recommend that to avoid such potential disasters, a company should make sure no one person has complete knowledge and responsibility for a computer system. While this strategy would provide no guarantee against catastrophe, at least such incidents would be somewhat less likely. Many companies planning to fire a systems analyst often contact computer security firms beforehand to see what they can do. Although it appears cold, callous, and humiliating (and it often is), many companies now escort laid off or fired employees to their desks, helping them collect their possessions, and then accompany them to the door. They hope this harsh procedure will eliminate any opportunity for the former employee to do harm to the company's computer system. While it may be necessary, this tactic is particularly hard on honest workers who have worked many years for the company and see this severe treatment as their reward.

Although infrequent, charges have at times been brought against those who destroy a company's computer system. In February of 1998 the U.S. Department of Justice brought charges against a former chief computer network program designer of Omega, a high-tech company that did work for NASA and the U.S. Navy. The designer had worked for the company for 11 years. After he was terminated, it was alleged that in retaliation he "intentionally caused irreparable damage to Omega's computer system by activating a 'bomb' that permanently deleted all of the company's sophisticated software programs." The loss cost the company at least $10 million in sales and contracts.

Juvenile Computer Hacking Is No Joke

Illegal accessing of a computer, known as hacking, is a crime committed frequently by juveniles. When it is followed by manipulation of the information of private, corporate, or government databases and networks, it can be quite costly. Another means of computer hacking involves creation of a "virus" program.

Cases of juvenile hacking have been going on for at least two decades and have included: six teens gaining access into more than 60 computer networks, including Memorial Sloan-Kettering Cancer Center and Los Alamos National Laboratory in 1983; several juvenile hackers accessing AT&T's computer network in 1987; and teens hacking into computer networks and Web sites for NASA, the Korean Atomic Research Institute, America Online, the U.S. Senate, the White House, the U.S. Army, and the U.S. Department of Justice in the 1990s.

In 1998 the U.S. Secret Service filed the first criminal case against a juvenile for a computer crime. The computer hacking of the unnamed perpetrator shut down the Worcester, Massachusetts, airport in 1997 for six hours. The airport is integrated into the Federal Aviation Administrative traffic system by telephone lines. The accused got into the communication system and disabled it by sending a series of computer commands that changed the data carried on the system. As a result, the airport could not function. (No accidents occurred during that time.) According to the Department of Justice, the juvenile pled guilty in return for two years' probation, a fine, and community service.

United States Attorney Donald K. Stern, lead attorney on the case against the juvenile observed that:

> Computer and telephone networks are at the heart of vital services provided by the government and private industry, and our critical infrastructure. They are not toys for the entertainment of teenagers. Hacking a computer or telephone network can create a tremendous risk to the public and we will prosecute juvenile hackers in appropriate cases....

On December 6, 2000, 18-year-old Robert Russell Sanford pled guilty to six felony charges of breach of computer security and one felony charge of aggravated theft in connection with cyber attacks on U.S. Postal Service computers. Sanford, a Canadian, was placed on five years probation, although he could have been sentenced to up to 20 years in prison. Sanford was also ordered to pay over $45,000 in restitution fines for the cyber attacks.

On September 21, 2000, a 16-year-old from Miami entered a guilty plea and was sentenced to six months detention for illegally intercepting electronic communications on military computer networks. The juvenile admitted that he was responsible for computer intrusions in August and October of 1999 into a military computer network used by the Defense Threat Reduction Agency

(DTRA), an arm of the Department of Defense. The DTRA is responsible for reducing the threat against the United States from nuclear, biological, chemical, conventional and special weapons.

Vulnerability of the Defense Department

Investigators from the U.S. General Accounting Office (GAO), in a report prepared for two Congressional committees, observed that the Pentagon experienced as many as 250,000 "attacks" on its computers in 1995, probably by computer hackers cruising the Internet. The Pentagon figures imply that in 65 percent of the attempts, hackers were able to gain entry into a computer network. The investigators warned, "The potential for catastrophic damage is great, especially if terrorists or enemy governments break into the Pentagon's systems." The report stated that the military's current security program was "dated, inconsistent and incomplete."

Even after this warning, in 1998, hackers broke into unclassified Pentagon networks and altered personnel and payroll data, in what Deputy Defense Secretary John Hamre called "the most organized and systematic attack the Pentagon has seen to date." In 1999 there were a reported 22,124 cyber attacks against the Department of Defense alone, costing the government an estimated $25 billion to bolster computer security procedures in order to ward off future attacks.

Internet Fraud

The Internet is no different than any other form of potential commerce. While most businesses are honest, potential frauds abound. The Internet Fraud Complaint Center (IFCC) was founded on May 8, 2000, by the National White Collar Crime Center and the FBI to monitor the problem of Internet fraud. According to the *IFCC 2002 Internet Fraud Report* (National White Collar Crime Center, 2003), in 2002 the IFCC received 75,063 complaints, an increase of 445 percent from 16,838 complaints in 2000. Internet auction fraud was the most common complaint (46.1 percent), followed by nondelivery of ordered merchandise (31.3 percent), and credit and debit card fraud (11.6 percent). The FTC reports that in 2003 victims of Internet fraud lost nearly $200 million, with a median loss of $195. Some 55 percent of all fraud reported to the FTC in 2003 involved the Internet, an increase from 45 percent in 2002. Investigation and prosecution of Internet fraud is difficult because the perpetrator and victim of the crime are often hundreds or even thousands of miles away from each other. But the IFCC recommends several steps consumers can take to minimize the risk that they will be victims of fraud.

- Before using an online auction service, learn as much as possible about how it works, what is expected from you, and what is expected from the seller.
- Learn as much as possible about the seller of any merchandise you are buying. Be cautious if the mailing address is a post office box. Call the seller's phone number to see if it is correct and working.
- Be aware that sellers in foreign countries operate under different laws that may be to your disadvantage if there is a later problem.
- Never give out your social security number or driver's license number to a seller. There is no need for this information and such actions may lead to identity theft.
- Use a credit card, which gives you the option to dispute charges later. Always make sure that the Web page is secure before giving out your credit card numbers.

ROBBING THE COMPANY

In March 1998 Gabriel Sagaz, former president of Domecq Importers, Inc., a subsidiary of Allied Domecq, P.L.C., the world's second-largest liquor company, pled guilty to fraud and avoiding income taxes. From 1989 through 1996 Sagaz and other top executives at Domecq Importers embezzled over $13 million from the company and received another $2 million in kickbacks from outside vendors.

Cooperative outside vendors would bill Domecq Importers, Inc. for goods never produced and services never performed. Sagaz and his fellow embezzlers would approve the payment of these invoices. The outside vendors would then deposit the money in accounts the criminals had set up in offshore banks. In addition Sagaz and the others took kickbacks from outside vendors to steer contracts to those vendors.

THE COMPANY ROBBING THE CONSUMER

Throughout most of the early 1990s, nine corporations colluded to fix the price of and to control an estimated $1 billion market for lysine, a widely used additive for animal feed. In September 1998 three former executives of the Archer Daniels Midland Corporation (ADM) were found guilty of having secretly met with other lysine producers to divide up marketing territories and establish prices.

Scott R. Lassar, the United States Attorney in Chicago, characterized the case as "one of the hardest-fought trials that I have ever been involved in, in terms of the firepower brought in by both sides." The case involved Michael D. Andreas, the son of ADM's owner and the one-time heir apparent to the $9.2 billion, privately owned food industry giant. In 1999 Andreas and Terrance S. Wilson were each sentenced to two years in jail and each ordered to pay a $350,000 fine. This could have been more, since the government is legally allowed to seek twice the amount gained in the crime or lost by the victims. The prosecutors asked for $25 million from

Andreas; the judge set the lower fine amount instead. In September 2000 the sentences of Andreas and Wilson were changed from two years to three years and from two years to nine months, respectively. Appeals brought by the two men were rejected by the U.S. Supreme Court in November 2000. Marc Whitacre, the other executive charged, was given immunity for his help taping conversations for the FBI, but later had it revoked after it was discovered that he also embezzled $9 million from the company. He was given a nine-year sentence, which had 20 months added to it in 1999.

The U.S. government's investigation of the food and feed additive industries resulted in eight criminal cases against nine corporations. Virtually all the companies pled guilty and paid almost $200 million in fines. In 1996 ADM agreed to pay $100 million in fines. In that deal, ADM was granted immunity against charges of price-fixing in the sale of high-fructose corn syrup, a major ADM product, if it cooperated with the federal government in its investigation of the industry.

Because prices for lysine were fixed, the animal feed bought by poultry and animal producers cost more than if there had been a free market in lysine. The food producers then passed this increased price on to consumers. Some estimated the cost of the price-fixing to the nation's consumers as high as $170 million. Although ADM and the other companies paid fines, and the convicted ADM executives were likely also to pay fines, none of this loss will likely ever be directly recovered by an individual consumer.

TAX FRAUD

For most Americans, failure to pay the correct amount of taxes to the Internal Revenue Service (IRS) results in agreement to pay off the taxes in some manner. However, when the IRS believes it has found a pattern of deception designed to avoid paying taxes, criminal charges can be brought. In 2003 the Criminal Investigations Division of the IRS initiated 1,814 cases. Of those, the IRS recommended prosecution in 974 cases, and in 770 cases criminal charges were filed or brought by indictment. In 2003 the IRS reported 688 convictions for tax fraud. Of those convicted for tax fraud, 79.8 percent were incarcerated, serving an average of 28 months.

BRIBERY

Some U.S. companies often feel they operate at a disadvantage in other countries because American law prohibits U.S.-based companies from using bribes to get foreign contracts, while some forms of bribery are allowed in most other industrialized countries. Until recently, the United States was the only major national economy with such laws. In fact, many foreign companies often deducted bribes as business expenses. In many countries, especially in Asia, the unwritten rule is that a senior official will get 5 percent of a $200,000 contract and a head of state requires 5 percent of a $200 million contract. The percentage increased in the 1990s, as some officials were demanding 10 to 15 percent before a bid for services or goods could be accepted.

Many businesses and diplomats from several European countries believe that changes in their tax laws would reduce the amount of bribery; others believe that because of stiff competition, businesses would find loopholes. Some American businesses hire middlemen to conduct the bribery of foreign officials; others invite prospective clients on junkets to the United States.

FORGERY AND COUNTERFEITING

As technology advances, forgers are able to use sophisticated computers, scanners (a machine that "reads" a document and transfers it to computer coding), and laser printers to make copies of more and more documents, including counterfeit checks, identification badges, driver's licenses, even dollar bills (though the bills may not have the right feel, they can be inserted into a stack of currency and an overworked bank teller may not catch the forgery).

The manufacturing of counterfeit United States currency or altering of genuine currency to increase its value is punishable by a fine of up to $5,000 and imprisonment of up to 15 years, or both. Possession of counterfeit U.S. currency is also a crime, punishable by a fine of up to $15,000, or imprisonment of up to 15 years, or both. Counterfeiting is not limited to paper money. The illegal manufacturing of a coin in any denomination above five cents is subject to the same penalties as counterfeiting paper currency, and increasing the numismatic value of a coin is punishable by a fine of up to $2,000, or imprisonment of up to five years, or both. The level of counterfeit bills in circulation worldwide is estimated to be less than 0.02 percent of all bills, about two counterfeit bills for every 10,000 genuine bills.

In response to the growing use of computer-generated counterfeit money, the U.S. Department of the Treasury redesigned the $50 and $100 bills in the 1990s. Noting that the $20 bill was the one most counterfeited, the Department of the Treasury introduced new $5, $10, and $20 dollar bills between 1998 and 2000. These bills contain a watermark making them harder to accurately copy. Another change in currency design was introduced in October 2003, a new $20 dollar bill with shades of green, peach, and blue colors in the background. A blue eagle and metallic green eagle and shield have also been added to the bill's design. In 2004 and 2005, respectively, similar enhancements are scheduled for the $50 and $100 bills.

According to the Department of the Treasury, advances in home computer technology and desktop publishing software have made counterfeiting easier than ever, despite the new designs of U.S. currency intended as safeguards against counterfeiting. In the past, fake money required some understanding of inks and how to mix them to achieve the exact tones needed to create authentic-looking currency. With advances in ink-jet printing, however, so-called P-notes (printer notes) require no such knowledge about inks or printing. In 1995 less than 1 percent of counterfeit notes were produced using digital technology. By 2002 some 40 percent of counterfeit notes were produced in this manner. The most popular denomination counterfeited overseas is the $100 bill, while domestic counterfeiters focus on the $20 bill.

Perhaps because of the ease of using computers and printers, overall arrests for counterfeiting have risen sharply, from 1,800 in 1995 to 4,900 in 2002. About 99 percent of those arrested for counterfeiting are convicted. Meanwhile, tracking counterfeiters has become more difficult because, increasingly, bills are made in smaller batches, often to be used only occasionally.

The U.S. Secret Service reports that one half of U.S. counterfeit currency distributed in the United States originated overseas. Other international counterfeiting schemes included reproducing financial instruments including commercial checks, traveler's checks, and money orders. Advanced reprographic capabilities made possible through computer technology, plus the growth of the worldwide Web, have extended counterfeiting knowledge to criminals throughout the world.

Counterfeit Products

Counterfeiting popular name brand products is a multibillion-dollar white-collar crime. Fake Chanel purses and Nike athletic shoes have been seized all over the world. In 2001 the GAO reported an International Chamber of Commerce estimate that counterfeit trademarked products account for 8 percent ($200 billion) of all world trade annually. Online counterfeit sales may account for $25 billion. In 1999 U.S. Customs seized a record $98.5 billion in counterfeit merchandise, reflecting an increase of $22 billion over the previous year. Relations between the United States and the People's Republic of China became strained due to the manufacture of counterfeit products in China, as well as the production of copyrighted software and compact disks. The Chinese government claimed to be initiating criminal action against such violators, but many observers wondered whether the few resulting arrests of copyright violators was nothing more than show.

A daring example of art forgery was announced by the Department of Justice on March 10, 2004. Ely Sakhai, owner of two prominent Manhattan art galleries, was charged with buying paintings by such famous artists as Marc Chagall, Henry Moore, Paul Gauguin, and Pierre-August Renoir, having expert forgeries made of them, and then selling both the forgeries and the originals to unsuspecting dealers around the world. Sakhai faces up to twenty years in prison for mail and wire fraud.

MONEY LAUNDERING

The U.S. General Accounting Office defines money laundering as "the disguising or concealing of illicit income to make it appear legitimate." Money laundering involves transferring illegally received monies into legal accounts so that when money is withdrawn from those accounts, it appears to the police or other government authorities to be legal earnings of the account or the business. When a money-laundering scheme is successful, the criminals can spend their illegally acquired money with little fear of being caught. Many of the techniques that launderers use would be perfectly legal business transactions if the source of the cash were not illegal activities.

The money-laundering scheme may be as simple as mailing a box of cash to an accomplice in another country where there is very little bank regulation. The accomplice deposits it in the local bank. The sender then writes a check on that bank and can use the money without fear of anyone knowing where the money came from. Other schemes may involve bribing a bank officer to permit illegal monies to be put in good accounts and then drawing the monies out.

Over the years, the federal government has enacted a number of laws to prevent money laundering. To prevent criminals from using financial institutions to hide or launder their illegally gained money from the authorities, the Bank Secrecy Act of 1970 required banks to report transactions involving currency of more than $10,000, the transfer of more than $10,000 into or out of the country, and any suspicious activity that may be illegal. The Money Laundering Control Act of 1986 criminalized money laundering, making it a crime to knowingly engage in any monetary transaction involving more than $10,000 obtained by criminal activity or to structure financial transactions to avoid the $10,000 reporting threshold. The Anti-Drug Abuse Act of 1988 called for banks to have stricter checks on customer identification and more stringent record keeping. The act also allowed the Treasury Department to monitor currency transactions by geographical region.

In 1994 the Money Laundering Suppression Act gave bank examiners stronger procedures for monitoring the activities of financial institutions. The Money Laundering and Financial Crimes Strategy Act of 1998 created the National Money Laundering Report, an intergovernmental national plan to coordinate all law enforcement activities against money laundering from local through federal levels. It also authorized the designation of High Intensity Financial Crime Areas, those with a high risk for money laundering or financial crimes, and Financial Crime-Free Communities, to allow law enforcement to focus their prevention efforts appropriately.

TABLE 7.3

Characteristics of convicted money laundering defendants, 2001

Defendant characteristics	Total		Laundering/racketeering (Title 18 offenses)		Monetary record and reporting (Title 31 offenses)	
	Number	Percent	Number	Percent	Number	Percent
Total	**1,243**	**100.0%**	**1,021**	**100.0%**	**222**	**100.0%**
Gender						
Male	912	80.0%	766	82.0%	146	70.9%
Female	228	20.0	168	18.0	60	29.1
Race/ethnicity						
White non-Hispanic	593	52.3%	521	56.1%	72	35.1%
Black non-Hispanic	186	16.4	162	17.5	24	11.7
Hispanic	292	25.8	193	20.8	99	48.3
Other	62	5.5	52	5.6	10	4.9
Age						
18–24 yr	55	4.9%	31	3.4%	24	11.8%
25–34 yr	286	25.3	231	25.0	55	27.0
35–44 yr	350	31.0	286	30.9	64	31.4
45–59 yr	335	29.7	289	31.2	46	22.6
60 or older	103	9.1	88	9.5	15	7.4
Citizenship						
U.S. citizen	867	76.6%	761	81.9%	106	52.2%
Non-U.S. citizen	265	23.4	168	18.1	97	47.8
Prior criminal history*						
No convictions	759	66.6%	596	63.8%	163	79.1%
Prior adult convictions	381	33.4	338	36.2	43	20.9

Note: Detail excludes defendants for whom a particular characteristic was not reported.
*A criminal record is limited to prior adult convictions. For some defendants in this table, it is further limited to the portion that is relevant for calculating sentences under the federal sentencing guidelines.

SOURCE: Mark Motivans, "Table 4: Characteristics of Convicted Money Laundering Defendants, 2001," in "Money Laundering Offenders, 1994–2001," in *Bureau of Justice Statistics Special Report,* July 2003

In 2001 the Strengthening America Act by Providing Appropriate Tools Required to Intercept and Obstruct Terrorism, informally called the Patriot Act, strengthened laws dealing with how U.S. banks use foreign correspondent banks to transfer money into and out of the country and the financing of terrorist organizations and activities. It also outlawed bulk cash smuggling, making it illegal to take more than $10,000 in concealed cash across the border to avoid reporting requirements. In addition to these federal measures, 36 states have adopted money laundering laws since 1985.

Increased awareness of money laundering is reflected in the number of Suspicious Activity Reports (SAR) submitted by banks to the U.S. Department of the Treasury. These reports, required whenever a bank has reason to believe that a transaction of at least $5,000 involves money derived from illegal activities, increased by 206 percent from 1997 to 2001. In 2002 over 273,000 reports were filed. The states of New York, Nevada, and California had the highest SAR levels, while the highest levels for metropolitan areas were found in New York and Los Angeles.

Of the 1,243 people convicted for money laundering in 2001, 1,021 were guilty of money laundering and racketeering charges and 222 for monetary record and reporting charges. Of those convicted, 52.3 percent were white, 25.8 percent were Hispanic, and 16.4 percent were black. Males made up 80 percent of those convicted, while 76.6 percent were U.S. citizens. Two-thirds (66.6 percent) of those convicted had no prior criminal convictions. (See Table 7.3.) The average prison sentence for money laundering in 2001 was 48 months.

The GAO reported in 2001 that it estimates the amount of money laundered worldwide each year to be as high as $1 trillion. Drug traffickers launder an estimated $300 to $500 billion each year, often using supposedly respectable financial institutions. Other crimes that need money laundered are fraud offenses, securities (stocks and bonds) manipulation, illegal gambling, bribery, extortion, tax evasion, illegal arms sales, political payoffs, and terrorism. Money laundering may account for as much as 2 to 5 percent of the world's gross domestic product, according to a former Managing Director of the International Monetary Fund.

In a recent case with international scope, the FBI announced in March 2004 that they had uncovered a money laundering operation involving Colombian drug lords, a Colombian terrorist group, and criminals in at least seven countries. Beginning with the investigation of a Utah loan fraud, the FBI eventually discovered that some $5 million had been laundered through U.S. banks in eight states by an international drug ring. The FBI investigation, called "Operation Utah Powder," found that

FIGURE 7.2

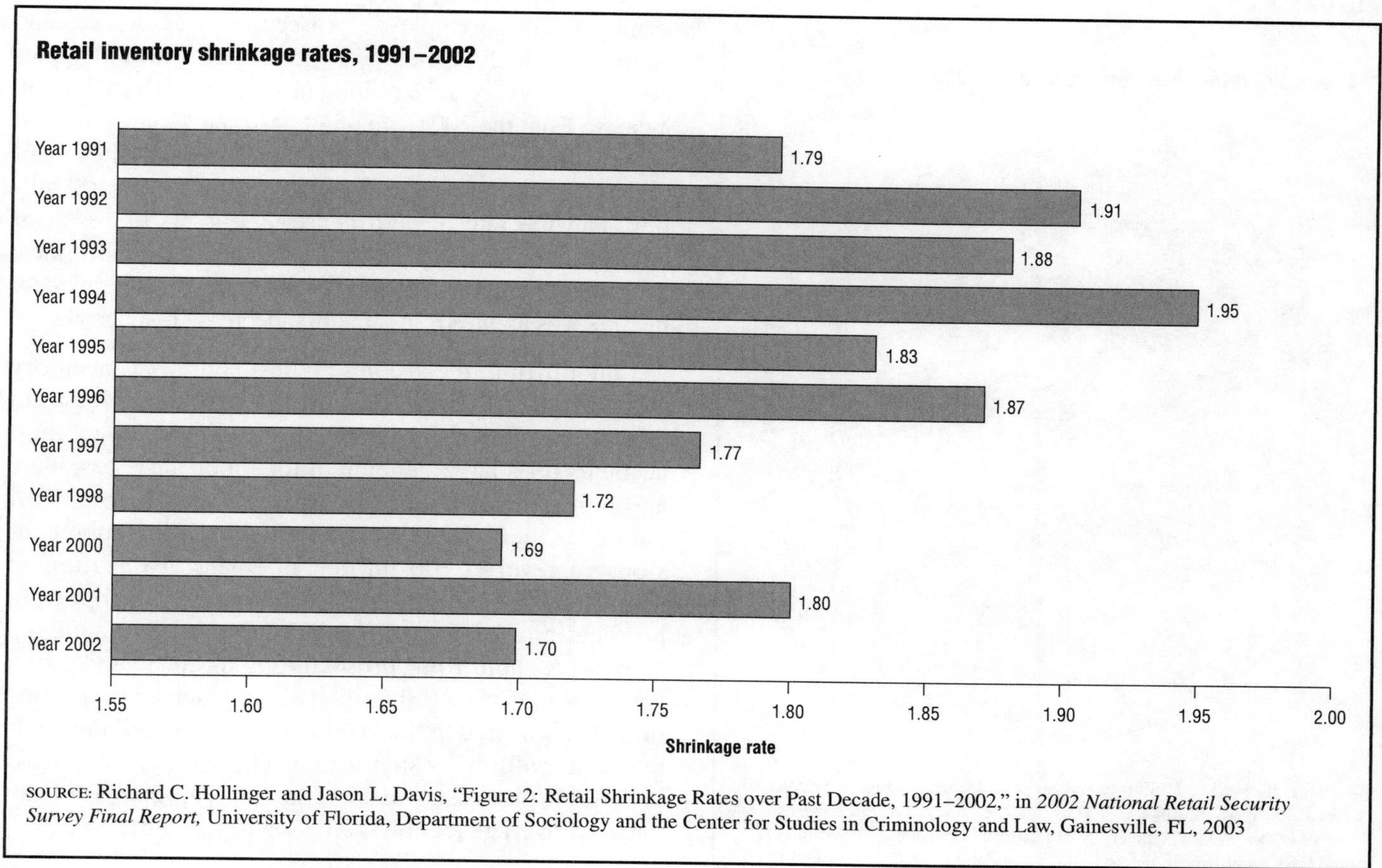

SOURCE: Richard C. Hollinger and Jason L. Davis, "Figure 2: Retail Shrinkage Rates over Past Decade, 1991–2002," in *2002 National Retail Security Survey Final Report,* University of Florida, Department of Sociology and the Center for Studies in Criminology and Law, Gainesville, FL, 2003

Colombian cocaine money was being laundered through U.S. banks to banks overseas using wire transfers, cashier's checks, falsified business invoices, and money orders. Authorities in Spain, the Cayman Islands, Panama, Mexico, Italy, the United Kingdom, and Latvia were soon involved in the investigation. The FBI found that the drug lords had also paid protection money to the Revolutionary Armed Forces of Colombia, the military wing of that country's Communist Party, and the United Self-Defense Forces of Colombia, a right-wing terrorist group, to guard their cocaine shipments. Four Utah residents were arrested as part of the ongoing operation.

The GAO, in *Money Laundering: Rapid Growth of Casinos Makes Them Vulnerable* (Washington, D.C., 1996), found that gambling was expanding rapidly across the United States. Along with this growth came a large increase in the amount of cash wagered at all casinos, which totaled about $439 billion in 1996. With this much cash changing hands, casinos may be particularly vulnerable to money laundering in the form of money from illegal activities being placed into legal gaming transactions.

Money laundering is a global problem requiring collective international efforts to combat. The United States has promoted multilateral efforts to combat money laundering. The United States and over 120 other nations signed the United Nations Convention on Transnational Organized Crime in order to combat money laundering as well as other international crimes in 2000.

The State Department is required by law (the International Narcotics Control Act of 1992, PL 102-583) to identify major money-laundering countries and to provide certain specific information for each country. The Department of State works with agencies of the Departments of the Treasury and Justice to put this information together. Countries are categorized by the degree to which they are at risk of money-laundering activities. Canada, Cayman Islands, Colombia, Germany, Hong Kong, Thailand, the United Kingdom, the United States, and Venezuela are examples of the countries placed on the high priority list.

RETAIL STORE THEFT

In the *2002 National Retail Security Survey Final Report* (University of Florida, Gainesville, FL, 2003), an annual survey of retail theft prepared for the National Retail Federation, authors Richard C. Hollinger, Ph.D., and Jason L. Davis found that the average retail store surveyed in 2002 lost about 1.7 percent of its inventory to shrinkage (the industry term for the difference between the recorded value of inventory bought and sold and the value of the actual inventory at the end of the year). The shrinkage rate in 2002 was down from the 2001 rate of 1.8 percent. (See Figure 7.2.)

FIGURE 7.3

Sources of retail inventory shrinkage, 2002

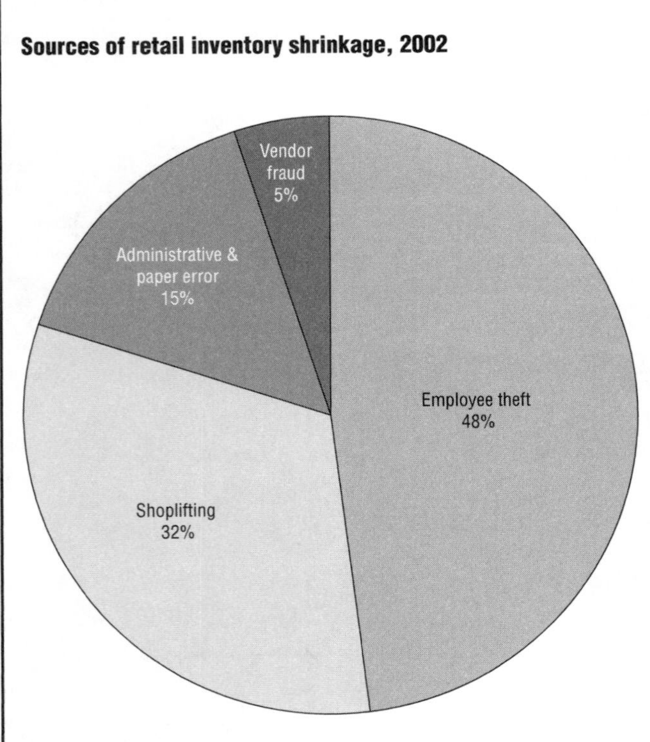

SOURCE: Richard C. Hollinger and Jason L. Davis, "Figure 4: Sources of Retail Inventory Shrinkage, 2002," in *2002 National Retail Security Survey Final Report,* University of Florida, Department of Sociology and the Center for Studies in Criminology and Law, Gainesville, FL, 2003

Shrinkage is generally attributed to shoplifting, employee theft, administrative error, or vendor fraud. Respondents to the 2002 survey reported that 48 percent of their losses were due to employee theft (up from 45.9 percent in 2001), 32 percent to shoplifting (up from 30.8 percent in 2001), 15 percent to administrative errors (down from 17.5 percent in 2001), and 5 percent to vendor fraud (down from 5.9 percent in 2001). (See Figure 7.3.)

As in previous surveys, employee theft was reported as the single most significant source of inventory shrinkage among retailers, accounting for a little over $15 billion in losses (nearly half of the total $31.3 billion in losses due to inventory shrinkage in 2002.) The highest rate of inventory shrinkage due to employee theft in 2002 was experienced in convenience stores (82.5 percent), followed by supermarkets and grocery stores (59 percent), and men's apparel retailers (57.5 percent). Office supply retailers reported a 57.4 percent rate and consumer electronics/appliances retailers reported that 57.3 percent of their inventory shrinkage was due to employee theft. The lowest rates of employee theft occurred among book and magazine vendors (33.3 percent), followed by drug retailers (40.4 percent), and cards/gifts/novelties retailers (41.4 percent) (See Figure 7.4.)

Responses to employee theft include apprehension and termination of the employee, prosecution, and civil demand or recovery. In 2002 there were 35.2 employee theft apprehensions for every $100 million in sales among retailers, an increase from the 2001 rate of 30.3. About 41 percent of all apprehensions resulted in criminal prosecution. The rate of employee theft prosecutions was 14.5 for each $100 million, and the rate of civil court actions as the result of employee thefts was 35.8 for every $100 million in sales. The average amount stolen by each employee theft incident in 2002 was about $1,341, the first decrease in a decade.

Shoplifting, the second highest source of inventory shrinkage in 2002, accounted for $10 billion in losses to American retailers in 2002. Though employee theft accounts for a larger amount of total monetary loss, there are more incidents of shoplifting than there are of employee theft. There were 134.8 shoplifting apprehensions for every $100 million in sales. Prosecution of shoplifters rose in 2002. There were 108.4 shoplifting prosecutions for every $100 million in sales in 2002, up from 92.8 shoplifting prosecutions in 2001, and 149.5 civil demands per $100 million as the result of shoplifting in 2002 compared to the 2001 rate of 133.7 civil demands per $100 million for shoplifting. The average dollar loss per shoplifting case was $207 in 2002, an increase from the 2001 average loss of $195. (See Figure 7.5.)

PUBLIC CORRUPTION

A broad definition of public corruption includes a public employee asking for money, gifts, or services in exchange for doing something such as giving a city contract or voting in a certain way. This abuse of public trust may be found wherever the interest of individuals or business and government overlap. It ranges from the health inspector who accepts a bribe from a restaurant owner or the police officer who "shakes down" the drug dealer, to the councilman or legislator who accepts money to vote a certain way. These crimes are often difficult to uncover, as often few willing witnesses are available.

Of the 27,283 people indicted for offenses involving the abuse of public office between 1973 and 2001, 11,687 (42.8 percent) were federal officials, 2,182 (7.9 percent) were state officials, and 6,526 (23.9 percent) were local officials. The rest of those indicted, 6,888 (25.2 percent), were not employed by the government. (See Table 7.4.)

Bribes, Kickbacks, and Racketeering

In May 2000 former Louisiana Governor Edwin Edwards was convicted of racketeering, extortion, mail fraud, and wire fraud in connection with a scheme to extort bribes from applicants for riverboat casino licenses. Edwards was convicted on 17 counts and his son, Stephen, was convicted on 18 counts involving the extortion of some $3 million. Two of the charges for which for-

FIGURE 7.4

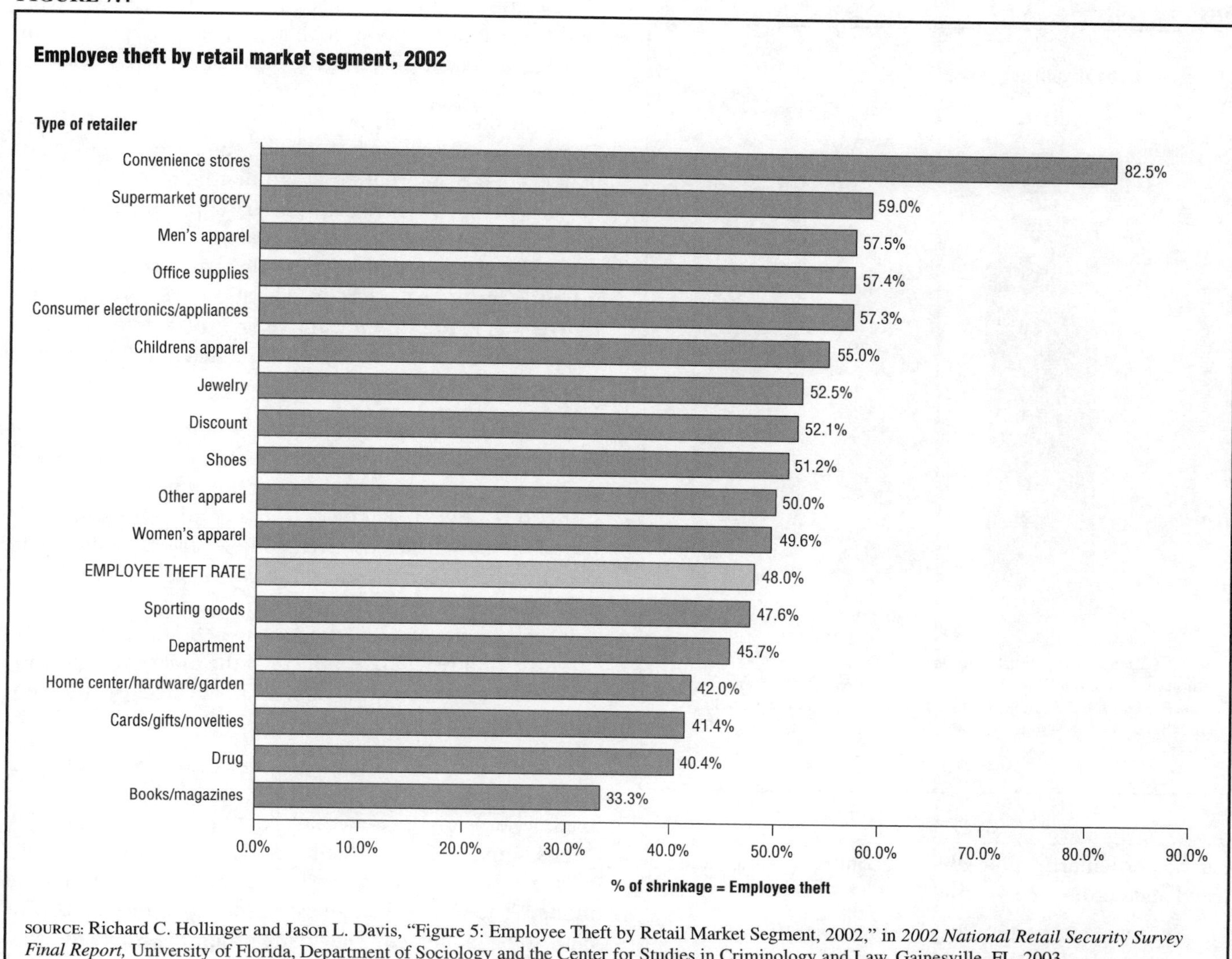

SOURCE: Richard C. Hollinger and Jason L. Davis, "Figure 5: Employee Theft by Retail Market Segment, 2002," in *2002 National Retail Security Survey Final Report,* University of Florida, Department of Sociology and the Center for Studies in Criminology and Law, Gainesville, FL, 2003

mer Governor Edwards was convicted carried prison terms of up 20 years and fines of up to $250,000.

In April 2002 U.S. Representative James A. Traficant was convicted of taking bribes and kickbacks from businessmen and his office staff. The nine-term Ohio Democrat was found guilty of 10 federal charges, including racketeering, bribery, and fraud, and was ordered to forfeit some $96,000 acquired as the result of illegal activities. As a result of the felony conviction, Traficant faced the possibility of being expelled from the U.S. House of Representatives. Expulsion would require a two-thirds vote by House members. The only such expulsion in recent history was in 1980, when Representative Michael Myers, a Democrat from Pennsylvania, was expelled for accepting money from undercover FBI agents posing as foreign dignitaries looking to buy influence in Congress.

The charges against Traficant included filing false tax returns, receiving gifts and free labor from business persons in return for political favors, and taking cash kickbacks from members of his staff. During the trial, prosecutors also accused Traficant of lobbying for contractors in exchange for free work, including paving a barn floor, fixing a drainage system, and removing trees at Traficant's farm.

In June 2002 Providence, Rhode Island, mayor Vincent A. Cianci Jr., was found guilty by a federal jury of conspiring to run a criminal enterprise from City Hall, although he was acquitted of 11 other charges against him. Cianci's conviction for racketeering conspiracy carried a maximum penalty of 20 years in prison and up to $250,000 in fines, or both. Two co-defendants in the case were also found guilty of racketeering conspiracy.

SCAMS ON THE ELDERLY

Because senior citizens are often retired and living on fixed incomes and savings, the promise of economic security can be very alluring. As a consequence, the elderly

FIGURE 7.5

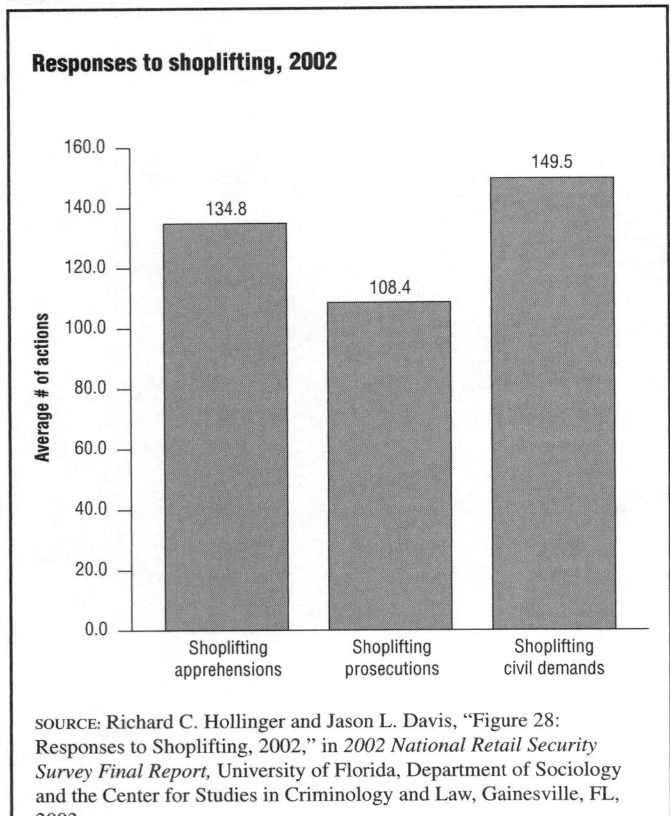

SOURCE: Richard C. Hollinger and Jason L. Davis, "Figure 28: Responses to Shoplifting, 2002," in *2002 National Retail Security Survey Final Report,* University of Florida, Department of Sociology and the Center for Studies in Criminology and Law, Gainesville, FL, 2003

can be particularly vulnerable to economic crimes such as fraud and confidence schemes.

Seniors are particularly vulnerable to con artists. Often, they are lonely, isolated from their families, and sometimes more willing than in earlier years to believe what they are told. Some suffer mental or physical frailties that leave them less able to defend themselves against high-pressure tactics. In addition, they may be financially insecure and may want to believe the con artist's promises of future wealth and security. Since many elderly are too embarrassed to admit that they have been fooled, many of these crimes are not reported.

Statistics on fraud against the elderly, sometimes called elder scams, are not collected by the major crime reporting agencies. In 2002 the National Fraud Information Center estimated that there were 14,000 illegal telemarketing operations in the United States, and that the elderly fell prey to unscrupulous telemarketers to the tune of $40 billion per year. Between 2002 and 2003, the 70 to 79 age group rose from 9 percent to 13 percent of all fraud victims, the steepest rise for any age group. Additionally, surveys conducted by the AARP (formerly the American Association of Retired Persons) indicated that most victims of telemarketing fraud were 50 years of age or older. In 2003 the top frauds committed against those 60 or older involved prizes/sweepstakes, lotteries/lottery clubs, and magazine sales.

Because the elderly are more likely to suffer from health-related problems such as diabetes, hypertension, arthritis, and heart disease, they can be especially susceptible to fraudulent claims for products marketed as treatments or cures for diseases. In 2001 the Federal Trade Commission initiated legal action against eight companies that used the Internet to fraudulently market medical devices, herbal products, and dietary supplements as treatments or cures for Alzheimer's disease, diabetes, arthritis and other diseases that affect senior citizens. The actions were the result of the FTC's Operation Cure.All. The initiative was to identify deceptive and misleading Internet promotions of products and services that purportedly treat or cure various diseases.

Another popular scam involves con artists calling or mailing information to elderly people announcing that they have won a free prize, but must pay postage and handling to receive it. They are told a credit card number is needed to pay these costs. The thieves then use the credit card number to buy items and to get cash. The elderly are also susceptible to repairmen who stop by and say they can fix their homes. The workers may do the repair work, but it is shoddy and overpriced. If the elderly try to complain, the repairmen are no longer in the area, possibly not even in the state.

A more elaborate scam involves a con artist, acting as a bank official, telling the elderly person that a particular bank teller is giving out counterfeit bills and that the bank needs help in catching the teller. The elderly person goes to the teller's window and withdraws a large sum of money. The victim then gives the money to the "bank official" to be examined. The "bank official" assures the customer that the money will be redeposited in his or her account; of course, it never is.

ENVIRONMENTAL CRIME

> *Environmental crime is a serious problem for the United States, even though the immediate consequences of an offense may not be obvious or immediately severe. Environmental crimes do have victims. The cumulative costs in environmental damage and the long range toll in illness, injury, and death may be considerable.*
>
> —Theodore M. Hammett and Joel Epstein, "Prosecuting Environmental Crime: Los Angeles County," *National Institute of Justice Program Focus,* 1993

Environmental crime involves illegally polluting the air, water, or ground. Sometimes firms dump hazardous materials and waste. To investigate properly, local, state, national, and international agencies often need to cooperate. It is not unusual for environmental criminals to transport hazardous waste across state or international borders for disposal in places with less stringent environmental enforcement.

According to the National Institute of Justice, several obstacles exist in prosecuting environmental crime.

TABLE 7.4

Persons indicted, awaiting trial on December 31, and convicted of offenses involving abuse of public office, 1973–2004

	Total			Elected or appointed official: Federal			Elected or appointed official: State			Elected or appointed official: Local			Others involved		
	Indicted	Awaiting trial on Dec. 31	Convicted	Indicted	Awaiting trial on Dec. 31	Convicted	Indicted	Awaiting trial on Dec. 31	Convicted	Indicted	Awaiting trial on Dec. 31	Convicted	Indicted	Awaiting trial on Dec. 31	Convicted
Total	**27,283**	**7,584**	**23,594**	**11,687**	**2,143**	**10,359**	**2,182**	**774**	**1,792**	**6,526**	**2,243**	**5,372**	**6,888**	**2,424**	**6,071**
1973	191	18	144	60	2	48	19	0	17	85	2	64	27	14	15
1974	305	5	213	59	1	51	36	0	23	130	4	87	80	0	52
1975	294	27	211	53	5	43	36	5	18	139	15	94	66	2	56
1976	391	199	260	111	1	101	59	30	35	194	98	100	27	70	24
1977	535	210	440	129	32	94	50	33	38	157	62	164	199	83	144
1978	530	205	418	133	42	91	55	20	56	171	72	127	171	71	144
1979	579	178	419	114	21	102	56	29	31	211	63	151	198	65	135
1980	727	213	602	123	16	131	72	28	51	247	82	168	285	87	252
1981	808	231	730	198	23	159	87	36	66	244	102	211	279	70	294
1982	813	186	671	158	38	147	49	18	43	257	58	232	349	72	249
1983	1,076	222	972	460*	58	424	81	26	65	270	61	226	265	77	257
1984	931	269	934	408	77	429	58	21	52	203	74	196	262	97	257
1985	1,157	256	997	563	90	470	79	20	66	248	49	221	267	97	240
1986	1,208	246	1,026	596	83	523	88	24	71	232	55	207	292	84	225
1987	1,276	368	1,081	651	118	545	102	26	76	246	89	204	277	135	256
1988	1,274	288	1,067	629	86	529	66	14	69	276	79	229	303	109	240
1989	1,348	375	1,149	695	126	610	71	18	54	269	122	201	313	109	284
1990	1,176	300	1,084	615	103	583	96	28	79	257	98	225	208	71	197
1991	1,452	346	1,194	803	149	665	115	42	77	242	88	180	292	67	272
1992	1,189	380	1,081	624	139	532	81	24	92	232	91	211	252	126	246
1993	1,371	403	1,362	627	133	595	113	39	133	309	132	272	322	99	362
1994	1,165	332	969	571	124	488	99	17	97	248	96	202	247	95	182
1995	1,051	323	878	527	120	438	61	23	61	236	89	191	227	91	188
1996	984	244	902	456	64	459	109	40	83	219	60	190	200	80	170
1997	1,057	327	853	459	83	392	51	20	49	255	118	169	292	106	243
1998	1,174	340	1,014	442	85	414	91	37	58	277	90	264	364	128	278
1999	1,134	329	1,065	480	101	460	115	44	80	237	95	219	302	89	306
2000	1,000	327	938	441	92	422	92	37	91	211	89	183	256	109	242
2001	1,087	437	920	502	131	414	95	75	61	224	110	184	266	121	261

Note: Questionnaires are sent annually to the U.S. attorneys' offices in each of the Federal judicial districts eliciting data concerning indictments and convictions during the year as well as prosecutions awaiting trial on December 31 of each year.
*The 1983 figures were reviewed to attempt to identify the reason for the substantial increase in prosecutions of federal officials. The explanation appeared to be two-fold: there had been a greater focus on federal corruption nationwide, and there appeared to have been more consistent reporting of lower-level employees who abused their office, cases that may have been overlooked in the past. For reference, the U.S. attorneys' offices were told: "For purposes of this questionnaire, a public corruption case includes any case involving abuse of office by a public employee. We are not excluding low-level employees or minor crimes, but rather focusing on the job-relatedness of the offense and whether the offense involves abuse of the public trust placed in the employee."

SOURCE: "Table 5.80: Persons Indicted, Awaiting Trial on December 31, and Convicted of Offenses Involving Abuse of Public Office, by Level of Government, 1973–2001," in *Sourcebook of Criminal Justice Statistics 2002,* U.S. Department of Justice, Bureau of Justice Statistics, Washington, DC, 2003

1. Some prosecutors feel unprepared to tackle environmental cases, which are perceived as hopelessly complicated and impossible to win.

2. Some corporate defendants regard civil penalties and one-time cleanup costs as part of doing business. Many prosecutors are now turning to civil suits only when criminal remedies are not available.

3. Some judges are not well-informed on environmental laws or are not sensitive to the seriousness of the crimes.

4. Individual juries may be reluctant to convict a community's business leaders and significant employers if the alleged environmental damage does not have immediate consequences.

The more common means of enforcing environmental laws is through regulatory action by the government's responsible agencies and the application of civil penalties to those who violate the regulations.

According to the U.S. Environmental Protection Agency (EPA), in fiscal year 2001 criminal charges were brought against 372 defendants for violations of environmental laws nationwide. Those found guilty were fined some $95 million and were sentenced collectively to 256 years in prison. One example of a successful criminal prosecution in fiscal year (FY) 2001 reported by the EPA, is the case of David D. Nuyen of Silver Springs, Maryland. In July 2001 Nuyen pled guilty to violations of the Lead Hazard Reduction Act and the Toxic Substances Control Act. Nuyen, who owned 15 low-income rental properties in Washington, D.C., admitted that he failed to notify tenants of lead paint hazards in one of his buildings. Nuyen was sentenced to two years in prison and fined $50,000.

In addition, the EPA reported the settlement of 222 civil actions in FY 2001, resulting in $125 million in civil penalties plus $25.5 million in settlements shared with states, including a multi-state enforcement case involving Morton International, Inc. In October 2001 the company agreed to resolve charges of violating clean air, water, and hazardous waste laws at its Moss Point, Mississippi facility. Under the terms of the settlement, Morton International agreed to pay $20 million in penalties and to spend up to $16 million on projects to enhance the environment.

In another civil action in FY 2001, the EPA reached settlements with four major refineries—Koch Petroleum, BP Amoco, Marathon Ashland Petroleum, and Motiva/Equilon/Shell. The settlements involved a total of 27 refineries in violation of hazardous air pollution laws. The EPA did not disclose the terms of the settlements. As a result of criminal prosecutions, civil actions, and administrative penalties, the EPA reported that in FY 2001 environmental violators paid a total of $4.3 billion for pollution controls and environmental clean-up.

In March 2002 the EPA and the Department of Justice announced that they had filed a civil action against Shell Pipeline Company LP and Olympic Pipeline Company in connection with a gasoline pipeline rupture near Bellingham, Washington, in 1999. The rupture released a three-inch thick layer of gasoline over a 1.33-mile stretch of creek water, resulting in a massive explosion that caused the deaths of three people, including two 10-year-old boys. The resulting fire destroyed some 2.5 miles of vegetation and created a burn zone encompassing 26 acres.

In April 2002 the Miami, Florida-based Carnival Company, which operates some 40 cruise ships, pled guilty to falsifying oil record books on several of its ships and agreed to pay $18 million in fines. The falsification of records occurred when Carnival employees ran fresh water past oil water separators, resulting in artificially low oil concentration readings that were officially recorded in the ships' oil records books. As a consequence, bilge water with higher levels of oil concentration than allowed under the law was released, threatening surrounding ocean life.

On May 13, 2002, Ashland, Inc., of Covington, Kentucky, pled guilty to negligent endangerment under the Clean Air Act for failing to properly seal a manhole cover on a sewer used to transport flammable hydrocarbons, resulting in an explosion that injured five people, one of them severely. Ashland, Inc., agreed to pay a total of $10.7 million in fines and payments to compensate the injured parties.

CHAPTER 8
CRIME, ALCOHOL, AND DRUGS

The connection between criminal activity and the use of drugs and alcohol has long been an issue in American society. Even before federal laws were passed in 1914 to control narcotics and other drugs, observers claimed that drug use and criminal activity were strongly linked. Drugs and alcohol are thought to encourage criminal behavior in several ways. Their use can reduce inhibitions, stimulate aggression, and interfere with critical thinking and motor skills (such as driving or operating machinery). Each of these factors may also reduce a person's ability to earn a legal income, which may lead the drug user to commit crimes in order to obtain money. For those using addictive drugs, the need to get money to support a drug habit may take priority over any other consideration. Illegal drug users may also find themselves more frequently exposed to situations that encourage crime.

For the poor and underprivileged, drug and alcohol abuse can become an additional negative social condition within their environment. The same circumstances leading a person to commit crimes may also lead to drug use. In addition, the same conditions limiting employment opportunity may also contribute to both drug abuse and criminal behavior. Table 8.1 shows the relationship between drugs and crime.

TABLE 8.1

How are drugs and crime related?

Drugs and crime relationship	Definition	Examples
Drug-defined offenses	Violations of laws prohibiting or regulating the possession, use, distribution, or manufacture of illegal drugs.	Drug possession or use. Marijuana cultivation. Methamphetamine production. Cocaine, heroin, or marijuana sales.
Drug-related offenses	Offenses in which a drug's pharmacologic effects contribute; offenses motivated by the user's need for money to support continued use; and offenses connected with drug distribution itself.	Violent behavior resulting from drug effects. Stealing to get money to buy drugs. Violence against rival drug dealers.
Interactional circumstances	Drug use and crime are common aspects of a deviant lifestyle. The likelihood and frequency of involvement in illegal activity is increased because drug users and offenders are exposed to situations that encourage crime.	A life orientation with an emphasis on short-term goals supported by illegal activities. Opportunities to offend resulting from contacts with offenders and illegal markets. Criminal skills learned from other offenders.

SOURCE "How Are Drugs and Crime Related?" in *Drugs, Crime and the Justice System,* U.S. Department of Justice, Bureau of Justice Statistics, Washington, DC, 1992

SUBSTANCE-RELATED ARRESTS

In *Crime in the United States, 2002* (Washington, D.C., 2003), the Federal Bureau of Investigation (FBI) reported that of the 13.7 million estimated arrests in 2002, drug abuse violations accounted for 1.5 million arrests, or about 11 percent, making drug abuse violations the highest single category of arrest, followed by driving under the influence (1.5 million arrests), simple assaults (1.3 million), and larceny/theft (1.2 million). (See Table 8.2.)

TABLE 8.2

Estimated totals of top 7 arrest offenses, 2002

Type of arrest	Number of arrests*
Total arrests*	13,741,400
Drug abuse violations	**1,538,800**
Driving under the influence	1,461,700
Simple assaults	1,288,700
Larceny/theft	1,160,100
Disorderlyconduct	669,900
Liquor laws	653,800
Drunkenness	572,700

*Arrest totals are based on all reporting agencies and estimates for unreported areas.

SOURCE: "Estimated Totals of Top 7 Arrest Offenses, United States, 2002," in *Drugs and Crime Facts,* U.S. Department of Justice, Bureau of Justice Statistics, Washington, DC, 2003 [Online] http://www.ojp.usdoj.gov/bjs/dcf/enforce.htm [accessed April 10, 2004]

FIGURE 8.1

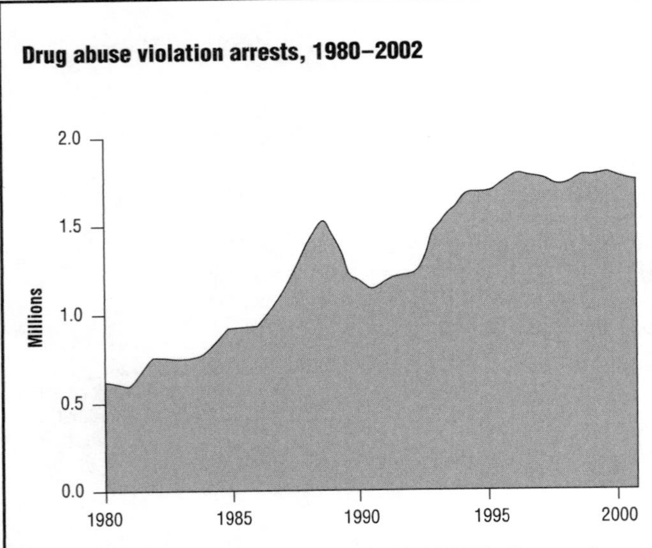

SOURCE: "Drug Abuse Violation Arrests, 1980–2002," in *Drugs and Crime Facts,* U.S. Department of Justice, Bureau of Justice Statistics, Washington, DC, 2003 [Online] http://www.ojp.usdoj.gov/bjs/dcf/correct

TABLE 8.3

Arrests for drug abuse violations, by region, 2002

Drug abuse violations	United States total	Northeast	Midwest	South	West
Total*	**100.0**	**100.0**	**100.0**	**100.0**	**100.0**
Sale/Manufacturing:*	19.7	27.9	23.1	17.2	16.4
Heroin or cocaine and their derivatives	8.8	19.1	6.0	7.8	6.2
Marijuana	5.4	6.5	7.4	4.8	4.4
Synthetic or manufactured drugs	1.4	1.0	1.3	2.6	0.8
Other dangerous nonnarcotic drugs	4.0	1.3	8.3	2.0	5.0
Possession:*	80.3	72.1	76.9	82.8	83.6
Heroin or cocaine and their derivatives	21.3	23.4	11.5	22.0	24.4
Marijuana	39.9	41.6	49.4	48.6	27.1
Synthetic or manufactured drugs	3.0	1.8	2.7	4.4	2.5
Other dangerous nonnarcotic drugs	16.0	5.4	13.3	7.8	29.7

*Because of rounding, the percentages may not add to 100.0.

SOURCE: "Table 4.1: Arrests for Drug Abuse Violations, by Region, 2002," in *Crime in the United States 2002,* Federal Bureau of Investigation, Washington, DC, 2003

Drug-Related Arrests

The federal government passed a number of anti-drug and anti-crime bills in the 1980s—the Comprehensive Crime Control Act of 1984 (PL 98-473), the Anti-Drug Abuse Act of 1986 (PL 99-570), and the Anti-Drug Abuse Act of 1988 (PL 100-690). Each of these requires increased mandatory sentencing (see below), harsher sentencing, preventive detention, and even the death penalty for certain drug-related crimes. These laws were a major factor in the rising rate of drug arrests and prison sentences for drug convictions in the late 1980s and 1990s. The number of drug arrests rose from 1980 to 1995 by roughly 250 percent but held level from 1995 to 2000. (See Figure 8.1.)

Possession of drugs accounted for 80.3 percent of drug abuse violations in the United States in 2002 and 19.7 percent were for the sale or manufacturing of drugs. Possession of marijuana accounted for almost 40 percent of drug abuse violations in 2002. Heroin or cocaine and their derivatives accounted for 21.3 percent of arrests for possession and 8.8 percent of arrests for the sale or manufacture of drugs. (See Table 8.3.) These patterns were nearly identical to 1999 arrests for drug abuse violations nationally. In the Northeast the figures for sale or manufacturing were significantly higher, at almost 28 percent of all drug abuse arrests. (See Table 8.3.) Since 1982, arrests for possession of drugs have far outpaced arrests for their manufacture and sale. (See Figure 8.2.) Heroin and cocaine arrests grew from 1982 to 2001, rising from 13 percent of all drug arrests to 33 percent. (See Table 8.4.)

DEMOGRAPHICS. Arrests for drug abuse violations in 2002 were prevalent among younger persons. A total of 49 percent (540,142) of those arrested for drug abuse violations were under age 25. Those under age 21 accounted for 31 percent (342,204) of arrests for drug violations while juvenile offenders under age 18 made up 12.1 percent (133,754) of arrests. Persons under age 15 accounted for 2 percent (21,836) of drug abuse arrests. Still, from 1970 to 1999, the number of adults arrested for drug abuse violations increased much more steeply than the number of juveniles. (See Figure 8.3.)

FIGURE 8.2

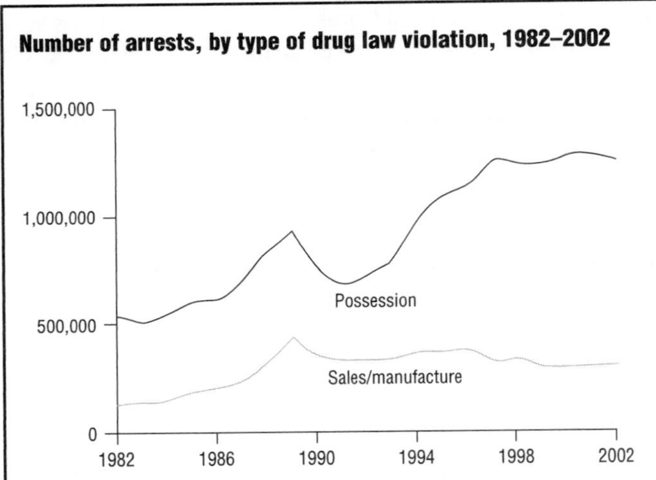

SOURCE: "Number of Arrests, by Type of Drug Law Violations, 1982–2002," in *Drugs and Crime Facts,* U.S. Department of Justice, Bureau of Justice Statistics, Washington, DC, 2003 [Online] http://www.ojp.usdoj.gov/bjs/dcf/enforce.htm [accessed April 10, 2004]

From 1993 to 2002 drug abuse arrests increased for all ages by 37 percent. Arrests of those under age 18 rose 59.1 percent. (See Table 1.5 in Chapter 1.) The number of females arrested for drug offenses rose 50 percent between 1993 and 2002, with arrests for females under 18 rising 120 percent during this time. (See Table 1.6 in Chapter 1.) Males continue to make up an overwhelming majority of drug abuse arrestees. In 2002 males accounted for 82 percent (798,695) of arrests for drug abuse violations, compared to 18 percent (175,387) for females.

In 2002 whites accounted for 66.2 percent of all arrests for drug abuse in the United States, while blacks accounted for 32.5 percent of all arrests. American Indians/Alaskan Natives (0.6 percent) and Asian/Pacific Islanders (0.7 percent) represented a very small proportion of total drug abuse arrests.

Alcohol-Related Arrests

In 2002 there were 840,384 arrests for driving under the influence of alcohol (DUI), down 2.8 percent from the 864,000 DUI arrests in 1998. Similarly, arrests for drunkenness were down by 16.9 percent, from a total of 455,225 in 1998, to 378,102 in 2002. Arrests for liquor law violations decreased from 395,831 in 1998 to 357,222 in 2002, down 9.8 percent. Liquor law violations are common among juvenile offenders, as it is illegal for juveniles to possess or purchase alcoholic beverages. Among persons under 18 years of age in 2002, there were 79,758 arrests for liquor law violations, a decline of 21.9 percent since 1998, compared to a decline of only 5.5 percent (277,464 arrests) among arrestees 18 or older.

White offenders are consistently involved in more arrests for alcohol violations than other races. In 2002 white arrests made up 87.8 percent of driving under the influence offenses, 87.7 percent of the liquor law violations, and 83.7 percent of drunkenness arrests. American Indians/Alaskan Natives accounted for 2.5 percent of liquor law arrests and 2.3 percent of drunkenness arrests.

PRESENCE OF DRUGS AT THE TIME OF ARREST

In 1987 the National Institute of Justice introduced the Drug Use Forecasting program (DUF) to determine the

FIGURE 8.3

Drug arrests by age, 1970–2002

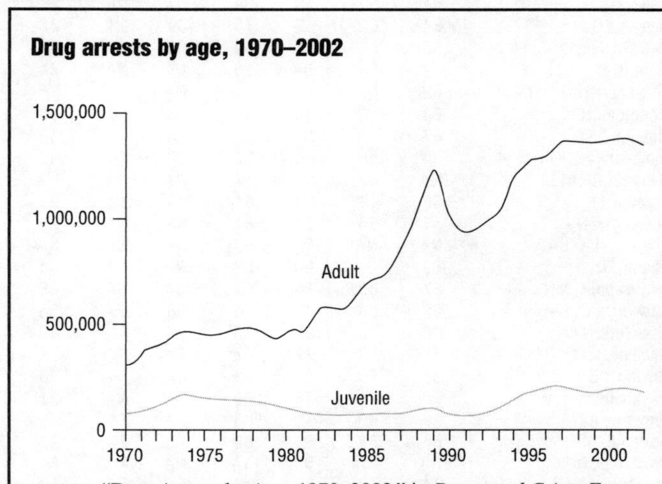

SOURCE: "Drug Arrests by Age, 1970–2002," in *Drugs and Crime Facts,* U.S. Department of Justice, Bureau of Justice Statistics, Washington, DC, 2003 [Online] http://www.ojp.usdoj.gov/bjs/dcf/enforce.htm [accessed April 10, 2004]

TABLE 8.4

Percent distribution of arrests for drug abuse violations, by type of drug, 1982–2001

	Total			Heroin/cocaine			Marijuana			Synthetic drugs			Other		
	Total	Sale/manufacture	Possession	Total	Sale/manufacture	Possession	Total	Sale/manufacture	Possession	Total	Sale/manufacture	Possession	Total	Sale/manufacture	Possession
1982	100%	20%	80%	13%	4%	9%	72%	10%	62%	4%	1%	2%	12%	5%	7%
1983	100	22	78	23	6	17	61	10	50	3	1	2	13	4	8
1984	100	22	78	26	7	19	59	10	48	3	1	2	12	4	9
1985	100	24	76	30	8	22	55	10	45	3	1	2	12	4	8
1986	100	25	75	41	13	28	44	8	36	3	1	2	13	4	9
1987	100	26	74	46	14	32	40	7	33	3	1	2	12	4	8
1988	100	27	73	52	17	35	34	6	28	3	1	2	11	4	7
1989	100	32	68	54	19	35	29	6	23	2	1	1	15	6	8
1990	100	32	68	54	21	33	30	6	24	2	1	2	14	4	10
1991	100	33	67	55	22	33	28	6	22	2	1	1	14	4	10
1992	100	32	68	53	21	32	32	7	26	2	1	1	13	4	9
1993	100	30	70	50	19	31	34	6	28	2	1	1	14	4	10
1994	100	27	73	47	17	30	36	6	30	2	*	1	16	4	12
1995	100	25	75	42	15	28	40	6	34	2	1	2	16	4	12
1996	100	25	75	40	14	26	43	6	36	2	1	1	16	4	12
1997	100	20	80	36	10	25	44	6	38	3	1	2	18	4	14
1998	100	21	79	37	11	26	44	5	38	3	1	2	17	4	13
1999	100	20	80	34	10	24	46	6	40	3	1	2	17	3	14
2000	100	19	81	34	9	24	46	6	41	3	1	2	17	3	14
2001	100	19	81	33	10	23	46	5	40	4	1	3	18	3	14

*Less than 0.5%.

SOURCE: "Table 4.29: Percent Distribution of Arrests for Drug Abuse Violations," in *Sourcebook of Criminal Justice Statistics 2002,* U.S. Department of Justice, Bureau of Justice Statistics, Washington, DC, 2003

TABLE 8.5

Drug use by adult arestees in 41 cities and counties, by sex and type of drug, 2000–2002

(Percent testing positive)

	Any drug[1]						Cocaine[2]						Marijuana					
	Male			Female			Male			Female			Male			Female		
Primary city	**2000**	**2001**	**2002**	**2000**	**2001**	**2002**	**2000**	**2001**	**2002**	**2000**	**2001**	**2002**	**2000**	**2001**	**2002**	**2000**	**2001**	**2002**
Albany, NY	65%	63%	70%	50%	62%	68%	25%	30%	26%	22%	44%	39%	45%	46%	54%	30%	40%	32%
Albuquerque, NM	65	64	62	58	66	70	35	37	38	41	46	49	47	38	34	18	25	27
Anchorage, AK	52	52	61	46	55	68	22	19	20	24	23	49	38	38	49	28	31	28
Atlanta, GA	70	NA	71	72	NA	NA	48	NA	49	58	NA	NA	38	NA	35	26	NA	NA
Birmingham, AL	65	63	64	53	NA	NA	33	29	34	42	NA	NA	45	49	42	18	NA	NA
Charlotte, NC	68	66	62	NA	68	64	44	32	34	NA	63	38	44	48	44	NA	18	38
Chicago, IL	76	84	85	80	NA	NA	37	41	48	59	NA	NA	46	50	49	26	NA	NA
Cleveland, OH	72	68	72	68	71	64	38	35	35	52	50	43	49	47	51	24	28	26
Dallas, TX	54	52	58	39	NA	NA	28	30	31	24	NA	NA	36	33	35	21	NA	NA
Denver, CO	64	62	62	70	64	68	35	34	33	47	45	45	41	40	40	34	33	33
Des Moines, IA	55	57	56	59	60	55	11	9	10	18	12	12	41	43	42	36	40	32
Detroit, MI	70	64	NA	70	NA	NA	24	22	NA	42	NA	NA	50	48	NA	24	NA	NA
Fort Lauderdale, FL	62	NA	NA	61	NA	NA	31	NA	NA	45	NA	NA	43	NA	NA	28	NA	NA
Honolulu, HI	63	59	63	62	50	60	16	11	9	19	10	7	30	30	32	19	14	21
Houston, TX	57	NA	NA	52	NA	NA	32	NA	NA	32	NA	NA	36	NA	NA	27	NA	NA
Indianapolis, IN	64	66	66	72	67	76	31	32	35	45	41	55	49	50	47	38	38	39
Kansas City, MO	NA	69	NA	NA	NA	NA	NA	34	NA	NA	NA	NA	NA	49	NA	NA	NA	NA
Laredo, TX	59	49	46	31	35	26	45	35	36	22	26	11	28	26	26	17	14	7
Las Vegas, NV	58	60	64	61	53	NA	22	21	24	27	26	NA	33	35	35	25	24	NA
Los Angeles, CA	NA	NA	62	65	NA	NA	NA	NA	32	33	NA	NA	NA	NA	36	32	NA	NA
Miami, FL	63	NA	NA	NA	NA	NA	44	NA	NA	NA	NA	NA	38	NA	NA	NA	NA	NA
Minneapolis, MN	67	69	74	NA	NA	NA	26	28	31	NA	NA	NA	54	54	54	NA	NA	NA
New Orleans, LA	69	68	72	56	56	59	35	37	42	41	38	42	47	45	47	28	25	26
New York, NY	80	76	81	75	77	61	49	45	49	53	57	39	41	40	44	28	32	31
Oklahoma City, OK	71	68	72	67	64	67	22	22	26	27	27	30	57	51	54	45	41	43
Omaha, NE	63	69	61	53	64	60	18	20	21	22	28	30	48	56	41	33	36	28
Philadelphia, PA	72	71	76	59	NA	NA	31	37	39	41	NA	NA	49	43	48	22	NA	NA
Phoenix, AZ	66	69	71	66	72	71	32	27	27	35	32	26	34	40	42	23	26	29
Portland, OR	64	68	66	69	73	67	22	27	22	30	37	28	36	36	38	26	24	22
Rio Arriba, NM	NA	NA	62	NA	NA	NA	NA	NA	30	NA	NA	NA	NA	NA	38	NA	NA	NA
Sacramento, CA	74	73	79	NA	81	NA	18	18	21	NA	30	NA	50	48	51	NA	28	NA
Salt Lake City, UT	54	54	60	59	49	74	18	16	19	14	22	31	34	34	36	25	19	25
San Antonio, TX	53	57	63	NA	NA	NA	20	30	32	NA	NA	NA	41	41	42	NA	NA	NA
San Diego, CA	64	62	64	66	67	69	15	14	13	26	16	21	39	36	38	27	28	33
San Jose, CA	53	62	58	68	71	67	12	13	13	8	15	12	36	38	34	29	34	27
Seattle, WA	64	64	70	NA	NA	NA	31	32	38	NA	NA	NA	38	35	36	NA	NA	NA
Spokane, WA	58	62	65	NA	NA	NA	15	18	16	NA	NA	NA	40	42	47	NA	NA	NA
Tucson, AZ	69	63	71	71	58	70	41	36	42	50	35	45	45	44	47	28	29	25
Tulsa, OK	NA	61	70	NA	NA	72	NA	20	22	NA	NA	27	NA	48	52	NA	NA	34
Washington, DC	NA	NA	64	NA	NA	74	NA	NA	28	NA	NA	38	NA	NA	41	NA	NA	33
Woodbury, IA	NA	NA	43	NA	NA	39	NA	NA	12	NA	NA	26	NA	NA	28	NA	NA	13
Median	64	64	64	62	64	67	31	29	30	33	31	31	41	43	42	27	28	28

Note: These data are from the Arrestee Drug Abuse Monitoring (ADAM) program sponsored by the U.S. Department of Justice, National Institute of Justice. ADAM data are collected in booking facilities in participating counties throughout the United States.

[1]Includes cocaine, marijuana, methamphetamine, opiates, and phencyclidine (PCP).

[2]Includes either crack or powder cocaine.

SOURCE: "Table 4.30: Drug Use by Adult Arrestees in 41 U.S. Cities and Counties, by Sex and Type of Drug," in *Sourcebook of Criminal Justice Statistics 2002,* U.S. Department of Justice, Bureau of Justice Statistics, Washington, DC, 2003

nature and extent of drug abuse in the nation by monitoring drug use of arrestees in 23 cities across the United States. In 1993 the DUF was criticized for producing data that were not generalized. This led to the redesign of the study, including its expansion to include 41 cities and new title, the Arrestee Drug Abuse Monitoring Program, or ADAM. The new program added elements to make the collected data more accurate and valuable to the local sites in monitoring local drug trends. The NIJ also plans to eventually expand the program to 75 cities. The data, collected quarterly in central booking facilities of each city, comes from voluntary and anonymous interviews and urine specimens from selected arrestees. Except for marijuana and PCP, which can remain in the system for several weeks, all the other drugs had been used by arrestees in the preceding two or three days.

Adult Arrestees

In 2002 the 41 cities collected data from adult male arrestees and published the results in *Preliminary Data on Drug Use and Related Matters among Adult Arrestees and Juvenile Detainees, 2002* (National Institute of Justice, Washington, D.C., 2003). The percentage of male arrestees who tested positive for any drug use ranged from a high of 85 percent in Chicago, Illinois to a low of 43

TABLE 8.6

Urine test results on drug use by adult male arrestees, 2002

Primary city	% of Arrestees testing positive for: Any of 5 drugs[1]	Multiple drugs (Any of 5)	Any of 10 drugs[2]	Multiple drugs (any of 10)	Interviews with completed urine tests (%)
Albany, NY	70.0	17.3	71.5	20.3	71.4
Albuquerque, NM	61.9	24.2	67.2	28.2	96.0
Anchorage, AK	61.4	11.0	64.5	15.0	90.2
Atlanta, GA	70.7	18.1	71.3	19.2	92.3
Birmingham, AL	63.6	17.6	65.2	20.9	85.5
Charlotte, NC	61.8	18.9	62.5	21.0	87.2
Chicago, IL	85.2	33.8	85.3	36.0	92.1
Cleveland, OH	71.9	23.4	73.2	25.4	92.0
Dallas, TX	58.0	17.8	59.2	20.3	95.8
Denver, CO	61.7	17.9	67.4	22.6	94.4
Des Moines, IA	56.0	18.5	57.3	19.8	91.2
Honolulu, HI	62.9	23.0	64.4	25.9	89.9
Indianapolis, IN	66.0	21.1	67.9	24.2	97.3
Laredo, TX	46.4	19.6	50.7	19.6	79.4
Las Vegas, NV	64.0	20.9	66.5	25.0	92.9
Los Angeles, CA	62.3	23.3	62.3	24.6	85.5
Minneapolis, MN	73.5	21.0	74.5	23.5	92.5
New Orleans, LA	71.6	29.3	73.4	32.1	97.4
New York, NY	81.0	26.1	82.7	31.5	97.3
Oklahoma City, OK	72.1	25.7	74.1	33.2	97.4
Omaha, NE	61.3	21.6	62.8	23.3	84.5
Philadelphia, PA	76.2	30.8	76.8	36.7	94.7
Phoenix, AZ	71.1	29.7	73.5	32.6	93.3
Portland, OR	66.3	24.2	68.7	27.7	93.5
Rio Arriba, NM	61.7	23.2	64.7	30.4	92.9
Sacramento, CA	78.7	31.3	80.1	36.7	96.1
Salt Lake City, UT	59.6	21.7	62.1	24.7	94.9
San Antonio, TX	62.9	20.0	64.4	22.0	95.9
San Diego, CA	63.8	22.5	66.1	25.6	96.5
San Jose, CA	58.5	21.1	60.2	22.7	90.9
Seattle, WA	70.1	23.8	71.0	25.1	92.5
Spokane, WA	64.8	23.0	66.6	24.5	94.8
Tucson, AZ	71.3	30.4	74.6	32.8	87.9
Tulsa, OK	70.4	24.3	72.2	29.6	98.4
Washington, DC	63.6	21.4	64.0	24.1	74.7
Woodbury, IA	42.8	12.8	43.3	14.5	86.5
Median	63.9	22.1	66.9	24.6	92.7

[1]The 5 drugs are cocaine, marijuana, methamphetamine, opiates, and phencyclidine (PCP).
[2]The 10 drugs are barbiturates, benzodiazepines, cocaine, marijuana, methadone, methamphetamine, methaqualone, opiates, phencyclidine (PCP), and propoxyphene.

SOURCE: "Table 3: Urine Test Results on Drug Use among Adult Male Arrestees, 2002," in *Preliminary Data on Drug Use & Related Matters among Adult Arrestees & Juvenile Detainees 2002,* U.S. Department of Justice, Office of Justice Programs, National Institute of Justice, Washington, DC, June 2002

percent in Woodbury, Iowa, with a median (half of the cities had higher percentages testing positive, half had lower) of 64 percent. (See Table 8.5.)

The findings are viewed as conservative estimates of drug use, since self-report studies tend to understate actual drug use. Urinalysis revealed that almost one-quarter (24.6 percent) of arrestees in about half of the cities had used more than one of 10 drugs. The use of more than one drug (any of 10) per arrestee ranged from 36.7 percent in Philadelphia, Pennsylvania and Sacramento, California to a low of 14.5 in Woodbury, Iowa. (See Table 8.6.) In most of the reporting cities, adult male arrestees were 32 years of age or older. In half the study sites, 30 percent or more of arrestees did not have a high school diploma. About 60 percent were employed, and over 80 percent had prior arrest records.

Data from the *1999 Annual Report on Drug Use Among Adult and Juvenile Arrestees* (National Institute of Justice, 2000), show the range of drug use among arrestees in 34 U.S. cities in 1999. Among white male arrestees, the highest rate of use of any drug was in Philadelphia, Pennsylvania, while the highest rate among African-American male arrestees was found in Albuquerque, New Mexico. Use of drugs among Hispanic male arrestees was highest in New York City, New York.

Among females, use of any drug by white arrestees was highest in New York City, while the largest proportion of African-American female arrestees were found to have used drugs in Albuquerque, and the largest proportion of Hispanic female arrestee drug users was found in Fort Lauderdale, Florida.

Juvenile Arrestees

In 2000 drug use by male juvenile arrestees showed common trends. Marijuana use occurred with the most fre-

FIGURE 8.4

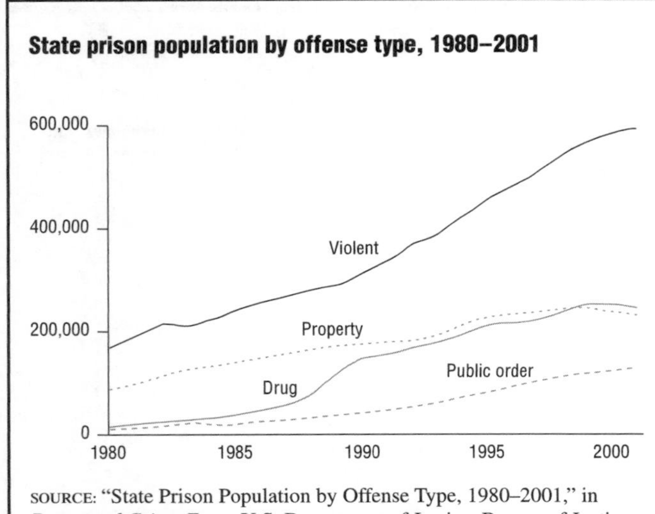

SOURCE: "State Prison Population by Offense Type, 1980–2001," in *Drugs and Crime Facts,* U.S. Department of Justice, Bureau of Justice Statistics, Washington, DC, 2003 [Online] http://www.ojp.usdoj.gov/bjs/dcf/correct.htm [accessed April 10, 2004]

quency, with the highest use in Phoenix (55 percent) and the lowest in Birmingham, Alabama (42 percent). Marijuana is the drug most commonly used by both male and female juvenile detainees, as reported in the *2000 Arrestee Drug Abuse Monitoring Program Report* (National Institute of Justice, April 2003). Cocaine was the second most common drug, although far behind marijuana in usage. In only three sites did more than 10 percent of juvenile detainees test positive for cocaine.

Generally, the older the juvenile arrestee, the more likely he was to test positive for drug use. Juvenile arrestees aged 17 showed the highest proportion of drug use. Less than 5 percent of detainees were homeless or living in a shelter, while some 93 percent lived in houses or apartments. Of those living with their families, 52 percent lived in two-parent families and 40 percent in single-parent families. Of those in single-parent families, 82 percent lived with their mothers.

JUVENILE DRUG USE

In 2002 juveniles who regularly smoked cigarettes were more likely to use alcohol or illicit drugs, according to the *2002 National Survey on Drug Use and Health* (Department of Health and Human Services, Substance Abuse and Mental Health Services, September 2003). The survey also reported that in 2002, 11.5 percent of juveniles between the ages of 12 and 17 reported that they currently used illicit drugs. Marijuana was the most frequently used (8.2 percent of all juveniles), followed by psychotherapeutic drugs (4 percent of all juveniles), and inhalants (1.2 percent). The percentages between boys and girls aged 12 to 17 varied slightly. For boys, 12.3 percent used illicit drugs, while the rate was 10.9 percent for girls. Boys used marijuana more frequently, with girls more likely to use psychotherapeutic drugs nonmedically. Illicit drug use also varied by race and ethnicity. Native Americans showed the highest rate of illicit drug use (10.1 percent), followed by blacks (9.7 percent), whites (8.5 percent), and Asians (3.5 percent).

So-called "club drugs" such as Ecstasy (MDMA), Rohypnol (known as the date rape drug), GHB, and ketamine have become popular among teenagers at dance clubs and "raves" in recent years. Because each of these club drugs is now scheduled under the Controlled Substances Act (Title II of the Comprehensive Drug Abuse Prevention and Control Act of 1970), they are illegal and their use constitutes a criminal offense.

According to the *2002 National Survey on Drug Use and Health* (Department of Health and Human Services, Substance Abuse and Mental Health Services, September 2003), 2.4 percent of 12- to 17-year-olds reported using Ecstasy, compared with 6.9 percent of 18- to 25-year-olds. Girls aged 12 to 17 (2.8 percent) were more likely to have used Ecstasy in the past year than were boys (1.9 percent), while those living in the Northeast and West were more likely to have used the drug than were those living in the Midwest. Numbers of new users of Ecstasy dropped from 1.9 million new users in 2000 to 1.8 million new users in 2001.

MORE DRUG OFFENDERS BEHIND BARS

At all levels—local, state, and federal—the number of drug offenders in prisons and jails increased dramatically from 1980 to 1993, far outstripping the generally sharp increase in the overall prison and jail populations. During this period, the total number of state prisoners almost tripled, and the number of federal prisoners increased fourfold. This trend changed by mid-decade. From 1995 to 2001 the largest growth in state prison population was in violent offenders. The number of drug offenders in state prisons increased by 30,600 inmates (15 percent of total growth) compared to violent offenders (63 percent of total growth) from 1995 to 2001.

From 1990 to 2001 the number of drug offenders in state prisons rose substantially. (See Figure 8.4.) From 1995 to 2001, female drug offenders accounted for 13 percent of the increase in total growth of female state prisoners sentenced, compared to a 49 percent growth in female violent offenders, and 22 percent growth in female property crime offenders. In comparison, male drug offenders accounted for 15 percent of the total growth of male state prison populations, with 64 percent of the growth attributed to male violent offenders. (See Table 8.7.) From 1995 to 2001 there was an increase of 19,100 black drug offenders in state prisons, accounting for 23 percent of the total growth of sentenced black prisoners under state jurisdiction. There were 16,200 additional white drug offenders in state prison and 1,400 fewer Hispanic drug offenders.

In 2002, of 14,054 homicides, 4.7 percent were drug-related, a slight decrease from 4.8 percent in 1998 but

FIGURE 8.5

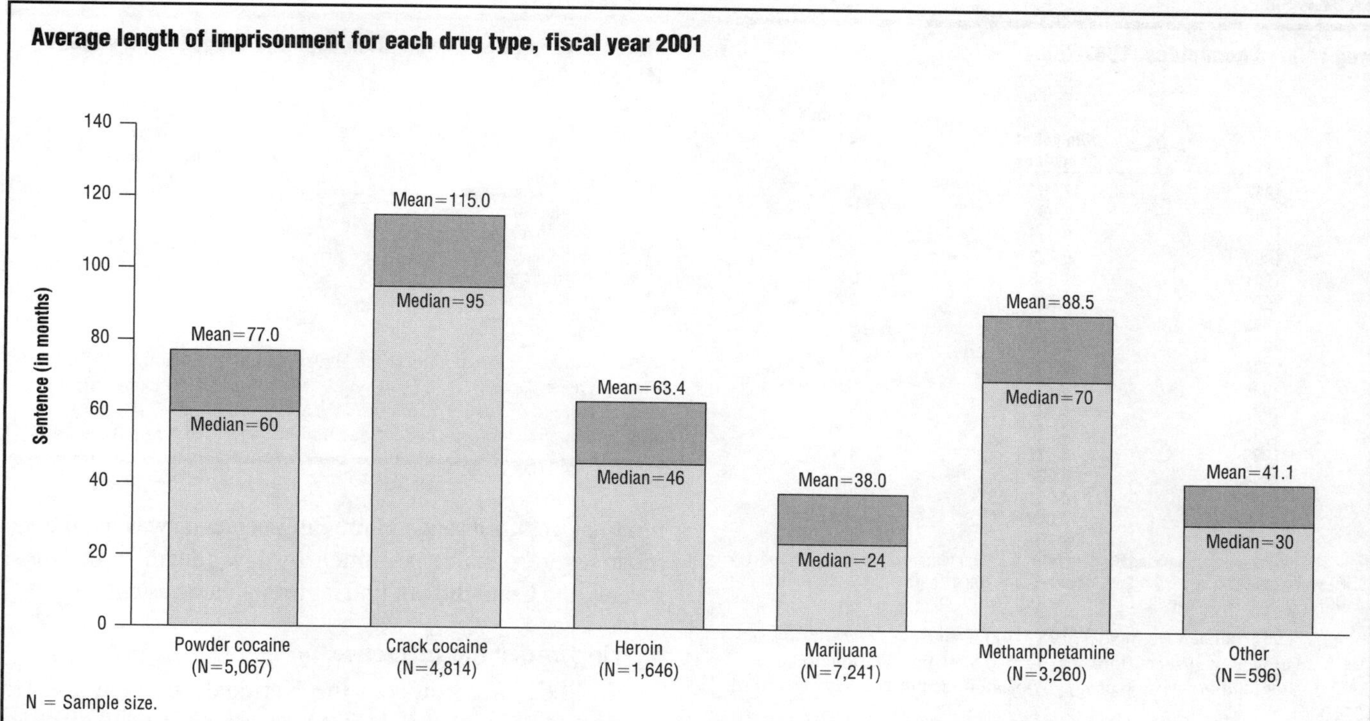

N = Sample size.

SOURCE: "Figure J: Average Length of Imprisonment for Each Drug Type, Fiscal Year 2001," in *2001 Sourcebook of Federal Sentencing Statistics,* U.S. Sentencing Commission, Washington, DC, 2001

higher than the 2001 rate of 4.1 percent. (See Table 8.8.) Of crime victims in 2002, about 10.2 percent reported that they believed the offender was using drugs, either alone or in combination with alcohol. (See Table 8.9.)

Drug Offender Sentences

Federal and state laws consider a number of factors in establishing penalties for violators of drug laws. In general, the penalties for drug violations are determined by:

- The dangerousness of the drug
- Whether the violation is for drug possession or drug trafficking
- The amount of the drug involved
- The criminal history of the offender
- The location of the transaction, such as near a school or in a crack house
- The ages of the buyer and seller

Figure 8.5 shows the mean (average) and median (half were more; half were less) lengths of prison sentences for each drug type in fiscal year 2001. The highest mean and median sentences were for crack cocaine (115 months and 95 months, respectively), followed by methamphetamine, with a mean of 88.5 months and a median sentence of 70 months. The lowest mean and median sentences (38 months and 24 months) were for the most widely used illicit drug, marijuana.

TABLE 8.7

Percent of total growth of sentenced prisoners under state jurisdiction, by offense and gender, 1995–2001

	Male	Female
Total	**100%**	**100%**
Violent	64	49
Property	—	22
Drug	**15%**	**13%**
Public-order	21	16

SOURCE: "Percent of Total Growth of Sentenced Prisoners under State Jurisdiction, by Offense and Gender, 1995–2001," in *Drugs and Crime Facts,* U.S. Department of Justice, Bureau of Justice Statistics, Washington, DC, 2003 [Online] http://www.ojp.usdoj.gov/bjs/dcf/correct.htm [accessed April 10, 2004]

MANDATORY MINIMUM SENTENCING. Mandatory minimum sentences limit the sentencing discretion of the judge. While the law sets the minimum length of time to which a convicted felon can be sentenced, it does allow judges to impose sentences longer than the mandatory minimums. A first-time offender in a federal court facing a 10-year mandatory minimum sentence could receive anything from 10 years up to and including life imprisonment. For example, offenders convicted of possessing at least five grams of crack cocaine for their first conviction, three grams for their second conviction, and one gram for their third conviction are sentenced to a mandatory minimum prison sentence of five years and a maximum sentence of 20 years.

TABLE 8.8

Drug-related homicides, 1987–2002

Year	Number of homicides	Percent drug related
1987	17,963	4.9%
1988	17,971	5.6
1989	18,954	7.4
1990	20,273	6.7
1991	21,676	6.2
1992	22,716	5.7
1993	23,180	5.5
1994	22,084	5.6
1995	20,232	5.1
1996	16,967	5.0
1997	15,837	5.1
1998	14,276	4.8
1999	13,011	4.5
2000	13,230	4.5
2001	14,061	4.1
2002	14,054	4.7

Note: The percentages are based on data from the Supplementary Homicide Reports (SHR) while the totals are from the Uniform Crime Reports (UCR). Not all homicides in the UCR result in reports in the SHR.

SOURCE: "Drug-Related Homicides, 1987–2002," in *Drugs and Crime Facts,* U.S. Department of Justice, Bureau of Justice Statistics, Washington, DC, 2003 [Online] http://www.ojp.usdoj.gov/bjs/dcf/duc.htm#to [accessed April 10, 2004]

Many law enforcement officials think some mandatory sentences are too harsh for the crime. As a result, some prosecutors charge the accused with lesser crimes than those for which they were arrested, and some judges ignore the mandatory sentencing and apply lesser punishments. In 2002 the U.S. Supreme Court agreed to decide on the constitutionality of mandatory sentencing as applied in two cases challenging California's Three Strikes law. In March 2003, in a 5–4 decision, the Supreme Court upheld the right of states to imprison repeat felony offenders for lengthy sentences.

MANDATORY LIFE TERM UPHELD. In June of 1991 the U.S. Supreme Court in *Harmelin v. Michigan* (501 US 957) upheld a Michigan law that imposed a mandatory life sentence without parole for possession of more than 650 grams of cocaine. Ronald Allen Harmelin's attorney argued that the mandatory sentence violated the Eighth Amendment's prohibition against cruel and unusual punishment. He claimed the sentence was "grossly disproportionate" to the crime. Also, the state law did not permit the judge to use his own discretion to reduce a sentence based on other mitigating factors, such as the fact that Harmelin had no prior felony convictions.

In a sharply divided 5–4 decision, the majority declared that the Eighth Amendment does not require a sentencing judge to be given discretion to reduce a sentence. The Court ruled that "cruel and unusual" came from the English Declaration of Rights of 1689 and was intended to prevent sentences of being burned or drawn and quartered (the criminal's hands and feet were tied to horses, which then pulled the victim to pieces). Although Harmelin's sentence was the second most severe penalty permitted by law (death is the most severe), the Court did not find it grossly inconsistent.

TABLE 8.9

Victim's perception of use of alcohol and drugs by the violent offender, 2002

	Percent of victims of violent crime
Alcohol only	17.0
Alcohol and drugs	4.6
Alcohol or drugs	1.5
Drugs only	5.6
No drugs or alcohol	27.7
Don't know	43.3

SOURCE: "Victim's Perception of the Use of Alcohol and Drugs by the Violent Offender, 2002," in *Drugs and Crime Facts,* U.S. Department of Justice, Bureau of Justice Statistics, Washington, DC, 2003 [Online] http://www.ojp.usdoj.gov/bjs/dcf/duc.htm#to [accessed April 10, 2004]

Driving under the Influence

In 2002, according to the National Highway Traffic Safety Administration (NHTSA), there were 17,419 alcohol-related traffic fatalities. In 1982 fatalities in alcohol-related crashes comprised 57 percent of all traffic fatalities, while the number had fallen to 41 percent in 2002. From 1997 to 2002 the alcohol-related fatality rate per 100 million vehicle miles traveled had fallen from .65 to .62. Some 310,000 people were injured in crashes in which law enforcement reported that alcohol was present. The rate of alcohol-related fatal crashes was more than three times higher at night (61 percent) than during the day (18 percent). For all crashes, the rate of alcohol involvement was four times as high at night (17 percent) than during the day (4 percent). The highest intoxication rates in fatal crashes in 2000 were recorded among drivers 21 to 24 years of age (27 percent), followed by drivers 25 to 34 years of age (24 percent), and 35 to 44 years of age (22 percent).

In 1983, the peak year for DUI arrests and fatalities, 33 states allowed persons under age 21 to purchase and sell alcoholic beverages. Since then, changes in the federal laws governing the way federal highway funds are distributed caused states to raise the legal drinking age to age 21. As of the year 2000, all states and the District of Columbia had a 21-year minimum drinking age. Observers link this change to the lowered incidence of DUI arrests and fatalities.

In addition, repeat offenders are now subject to four alternative sanctioning approaches to keep them from driving drunk: automobile impoundment, ignition interlock (ignitions that will not operate if the driver's breath shows alcohol), electronically monitored house arrest, and intensive probation supervision in which counseling targets an offender's drinking habits. Social attitudes toward drinking and driving also have changed through the 1980s and 1990s. By the end of the twentieth century, driving after

FIGURE 8.6

National drug control budget, in billions, 2002–2005

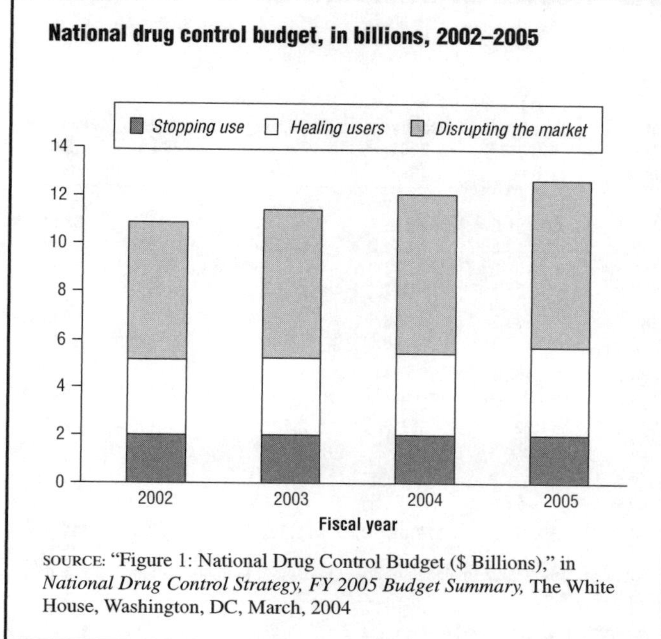

SOURCE: "Figure 1: National Drug Control Budget ($ Billions)," in *National Drug Control Strategy, FY 2005 Budget Summary,* The White House, Washington, DC, March, 2004

TABLE 8.10

Agency summary of drug control funding, 2003–2005

(Budget authority in millions)

	Fiscal year 2003 final	Fiscal year 2004 enacted	Fiscal year 2005 request
Department of Defense	$905.9	$908.6	$852.7
Department of Education	644.0	624.5	611.0
Department of Health and Human Services			
National Institute on Drug Abuse	960.9	990.8	1,019.1
Substance Abuse and Mental Health Services Administration	2,354.3	2,488.7	2,637.7
Total HHS	3,315.2	3,479.5	3,656.8
Department of Homeland Security			
Immigration and Customs enforcement	518.0	538.7	575.8
Customs and border protection	873.9	1,070.5	1,121.4
U.S. Coast Guard	648.1	773.7	822.3
Total HLS	2,040.0	2,382.9	2,519.4
Department of Justice			
Bureau of Prisons	43.2	47.7	49.3
Drug Enforcement Administration	1,639.8	1,703.0	1,815.7
Interagency Crime and Drug Enforcement[1]	477.2	550.6	580.6
Office of Justice Programs	269.6	181.3	304.3
Total Department of Justice	2,429.8	2,482.7	2,749.9
ONDCP			
Operations	26.3	27.8	27.6
High Intensity Drug Trafficking Area Program	226.0	225.0	208.4
Counterdrug Technology Assessment Center	46.5	41.8	40.0
Other Federal Drug Control Programs	221.8	227.6	235.0
Total ONDCP	520.6	522.2	511.0
Department of State			
Bureau of International Narcotics and Law Enforcement Affairs	874.3	914.4	921.6
Department of Veterans Affairs			
Veterans Health Administration	663.7	765.3	822.8
Other presidential priorities[2]	3.4	2.2	3.5
Total, federal drug budget	$11,397.0	$12,082.3	$12,648.6

[1]Prior to FY 2004, funds for the Interagency Crime and Drug Enforcement programs were appropriated into two accounts, one in the Justice Department and one in the Treasury Department. Beginning in fiscal year 2004 those accounts wer e consolidated. In this table funding is shown as combined for all three years.
[2]Includes the Small Business Administration's Drug Free Workplace grants and the National Highway Traffic Safety Administration's Drug Impaired Driving program.

SOURCE: "Table 2: Drug Control Funding: Agency Summary, Fiscal Year 2003–Fiscal Year 2005," in *National Drug Control Strategy, FY 2005 Budget Summary,* The White House, Washington, DC, March, 2004

several drinks was considered far less socially acceptable than just a generation earlier.

THE FEDERAL GOVERNMENT'S ROLE

The federal government has addressed the drug problem in two ways: reduction of supply through enforcement and interdiction, and reduction of demand through education, prevention, and treatment. According to the Office of National Drug Control Policy, actual federal spending on drug control programs increased from $1.5 billion in 1981 to $12.1 billion in FY 2004. A total of $12.6 billion has been proposed for the 2005 budget year, an increase of 4.7 percent over 2004. The money is spent in three distinct areas: stopping drug use, healing drug users, and disrupting the market for drugs. (See Figure 8.6.) Among the programs meant to stop drug use are the National Youth Anti-Drug Media Campaign, an ongoing series of anti-drug advertising messages, and the Drug-Free Communities Program, which supports local anti-drug coalitions. To assist drug users in their efforts to quit using drugs, the Access to Recovery initiative provides vouchers for those wishing medical care. To disrupt the drug market, the Organized Crime Drug Enforcement Task Forces focus law enforcement efforts on major drug trafficking organizations.

Drug control spending by individual departments in FY 2004 included: $3.5 billion for the Department of Health and Human Services; $1.7 billion for the Drug Enforcement Administration; and $1.1 billion for Customs and Border Protection. (See Table 8.10.) By function, the FY 2004 budget spent $5.4 billion on demand reduction efforts, $3.1 billion on domestic law enforcement, $2.5 billion on interdiction, and $1.1 billion on international efforts. (See Table 8.11.)

Federal drug seizures, as reported by five federal law enforcement agencies, increased for most types of drugs from 1989 to 2002. In 1989 about 1.3 million pounds of drugs were seized, compared to 2.6 million in 2002. A large rise in drug seizures occurred for heroin, more than doubling from 2,415 pounds in 1989 to 6,900 pounds seized in 2002. (See Table 8.12.) In FY 2002, drug interdiction efforts by the federal government accounted for the seizure of 225,122 pounds of cocaine, 2.4 million pounds of marijuana, and 193 pounds of hashish. Seizures of hashish in 2002 showed a marked decline from the amounts seized in some earlier years, perhaps due to less demand for the drug.

TABLE 8.11

Historical drug control funding by function, 1996–2005

(budget authority in millions)

Functional areas*	Fiscal year 1996 actual	Fiscal year 1997 actual	Fiscal year 1998 actual	Fiscal year 1999 actual	Fiscal year 2000 final	Fiscal year 2001 final	Fiscal year 2002 final	Fiscal year 2003 final	Fiscal year 2004 enacted	Fiscal year 2005 request
Demand reduction										
Drug abuse treatment	$1,928.7	$2,132.7	$1,947.4	$2,175.6	$2,241.6	$2,491.6	$2,544.7	$2,612.5	$2,775.3	$3,084.8
Drug abuse prevention	902.0	1,106.9	1,330.8	1,407.6	1,445.8	1,540.8	1,639.0	1,583.6	1,579.2	1,566.1
Treatment research	281.6	309.6	322.2	373.5	421.6	489.0	547.8	611.4	616.7	632.5
Prevention research	187.4	206.5	219.6	249.9	280.8	326.8	367.4	382.9	406.0	411.5
Total demand reduction	3,299.7	3,755.6	3,819.9	4,206.6	4,389.7	4,848.3	5,098.9	5,190.3	5,377.3	5,694.9
percentage	52.6%	49.9%	50.1%	45.7%	43.2%	49.4%	46.8%	45.5%	44.5%	45.0%
Domestic law enforcement	1,624.1	1,836.3	1,937.5	2,100.6	2,238.3	2,462.8	2,794.7	2,954.1	3,080.5	3,201.1
percentage	25.9%	24.4%	25.4%	22.8%	22.0%	25.1%	25.7%	25.9%	25.5%	25.3%
Interdiction	1,106.7	1,549.3	1,406.5	2,155.6	1,904.4	1,895.3	1,913.7	2,147.5	2,490.6	2,602.7
percentage	17.6%	20.6%	18.4%	23.4%	18.8%	19.3%	17.6%	18.8%	20.6%	20.6%
International	243.6	389.9	464.0	746.3	1,619.2	617.3	1,084.5	1,105.1	1,133.9	1,149.9
percentage	3.9%	5.2%	6.1%	8.1%	15.9%	6.3%	10.0%	9.7%	9.4%	9.1%
Totals	**$6,274.1**	**$7,531.2**	**$7,628.0**	**$9,209.1**	**$10,151.5**	**$9,823.8**	**$10,891.9**	**$11,397.0**	**$12,082.3**	**$12,648.6**

*Consistent with the restructured drug budget, ONDCP has adjusted the amounts reported for fiscal years 1996–2002 to eliminate the BYRNE grant funding from this table and have included funding for the National Highway Traffic Safety Administration's Drug Impaired Driving program.

SOURCE: "Table 3: Historical Drug Control Funding by Function FY 1996–2005," in *National Drug Control Strategy, FY 2005 Budget Summary,* The White House, Washington, DC, March 2004

TABLE 8.12

Federal drug seizures, by drug type, 1989–2002

	Pounds seized*				
Fiscal year	Total	Heroin	Cocaine	Marijuana	Hashish
1989	1,343,702	2,415	218,697	1,070,965	51,625
1990	738,004	1,704	235,885	483,353	17,062
1991	926,700	3,067	246,325	499,097	178,211
1992	1,093,366	2,552	303,289	783,477	4,048
1993	1,045,997	3,516	244,315	772,086	26,080
1994	1,355,678	2,898	309,710	1,041,445	1,625
1995	1,576,865	2,569	234,105	1,308,171	32,020
1996	1,718,552	3,373	253,297	1,429,786	32,096
1997	1,796,863	3,121	252,329	1,488,362	53,051
1998	2,047,558	3,499	266,029	1,777,434	596
1999	2,571,355	2,733	284,631	2,282,313	1,678
2000	2,894,200	6,640	248,827	2,614,746	23,987
2001	2,919,608	4,392	239,957	2,674,826	433
2002	2,644,580	6,900	225,122	2,412,365	193

*Figures are rounded to the nearest pound.

SOURCE: "Table 4.36: Federal Drug Seizures, Fiscal Years 1989–2002," in *Sourcebook of Criminal Justice Statistics 2002,* U.S. Department of Justice, Bureau of Justice Statistics, Washington, DC, 2003

CHAPTER 9

LAW ENFORCEMENT, CRIME PREVENTION, AND PUBLIC OPINIONS ABOUT CRIME

After a crime has been committed, the justice system of the United States goes into action. The system has three major components that work together:

- Law enforcement agencies gather evidence and capture suspected perpetrators.
- The judicial system tries perpetrators in a court of law and, if they are found guilty, sentences them to a period of incarceration or some other form of punishment, restitution, and/or treatment.
- Correction agencies house convicted criminals in prisons, jails, treatment centers, or other places of confinement.

CITY, COUNTY, AND STATE LAW ENFORCEMENT

In 2002 the United States had 13,981 city, county, and state police agencies and nine major federal law enforcement agencies. As of October 31, 2002, there were 957,502 full-time law enforcement employees. Of the total, 665,555 were sworn police officers and civilian employees accounted for 291,947. Almost 90 percent of police officers were male, while 62.1 percent of civilian employees were female. Suburban counties employed 268,044 law enforcement personnel, and the 70 cities in the nation with populations of 250,000 or more employed 205,573 law enforcement personnel. The 10 cities with populations of one million or more employed 112,183 law enforcement personnel. (See Table 9.1.)

Killed in the Line of Duty

Wearing a badge is a dangerous profession.... While progress is being made, violence remains a serious threat to those who have sworn to protect society.

—The Federal Bureau of Investigation, *Law Enforcement Officers Killed and Assaulted, 1996*

From 1993 through 2002, felons killed 636 law enforcement officers, an average of about 73 officers per year. Law enforcement murders were higher in the mid-1990s than other years during this time. From a peak of 80 in 1994, the number of officers killed declined to 61 in 1996, rose to 71 in 1997 and dropped in 1999 to 42. In 2002, 56 law enforcement officers were killed in the line of duty, down from 70 in 2001. (See Table 9.2.)

In 2002, 15 officers were killed in ambush situations. Ten officers died during arrest situations, such as drug-related arrests. Ten died in traffic stops or pursuits, nine were killed answering disturbance calls, and eight officers died while investigating suspicious persons or circumstances. Being in a one-officer vehicle was the most dangerous situation: 17 officers were in one-officer vehicles without assistance when they were killed. (See Table 9.3.)

WEAPONS USED. Firearms claimed the lives of 591 of the 636 officers killed in the line of duty from 1993 through 2002. Of these murders, 443 were committed with handguns, 112 with rifles, and 36 with shotguns. Bombs killed nine officers, while knives (eight), personal weapons (three), and other weapons (25) killed the remainder of officers. (See Table 9.4.) During 2002, firearms were used in 51 of the 56 slayings, and handguns were used in 38 of those killings. Ten were killed with rifles and three with shotguns.

ASSAILANTS. In 2002, 61 suspects were arrested for the murders of law enforcement officers; 59 were male and two were female. Thirty-seven of the arrestees were white, and 24 were black. Thirty-six assailants were under the age of 31, and 24 were ages 18 to 24. The average age was 32. (See Table 9.5 and Table 9.6.)

Among the 785 persons arrested and charged for their involvement in killing officers from 1993 to 2002, the average age was 28. Some 528 had been previously arrested for criminal activities (245 of them for crimes of violence), and 373 had been convicted, while 158 were on parole at the time of the killings. (See Table 9.7.)

TABLE 9.1

Full-time law enforcement employees, as of October 31, 2002

Population group	Total	Percent law enforcement employees		Total	Percent officers		Total	Percent civilians	
		Male	Female		Male	Female		Male	Female
Total agencies: 13,981 agencies; population 271,240,537	**957,502**	**73.2**	**26.8**	**665,555**	**88.7**	**11.3**	**291,947**	**37.9**	**62.1**
Total cities: 10,653 cities; population 182,456,027	**558,892**	**75.1**	**24.9**	**428,365**	**88.7**	**11.3**	**130,527**	**30.2**	**69.8**
Group I 70 cities, 250,000 and over; population 52,879,728	205,573	70.5	29.5	154,116	83.5	16.5	51,457	31.8	68.2
10 cities, 1,000,000 and over; population 24,682,265	112,183	69.6	30.4	83,925	82.5	17.5	28,258	31.4	68.6
22 cities, 500,000 to 999,999; population 14,767,287	52,626	72.6	27.4	40,101	84.0	16.0	12,525	36.1	63.9
38 cities, 250,000 to 499,999; population 13,430,176	40,764	70.4	29.6	30,090	85.6	14.4	10,674	27.8	72.2
Group II 162 cities, 100,000 to 249,999; population 24,457,039	61,739	73.2	26.8	46,124	89.0	11.0	15,615	26.4	73.6
Group III 389 cities, 50,000 to 99,999; population 26,808,264	62,203	76.3	23.7	47,762	91.3	8.7	14,441	26.9	73.1
Group IV 760 cities, 25,000 to 49,999; population 26,374,112	61,343	78.0	22.0	47,960	92.2	7.8	13,383	27.3	72.7
Group V 1,763 cities, 10,000 to 24,999; population 27,930,903	68,513	79.4	20.6	54,413	93.1	6.9	14,100	26.5	73.5
Group VI 7,509 cities, under 10,000; population 24,005,981	99,521	79.9	20.1	77,990	92.1	7.9	21,531	35.8	64.2
Suburban counties 964 agencies; population 57,536,474	268,044	69.8	30.2	158,104	86.9	13.1	109,940	45.3	54.7
Rural counties 2,364 agencies population 31,248,036	130,566	72.1	27.9	79,086	92.1	7.9	51,480	41.5	58.5
Suburban area* 6,528 agencies; population 108,747,307	418,093	73.3	26.7	275,584	89.2	10.8	142,509	42.5	57.5

*Suburban area includes law enforcement agencies in cities with less than 50,000 inhabitants and county law enforcement agencies that are within a Metropolitan Statistical Area. Suburban area excludes all metropolitan agencies associated with a central city. The agencies associated with suburban areas also appear in other groups within this table.

SOURCE: "Table 74: Full-Time Law Enforcement Employees as of October 31, 2002: Employees, Percent Male and Female by Population Group," in *Crime in the United States 2002,* Federal Bureau of Investigation,Washington, DC, 2003

FEDERAL LAW ENFORCEMENT

According to a Bureau of Justice Statistics (BJS) survey, in June of 2002 federal agencies employed more than 93,000 full-time officers authorized to make arrests and carry guns. This figure reflects an almost 6 percent increase from June of 2000. Of the major federal employers in 2002, the Immigration and Naturalization Service (INS) employed the most officers (19,407), almost half of whom were Border Patrol agents. The Federal Bureau of Prisons (BOP) accounted for 14,457 officers, the U.S. Customs Service for 11,977, and the FBI for 11,398. (See Table 9.8.)

In 2002, 85.2 percent of federal officers were male. The Internal Revenue Service (IRS), one of the agencies with 500 or more officers, had the largest proportion of female agents, at 28 percent. The DEA (Drug Enforcement Agency) had the smallest proportion of female officers, only 8.6 percent. Racial or ethnic minorities filled 32.4 percent of all federal law enforcement positions. Hispanics, who can be of any race, accounted for 16.8 percent of federal officers, and non-Hispanic blacks made up another 11.7 percent. Asian/Pacific Islanders (2.5 percent) and American Indians (1.2 percent) were also represented in the federal force. (See Figure 9.1.)

Federal Officers Assaulted and Killed

From 1998 to 2002 a total of 2,772 federal officers were assaulted. The assaults resulted in eight fatalities, one of which occurred in 2002. The 374 federal officers assaulted in 2002 was the lowest number of assaults during this period, with 653 assaults in 1998 being the highest. In

TABLE 9.2

Law enforcement officers feloniously killed, by circumstances at scene of incident, 1993–2002

Circumstance	Total	1993	1994	1995	1996	1997	1998	1999	2000	2001	2002
Total	**636**	**70**	**80**	**74**	**61**	**71**	**61**	**42**	**51**	**70**	**56**
Disturbance calls	98	10	8	8	4	14	16	7	8	14	9
Bar fights, person with firearm, etc.	41	5	4	2	1	3	7	6	4	5	4
Family quarrels	57	5	4	6	3	11	9	1	4	9	5
Arrest situations	205	28	34	21	26	22	16	12	12	24	10
Burglaries in progress/ pursuing burglary suspects	23	1	4	4	3	5	0	0	3	3	0
Robberies in progress/ pursuing robbery suspects	73	9	18	7	12	11	3	4	1	4	4
Drug-related matters	38	3	4	4	3	1	7	2	3	8	3
Attempting other arrests	71	15	8	6	8	5	6	6	5	9	3
Civil disorders (mass disobedience, riot, etc.)	0	0	0	0	0	0	0	0	0	0	0
Handling, transporting, custody of prisoners	20	1	1	4	0	4	4	2	2	2	0
Investigating suspicious persons/circumstances	105	15	15	17	13	10	6	7	6	8	8
Ambush situations	96	5	8	14	6	12	10	6	10	10	15
Entrapment/premeditation	34	3	1	6	2	5	4	4	2	3	4
Unprovoked attacks	62	2	7	8	4	7	6	2	8	7	11
Mentally deranged assailants	15	1	4	1	1	1	0	0	0	3	4
Traffic pursuits/stops	97	10	10	9	11	8	9	8	13	9	10

Note: The 72 deaths that resulted from the events of September 11, 2001, are not included in this table.

SOURCE: Table 18: Law Enforcement Officers Feloniously Killed, by Circumstance at Scene of Incident, 1993–2002," in *Crime in the United States, 2002: Uniform Crime Reports,* Federal Bureau of Investigation, Washington, DC, 2003

2002 personal weapons (hands, feet, etc.) were used in 173 incidents, firearms were used in 34 incidents, and threats accounted for 65 incidents.

In July of 1998 the nation was shocked by a shooting in the Capitol Building in Washington, D.C. Russell E. Weston, Jr., was charged with fatally shooting two Capitol police officers, Jacob J. Chestnut and John M. Gibson. Both [illegible] were buried with honors in Arlington National Cemet[illegible]. Weston himself was wounded in the gunfire exchange but recovered. Also wounded was a young female tourist.

CRIME PREVENTION

Crime prevention programs implemented by state and local agencies receive over $3.2 billion in U.S. Department of Justice grant funds each year. In 1996 the United States Congress issued a mandate to the Attorney General to authorize an evaluation of the effectiveness of these programs. The University of Maryland's Department of Criminology and Criminal Justice was selected to conduct the evaluation and issue a report. That report, "Preventing Crime: What Works, What Doesn't, What's Promising," was published in July 1998 as a *Research in Brief* by the National Institute of Justice (Office of Justice Programs, U.S. Department of Justice, Washington, DC).

[illegible] evaluating crime prevention programs througho[illegible] the United States, researchers looked at both the process employed by each program (how it was designed to work), and the impact of each program on reducing crime in a number of categories, such as in schools, families, communities, businesses, and high-crime areas. Based on ratings of between one (weakest) and five (strongest) in each category, researchers divided crime prevention programs into those that worked and those that did not work. Programs that worked had ratings of three or higher in at least two categories, while those that did not work had ratings of less than three in all categories or in all but one category. Crime prevention programs were rated as "promising" if there was no conclusive evidence of overall success or failure but the program received a level three evaluation or higher in at least one category and was "found to be effective by the remaining evidence."

What Worked

For small children, frequent home visits to infants under the age of two by trained nurses or aides reduced the incidence of child abuse as well as other injuries to children, and an arrest by age 15 occurred less frequently among preschoolers under the age of five who received weekly ho[illegible]s from teachers. Among adolescents, risk factors fo[illegible]quency such as aggression and hyperactivity were more effectively dealt with by parents who had participated in some type of family therapy or parenting classes.

Several types of school-based programs were identi[illegible]ied as being effective. A combination of consistency with school rules, reinforcing positive behavior among students, and implementing school-wide programs such as anti-bullying campaigns reduced the incidence of crime and delinquency. Long-term programs such as Life Skills

TABLE 9.3

Law enforcement officers feloniously killed, by type of assignment, 1993–2002

Circumstance at scene of incident by type of assignment

Circumstance	Total	2-officer vehicle	1-officer vehicle		Foot patrol		Other*		Off duty
			Alone	Assisted	Alone	Assisted	Alone	Assisted	
Total	**56**	**6**	**17**	**15**	**1**	**0**	**2**	**10**	**5**
Disturbance calls	9	2	1	5	0	0	0	1	0
Bar fights, person with firearm, etc.	4	0	1	3	0	0	0	0	0
Family quarrels	5	2	0	2	0	0	0	1	0
Arrest situations	10	1	1	1	0	0	0	5	2
Burglaries in progress/ pursuing burglary suspects	0	0	0	0	0	0	0	0	0
Robberies in progress/ pursuing robbery suspects	4	1	0	1	0	0	0	0	2
Drug-related matters	3	0	0	0	0	0	0	3	0
Attempting other arrests	3	0	1	0	0	0	0	2	0
Civil disorders (mass disobedience, riot, etc.)	0	0	0	0	0	0	0	0	0
Handling, transporting, custody of prisoners	0	0	0	0	0	0	0	0	0
Investigating suspicious persons/circumstances	8	0	4	2	0	0	0	2	0
Ambush situations	15	2	3	3	1	0	2	1	3
Entrapment/premeditation	4	0	0	0	0	0	1	1	2
Unprovoked attacks	11	2	3	3	1	0	1	0	1
Mentally deranged assailants	4	0	1	3	0	0	0	0	0
Traffic pursuits/stops	10	1	7	1	0	0	0	1	0

*Includes detectives, officers on special assignments, undercover officers, and officers on other types of assignments that are not listed.

SOURCE: "Table 22: Law Enforcement Officers Feloniously Killed, by Circumstance at Scene of Incident Type of Assignment, 2002," in *Crime in the United States, 2002: Uniform Crime Reports,* Federal Bureau of Investigation, Washington, DC, 2003

TABLE 9.4

Law enforcement officers feloniously killed, by type of weapon, 1993–2002

Type of weapon

Weapon	Total	1993	1994	1995	1996	1997	1998	1999	2000	2001	2002
Total	**636**	**70**	**80**	**74**	**61**	**71**	**61**	**42**	**51**	**70**	**56**
Firearms	591	67	79	62	57	68	58	41	47	61	51
Handgun	443	51	67	43	50	50	40	25	33	46	38
Rifle	112	13	8	14	6	12	17	11	10	11	10
Shotgun	36	3	4	5	1	6	1	5	4	4	3
Knife or cutting instrument	8	0	0	2	1	2	1	0	1	0	1
Bomb	9	0	0	8	0	0	1	0	0	0	0
Personal weapons	3	0	0	0	1	1	0	0	0	1	0
Other	25	3	1	2	2	0	1	1	3	8	4

Note: The 72 deaths that resulted from the events of September 11, 2001, are not included in this table.

SOURCE: "Table 26: Law Enforcement Officers Feloniously Killed, by Type of Weapon, 1993–2002," in *Crime in the United States, 2002: Uniform Crime Reports,* Federal Bureau of Investigation, Washington, DC, 2003

Training in the areas of stress control, anger management, and problem solving helped to reduce delinquency and substance abuse, as did the use of behavior modification techniques in teaching thinking skills to juveniles at high risk of delinquency.

Police programs rated effective in reducing crime included extra police patrols in high-crime areas and the use of specialized units that identified and monitored repeat offenders once they were released into the community. The study found that the arrest of employed domestic abusers reduced the rate of future incidents of domestic abuse by the same individuals.

Among other programs, the threat of filing civil actions against landlords for not reporting drug offenses helped to reduce the incidence of drug crime on their premises, while drug treatment programs in prison reduced the rate of repeat drug offenses by prison parolees. Treatment also proved effective in reducing overall repeat offender rates among both juveniles and adults when the treatment program was targeted at risk

TABLE 9.5

Law enforcement officers feloniously killed, by profile of known assailants and age groups, 1993–2002

Profile of known assailants, age groups

Known assailants	Total	1993	1994	1995	1996	1997	1998	1999	2000	2001	2002
Total	**785**	**93**	**114**	**93**	**85**	**76**	**77**	**49**	**64**	**73**	**61**
Age											
Under 18 years	83	16	18	17	7	3	11	3	4	2	2
18–24 years	290	32	38	31	37	25	27	24	20	32	24
25–30 years	150	12	24	14	23	19	17	10	11	10	10
31–40 years	117	9	15	17	6	17	10	10	8	13	12
Over 40 years	109	13	13	11	10	12	11	2	14	10	13
Age not reported	36	11	6	3	2	0	1	0	7	6	0
Average years of age	28	28	27	27	27	30	27	27	32	29	32

Note: The 72 deaths that resulted from the events of September 11, 2001, are not included in this table.

SOURCE: "Table 38: Law Enforcement Officers Feloniously Killed, Profile of Known Assailants, Age Groups, 1993–2002," in *Crime in the United States, 2002: Uniform Crime Reports,* Federal Bureau of Investigation, Washington, DC, 2003

TABLE 9.6

Law enforcement officers feloniously killed, by profiles of known assailants, race, and sex, 1993–2002

Known assailants	Total	1993	1994	1995	1996	1997	1998	1999	2000	2001	2002
Total	**785**	**93**	**114**	**93**	**85**	**76**	**77**	**49**	**64**	**73**	**61**
Race											
White	417	37	60	50	34	38	45	27	44	45	37
Black	307	46	46	38	39	31	24	19	16	24	24
Asian/Pacific Islander	15	0	2	2	3	4	2	0	0	2	0
American Indian/Alaskan Native	14	0	1	2	2	3	3	2	0	1	0
Race not reported	32	10	5	1	7	0	3	1	4	1	0
Sex											
Male	750	84	105	85	84	76	76	47	62	72	59
Female	22	1	5	7	1	0	1	2	2	1	2
Sex not reported	13	8	4	1	0	0	0	0	0	0	0

Note: The 72 deaths that resulted from the events of September 11, 2001, are not included in this table.

SOURCE: "Table 39: Law Enforcement Officers Feloniously Killed, Profile of Known Assailants, Race and Sex, 1993–2002," in *Crime in the United States, 2002: Uniform Crime Reports,* Federal Bureau of Investigation, Washington, DC, 2003

TABLE 9.7

Law enforcement officers feloniously killed, by profile of known assailants and criminal history, 1993–2002

Known assailants	Total	1993	1994	1995	1996	1997	1998	1999	2000	2001	2002
Total	**785**	**93**	**114**	**93**	**85**	**76**	**77**	**49**	**64**	**73**	**61**
Prior criminal arrest	528	55	62	62	48	59	54	41	51	48	48
Convicted on prior criminal charge	373	31	41	38	42	55	34	30	29	37	36
Received juvenile conviction on prior criminal charge	67	6	6	4	6	5	12	6	1	12	9
Received parole or probation on prior criminal charge	287	25	35	31	31	35	23	22	25	29	31
Prior arrest for											
Crime of violence	245	19	45	43	28	24	18	11	20	19	18
Murder	22	3	4	1	1	1	5	1	3	1	2
Drug law violation	252	24	26	34	22	34	27	21	13	23	28
Assaulting an officer or resisting arrest	146	15	25	20	11	13	7	19	9	17	10
Weapons violation	240	26	40	28	26	27	17	19	19	19	19

Note: The 72 deaths that resulted from the events of September 11, 2001, are not included in this table.

SOURCE: "Table 42: Law Enforcement Officers Feloniously Killed, Profile of Known Assailants, Criminal History, 1993–2002," in *Crime in the United States, 2002: Uniform Crime Reports,* Federal Bureau of Investigation, Washington, DC, 2003

TABLE 9.8

Gender and race or ethnicity of full-time federal officers with arrest and firearm authority in agencies employing 500 or more full-time officers, June 2002

		Percent of full-time federal officers with arrest and firearm authority						
		Gender		Race/ethnicity				
Agency	Number of officers*	Male	Female	Total minority	American Indian	Black or African American	Asian or Pacific Islander	Hispanic or Latino, any race
Immigration and Naturalization Service	19,407	87.9%	12.1%	46.7%	0.5%	5.0%	2.7%	38.1%
Federal Bureau of Prisons	14,457	86.4	13.6	40.0	1.4	24.9	1.5	12.3
U.S. Customs Service	11,977	81.4	18.6	36.4	0.8	6.9	3.7	24.7
Federal Bureau of Investigation	11,398	82.0	18.0	16.8	0.4	6.1	3.0	7.3
U.S. Secret Service	4,266	90.3%	9.7%	20.3%	0.8%	11.9%	1.9%	5.6%
Drug Enforcement Administration	4,111	91.4	8.6	17.7	0.5	7.9	2.0	7.3
U.S. Postal Inspection Service	3,175	82.3	17.7	37.2	0.4	23.2	4.2	9.4
Internal Revenue Service	2,868	72.0	28.0	22.1	0.9	9.8	4.4	7.1
U.S. Marshals Service	2,692	88.4	11.6	17.6	0.6	7.1	2.1	7.6
Bureau of Alcohol, Tobacco and Firearms	2,362	87.1%	12.9%	19.8%	1.1%	9.2%	1.9%	7.4%
National Park Service	2,148	84.8	15.2	12.8	1.6	5.1	2.1	4.1
Ranger Activities Division	1,558	83.1	16.9	9.9	2.1	2.1	1.9	3.9
U.S. Park Police	590	89.3	10.7	20.7	0.2	13.1	2.7	4.7
Veterans Health Administration	1,649	91.4	8.6	40.8	1.2	28.3	1.3	9.8
U.S. Capitol Police	1,225	81.2%	18.8%	33.0%	0.2%	29.0%	1.0%	2.8%
U.S. Fish and Wildlife Service	728	88.9	11.1	12.0	3.6	1.8	0.4	6.0
GSA-Federal Protective Service	709	90.7	9.3	40.3	0.4	30.4	1.1	8.5
USDA Forest Service	611	78.1	21.9	18.8	7.1	3.6	1.5	6.5
Bureau of Diplomatic Security	592	90.4	9.6	16.7	0.8	7.3	3.7	4.9

Note: Data on gender and race or ethnicity of officers were not provided by the Administrative Office of the U.S. Courts.
Detail may not add to total because of rounding or because of personnel classified as "other" race.
*Includes employees in U.S. Territories.

SOURCE: Brian A. Reaves and Lynn M. Bauer, "Table 5: Gender and Race or Ethnicity of Federal Officers with Arrest and Firearm Authority, Agencies Employing 500 or More Full-Time Officers, June 2002," in *Federal Law Enforcement Officers, 2002,* U.S. Department of Justice, Bureau of Justice Statistics, Washington, DC, August 2003

factors related to the underlying criminal offense, such as aggression or childhood abuse.

What Did Not Work

Despite their popularity and widespread use, gun buy-back programs, Drug Abuse Resistance Education (D.A.R.E.), and "Scared Straight" programs that brought juvenile offenders face-to-face with hardened prison inmates were among programs rated ineffective by researchers. Among other popular programs, boot camps using military-like discipline and regimentation failed to reduce the rate of repeat offenders among both juveniles and adults. Similarly, shock probation, shock parole, and split sentences under which offenders were briefly incarcerated before being released to a supervised community setting did not reduce the incidence of repeat offending any more than programs that placed similar offenders directly under community supervision without an initial period of incarceration.

According to the report, the incarceration of serious offenders at high risk of re-offending was effective in preventing future crimes; however, the less serious the offender, the less likely incarceration was to have a demonstrable impact on future crimes.

As discussed earlier, the arrest of employed domestic abusers reduced repeat offenses of domestic abuse; however, the opposite occurred among domestic abusers who were unemployed. According to the report, "Arrests of unemployed suspects for domestic assault caused higher rates of repeat offending over the long term than nonarrest alternatives" that addressed the underlying problems that contributed to the unemployment, such as substance abuse.

Summer-job and subsidized work programs also failed to reduce crime or arrests, as did police newsletters with local crime information.

What Was Promising

The report lists the following programs as among those that are potentially helpful in reducing certain types of criminal activity or repeat offending:

- Proactive drunk driving arrests with breath tests may reduce accident deaths.
- Community policing, including meetings with area residents, may reduce inaccurate perceptions of crime.
- Mailing arrest warrants to domestic violence suspects who leave the scene before police arrive may reduce repeat offenses.

TABLE 9.9

Public opinion poll on attitudes of respondents toward most important problem facing the country, 1983–2003

QUESTION: "WHAT DO YOU THINK IS THE MOST IMPORTANT PROBLEM FACING THIS COUNTRY TODAY?"

	Oct. 7–10, 1983	Feb. 10–13, 1984	Jan. 25–28, 1985	July 11–14, 1986	Apr. 10–13, 1987	Sept. 9–11, 1988	May 4–7, 1989	July 19–22, 1990	Mar. 7–10, 1991	Mar. 26–29, 1992	Jan. 8–11, 1993	Jan. 15–17, 1994	Jan. 16–18, 1995	May 9–12, 1996	Jan. 10–13, 1997	Apr. 17–19, 1998	May 23–24, 1999	Mar. 10–12, 2000	Jan. 10–14, 2001	Mar. 4–7, 2002	Feb. 3–6, 2003
High cost of living; inflation; taxes	12%	10%	11%	4%	5%	2%	3%	2%	2%	8%	4%	4%	7%	11%	6%	7%	3%	13%	6%	2%	2%
Unemployment	41	29	20	23	13	9	6	3	8	25	22	18	15	13	NA	5	4	2	48		10
International problems; foreign affairs	7	11	NA	NA	NA	4	4	NA	1	3	8	3	2	4	3	4	3	4	4	2	8
Crime; violence	5	4	4	3	3	2	6	1	2	5	9	37	27	25	23	20	17	13	9	1	2
Guns/gun control	NA	NA	NA	NA	NA	NA	NA	NA	NA	NA	NA	NA	(a)	NA	NA	1	10	7	1	NA	NA
Fear of war/nuclear war; international tensions	14	11	27	22	23	5	2	1	2	NA	NA	NA	(a)	NA	NA	NA	2	NA	(a)	12	35
Ethics, moral, family decline	5	7	2	3	5	1	5	2	2	5	7	8	6	14	9	16	18	15	13	7	4
Terrorism	NA	NA	NA	NA	NA	NA	NA	NA	NA	NA	NA	NA	NA	NA	NA	NA	NA	NA	NA	22	10
Excessive government spending; Federal budget deficit	4	12	18	13	11	12	7	21	8	8	13	5	14	15	8	5	1	4	1	1	3
Dissatisfaction with government	2	2	NA	NA	5	NA	2	1	NA	8	5	6	5	12	7	8	5	11	9	4	2
Economy (general)	4	5	6	7	10	12	8	7	24	42	35	14	10	12	21	6	3	6	7	18	34
Poverty; hunger; homelessness	NA	NA	6	6	5	7	10	7	10	15	15	11	10	7	10	10	7	5	4	4	3
Drugs; drug abuse	NA	NA	2	8	11	11	27	18	11	8	6	9	6	10	17	12	5	5	7	3	2
National security	NA	NA	NA	NA	NA	NA	NA	NA	NA	NA	NA	NA	NA	NA	NA	NA	NA	NA	NA	6	3
Trade deficit; trade relations	NA	NA	NA	NA	NA	3	3	1	1	4	3	2	1	2	1	1	1	1	(a)	NA	NA
Education; quality of education	NA	NA	NA	NA	NA	2	3	2	2	8	8	7	5	13	10	13	11	16	12	7	4
Environment; pollution	NA	NA	NA	NA	NA	NA	4	5	2	3	3	1	1	3	1	2	2	2	2	2	1
AIDS	NA	NA	NA	NA	NA	NA	1	2	*	3	2	2	1	*	1	1	*	*	*	NA	NA
Abortion	NA	NA	NA	NA	NA	NA	*	NA	NA	NA	NA	NA	1	0	1	1	*	2	1	*	1
Health care	NA	NA	NA	NA	NA	NA	NA	NA	NA	12	18	20	12	10	7	6	5	8	7	6	5
No opinion; don't know	4	4	3	3	4	12	7	5	6	2	2	2	2	7	6	4	2	6	8	4	5

Note: Exact wording of response categories varies across surveys. Multiple responses are possible; the Source records up to three problems per respondent. Some problems mentioned by a small percentage of respondents are not included in the table. Sample sizes vary from year to year; the data for 2003 are based on telephone interviews with a randomly selected national sample of 1,001 adults, 18 years of age and older, conducted Feb. 3-6, 2003.
*Less than 0.5%.

SOURCE: "Table 2.1: Attitudes toward the Most Important Problem Facing the Country," in *Sourcebook of Criminal Justice Statistics 2002,* U.S. Department of Justice, Bureau of Justice Statistics, Washington, DC, 2003. The Gallup Organization, Inc.

FIGURE 9.1

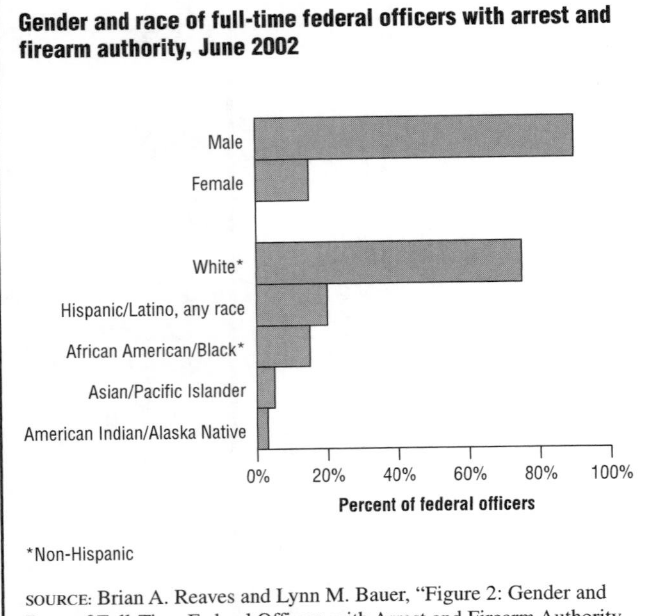

*Non-Hispanic

SOURCE: Brian A. Reaves and Lynn M. Bauer, "Figure 2: Gender and Race of Full-Time Federal Officers with Arrest and Firearm Authority, June 2002," in *Federal Law Enforcement Officers, 2002,* U.S. Department of Justice, Bureau of Justice Statistics, Washington, DC, August 2003

- Battered women's shelters may help some women reduce the likelihood of being victimized again.
- Gang monitoring by community workers and probation and police officers may reduce criminal gang activity.
- Community-based mentoring by Big Brothers/Big Sisters of America may prevent drug abuse.
- Schools that group students into smaller units, like a school within a school, may prevent school crime.
- Job Corps residential training programs for at-risk youth may reduce the incidence of felony offenses.
- Prison-based vocational education programs for adult inmates in federal prisons may reduce repeat offending.
- Adding a second clerk in a convenience store that was previously robbed may reduce store robberies.
- Drug courts may reduce repeat drug offending.
- Drug treatment in jails with follow-up urine testing in the community may reduce the rate of drug re-offenses.
- Intensive supervision and aftercare of juvenile offenders may reduce the rate of re-offending for both minor and serious crimes.
- Community-based after-school recreation programs may reduce local juvenile crime.

Neighborhood Watch

According to the report, "Neighborhood watch programs organized with police failed to reduce burglary or other target crimes, especially in higher crime areas where voluntary participation often fails." The latter point on voluntary participation was echoed by The National Sheriffs' Association, which founded the current National Neighborhood Watch Program in 1972 with funding from the Law Enforcement Assistance Administration. According to information provided by the National Sheriffs' Association, "Communities that need neighborhood watches the most are the ones that find it the hardest to keep them. This is particularly the case with lower income neighborhoods. Typically, adults in these neighborhoods work multiple jobs with odd hours, making it difficult to schedule meetings and organize events. It also makes it difficult for neighbors to get to know and care about one another in a way that makes them feel comfortable watching out for one another."

TABLE 9.10

Public opinion poll on respondents' attitude toward level of crime, 1989–2002

QUESTION: "IS THERE MORE CRIME IN THE U.S. THAN THERE WAS A YEAR AGO, OR LESS?"

	More	Less	Same*	No opinion
1989	84%	5%	5%	6%
1990	84	3	7	6
1992	89	3	4	4
1993	87	4	5	4
1996	71	15	8	6
1997	64	25	6	5
1998	52	35	8	5
2000	47	41	7	5
2001	41	43	10	6
2002	62	21	11	6

*Response volunteered.

SOURCE: "Table 2.31: Attitudes toward Level of Crime in the United States 1989–2002," in *Sourcebook of Criminal Justice Statistics 2002,* U.S. Department of Justice, Bureau of Justice Statistics, Washington, DC, 2003. The Gallup Organization, Inc.

Still, according to the National Sheriffs' Association, the National Neighborhood Watch Program has proved successful in reducing crime in many neighborhoods across the country. For example, in Minnesota in the late 1990s, existing Neighborhood Watch programs mobilized in response to a rise in crime and assisted local police in clearing an average of 25 percent of cases. Similarly, in the late 1990s, with the help of Neighborhood Watch programs in Fairfax County, Virginia, burglary rates dropped by 90 percent.

According to the National Sheriffs' Association, "Although not all Neighborhood Watches report success, and most of the time they fail to fully mobilize the residents, most of these programs are successful. Further, these programs often produce positive results beyond reducing crime, such as social interaction or cleaning up the neighborhood."

TABLE 9.11

Public opinion poll on respondents' attitudes toward crime in own area, 1972–2002

QUESTION: "IS THERE MORE CRIME IN YOUR AREA THAN THERE WAS A YEAR AGO, OR LESS?"

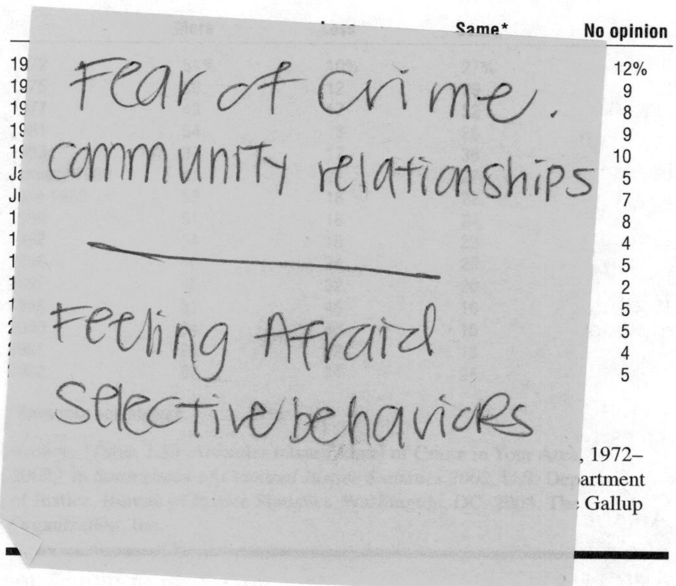

	More	Less	Same*	No opinion
19[illegible]	[illegible]	[illegible]	[illegible]	12%
19[illegible]	[illegible]	[illegible]	[illegible]	9
19[illegible]	[illegible]	[illegible]	[illegible]	8
19[illegible]	[illegible]	[illegible]	[illegible]	9
19[illegible]	[illegible]	[illegible]	[illegible]	10
Ja[illegible]	[illegible]	[illegible]	[illegible]	5
Ju[illegible]	[illegible]	[illegible]	[illegible]	7
1[illegible]	[illegible]	[illegible]	[illegible]	8
1[illegible]	[illegible]	[illegible]	[illegible]	4
1[illegible]	[illegible]	[illegible]	[illegible]	5
1[illegible]	[illegible]	[illegible]	[illegible]	2
1[illegible]	[illegible]	[illegible]	[illegible]	5
[illegible]	[illegible]	[illegible]	[illegible]	5
[illegible]	[illegible]	[illegible]	[illegible]	4
[illegible]	[illegible]	[illegible]	[illegible]	5

[illegible], 1972–[illegible] [illegible]artment [illegible] Gallup [illegible]

TABLE 9.12

Public opinion poll on respondents' fear of walking alone at night, within one mile of own area, 1965–2002

QUESTION: "IS THERE ANY AREA NEAR WHERE YOU LIVE—THAT IS, WITHIN A MILE—WHERE YOU WOULD BE AFRAID TO WALK ALONE AT NIGHT?"

	Yes	No
1965	34%	66%
1967	31	67
1968	35	62
1972	42	57
1975	45	55
1977	45	55
1979	42	58
1981	45	55
1982	48	52
1983	45	55
1989	43	57
1990	40	59
1992	44	56
1993	43	56
1994	39	60
1996	39	60
1997	38	61
2000	34	66
2001	30	69
2002	35	64

SOURCE: "Table 2.35: Respondents Reporting Fear of Walking Alone at Night, Selected Years 1965–2002," in *Sourcebook of Criminal Justice Statistics 2002,* U.S. Department of Justice, Bureau of Justice Statistics, Washington, DC, 2003. The Gallup Organization, Inc.

THE FEAR OF CRIME

The fear of becoming a victim of crime can undermine community relationships. People may withdraw physically and emotionally, losing contact with their neighbors and weakening the social fabric of their lives and communities. In a 2003 Gallup Poll, 2 percent of those polled named crime and violence as the most important problem facing the country. This percentage was down significantly from 37 percent in 1994, the highest percentage recorded in the past 20 years. The mid-1990s saw the highest percentages of those who saw crime and violence as the most important issue. Since that time the percentages have decreased dramatically. By 2001 the number had fallen to only 1 percent, and only 2 percent in 2002. (See Table 9.9.)

More Crime or Less Crime Today?

Another Gallup Poll reported that 62 percent of Americans thought there was more crime in the United States in 2002 than in the year before. (See Table 9.10.) That figure is higher than the 41 percent of respondents in 2001 who felt there was more crime than the year before, and the 47 percent of respondents in 2000 who felt the same. But in 1989, 84 percent of respondents felt there was more crime than the year before.

In 2002 more women (70 percent) felt there was more crime than there had been the year before than did men (53 percent). Seventy-six percent of blacks thought so, compared to 60 percent of whites. Fifty-eight percent of the youngest respondents (18 to 29 years of age) and 68 percent of the oldest (65 or older) felt that there was more crime in the United States than the year before. Those who were less educated and had more limited earnings were more likely to feel that there was more crime in the United States than the year prior.

Some 37 percent of respondents in another Gallup Poll said that they believed there was more crime in their area in 2002 than there was a year ago. This is up from the 26 percent who perceived more crime in their area in 2001, but well below the over 50 percent during the years from June 1989 to 1992 and the 46 percent in 1996 and 1997. (See Table 9.11.)

Feeling Afraid

In 2002 the Gallup Poll found that about one in three Americans (35 percent) was afraid to walk alone at night. Almost the same proportion of Americans felt that way in 1965 (34 percent). Through the 1970s, 1980s, and early 1990s the proportion increased to between 40 and 45 percent, and declined steadily from 1993 to 2001, before rising again in 2002. (See Table 9.12.)

Asked if they engaged in selective behaviors because of concern over crime, 43 percent of Gallup Poll respondents in 2002 reported avoiding going to certain places or neighborhoods, 30 percent kept a dog for protection, 24 percent had a burglar alarm, and 21 percent reported buying a gun for protection. (See Table 9.13.)

TABLE 9.13

Public opinion poll on selected behaviors of respondents because of concern over crime, 2002

QUESTION: "PLEASE TELL ME WHICH, IF ANY, OF THESE THINGS YOU, YOURSELF, DO OR HAVE DONE."

		Sex	
	Total	Male	Female
Avoid going to certain places or neighborhoods you might otherwise want to go to	43%	37%	49%
Keep a dog for protection	30	26	34
Had a burglar alarm installed in your home	24	25	23
Bought a gun for protection of yourself or your home	21	27	16
Carry mace or pepper spray	16	9	22
Carry a knife for defense	11	15	7
Carry a gun for defense	10	16	5

SOURCE: "Table 2.38: Respondents Reporting Whether They Engaged in Selected Behaviors Because of Concern over Crime, 2002," in *Sourcebook of Criminal Justice Statistics 2002,* U.S. Department of Justice, Bureau of Justice Statistics, Washington, DC, 2003. The Gallup Organization, Inc.

JUVENILES AND CRIME

Worrying about Crime

Each year the Institute for Social Research at the University of Michigan conducts the *Monitoring the Future* survey of students and young adults. Primarily, the survey asks questions about social behaviors, such as sexual activity, drug use, violence, and crime. In 2002, 75.5 percent of high school seniors said that they often or sometimes worried about crime and violence. Female students (83.1 percent) were more likely to worry than were male students (66.5 percent). Black students (80.8 percent) were more worried about crime and violence than white students (73.4 percent). (See Table 9.14.)

According to the same study, when asked how often they worried about certain major problems facing the nation, high school seniors in the class of 2002 said they worried about crime and violence the most (75.5 percent), followed by drug abuse (56.9 percent), hunger and poverty (49.7 percent), and economic problems (47 percent). From 1990 to 2002 crime and violence was the number one worry of high school seniors participating in the study.

Juvenile Punishment

In 2000 nearly two-thirds of respondents to a national Gallup Poll thought that juveniles between the ages of 14 and 17 who commit violent crimes should be tried as adults. Male respondents were more likely to feel that way than females. Sixty-eight percent of those interviewed who had "some college" education believed juveniles should be tried as adults, while only 55 percent of those with post-college graduate education felt that way.

In 2003 the Survey Research Program of the College of Criminal Justice at Sam Houston State University asked for opinions regarding whether those under the age of 18 should be eligible for the death penalty. Just over 52 percent believed they should be eligible, while 32.6 percent believed the death penalty should be only for those over the age of 18. Of those who believed the death penalty should be applied to those under the age of 18, 37.7 percent thought the youngest aged offenders should be 16 years old.

THE DEATH PENALTY

A Gallup Poll found that although a majority of Americans still favored the death penalty in 2001, the percentage of those supporting the death penalty was 67 percent, down from a high of 75 percent in 1997. In 2003 a Gallup Poll found that 60 percent believed the death penalty was applied fairly, with 65 percent of whites stating this view as compared to 26 percent of blacks. (See Table 9.15.)

CONFIDENCE IN THE CRIMINAL JUSTICE SYSTEM

Each year the Gallup Organization, Inc., asks the American people about their confidence in the major institutions of society. Twenty-nine percent of those polled in 2003 said that they had a great deal or quite a lot of confidence in the criminal justice system, with 45 percent reporting some confidence. (See Table 9.16.) Those with less education and lower income levels had the least confidence in the criminal justice system. Those aged 18 to 29 years old had the highest level of confidence (35 percent) of any age group. Of Democrats, 29 percent expressed a great deal of confidence, compared with 32 percent of Republicans.

In 2003 one-fourth of all respondents had either very little or no confidence in the criminal justice system. Fewer whites (24 percent) than blacks (42 percent) had little or no confidence in the system. Fewer Republicans (24 percent) than Democrats (26 percent) expressed a lack of confidence in the criminal justice system. Those who earned less than $20,000 a year (35 percent) were more likely than those who earned more than $75,000 a year (19 percent) to feel little or no confidence in the system.

CONFIDENCE IN THE POLICE

In the 2003 Gallup Poll, Americans expressed much more confidence in the police than they did in the criminal justice system. Sixty-one percent stated they had a great deal or quite a lot of confidence in the police, and 29 percent said they had some confidence. Only 10 percent claimed to have little or no confidence in the police. (See Table 9.17.)

Blacks (43 percent) were significantly less likely than whites (65 percent) to have a high level of confidence in the police. Suburban dwellers (64 percent) and Republicans (70 percent) were more likely than rural residents

TABLE 9.14

Public opinion poll of high school seniors reporting that they worry about crime and violence, by sex, race, region, college plans, and illicit drug use, 1990–2001

QUESTION: "OF ALL THE PROBLEMS FACING THE NATION TODAY, HOW OFTEN DO YOU WORRY ABOUT. . . CRIME AND VIOLENCE?"

(Percent responding "sometimes" or "often")

	Class of 1990 (N=2,595)	Class of 1991 (N=2,595)	Class of 1992 (N=2,736)	Class of 1993 (N=2,807)	Class of 1994 (N=2,664)	Class of 1995 (N=2,646)	Class of 1996 (N=2,502)	Class of 1997 (N=2,651)	Class of 1998 (N=2,621)	Class of 1999 (N=2,348)	Class of 2000 (N=2,204)	Class of 2001 (N=2,222)	Class of 2002 (N=2,267)
Total	**88.8%**	**88.1%**	**91.6%**	**90.8%**	**92.7%**	**90.2%**	**90.1%**	**86.5%**	**84.4%**	**81.8%**	**83.5%**	**81.0%**	**75.5%**
Sex													
Male	84.8	82.6	87.6	85.7	88.4	85.8	84.8	79.4	76.5	74.4	76.0	71.7	66.5
Female	93.4	93.6	95.7	95.6	96.5	95.1	95.4	93.7	91.7	89.5	90.2	90.1	83.1
Race													
White	88.1	86.6	90.5	89.4	92.9	90.0	89.5	84.5	83.5	80.8	82.6	78.7	73.4
Black	92.7	94.5	96.9	95.1	90.7	93.0	92.9	90.4	85.7	84.8	91.1	90.2	80.8
Region													
Northeast	87.7	86.0	92.0	90.6	91.0	91.7	89.4	83.2	83.1	85.4	82.2	79.8	70.8
North Central	87.0	88.8	87.6	90.2	93.2	86.7	87.4	85.1	80.7	80.0	84.6	79.4	75.0
South	90.4	88.4	93.8	91.2	93.3	91.3	91.1	88.7	87.0	81.1	85.8	83.6	79.2
West	89.4	89.0	93.0	91.4	92.4	92.2	93.4	88.2	85.4	82.0	79.3	80.7	74.6
College plans													
Yes	89.8	89.9	93.1	92.4	94.1	92.6	91.6	88.4	85.3	84.5	85.0	83.5	76.9
No	88.0	83.9	87.7	85.8	89.4	84.0	86.2	80.7	82.2	72.3	77.9	72.7	69.0
Lifetime illicit drug use													
None	90.6	90.7	92.9	91.9	94.1	91.8	90.5	89.1	86.8	84.3	85.4	82.3	77.1
Marijuana only	87.1	85.4	89.6	91.1	91.5	90.9	91.9	85.7	82.3	82.8	85.8	85.2	77.0
Few pills	87.6	86.6	89.4	90.7	95.6	92.6	91.0	88.3	84.6	84.3	79.1	83.1	77.8
More pills	85.7	84.8	90.6	87.4	89.5	84.1	87.4	81.0	83.3	75.6	79.9	73.8	69.7

Note: Data are given for those who identify themselves as white or Caucasian and those who identify themselves as black or African-American; data are not given for the other ethnic categories because each of these groups constitutes a small portion of the sample in any given year and therefore would yield unreliable estimates

SOURCE: Adapted from Lloyd D. Johnston, Jerald G. Bachman, and Patrick M. O'Malley, "Table 2.69: High School Seniors Reporting that They Worry about Crime and Violence, by Sex, Race, Region, College Plans, and Illicit Drug Use, United States, 1990–2002," *Monitoring the Future 2000,* University of Michigan, Institute for Social Research, Ann Arbor, MI. updated. *Sourcebook of Criminal Justice Statistics,* U.S. Department of Justice, Bureau of Justice Statistics, Washington, DC, 2003

(55 percent) and Democrats (58 percent) to express high levels of confidence. A strong majority in all demographic groups had at least some confidence in the police.

According to *Factors That Influence Public Opinion of the Police* (U.S. Department of Justice, Office of Justice Programs, National Institute of Justice, 2003), police can improve public opinion in the community by increasing the number of informal contacts they have with citizens. These contacts can include community meetings, talking with citizens, and increasing police visibility in the neighborhoods. Such contacts improved public opinion even when the local crime rate was high. They also lessened the negative impact when residents had formal contacts with police, such as being arrested or questioned. These improvements were found regardless of the residents' race or ethnicity.

GUNS

Guns in the Home

In 2002, 41 percent of Americans told the Gallup Poll they had guns in their homes, up from 40 percent in 2001. The proportion of gun ownership stayed relatively stable the last four decades of the twentieth century, ranging from a low of 36 percent in 1999 to a high of 51 percent in October 1993. (See Table 9.18.)

In 2002 the most likely people to own guns were male, with some college, aged 50 to 64 years old, making $50,000 to $74,999 per year, and living in the South (48 percent) or Midwest (45 percent).

Laws Governing Firearm Sales

The regulation of gun sales remained a controversial issue for the nation's citizens into the new century. In 2002 the Gallup Poll reported that 51 percent of those polled felt that laws covering firearm sales should be stricter, a drop from 62 percent in 2000. Thirty-six percent favored keeping the laws as they were, and 11 percent believed the gun laws should be less strict. Fifty-eight percent of females, 59 percent of blacks, and 62 percent of Democrats supported stricter laws, compared to 43 percent of males, 49 percent of whites, and 40 percent of Republicans. Fifty-nine percent of persons living in urban areas felt that firearm sales laws should be stricter, a drop from 67 percent in 2000, while 42 percent of rural residents supported stricter gun laws, a decrease from 53 percent in 2000. (See Table 9.19.)

TABLE 9.15

Public opinion poll on respondents' attitudes toward fairness of application of death penalty, 2003

QUESTION: "GENERALLY SPEAKING, DO YOU BELIEVE THE DEATH PENALTY IS APPLIED FAIRLY OR UNFAIRLY IN THIS COUNTRY TODAY?"

	Applied fairly	Applied unfairly	Don't know/ refused
National	60%	37%	3%
Sex			
Male	63	35	2
Female	59	38	3
Race			
White	65	32	3
Nonwhite	44	54	2
Black	26	71	3
Age			
18 to 29 years	64	35	1
30 to 49 years	67	31	2
50 to 64 years	54	44	2
50 years and older	52	44	4
65 years and older	51	44	5
Education			
College post graduate	46	51	3
College graduate	54	39	7
Some college	61	36	3
High school graduate or less	67	32	1
Income			
$75,000 and over	58	38	4
$50,000 to $74,999	66	32	2
$30,000 to $49,999	66	33	1
$20,000 to $29,999	60	39	1
Under $20,000	52	45	3
Community			
Urban area	53	46	1
Suburban area	66	30	4
Rural area	58	40	2
Region			
East	55	42	3
Midwest	61	37	2
South	59	37	4
West	68	30	2
Politics			
Republican	73	24	3
Democrat	50	47	3
Independent	57	41	2

SOURCE: "Table 2.52: Attitudes Toward Fairness of the Application of the Death Penalty," in *Sourcebook of Criminal Justice Statistics 2002,* U.S. Department of Justice, Bureau of Justice Statistics, Washington, DC, 2003. The Gallup Organization, Inc.

TABLE 9.16

Public opinion poll on respondents' reported confidence in criminal justice system, 2003

QUESTION: "I AM GOING TO READ YOU A LIST OF INSTITUTIONS IN AMERICAN SOCIETY. PLEASE TELL ME HOW MUCH CONFIDENCE YOU, YOURSELF, HAVE IN EACH ONE—A GREAT DEAL, QUITE A LOT, SOME, OR VERY LITTLE: THE CRIMINAL JUSTICE SYSTEM?"

	Great deal/quite a lot	Some	Very little	None[1]
National	29%	45%	25%	1%
Sex				
Male	29	42	27	2
Female	28	47	24	1
Race				
White	30	46	23	1
Nonwhite	23	39	35	3
Black	26	32	37	5
Age				
18 to 29 years	35	49	15	1
30 to 49 years	26	44	28	2
50 to 64 years	26	49	24	1
50 years and older	28	44	27	1
65 years and older	30	40	29	[2]
Education				
College post graduate	35	48	17	[2]
College graduate	40	44	15	1
Some college	29	50	20	1
High school graduate or less	23	39	36	2
Income				
$75,000 and over	35	46	18	1
$50,000 to $74,999	31	46	23	[2]
$30,000 to $49,999	31	45	22	2
$20,000 to $29,999	20	43	34	2
Under $20,000	24	41	34	1
Community				
Urban area	27	46	26	1
Suburban area	32	44	23	1
Rural area	26	45	28	1
Region				
East	29	44	26	1
Midwest	30	48	21	1
South	30	42	26	2
West	25	46	28	1
Politics				
Republican	32	44	24	[2]
Democrat	29	45	24	2
Independent	26	45	27	2

[1]Response volunteered.
[2]Less than 0.5%

SOURCE: "Table 2.12: Reported Confidence in the Criminal Justice System, 2003," in *Sourcebook of Criminal Justice Statistics 2002,* U.S. Department of Justice, Bureau of Justice Statistics, Washington, DC, 2003. The Gallup Organization, Inc.

TABLE 9.17

Public opinion poll on respondents' confidence in police, 2003

QUESTION: "I AM GOING TO READ YOU A LIST OF INSTITUTIONS IN AMERICAN SOCIETY. PLEASE TELL ME HOW MUCH CONFIDENCE YOU, YOURSELF, HAVE IN EACH ONE—A GREAT DEAL, QUITE A LOT, SOME, OR VERY LITTLE: THE POLICE?"

	Great deal/quite a lot	Some	Very little	None[1]
National	61%	29%	9%	1%
Sex				
Male	60	28	11	1
Female	61	31	7	1
Race				
White	65	27	7	1
Nonwhite	43	37	18	2
Black	43	30	24	3
Age				
18 to 29 years	61	25	12	2
30 to 49 years	59	31	10	[2]
50 to 64 years	63	28	8	1
50 years and older	64	28	8	[2]
65 years and older	66	27	6	0
Education				
College post graduate	67	30	3	[2]
College graduate	70	26	4	0
Some college	64	27	8	1
High school graduate or less	53	31	15	1
Income				
$75,000 and over	70	26	4	[2]
$50,000 to $74,999	68	24	8	0
$30,000 to $49,999	64	26	9	1
$20,000 to $29,999	48	32	16	3
Under $20,000	49	36	14	1
Community				
Urban area	59	26	14	1
Suburban area	64	30	6	[2]
Rural area	55	33	11	1
Region				
East	58	30	10	2
Midwest	62	29	9	[2]
South	64	26	10	[2]
West	57	33	9	1
Politics				
Republican	70	24	6	0
Democrat	58	30	11	1
Independent	55	32	11	2

[1]Response volunteered.
[2]Less than 0.5%.

SOURCE: "Table 2.13: Reported Confidence in the Police 2003," in *Sourcebook of Criminal Justice Statistics 2002,* U.S. Department of Justice, Bureau of Justice Statistics, Washington, DC, 2003. The Gallup Organization, Inc.

TABLE 9.18

Public opinion poll on respondents' reporting having a gun in their home, 1959–2002

QUESTION: "DO YOU HAVE A GUN IN YOUR HOME?"

	Yes	No
1959	49%	51%
1965	48	52
1968	50	50
1972	43	55
1975	44	54
1980	45	53
1983	40	58
1985	44	55
1989	47	51
1990	47	52
1991	46	53
March 1993	48	51
October 1993	51	48
July 1996	38	60
November 1996	44	54
1997	42	57
1999	36	62
April 2000	42	57
August 2000	39	60
2001	40	59
2002	41	58

SOURCE: "Table 2.56: Respondents Reporting Having a Gun in Their Home, Selected Years 1959–2002," in *Sourcebook of Criminal Justice Statistics 2002,* U.S. Department of Justice, Bureau of Justice Statistics, Washington, DC, 2003. The Gallup Organization, Inc.

TABLE 9.19

Public opinion poll on respondents' attitudes toward laws governing firearm sales, 2002

QUESTION: "IN GENERAL, DO YOU FEEL THAT THE LAWS COVERING THE SALE OF FIREARMS SHOULD BE MADE MORE STRICT, LESS STRICT, OR KEPT AS THEY ARE NOW?"

	More strict	Less strict	Kept as they are now
National	51%	11%	36%
Sex			
Male	43	17	39
Female	58	6	34
Race			
White	49	11	38
Nonwhite	58	14	28
Black	59	12	29
Age			
18 to 29 years	51	10	39
30 to 49 years	52	13	34
50 to 64 years	51	12	34
50 years and older	49	10	38
65 years and older	46	9	42
Education			
College post graduate	61	10	28
College graduate	59	5	34
Some college	47	16	36
High school graduate or less	47	11	40
Income			
$75,000 and over	57	11	31
$50,000 to $74,999	49	12	38
$30,000 to $49,999	53	13	32
$20,000 to $29,999	52	10	38
Under $20,000	48	8	42
Community			
Urban area	59	11	30
Suburban area	51	12	35
Rural area	42	11	45
Region			
East	59	10	29
Midwest	49	10	39
South	47	12	40
West	49	13	36
Politics			
Republican	40	12	46
Democrat	62	8	29
Independent	51	12	35

SOURCE: "Table 2.61: Attitudes toward Laws Covering the Sale of Firearms 2002," in *Sourcebook of Criminal Justice Statistics 2002,* U.S. Department of Justice, Bureau of Justice Statistics, Washington, DC, 2003. The Gallup Organization, Inc.

IMPORTANT NAMES AND ADDRESSES

American Civil Liberties Union
125 Broad St., 18th Floor
New York, NY 10004
(212) 234-3005
E-mail: infoaclu@aclu.org
URL: http://www.aclu.org

Anti-Defamation League
823 United Nations Plaza
New York, NY 10017
(212) 885-7700
FAX: (212) 867-0779
E-mail: webmaster@adl.org
URL: http://www.adl.org

Bureau of Alcohol, Tobacco, and Firearms
650 Massachusetts Ave. NW, Room 8290
Washington, DC 20226
(202) 927-7970
FAX: (202) 927-7756
E-mail: atfmail@atfhq.atf.treas.gov
URL: http://www.atf.treas.gov

Bureau of Engraving and Printing
Department of the Treasury
14th and C Streets, SW
Washington, DC 20228
(202) 874-3019
URL: http://www.bep.treas.gov

Bureau of Justice Statistics
810 7th St. NW
Washington, DC 20531
(202) 307-0765
E-mail: askbjs@ojp.usdoj.gov
URL: http://www.ojp.usdoj.gov/bjs

Bureau of Labor Statistics
Postal Square Building
2 Massachusetts Ave. NE
Washington, DC 20212-0001
(202) 691-5200
FAX: (202) 691-6325
E-mail: feedback@bls.gov
URL: http://www.bls.gov/home.htm

Coalition for Juvenile Justice
1211 Connecticut Ave. NW, Suite 414
Washington, DC 20036-2072
(202) 467-0864
FAX: (202) 887-0738
E-mail: info@juvjustice.org
URL: http://www.juvjustice.org

Drug Enforcement Administration
2401 Jefferson Davis Highway
Mailstop AXS
Alexandria, VA 22301
(202) 307-1000
FAX: (202) 307-7335
URL: http://www.usdoj.gov/dea

Federal Bureau of Investigation
935 Pennsylvania Ave. NW, #7116
Washington, DC 20535-0002
(202) 324-3444
FAX: (202) 324-4705
URL: http://www.fbi.gov

Federal Bureau of Investigation: Terrorism and Violent Crime
935 Pennsylvania Ave. NW, #5222
Washington, DC 20535-0002
(202) 324-4664
FAX: (202) 324-1524
http://www.fbi.gov

Federal Bureau of Prisons
320 1st St. NW
Washington, DC 20534
(202) 307-3198
E-mail: webmaster@bop.gov
URL: http://www.bop.gov

Federal Trade Commission
600 Pennsylvania Ave. NW
Washington, DC 20580
(202) 326-2222
URL: http://www.ftc.gov

Highway Loss Data Institute
1005 North Glebe Rd., Suite 800
Arlington, VA 22201
(703) 247-1600
FAX: (703) 247-1595
URL: http://www.hwysafety.org

Internal Revenue Service Criminal Investigation Division
Washington, DC 20066-6096
(202) 283-9665
Toll-free: 1-800-829-0433
URL: http://www.ustreas.gov/irs/ci

National Association for the Advancement of Colored People
4805 Mt. Hope Dr.
Baltimore, MD 21215
Toll-free: 1-800-NAACP-98
(1-800-622-2798)
E-mail: dcbureau@naacp.org
URL: http://www.naacp.org

National Center for Victims of Crime
2000 M St. NW, Suite 480
Washington, DC 20036
(202) 467-8700
FAX: (202) 467-8701
E-mail: webmaster@ncvc.org
URL: http://www.ncvc.org

National Conference of State Legislatures
1560 Broadway, #700
Denver, CO 80202
(303) 830-2200
E-mail: Info@ncsl.org
URL: http://www.ncsl.org

National Consumers League
1701 K St. NW, Suite 1200
Washington, DC 20006
(202) 835-3323
FAX: (202) 835-0747
E-mail: info@nclnet.org
URL: http://www.nclnet.org

National Crime Prevention Council
1000 Connecticut Ave. NW, 13th Floor

Washington, DC 20036
(202) 466-6272
FAX: (202) 296-1356
URL: http://www.ncpc.org

National Criminal Justice Association
720 7th St., 3rd Floor
Washington, DC 20001-3716
(202) 628-8550
FAX: (202) 628-0080
E-mail: info@ncja.org
URL: http://www.ncja.org

National Criminal Justice Reference Service
P.O. Box 6000
Rockville, MD 20849-6000
(301) 519-5500
Toll-free: 1-800-627-6872
FAX: (301) 519-5212
E-mail: askncjrs@ncjrs.org
URL: http://ncjrs.org

National Highway Traffic Safety Administration
400 7th St. SW
Washington, DC 20590
(202) 366-0123
Toll-free: 1-800-424-9393
URL: http://www.nhtsa.dot.gov

National Institute of Justice
810 7th St. NW
Washington, DC 20531
(202) 307-2942
FAX: (202) 307-6394
URL: http://www.ojp.usdoj.gov/nij

National Organization for Victim Assistance
1730 Park Rd. NW
Washington, DC 20010
(202) 232-6682
Toll-free: 1-800-879-6682 (information hotline)
FAX: (202) 462-2255
E-mail: nova@try-nova.org
URL: http://www.try-nova.org

National White Collar Crime Center
7401 Beaufont Springs Dr., Suite 300
Richmond, VA 23225-5504
URL: http://www.nw3c.org

National Youth Gang Center
P.O. Box 12729
Tallahasee, FL 32317
(850) 385-0600
E-mail: nygc@iir.com
URL: http://www.iir.com/nygc

Office for Victims of Crime
810 7th St. NW, 8th Floor
Washington, DC 20531
(202) 307-5983
FAX: (202) 514-6383
E-mail: askovp@ojp.usdoj.gov
URL: http://www.ojp.usdoj.gov/ovc

Office of Juvenile Justice and Delinquency Prevention
810 7th St. NW, 6th Floor
Washington, DC 20531
(202) 307-5911
Toll-free: 1-800-638-8736
FAX: (202) 307-2093
E-mail: askjj@ncjrs.org
URL: http://www.ojjdp.ncjrs.org

Office of National Drug Control Policy
Drug Policy Information Clearinghouse
P.O. Box 6000
Rockville, MD 20849-6000
Toll-free: 1-800-666-3332
FAX: (301) 519-5212
Email: ondcp@ncjrs.org
URL: http://www.whitehousedrugpolicy.gov

Office on Violence against Women
810 7th St. NW
Washington, DC 20531
(202) 307-6026
FAX: (202) 307-3911
http://www.ojp.usdoj.gov/vawo

The Sentencing Project
514 10th St. NW
Washington, DC 20004
(202) 628-0871
FAX: (202) 628-1091
E-mail: staff@sentencingproject.org
URL: http://www.sentencingproject.org

Southern Poverty Law Center
400 Washington Ave.
Montgomery, AL 36104
(334) 956-8200
URL: http://www.splcenter.org

Supreme Court of the United States
One 1st St. NE
Washington, DC 20543
(202) 479-3211
URL: http://www.supremecourtus.gov

U.S. Census Bureau
Washington, DC 20233
(301) 457-1722
E-mail: webmaster@census.gov
URL: http://www.census.gov

U.S. Department of Justice
950 Pennsylvania Ave. NW
Washington, DC 20530-0001
(202) 353-1555
E-mail: askdoj@usdoj.gov
URL: http://www.usdoj.gov

U.S. Postal Inspection Service
P.O. Box 96096
Washington, DC 20066-6096
(202) 636-2300
FAX: (202) 636-2287
URL: http://www.usps.com/postalinspectors

U.S. Secret Service
Office of Liaison and Public Affairs
950 H Street NW, Suite 8400
Washington, DC 20223
(202) 406-5708
URL: http://www.treas.gov/usss

U.S. Securities and Exchange Commission
450 5th St. NW
Washington, DC 20549
(202) 942-7040
E-mail: help@sec.gov
URL: http://www.sec.gov

U.S. Sentencing Commission
Office of Public Affairs
1 Columbus Circle NE
Washington, DC 20002-8002
(202) 502-4500
E-mail: pubaffairs@ussc.gov
URL: http://www.ussc.gov

Violence Policy Center
1140 19th St. NW, #600
Washington, DC 20036
E-mail: info@vpc.org
URL: http://www.vpc.org

RESOURCES

The various agencies of the U.S. Department of Justice are the major sources of crime and justice data in America. The Bureau of Justice Statistics (BJS) compiles statistics on virtually every area of crime and reports that data in a number of publications. The annual BJS *Sourcebook of Criminal Justice Statistics*, prepared by the Hindelang Criminal Justice Research Center, State University of New York at Albany, is a comprehensive compilation of criminal justice statistics. The annual BJS *National Crime Victimization Survey* provides data for several studies, the most important of which is *Criminal Victimization in the United States*. Other valuable BJS publications include *Education and Correctional Populations* (2003), *Prison and Jail Inmates at Midyear 2002* (2003), *Money Laundering Offenders, 1994-2001* (2003), *Mental Health Treatment in State Prisons, 2000* (2002), *Prisoners in 2002* (2003), and *Capital Punishment, 2002* (2003).

The Federal Bureau of Investigation (FBI) collects crime data from state law enforcement agencies through its Uniform Crime Reports program. The FBI annual *Crime in the United States* is the most important source of information on crime reported to law enforcement agencies. Other important annual publications include *Law Enforcement Officers Killed and Assaulted*, *Terrorism in the United States*, *Hate Crime Statistics*, and *The Measurement of White Collar Crime Using Uniform Crime Reporting (UCR) Data*.

The Office of Juvenile Justice and Delinquency Prevention (OJJDP) published the following: *Short- and Long-Term Consequences of Adolescent Victimization* (2002), *Juvenile Court Statistics, 1999* (2003), *Highlights of the 2001 National Youth Gang Survey* (2003), *National Youth Gang Survey Trends, 1996 to 2000* (2002), *Statistical Briefing Book (Online)* (2004), and *Detention in Delinquency Cases, 1990–1999*. The OJJDP *Juvenile Justice Bulletin* is a major source of current information about juvenile crime; its "Juvenile Arrests 2001" (Howard N. Snyder, 2003) was also helpful.

The Bureau of Alcohol, Tobacco, and Firearms (ATF) of the U.S. Department of the Treasury provides data on bombings, arson, and weapons offenses. Of special importance was the *First Year Report for the President* (1997) of the National Church Arson Task Force, which is jointly headed by the FBI and the ATF. The Office of National Drug Control Policy provided information from its reports, *National Drug Control Strategy* (2004) and *The Economic Costs of Drug Abuse in the United States, 1992–1998* (2001). The National Criminal Justice Association (Washington, DC) monitors crime legislation and issues, as reported in its periodical *Justice Bulletin*.

The Federal Trade Commission, through its Identify Theft Clearinghouse, published *National and State Trends in Fraud and Identity Theft, January-December, 2003* (2004). The National Institute of Justice provided information on drug use among persons arrested in *Preliminary Data on Drug Use and Related Matters among Adult Arrestees and Juvenile Detainees, 2002* (2003) and the *2000 Arrestee Drug Abuse Monitoring: Annual Report* (2003). The Department of Health and Human Services' Office of Applied Studies published *Results from the 2002 National Survey on Drug Use and Health: National Findings* (2003).

Several organizations are devoted to combating prejudice and civil rights abuses in the United States. The Anti-Defamation League produces *Map of State Statutes for Hate Crimes* as a reference guide on the nation's hate crime legislation. The Southern Poverty Law Center (Montgomery, Alabama) publishes data on hate crimes in its periodical *Intelligence Report*.

The Sentencing Project conducts research on criminal justice issues and promotes sentencing reform. They published *Comparative International Rates of Incarceration: An Examination of Causes and Trends* by Marc Mauer, (2003). Key information was also acquired from polling results reported by the Gallup Organization. Also used was *Monitoring the Future Study National Results on Adolescent Drug Use: Overview of Key Findings 2001* (2002), completed by the Survey Research Center of the Institute for Social Research at the University of Michigan (Ann Arbor). The National Law Journal provided valuable survey data on Americans' opinions of the death penalty. The Violence Policy Center reported on the use of guns in high-profile shootings in its report *Where'd They Get Their Guns? An Analysis of the Firearms Used in High-Profile Shootings, 1963 to 2001* (2002).

Other publications used in this book include the *2002 National Retail Security Survey* (Richard Hollinger et al., University of Florida, Gainesville, FL, 2003). The Highway Loss Data Institute provided valuable information on trends in motor vehicle thefts. The Computer Security Institute published the *2003 Computer Crime and Security Survey* (2003).

INDEX

Page references in italics refer to photographs. References with the letter t *following them indicate the presence of a table. The letter* f *indicates a figure. If more than one table or figure appears on a particular page, the exact item number for the table or figure being referenced is provided.*

C

D

E

K

L

Q

R

S

Y

Z